Nancy and the Political

Critical Connections

A series of edited collections forging new connections between contemporary critical theorists and a wide range of research areas, such as critical and cultural theory, gender studies, film, literature, music, philosophy and politics.

Series Editors
Ian Buchanan, University of Wollongong
James Williams, University of Dundee

Editorial Advisory Board

Nick Hewlett
Gregg Lambert
Todd May
John Mullarkey
Paul Patton
Marc Rölli
Alison Ross
Kathrin Thiele
Frédéric Worms

Titles available in the series
Badiou and Philosophy, edited by Sean Bowden and Simon Duffy
Agamben and Colonialism, edited by Marcelo Svirsky and Simone Bignall
Laruelle and Non-Philosophy, edited by John Mullarkey and Anthony Paul Smith
Virilio and Visual Culture, edited by John Armitage and Ryan Bishop
Rancière and Film, edited by Paul Bowman
Stiegler and Technics, edited by Christina Howells and Gerald Moore
Badiou and the Political Condition, edited by Marios Constantinou
Nancy and the Political, edited by Sanja Dejanovic
Butler and Ethics, edited by Moya Lloyd

Forthcoming titles
Latour and the Passage of Law, edited by Kyle McGee
Agamben and Radical Politics, edited by Daniel McLoughlin
Rancière and Literature, edited by Julian Murphet and Grace Hellyer
Nancy and Visual Culture, edited by Carrie Giunta and Adrienne Janus
Balibar and the Citizen/Subject, edited by Warren Montag and Hanan Elsayed

Visit the Critical Connections website at www.euppublishing.com/series/crcs

Nancy and the Political

Edited by Sanja Dejanovic

Edinburgh University Press is one of the leading university presses in the UK. We publish academic books and journals in our selected subject areas across the humanities and social sciences, combining cutting-edge scholarship with high editorial and production values to produce academic works of lasting importance. For more information visit our website: www.edinburghuniversitypress.com

© editorial matter and organisation Sanja Dejanovic, 2015, 2017
© the chapters their several authors, 2015, 2017

Edinburgh University Press Ltd
The Tun – Holyrood Road
12 (2f) Jackson's Entry
Edinburgh EH8 8PJ
www.euppublishing.com

First published in hardback by Edinburgh University Press 2015

Typeset in 11/13 Adobe Sabon by
Servis Filmsetting Ltd, Stockport, Cheshire

A CIP record for this book is available from the British Library

ISBN 978 0 7486 8317 8 (hardback)
ISBN 978 0 7486 8318 5 (paperback)
ISBN 978 0 7486 8319 2 (webready PDF)
ISBN 978 0 7486 8320 8 (epub)

The right of Sanja Dejanovic to be identified as Editor of this work has been asserted in accordance with the Copyright, Designs and Patents Act 1988, and the Copyright and Related Rights Regulations 2003 (SI No. 2498).

Contents

List of Contributors — vii

Introduction: Sense, Praxis, and the Political — 1
Sanja Dejanovic

Event of Sense: Being-With, Ethics, Democracy

1. 'We Must Become What We Are': Jean-Luc Nancy's Ontology as *Ethos* and *Praxis* — 21
   Marie-Eve Morin

2. Badiou and Nancy: Political Animals — 43
   Christopher Watkin

3. Nancy and Hegel: Freedom, Democracy and the Loss of the Power to Signify — 66
   Emilia Angelova

4. The Event of Democracy — 88
   François Raffoul

5. Thinking Nancy's 'Political Philosophy' — 116
   Ignaas Devisch

Everything is Not Political

6. Image-Politics: Jean-Luc Nancy's Ontological Rehabilitation of the Image — 139
   Alison Ross

7. Immanent Surface: Art and the Demand for Signification — 164
   Jonathan Lahey Dronsfield

8. The Separated Gesture: Partaking in the Inoperative
   Praxis of the Already-Unmade   192
   John Paul Ricco

The Political Between Two Infinities: Evaluations

9. *Im-mundus* or Nancy's Globalising-World-
   Formation   219
   Jean-Paul Martinon

10. Precarity/Abandonment   245
    Philip Armstrong

11. 'A Struggle between Two Infinities': Jean-Luc
    Nancy on Marx's Revolution and Ours   272
    Jason E. Smith

    Index   290

List of Contributors

Emilia Angelova is Associate Professor of Philosophy at Concordia University. Her research focuses on problems of the constitution of self, singularity and subjectivity in twentieth-century continental philosophy. She has published a number of journal articles that engage with the thought of Kant, Heidegger, and Levinas. She is the recipient of Trent's Symons Award for Excellence in Teaching.

Philip Armstrong is Associate Professor at Ohio State University. He is the author of *Reticulations: Jean-Luc Nancy and the Networks of the Political* (University of Minnesota Press, 2009). He has co-edited issues of *La Part de L'Oeil* (with Laura Lisbon and Stephen Melville, 2001), and, *Res* (with Stephen Melville and Erica Naginski, 2004). Current research includes a book on a genealogy of networks, and essays on the relation between photography and phenomenology in the writings of Barthes, Damisch, and Nancy.

Sanja Dejanovic received her PhD from York University. Her dissertation deals with the paradox of sense or event of thought in Gilles Deleuze's philosophy. She is the author of various journal articles, including, 'The Sense of the Transcendental Field: Deleuze, Sartre, Husserl' with the Journal of Speculative Philosophy. She is working on a book project provisionally entitled *Freedom: On the Mutually Reflected Affirmation*.

Ignaas Devisch is Professor in Social Philosophy, Ethics and Philosophy of Medicine at University College Arteveldehogeschool and Ghent University, Belgium. He is co-editor of *Re-treating Religion: Deconstructing Christianity with Jean-Luc Nancy* (Fordham University Press, 2011).

Jonathan L. Dronsfield is Reader in Theory and Philosophy of Art at the University of Reading, and sits on the Executive Committee of the Forum for European Philosophy, London School of Economics. He has two forthcoming works, *Derrida and the Visual*, and, *Headlessness* (with Marcus Steinweg and Thomas Hirschhorn).

Jean-Paul Martinon is a lecturer in the Department of Visual Cultures at Goldsmiths College, London, UK. He was the co-founder and curator of *Rear Window* (1991–8), an independent arts trust that staged a series of exhibitions and conferences in temporary sites across London. He has published numerous essays in exhibition catalogues and academic journals on museum theory and contemporary French deconstruction. He is the author of *On Futurity: Malabou, Nancy and Derrida* (Palgrave Macmillan, 2007).

Marie-Eve Morin is Professor of Philosophy at University of Alberta. She is the author of *Jean-Luc Nancy* (Polity, 2012) and has co-edited *Jean-Luc Nancy and Plural Thinking: Expositions of World, Ontology, Politics, and Sense* (New York Press, 2012). She is currently working on a project on *Merleau-Ponty and Nancy at the Limits of Phenomenology*.

François Raffoul is Professor of Philosophy at Louisiana State University. He is the author of *Heidegger and the Subject* (Prometheus Books, 1999), *A Chaque fois Mien* (Galilee, 2003), and *The Origins of Responsibility* (forthcoming, Indiana University Press). He is the co-author (with David Pettigrew) of *Disseminating Lacan* (SUNY Press, 1996), *Heidegger and Practical Philosophy* (SUNY Press, 2002), and, more recently, *Rethinking Facticity* (SUNY Press, 2008). He has jointly translated Jean-Luc Nancy's *The Creation of the World or Globalization*, and *The Gravity of Thought*.

John Paul Ricco is Associate Professor of Contemporary Art, Media Theory, and Criticism in the Department of Visual Studies at University of Toronto. He is completing two books. One is entitled, *The Decision Between Us*, which is a theorisation of the aesthetic staging of the space of decision in late-twentieth century art and visual culture. The other, *Non-Consensual Futures*, is on the politics and ethics of the contractual, trust, faith, and futurity in the contemporary era of the simulacrum and spectacle.

Alison Ross is a member of the Research Unit in European Philosophy in the Arts Faculty at Monash University. She is the author of *The Aesthetic Paths of Philosophy: Presentation in Kant, Heidegger, Lacoue-Labarthe and Nancy* (Stanford University Press, 2007).

Jason E. Smith is Assistant Professor in the Graduate Art Department at Art Center College of Design. He writes on contemporary art, continental philosophy and political theory, and his work has recently appeared in *Critical Inquiry, Critical Companion to Contemporary Marxism, Grey Room, Parrhesia* and *Theory & Event*, among other places. With Philip Armstrong, he recently published a long interview with Jean-Luc Nancy, *Politique et au-delà* (Galilée, 2011). He is currently writing a book on the films of Guy Debord.

Christopher Watkin specialises in twentieth-century and contemporary French literature and philosophy. He has recently published *Phenomenology or Deconstruction* (Edinburgh University Press, 2008), and his most recent work deals with the theme of atheism in contemporary French thought, with particular reference to the works of Alain Badiou, Quentin Meillassoux and Jean-Luc Nancy, entitled *Difficult Atheism* (Edinburgh University Press, 2011). He is part of the Contemporary European Thought Research Group.

Introduction
Sense, Praxis, and the Political
Sanja Dejanovic

1. Replaying the Question

One of the most interesting claims made by Jean-Luc Nancy is that 'politics and philosophy have an original feature in common: both are born from the disappearance of the gods'.[1] With the disappearance of any figure that could occupy the place of power, found community or a totality of being-together in the form of the One, thereby re-inscribing another onto-theology, it becomes possible to retrace the political, putting into question yet again. If it is not a matter of reinstalling another figure, foundation or representation, which would ensure what he has referred to with Phillippe Lacoue-Labarthe as the closure of the political, then, it is a matter of, as he says, going 'deeper into the *nihil* of nihilism'; the nihilism opened up by the flight of sense, which must now be rethought as a separate domain in relation to power according to Nancy.[2] The political is born from this disappearance as it suspends us upon a void, the horizon of the political from which point we must retrace it, or from which point the political must itself be put into question. This question of the political, or the political put into question, is suggestive of the absence of any predestined project, design or end to which the political would be addressed. By going deeper into the *nihil* of nihilism, we can only anticipate so far that the question of the political arises with the event as an always renewed questioning. As Roberto Esposito notes after Walter Benjamin, it is nihilism which constitutes 'the method of world political action',[3] perhaps because each time it is its own 'struggle for a world' without a predetermined response to the question. This is why we must replay the question and rethink the political along with Nancy, all the while taking great care not to displace the act of its opening.

When raising the question of the political, the recognisable question, one that has been posed in myriad ways, is never far behind: What is to be done? Directed at Nancy's philosophy, such a question might easily become an inquiry into what sort of tools does the philosopher produce to facilitate political action, or what he calls a 'struggle for a world'. With such an inquiry it appears as though the problematic has been determined, while the question of the political merely arises as a way to facilitate action.

The question 'What is to be done?', is also the title of a short piece by Nancy included in *Retreating the Political*, a co-authored work with Phillippe Lacoue-Labarthe that serves as the culmination of the research agenda of the *Centre for Philosophical Research on the Political*. This question is of interest for many reasons, one of which is that it returns us to a traditional approach embedded in political philosophy concerning the relationship of thinking and doing or acting, and theory and practice. As Nancy writes, the question, 'What is to be done?' is perceived as posed from the position of knowledge; 'one already knows what it is right to think, and that the only issue is how one might then proceed to act'.[4] More than this, however, there is the presupposition that the philosophical stages the political act by way of the figure of the subject, the human, the citizen and so on, while the essence of the political lies in realising the representations, evaluations or values, and relations prefigured by the philosophical. But, as Nietzsche once pointed out, what if this bridge between knowledge and action was never finally built? What if this 'bridge' is precisely the interstice of questioning, of suspension, where the doing, as Nancy notes, is thought anew each time, or this thinking is itself a doing; a making of a world in which the question of doing, 'perpetually reopened ... prevents us from ever knowing in advance *what is* to be done, but imposes upon us the task of never making anything that is not a world'.[5] This is why Nancy often reminds us that he does not seek to produce a new politics. Instead, he places the political into question from the perspective of the philosophical, which resolutely keeps open this question by being itself an inquiry into the event of sense. It is with this event of sense that Nancy manages to rethink the co-emergence of the political and the philosophical with their distinct orientations. And it is precisely this event of sense, along with Nancy's novel contribution of the ontology of singular plural that prompted the opening up of this questioning, which is thought in relation to the political in this collection.

By emphasising the retracing of the political, kept open and alive through this very questioning, it is not Nancy's intention to 'deprive us of the means to action'.[6] Rather, for him, it is a matter of inquiring in what name we carry out the 'struggle for the world', or alternatively, the question becomes what is at stake in the political itself. If we are to rethink the political, an exigency that was ignited for Nancy with the events of '68, then we need to dive deeper into the *nihil* of nihilism, or inquire into our abandonment to finitude, which, for him, exposes to us that we are nothing else than shared existence, *with nothing transcendent interposed between us and action*.

For Nancy, 1968 marks the transition from one kind of being, thought in terms of cohesion, coherence, conformity, to another being-together; from a 'become what you are' to '"be what you are [in the plural singular sense] becoming" . . . without any final consecration'.[7] What is at stake in the political becomes the relation itself, our *being-with-one-another* or *being-together*, the poverty at the 'basis' of our making sense, which opens up the questioning of the political from a position of non-totality. This was the concluding achievement of the *Centre for Philosophical Research on the Political*: 'The so-called question of relation remains, to our mind, *the* central question; as such, it is even, perhaps, the question of the essence of the political'.[8]

Our consideration of the political has to be situated with respect to Nancy's conception of this relation. Since *The Inoperative Community* (1991), his concern has been to rearticulate community, to conceive of a new lexicon that 'does not put into effect any community . . . From "being-in-common", "being-together", and "separation", arriving at "being-with" or the pure and simple "with"' as being singular plural, Nancy's effort has been directed at conceiving of Being as a relation, as a *co-* or shared existence, that remains opened as such; the never finished with finite affirmations of sharing which displace the notion that everything is political.[9] It remains to be seen how this new ontology of sociality displaces the notion that everything is political, or how upholding the 'relation of the relation' is pivotal to politics becoming an activity that de-totalises.[10] For now, it is important for us to inquire, along with Nancy, as to what sort of politics we have once we are exposed to the finitude of sense, once we engage in a finite thinking that addresses our time.[11] It is only with such an engagement, an engagement with our being-with-one-another, that we are able to replay the question of the political as one that beckons to be reopened at the interstice between the affirmation of a world and a refutation of it; in other words, as becoming a struggle for a world.

2. Co-existence, Freedom, Original Ethics

Nancy first takes up the theme of relation in *The Inoperative Community* as a problem of immanence. In that text he endeavours to redefine Being as relational, while proposing that relation 'undoes, in its very principle . . . the autarchy of absolute immanence'.[12] What is at issue in this notion of relation is a sharing of existence that constitutes beings in their singularity. In other words, community is not a being-together that represses singularity, but must be the co-existence without which one could not become a singular being as such. Nancy writes:

> These singular beings are themselves constituted by sharing, they are distributed and placed, or rather *spaced*, by the sharing that makes them *others*: other for one another, and other, infinitely other for the Subject of their fusion, which is engulfed in then sharing, in the ecstasy of the sharing: 'communicating' by not communing. These places of communication are no longer places of fusion, even though in them one *passes* from one to the other; they are defined and exposed by their dislocation. Thus, the communication of sharing would be this very dis-location.[13]

Articulated as the ever transforming relation that singular beings share, community is essentially an incomplete one, an 'infinite birth of finitude'; it does not suppose a common being, but a finite existence that undoes any completion by being the sort of sharing that is a dis-location or an event of singularisation each time. This is the reason behind Nancy's claim that 'community is, in a sense, resistance itself: namely, resistance to immanence'.[14]

Although the emphasis shifts in *Being Singular Plural* (2000), *The Sense of the World* (1997), *The Birth to Presence* (1993) and other texts, towards an exposition of meaning or sense, Nancy's core aim remains, which is to conceive of Being as relational. In *Being Singular Plural*, Nancy seems to be taking up Nietzsche's claim that 'we are unknown to ourselves, we men of knowledge – and with good reason. We have never sought ourselves – how could it happen that we should find ourselves?'[15] Nietzsche's call that we must seek ourselves finds a response in Nancy's deceptively simple response of how we are what we are becoming: '*We are* meaning ... whether realized or not'.[16] In turn, meaning is 'our being-with-one-another. We do not "have" meaning anymore, because we ourselves are meaning – entirely, without reserve, infinitely, with no meaning other than "us"'.[17]

With this sort of formulation of meaning, Nancy is arguing that our being-together is the constitution of meaning, a meaning that is never finally determined, nor given in advance. Distinct from Heidegger for whom meaning emerges with *Dasein's* being in the world, Nancy's *co*-existential analytic stresses that 'Being itself, the phenomenon of Being, is meaning that is, in turn, its own circulation and *we* are this circulation.'[18] Or alternatively, Being is nothing else than the 'with' of being-with. He stresses that this being-with is not added to a prior Being or secondary to it, but '"with" is at the heart of Being'.[19] The reframing of the problem of being is not a footnote to the Heideggerian project by placing *Mitsein* at the forefront; a claim that can be made with regard to Nancy's reflections on Freud, Hegel, Rousseau, Marx, and others. A more valid estimation of Nancy's approach would be that he seeks to deconstruct where Heidegger's philosophy begins, which, for him, 'reverses the order of philosophical exposition' entirely.[20] His distinction from Heidegger's philosophy becomes evident when one considers that, for Nancy, the present is born in its division, that is to say, in being-shared, or said in other words, '*Being itself is given to us as meaning*. Being does not *have* meaning' while 'there is no meaning if meaning is not shared'; co-appearance is this sharing of meaning, the *birth to presence* being the division of meaning.[21]

While Heidegger and Nancy agree that the task of philosophy is to think finitude, Nancy's philosophy is one of surfaces not of depth. It concerns the self-referential sense of the world, not an authentic dwelling in the world. His ontology has received a great deal of attention, because he has managed to reverse the ontological exposition by beginning with the singular plural. According to him, the plural singularity of sense, its circulation, is the sharing and creation of the world anew every instance. The sharing of meaning is itself the creation of a world, this creation being nothing more than us being-with-one-another. Meaning is created precisely in the sharing of presence. Nancy understands this sharing and circulation of meaning as happening each time singularly in its plurality:

> Circulation goes in all directions: this is the Nietzschean thought of the 'eternal return', the affirmation of meaning as the repetition of the instant, nothing but this repetition, and as a result, nothing (since it is a matter of the repetition of what essentially does not return). But it is a repetition already comprised in the affirmation of the instant, in this affirmation/request seized in the letting go of the instant, affirming the passage of presence and itself passing with it, affirmation abandoned in its very movement.[22]

The present is the eternal repetition of the originary plurality of singularity, rather than the origin of *Dasein's* authentic mode of being. Nancy thus claims that there is no supplemental truth of Being other than the banal, yet confused, notion that the birth to presence of singularity is itself a plurality of singularities. In addition to this, the articulation of our being-with-one-another, the singular plural ontology, is not only an exposition of the singularity of being-with each instance, it is the plural exposition of beings in their singularity. In this respect, being singular plural manages to trace the entire ontological domain. The singular, Nancy writes, supposes the plural, it is '*each one* and, it is *each time* one, one among' all the others, and vice versa.[23]

This singularity is always a different constellation of singularities making sense anew out of nothing; hence, his formulation of this *nihil* in relation to community as its sovereignty. Though this sense is shared, it is shared insofar as it is spaced by the nothing or the void of the world. The nothing, which Nancy refers to as sovereignty in *The Inoperative Community*, becomes the truth of creation; what he will call the empty time of the event, which is the truth of every weaving of sense in the creation of a world, discussed primarily in *The Sense of the World*. To reiterate in Nancy's words, the '*nihil* of creation is the *truth* of meaning, but meaning is the originary sharing of this truth'.[24] Sense is then this beginning of a world, each time a birth to presence which presupposes nothing, each time reconstituted with the passage of time itself as the passage of time. With this continuous singularisation, Nancy wants to argue that the 'creation takes place everywhere and always – but it is this unique event, or advent, only on the condition of being each time what it is, or being what it is only "at each time" each time appearing singularly'.[25] Being a singular exposition, creation as the birth to presence is itself existence, or 'existence is creation, *our* creation; it is the beginning and end that we are'.²⁶ There is nothing more or less at stake in the world than the singular plural that extends the world out of nothing; the creation of a world 'begins its turn' with you, me, or, anybody. By creating the world out of nothing, this sense, existence itself affirmed, as Nancy notes, has absolute value in itself: '*we as* the beginning and end of the world, inexhaustible in the circumscription that nothing circumscribes, that 'the' nothing circumscribes. *We make sense*, not by setting a price or value, but by exposing the absolute value that the world *is* by itself'.²⁷ Of course such ontology does not limit the world-forming of the world to human relations, nor does it treat the world as a sphere of human activity. Instead, as Nancy writes: 'it is not so much the world of humanity, as it is the world of the non-human to which humanity is exposed and which humanity, in turn, exposes'.²⁸ Or, if you will, whereas humanity exposes the world in speech, in this sense speaking for all beings, the exposition of the world itself is always created by the sharing of the present, or by the co-appearing *there* of the human and non-human (if we can even presuppose such division, which is a point of contention). Having this awareness does not lead us to conclude that all beings have common dignity insofar as they are creatures created by God – a conclusion that translates into the mastery of humanity over nature – rather that *we* are ethically responsible in our expositions of the world. With this thought, let us turn to Nancy's ethics.

Nancy's ontological ethics addresses itself to the finite sense of existing. Defining one of the tasks of philosophy, he notes in 'Originary Ethics' that 'it isn't philosophy's job to prescribe norms or values: instead, it must think the essence or the sense of what makes up *action* as such', or what is also referred to in his work as *praxis*.²⁹ Before we can address the *thinking* of this action, which is itself a thinking of freedom for Nancy just as it is for Heidegger, let us place the emphasis on thinking this *action*.³⁰ For Nancy, action is not a characteristic of being, but being itself is action. Said in other words, if 'being is a matter of action, it is because being ... *is* what is at stake in its conduct, and its conduct is the bringing into play of being'.³¹ In accordance with this thought of being, then, an existent would not think of itself as distinct from being, but would rather think its relation 'with the proper fact of being' in its very conduct.³² Nancy goes on to note that a being's relation to Being is 'one of sense' or the 'very fact of being is one of making sense'. What he means by this is that action itself is sense or the making of sense. Existence is deceptively simple, 'to be is to make sense', with this 'to be' itself being a praxis, a making of a world that involves the thinking of being. He goes on to write in *A Finite Thought* (2003) that 'as sense's conduct, or as the conduct of sense, [an act] is essentially thinking. The essential act is thinking. But that doesn't close action back up on a "merely theoretical practice"'.³³

Why would Nancy claim that action is itself thinking? He writes that, in 'in reality, "thinking" is the name for action because sense is at issue in action'.³⁴ I will delve into this thinking a little more in a moment; for now, it suffices to say that the act of thought is itself the thinking of how sense emerges singularly.³⁵ Thinking arises with the infinite, the truth of sense, as the finite, the sharing of sense in the creation of the world. In Nancy's words, if it is to be a finite thinking, thinking must '*expose itself* to what is finite about sense'.³⁶ What is finite about sense is its un-accomplishment; never being finished with it. That is to say, finitude is the 'non-fixing of . . . signification; not, however, as the powerlessness to fix it, but as the power to leave it open'.³⁷ This praxis of sense without accomplishment is the 'condition' of action, or the 'condition' of actions making sense. According to Nancy, what is supposed here is the groundless decision for existence, *letting beings be*, that is the thinking of freedom at the heart of the creation of the world. Addressing this letting be, Nancy notes that: 'Making-sense is not of sense's making; it is making being be, or *letting* it be . . . (to have something constructed, also means to let or to give to the constructing activity as such; *sein lassen* means to let be, to give, to entrust to the activity of being as such). Letting be isn't passive; it is action itself'.³⁸ The groundlessness at the heart of sharing of finitude in which the letting be is affirmed is freedom, while freedom, as Nancy notes in *The Experience of Freedom* (1993), is the advent of co-existence.

Nancy's original ethics then consists of the affirmation of the '*fact*' of existing', with such affirmation being precisely the letting be of making-sense itself in our being-with-one-another.³⁹ This letting be is the decision for existing, a decision which is made for the finitude of sense, the never finished with sharing of sense, or alternatively, the 'infinite absenting of the appropriation of sense itself'.⁴⁰ This infinite absenting of the appropriation of sense as freedom thought in our being-with-one-another is an interesting way to posit ethical responsibility for existence. Nancy frames this in a powerful way when writing that:

Sense is the engagement between several beings, and truth always, inevitably, lies between or in this with. This is our responsibility: it isn't a task assigned to us, but an assignment that constitutes our being. We exist *as* this responsibility ... This responsibility is empty as it is absolute. This emptiness is its truth: the opening of sense. This emptiness is everything, therefore, everything except nothingness in the sense that nihilism understands it. Nihilism affirms that there is no sense, that the heavens of sense are empty. *In a sense*, absolute responsibility says the same thing: that there is no given ... sense, that sense can never be given.[41]

We exist as responsibility because our existence is affirmed in our being-with others. It is by being-with that we manage to create a world as such. This responsibility is absolute precisely because we are abandoned beings, making sense by virtue of groundlessness, senselessness, which is our freedom. Indeed, for Nancy this groundlessness is an essential aspect of the ethics insofar as we are, as Nietzsche claimed, an 'undetermined animal'. This indetermination at the heart of things is not some vague being-towards the world, but that which gives to beings future possibility insofar as they affirm the finite making of sense as the absenting of appropriation. This affirmation of future possibility – what was referred to as a letting be above – is intimate to thinking. As Nancy notes, thinking emerges with this absenting of sense, which is the resistance at the heart of things, a resistance that gives to singular beings, including the worlds that they create, measureless value; a valueless value that they partake of equally even while they are non-equivalent or different. He rightly identifies this resistance, along with the expropriation of the condition of existence, to be the most difficult to think through, all the while being precisely that which finite thought must address itself to. This sort of thinking defines the task of philosophy according to Nancy. It is a kind of thinking that 'commits itself to sense and thus to a sense that is still to come, to sense's future, rather than merely describing or delivering sense as if it were already in place'.[42] Indeed, a philosophy that is dedicated to finite thought, to the event of sense as such, as he notes, does not re-inscribe a horizon of signification, but seeks to do justice to the finite sense of being-with by responding to the exigencies of its time.

The question that arises with this original ethics is 'how do we answer for existence – and to existence'?[43] This question, which at its core is one of justice, is not only the concern for the philosophical, but frames the interstice where the inquiry into the political arises. This is what we might understand as the co-emergence of the philosophical and the political. Of course, the positing of this question is from the perspective of being-with, from the point of view of an incommensurable singularity in our co-existence, or as Nancy puts it, from the position of the 'in-appropriable property' at the heart of things. It is from the perspective of such evaluation that we manage to pose the question itself by answering the call to take it up, again. The question of the political itself emerges with our being-with-one-another each time in a singular sense, even while this being-with, our co-existence, is not, as Nancy says, political. He writes:

> If politics is again to mean something, and mean something new, it will only be in touching this 'essentiality' of existence which is itself its own 'essence', that is to say, which has no essence, which is 'arch-essentially' *exposed* to that very thing. In its structure and nature, such an exposure contains at the same time the finitude of all singularity and the *in*-common of its sharing ... 'Politics' must designate what interests each point of existence in the 'common'. The stake is the interest (that which matters) ... Thus that which interests is necessarily that which is the most common. But that which interests is most common because it is not given. It is a matter of the interval, of the 'in' or 'in between'.[44]

There is much said in this passage to orient us in this volume in thinking through the political in Nancy's philosophy. It demonstrates why it is that he is not interested in merely putting forth another politics. In the first place, the political, for Nancy, is not meant to put forth another model of the relation, community, or subjectivity, but would arise in light of that which is shared between us. With the new ontology of the singular plural, the political itself is rethought in a unique way. It is not only a post-foundational politics. It is more than this. It is true that its lack of grounding implies a being in common that is never completely determined. It is in this sense that we might talk about the political as concerning itself with the task of de-totalisation.[45] That is to say, the political itself arises in response to a relation that *it seeks to uphold as relation*, the plurality it implies in its singularity, its non-totality. This is what Nancy is getting at when claiming as early as *The Inoperative Community* that politics must be an un-working of community. But the absence of ground, thought with respect to our being-with, lends to the political a kind of revolutionary spirit, captured in the first place in the form of the question. It allows the positing of the political anew always with respect to shared existence, as a novel problematic, 'issue', or 'interest'; a notion that we must think through for ourselves each time. Addressed from the view of Nancy's ontology of singular plural, the political is concerned with plural meaning, what will later be called, the tying of sense, or alternatively, it emerges each time with singular creation of a world as a struggle for a world. This is why we cannot put forth another model of the political, but must always pose the question of the political as a function of the event. As Nancy argues, with the singular plural, a unique existence is at stake in each gesture, encounter, and act, which means that each time the political arises as a novel struggle for a world hitherto unheard, unrecognised, unexpressed. This means that not only is the relation of the relation upheld, opened up the future possibility of making a world, but the political itself is incomplete. But how exactly would the political itself be this struggle to leave the relation undetermined as such, or open to its future possibility (a thought which is central to the original ethics)? This is one of the central themes to which this collection of essays is dedicated to exploring. It is a matter of the question of the political itself arising at the interstice that conjoins two infinities.

3. World, Infinities, the non-Equivalence of Evaluations

The central problem that we must reckon with today, according to Nancy, is the closure of sense – not its infinite absenting or restlessness in world-formation, but by the workings of capital, or what he also refers to as globalisation in *The Creation of the World or Globalization* (2007). In that text, the title of which prompts us to make a decisive evaluation, he writes that 'the world has lost its capacity to "form a world": it seems only to have gained the capacity of proliferating, to the extent of its means, the "unworld"'.[46] The proliferation of the un-world is understood by Nancy as a destruction of the world, because it renders the valueless or measureless value of the singular senses of being-with equivalent. In other words, it levels them, renders them uniform, open to circulation, exchange and consumption. Capitalism exposes our being-with, but as an incapacity to create a world. In 'The Measure of the "With"' Nancy argues that 'capital exposes [the sharing of the world] as a certain violence, where being-together becomes being-of-market-value and haggled over. The being-with that is thus exposed vanishes at the same time it is exposed, stripped bare'.[47] To reiterate, in its indefinite proliferation, capitalism seems to expose the sharing of the world, even reaps the potentials of this sharing, but in the process of expropriating the possibilities of creating a world. Here being-with has weight, is given value, only insofar as it can serve as instrument, be made productive, in the creation of value.

To this creation of value, Nancy opposes the value of creation of worlds. Here what becomes at stake is the very notion of creation. To create a world according to him means, as noted, to create the world out of nothing, out of the poverty (without principle, reason, ground which would be a sort of original gift) of the world to which we are abandoned to remake anew every instance. In this sense, a world in its simplicity is a world 'for only those who inhabit it'; it does not refer to anything external to it that would give it its sense.[48] Therefore, 'thought in terms of a world, meaning refers to nothing more than to the possibility of the meaning of the world, to the proper mode of its stance insofar as it circulates between all those who stand in it'.[49] This sort of creation of the world, which Nancy calls a *praxis* or *ethos*, has as its final goal nothing else than the enjoyment of making a world, that is to say, it properly speaking has no end being itself the 'finite inscription of infinity' which is existence making sense. Or alternatively, this sort of creation is enjoyment itself, an enjoyment with incommensurable value.

However, Nancy recognises that this kind of infinite creation of worlds, particularly the excess of enjoyment as creation, seems to be one and the same thing as the infinite creation of value by capitalism. In *The Creation of the World* he posits two types of absolute value which appear to be the sides of the infinite, one of the two continuously appropriating the excess of the other. He writes that, on the one hand, 'value has value through this endless autistic process, and this infinite has no other act than the reproduction of its *potentiality* (thus in both sense of the word, power and potentiality). The "bad infinite", following Hegel, is indeed the one that cannot be *actual*'.[50] On the other hand, there is value in the Marxist sense of a 'beyond of production itself' which is enjoyment as excess.[51] But it is this excess, the creation of shared worlds as the finite of the infinite, which both evades general equivalence with respect to capitalism and with respect to itself, while also being subsumed by its other, the 'bad infinite'.

> A troubling circumstance – that such an excess of enjoyment (and enjoyment is excessive or it is not enjoyment) constitutes something like the exact parallel of profit that is the law of capital, but a parallel that inverts the sign of surplus-production. This is the case in the sense that the extortion of surplus-value profits from the value created by the work to deposit it in the account of the accumulation in general equivalency (according to the law of an indefinite addition, the principle of which is also excessive, but an excess whose *raison d'etre* is accumulation, the end/goal being to indefinitely reproduce the cycle of production and alienation). In that sense enjoyment would be shared appropriation – or appropriating sharing – of what cannot be accumulated or what is not equivalent, that is, of value itself (or of meaning) in the singularity of its creation . . . What matters is to be able to think how the proximity of the two 'ex-' or this twofold excess is produced, how the same world is divided in this way. In a way, profit and enjoyment placed back to back behave like two sides of the infinite.[52]

Now that we are brought to the 'crossroads of two infinities', the question for Nancy becomes – How can we make decisive evaluations which in one and the same gesture do justice to the sharing of worlds as incalculable and non-equivalent, while exposing the nonsense of capital? In other words, it is insufficient to say that capitalism itself discloses its own meaninglessness, as excess or surplus here becomes the potential for evermore accumulation. We must instead, according to him, venture to ask how to do 'justice to the infinite in act', to this enjoyment which is the creation of shared worlds of sense, to the value of creation which finds value in its making sense in itself.[53] This is the task to which *The Truth of Democracy* (2010) is dedicated to thinking through. In that text Nancy puts forth a novel conception of democracy, no longer being one political form amongst others, but as consisting of evaluative gestures of non-equivalence, akin to Nietzsche's re-evaluation of values, that displace the levelling of sense by capital. Since capitalism nullifies meaning by rendering singular worlds indistinguishable, exchangeable, or substitutable, a democracy of non-equivalence that deposes economic domination would be one in which each making of sense is an evaluative affirmation with incommensurable value.⁵⁴ Such evaluation, discussed above as the decision of existence, is understood by Nancy as the 'sharing out of the incalculable' which no measure can appropriate. This kind of sharing of the incalculable, the infinite excess of sharing, is the *truth* of democracy, since it is the perpetual reopening of the infinite in the finite, or the re-evaluation and un-working of our being-with on the basis of nothing else than shared existence; embraced finitude in the infinite surpassing of the being-with one another (Pascal's transcendence) that allows us to renegotiate what justice indeed is when faced with the exigencies of our time. Democracy, here conceived of as closer to anarchy with Bataille's claim that sovereignty is nothing, becomes an event, an event of sense, unique each time, awaiting to be remade in our being-together. In other words, democracy, as with Rousseau's social contract, does not presuppose a grounding of any sort, but is itself invented in each encounter with one another; an encounter in which we keep open the infinite sharing of the incalculable, the incommensurable value of each singular sense, by resisting the imposition of any form that transcends the very creation of worlds.

How is such a resistance against the levelling of singular affirmation political, however, if at all? Nancy's argument in *The Truth of Democracy* is that democracy as the groundless ground of any decisive evaluation is metaphysics, not politics. One of his major aims in that text, as with a number of others, is to sever politics from the praxis of sense. Here the concern arises yet again as to whether Nancy's philosophy is able to orient politics at all. 'Someone will say to me: So you are declaring openly that, for you, democracy is not political! And then you just leave us hanging, without any means to action, intervention, or struggle, as you gaze off dreamily towards your "infinite"'.⁵⁵ His response to this sort objection is that the 'political question can no longer seriously be asked except by considering what democracy engages as a sort of principal going beyond the political order'. In other words, it is not a question of doing without politics, rather, the political question itself arises along with such evaluative affirmations which are not political as such. The political, then, would be 'born in the separation between itself and another order ... a separation that might be said to be that of truth or of sense, of this sense of the world'.⁵⁶ Born in the separation, politics, for Nancy, is the opening up the space for such affirmations or it is in the service of making possible the tying of sense by art, love, thought, existence and so on, but it does not itself create sense as such. As he notes, while the praxis of sense in any of the mentioned, art, love, thought, existence, is the 'finishing off of the infinite', politics is itself indefinite.⁵⁷

What does Nancy mean when arguing that politics is indefinite? In *The Sense of the World* (1998) he writes that though 'politics begins with sense (undifferentiated and vague being-toward), [it] must punctuate itself into truth (the first punctuation being the form of power)'. So as to 'punctuate itself into truth', politics needs to be understood, not as the fulfilment of desire to form sense where it lacks, as reinforcing another place of power, or as accomplishing itself in any sense, but rather, as opening up space for events of sense by severing the register of the non-political from the imperatives of power. In order to be in the service of democratic evaluations, politics would enable, Nancy writes, 'goals over which power as such is powerless', or a 'surpassing of power' in the re-negotiation of community.⁵⁸ Politics here would then enable the 'power of reversal' of one infinite into another, by opening up the space for events of sense. While democracy consists of singular evaluative affirmations, the struggle for a world, which makes possible the inversion of one infinite into another, would be a political one. Because what is at stake in the political is not simply this inversion, but the creation of sense by way of which the question of the political arises to begin with, politics is a struggle for a world that is each time re-animated by a novel claim for justice that disputes power in its many manifestations. What is at stake in the question of the political, for Nancy, is thus not some definite form or end, but doing justice to the incalculable value of each singular being-with by making possible the weaving of sense. The question of the political born in the interstice that conjoins two infinities is a radical rethinking of its essence, one deserving the spirited responsiveness it receives in this collection.

Notes

1. Roberto Esposito and Jean-Luc Nancy, 'Dialogues on the Philosophy to Come', trans. Timothy Campbell, *Minnesota Review*, Number 75, Fall 2010, pp. 71–88 (p. 76).
2. Ibid., p. 76. This separation is discussed by Jean-Luc Nancy in *The Truth of Democracy*, trans. P. A. Brault and M. Naas (New York: Fordham University Press, 2010).
3. Ibid., p. 77.

4. Nancy, 'What is to be Done?' in Nancy and Lacoue-Labarthe, *Retreating the Political* (London: Routledge, 1997), p. 151. I've also considered this relationship between knowledge and action as Nietzsche questions it in 'The Paradox of Sense, or on the Event of Thought in Gilles Deleuze's Philosophy', York University 2013, unpublished manuscript.
5. Ibid., p. 152; original emphasis.
6. Nancy, 'What is to be Done?' and in *The Truth of Democracy*, p. 29 on political action in relation to democracy.
7. Jean-Luc Nancy, *A Finite Thinking*, ed. Simon Sparks (Stanford: Stanford University Press, 2003), p. 302. For a study of becoming and its ethical implications see Morin's '"We Must Become What We Are": Jean-Luc Nancy's Ontology as Ethos and Praxis' in this collection.
8. Nancy and Lacoue-Labarthe, *Retreating the Political* (London: Routledge, 1997), p. 127 original emphasis.
9. Roberto Esposito and Jean-Luc Nancy, 'Dialogues on the Philosophy to Come', p. 81.
10. For other considerations of the political see Oliver Marchart's 'Retracing the Political Difference: Jean-Luc Nancy' in *Post-Foundational Political Thought* (Edinburgh: Edinburgh University Press, 2007), Philip Armstrong's *Reticulations: Jean-Luc Nancy and the Networks of the Political* (Minneapolis: University of Minnesota Press, 2009), Ignaas Devisch's *Jean-Luc Nancy and the Question of Community* (New York: Bloomsbury, 2013), the section 'Expositions of the Political: Justice, Freedom, Equality' in Petter Gratton and Marie-Eve Morin's *Jean-Luc Nancy and Plural Thinking: Expositions of World, Ontology, Politics, and Sense* (Albany, NY: SUNY Press, 2012), Simon Critchley's *Ethics, Politics, Subjectivity: Essays on Derrida, Levinas and Contemporary French Thought* (New York: Verso, 2009), Walter Brogan's 'The Parting of Being: On Creation and Sharing in Nancy's Political Ontology', *Research in Phenomenology*, 40:3, 2010, Agamben et al., *Democracy in What State?* (New York: Columbia University Press, 2012), and Jean-Luc Nancy, Philip Armstrong and Jason E. Smith, *Politique et au-delà* (Paris: Galilée, 2011).
11. Nancy, *A Finite Thinking*, pp. 10–20 or see the first section on 'Thinking'.
12. Jean-Luc Nancy, *The Inoperative Community*, ed. Peter Connor (Minneapolis: University of Minnesota Press, 1991), p. 4.
13. Ibid., p. 25.

14. Ibid., p. 35.
15. Nietzsche, *On the Genealogy of Morals* (New York: Vintage Books, 1989), p. 15.
16. Jean-Luc Nancy, *Being Singular Plural*, trans. R. D. Richardson and A. E. O'Byrne (Stanford: Stanford University Press, 2000), p. 1.
17. Ibid.
18. Ibid., p. 2; original emphasis.
19. Ibid., p. 30. For an excellent discussion of the 'being-with' also see Christopher Fynsk's *Heidegger: Thought and Historicity* (Ithaca: Cornell University Press, 1994).
20. Ibid. [minor change to quotation from 'reverse' to 'reverses'].
21. Ibid., p. 2; original emphasis.
22. Ibid., p. 4.
23. Ibid., p. 11; original emphasis.
24. Ibid., p. 3; original emphasis.
25. Ibid., p. 16.
26. Ibid., p. 17; original emphasis.
27. Ibid., p. 4; original emphasis.
28. Ibid., p. 18.
29. Nancy, *A Finite Thinking*, p. 173; original emphasis.
30. On the question of freedom also see Jean-Luc Nancy, *The Experience of Freedom*, trans. B. McDonald (Stanford: Stanford University Press, 1993), and a study of it by Patrick Roney, 'Evil and the Experience of Freedom: Nancy on Schelling and Heidegger', *Research in Phenomenology*, 9:3, 2009, pp. 374–400.
31. Nancy, *A Finite Thinking*, p. 175.
32. Ibid.
33. Ibid.
34. Ibid.
35. Ibid., p. 4.
36. Ibid., p. 30; original emphasis.
37. Ibid., p. 178.
38. Ibid., p. 177.
39. Ibid., p. 13.
40. Ibid., p. 13.
41. Ibid., p. 296.
42. Ibid., p. 293.
43. Jean-Luc Nancy, 'The Compearance: From the Existence of "Communism" to the Community of "Existence"', *Political Theory*, 20:3, August 1992, pp. 371–98 (p. 373).
44. Ibid., p. 390; original emphasis.

45. See 'Is Everything Political?' in Nancy's *The Truth of Democracy*.
46. Jean-Luc Nancy, *The Creation of the World, or Globalization*, trans. F. Raffoul and D. Pettigrew (Albany: SUNY Press, 2007), p. 43. For a study of violence in Nancy's philosophy see Morin's 'Nancy, Violence and the World', *Parrhesia*, 16, 2013, pp. 61–72.
47. Nancy, *Being Singular Plural*, p. 74.
48. Nancy, *The Creation of the World, or Globalization*, p. 42.
49. Ibid., p. 43.
50. Ibid., p. 39; original emphasis. For Nancy's reading of Hegel see his text *On Hegel: The Restlessness of the Negative* (Minneapolis: University of Minnesota Press, 2002). Also see Jason Smith's excellent introduction to that text, his discussion of the relationship of the political to the non-political, and Angelova's paper 'Nancy and Hegel: Freedom, Democracy and the Loss of the Power to Signify' included in this collection.
51. Ibid., p. 45.
52. Ibid., p. 46. For a more exhaustive study of the crossroads of these two infinities see Smith's paper entitled '"A Struggle Between Two Infinities": Jean-Luc Nancy on Marx's Revolution and Ours'.
53. Ibid., p. 40.
54. For Nancy, this exigency to redefine democracy as an overturning of the nihilism or nullification of meaning arose with the events of '68. For a considerable discussion of democracy as event see Raffoul's 'The Event of Democracy' in this volume.
55. Nancy, *The Truth of Democracy*, p. 29.
56. Ibid., p. 18.
57. Nancy, 'Finite and Infinite Democracy' in Agamben et al., *Democracy in What State?*, p. 74. The separation of aesthetics and politics is explicated in this volume in the subsection entitled 'Everything is Not Political'.
58. Ibid., p. 70.

Event of Sense:
Being-With, Ethics,
Democracy

I

'We Must Become What We Are': Jean-Luc Nancy's Ontology as *Ethos* and *Praxis*

Marie-Eve Morin

In *Being Singular Plural*, Jean-Luc Nancy asserts that the ontology of being-with, or the thinking of the 'we' he is developing in this book, is at the same time an ethos and a praxis.[1] Nancy goes so far as to say that: 'There is no difference between the ethical and the ontological: the "ethical" exposes what the "ontological" disposes.'[2] From a cursory reading of various passages, we can glean Nancy's reasons for affirming this equivalence. His ontology is an ethos and a praxis because there can be no appropriation of the meaning of the 'with', no representation of the 'we'. More than ten years later, in a text about democracy the aim of which is more specifically to carve out the respective spaces of the political and the ontological, Nancy affirms: '"communism" must . . . be posited as a given, as a fact: our first given. Before all else, we are in common. Then we must become what we are: the given is an exigency, and this exigency is infinite.'[3] This affirmation echoes another one found in Nancy's earlier book on community, where we can read: 'Community is given to us with being and as being, well in advance of all our projects, desires, and undertakings. At bottom, it is impossible for us to lose it . . . We cannot not compear . . . Community is given to us . . . it is not a work to be done or produced. But it is a task, which is different – an infinite task at the heart of finitude.'[4]

In *Being Singular Plural*, the understanding of our being-in-common as *ethos* and *praxis*, as task and exigency, is developed explicitly against what Nancy calls philosophical politics or political philosophy – that is, against the reciprocal determination of philosophy and politics. In this reciprocal determination, each is the subject of the other. The *polis*, as the place where the *logos* is articulated, makes possible philosophy in its metaphysical institution, as the science that provides a ground for beings.

At the same time, philosophy, insofar as it produces a common reason, makes possible the *polis* as the gathering of rational men (*anthrōpos logikos*).⁵ As the middle term between politics and philosophy, the *logos* guarantees both the gathering of the *polis* and the unity of philosophy. If Nancy calls for a recommencement of philosophy from itself against this philosophical politics, it is because such a recommencement of philosophy apart from its overdetermination by politics (as founded in and as founding the *polis*) lays bare our ontological situation: not the commonality of reason as the 'one-origin' but the dis-position and ex-position of a plurality of singular origins without common ground. Without common ground, our existences derive their consistency not from something common but from the 'in' or the 'between' of existences, their sharing out. Yet, Nancy is clear that he 'does not plan to propose an "other politics"'⁶ under the heading of an ontology of the singular plural or the in-common. His ontology is an *ethos* and a *praxis*, but it does not propose an 'other politics'. This of course does not mean that it does not propose something else than a politics understood within the horizon of metaphysics (as the production or management of a given common).

In order to understand the role and place of 'another politics' or of 'another of politics' in Nancy's ontology, it is first crucial to elucidate the way in which Nancy's ontology is an *ethos* and a *praxis*. In order to do so, I will make a long detour through Nancy's description of existence as abandonment and as freedom, and then as decision. I will draw on the texts in which Nancy engages most directly with Heidegger's thought (in particular, *The Experience of Freedom*, 'Heidegger's "Originary Ethics"', and 'The Decision of Existence'), and I will use Heidegger's own works, when necessary, in order to flesh out and sometimes extrapolate from Nancy's evocative claims. The danger of proceeding in this way is that we run the risk of conflating Nancy with Heidegger. Indeed, Nancy often uses Heideggerian syntagms in such a way that the reader is unclear whether he is merely explicating a Heideggerian thought or speaking in his own name. Hence, I will also try to pay attention to the changes in emphasis in Nancy's reappropriation of Heidegger's thought: from '*es gibt*' to '*il y a*', from gift to freedom, from guarding and sheltering to opening and exposing. Throughout it will seem that Nancy is confusing existence with Being. The reason for this apparent confusion will become clear at the end of this chapter. Despite its Heideggerian connotation, existence in Nancy's sense is not limited to Dasein but applies to each being: star, rose, god, city, stone. In the end, it is the way in which existence is a struggle for the world in which other beings are implicated from the start that will differentiate Nancy's ontology, and hence its *ethos* and *praxis*, most radically from Heidegger's.

1. Abandonment of Being: From Gift to Freedom

In the simplest terms, Being means, for Nancy, *Setzung*, position or positioning. An essence doesn't exist or it exists only when it is positioned. This is how Nancy reads the Kantian thesis that is also discussed by Heidegger in *Basic Problems of Phenomenology*: 'Being is not a real predicate', or in its positive formulation: 'Being is absolute position of a thing.'[7] Nancy explains in the following words:

> Being is neither substance nor cause of the thing, rather, it is a being-the-thing in which the verb 'to be' has a transitive value of 'positioning', but one in which the 'positioning' is based on and caused by nothing else but Dasein, being-there, being thrown down, given over, abandoned, offered up by existence.[8]

The existence of an essence lies in its taking place, its arrival or coming 'here and now'. 'Existence' (that there is such and such, rather than what there is as such) is, in Nancy's terms, abandoned being. This expression has a double meaning. First, Being is abandoned or left behind as a cause or ground, or a condition of possibility that would precede what is and serve to explain why what is, is. In other words, the answer to the fundamental question of metaphysics, 'Why are there beings rather than nothing?', is not to be sought in the antecedence of Being. The answer already lies in the question: 'Since there is something, and not everything, it is because this thing is in abandonment, it is because everything is abandoned.'[9] This is the second sense of abandonment: the cause/ground of the thing withdraws into the thing itself. The notion of creation *ex nihilo* is another way of thematising this abandonment or withdrawal of the cause/ground of beings. That the world – beings as a whole – is 'created' does not mean that it is produced by a very powerful Demiurge on the basis of a pre-existing nothing. The nothing is not that on the basis of which the world is made, since such a thought of the nothing would turn it into a pre-given substrate. To think of a creation *ex nihilo*, it is not enough to get rid of a God-Maker; the nihil must also be emptied out of its role as underlying, pre-given substrate. Ultimately, what needs to be emptied out or deconstructed, is the place of the transcendent principle that grounds the world, a place that can be occupied by a God-Maker, by the 'Man' of humanism, or by the 'Nothing'. What we are left with after the deconstruction of the transcendent principle – though speaking of a 'remainder' can mislead us into thinking that this process is negative and leads to a loss – is the world in its proper sense: 'nothing but that which grows [*rien que cela qui croît*] (*creo, cresco*), lacking any growth principle'.[10]

The abandonment of Being in the double sense in which Nancy uses the phrase shows deep affinities with Heidegger's *Seinsverlassenheit*. Yet, according to Nancy, Heidegger's *Seinsverlassenheit* still has the connotations of withdrawing, leaving behind in one's retreat and hence holding to oneself, connotations from which Nancy will try to distance himself. Indeed, in *Der Spruch des Anaximander*, Heidegger characterises the way in which Being discloses itself in the unconcealment of what is as a *Ansichhalten*, a keeping to oneself.[11] On the other hand, what Nancy emphasises in the abandonment is an expenditure without reserve, and hence a certain disponibility and abundance of what is. Indeed, while *abandonner* has the connotation of a withdrawing or leaving behind, and hence of a neglecting, not caring for, *être à l'abandon* does not only have this connotation of destituteness, but also points to a certain freedom, availability or even abundance, as a garden *à l'abandon* is an overgrown garden.[12]

What we witness then, from Heidegger to Nancy, is a subtle shift in the meaning of Being, and more specifically in the significance of the abandonment or withdrawal of Being. The crux of the problem could be formulated in the following way: in the withdrawal or abandonment of Being, is Being kept in reserve, hidden and withdrawn, or is it rather the case that Being is nothing more than the thing itself in its sheer existence? Rightly or wrongly, Nancy sees Heidegger as holding on to the first option: Being withdraws, it is effaced by the presencing of beings; it holds itself back and can only 'appear' as nothing. For Heidegger, the 'free gesture' of the disclosure of Being – the gesture that lets beings be encountered meaningfully in the world – is also at the same time a holding back that is responsible for the history of Being as errancy.

Only beings are, so that when Being is thought, it is thought as an exemplary or supreme being. This forgetting or oblivion of Being is a consequence of the essential withdrawal of Being (the fact that Being, which is not a being, is only the 'letting-be' of beings).

For Nancy, Heidegger's thought of the concealing of Being is an ontodicy, a justification of evil.[13] This is the case because evil is made possible by the withdrawal of Being, but it does not ruin Being as such. Rather Being holds itself back, and in this way enables both das *Grimmige* und das *Heile*, fury and grace, by enabling good and evil. Thought in such a way, the withdrawal of Being holds within itself the possibility of a 'saving'. Being withdraws behind good and evil, remains the potential for both good and evil, even in the midst of fury. Even though evil does not necessarily lead to its reversal into the good, that is, even though the history of metaphysics is not necessarily the history of a redemption, evil is still justified. In 'The Question Concerning Technology', reading the two verses of Hölderlin's *Patmos*, 'But where *danger* is, *grows* / The *saving power* also', Heidegger shows how the saving power [*das Rettende*] is the flip side of revealing [*Entbergen*] in so far as the latter happens or comes to pass 'from out of a granting [*Gewähren*] and as such a granting'.[14] As the translator points out, the verb *gewähren* is connected, for Heidegger, to both *wahren*, to watch over, keep safe or protect, and *währen*, to endure, and means, besides to grant, also to guarantee or vouchsafe.[15] The highest dignity of the human being lies in keeping watch over the unconcealment insofar as it is a granting, that is, insofar as it harbours a granting gesture that necessary conceals itself in granting that what is unconceals itself.

In the *Letter on Humanism*, Heidegger speaks instead of *wahren* or *Wahrnis* of a guarding [*hüten*] or shepherding [*hirten*] of the truth of Being.[16] What is so shepherded is not what is in so far as its appearance is granted to us, but the 'source' of the meaningful appearance of what is. What Heidegger comes to realise after *Being and Time* is the inadequacy of transcendental-horizonal thinking to grasp this source in its giving or granting gesture, to think from out of this source rather than towards it. That the transcendental-horizonal way of thinking is inadequate to think the source of meaningfulness comes to the fore in the essay 'On the Essence of Truth' as soon as this source is shown to be hidden: both concealed and overlooked. Thought as the mystery, *das Geheimnis*, this source is not only responsible for the giving or sending, the opening up of a world, but it also holds open the inexhaustible possibility of other worlds. This source will later be thought as *Ereignis*, as the 'event' that binds the human being to Being and vice versa, by throwing the human being into a specific meaning-formation (a specific world with its specific way of understanding what it means to be and hence of relating to what is), and calling forth the human being to sustain this meaning-formation. If the source is hidden, it is not because it stands behind something that blocks our access to it but because, as the bond between the human being and Being, it cannot be surveyed or mastered by the human being. This would require that the human being step out of its bond with Being. At the same time, if there is an 'experience' of the mystery that does not betray this mystery by making it present, but at the same time still lets us experience it as holding in reserve possibilities of radical transformation of the human being–Being bond, then this experience must be the experience of the contingency of our current bond to Being. Such is the experience of the history of Being in its epochal character, that is, as both a granting and a refusal, or as granting refusal. The sheltering or guarding of the mysterious source of the meaningfulness of beings requires that we hold on to the reciprocal bond between the human being and Being, that we become the grounder of the 'there' or the 'open' that is opened through this reciprocal bond. But what is guarded then is not a thing but an opening. As Nancy points out, an opening cannot be guarded by protecting it from or guaranteeing it against closure since such a move would turn the opening into something given, stable, fixed. The guard of the open can only happen through its opening without protection or guarantee.[17] There is nothing 'there' to be safeguarded.

To avoid this subtle shift in the understanding of Being from a letting/opening to a giving that has to be received and kept, Nancy insists on shifting the emphasis from a granting or giving of Being toward the freedom of this granting. In this way, the granting does not becomes subordinated to a *truth* of Being as concealing, refusal, mystery, a truth that would have to be retrieved, remembered and kept. A *free* giving is not a movement of concealing in the unconcealing of beings, a concealing of Being's own giving in the given beings. Such a giving gesture is not 'free' since it runs the risk of turning into the (mysterious) 'origin' or ground of beings. Or at least it is not free of the metaphysical thought of freedom that questions what is with regards to its ground. In the shift of emphasis Nancy proposes, Being is not thought as '*es gibt*' but as '*il y a*': that there are beings. While the '*es gibt*' is the formulation of a *Verlassenheit/Vergessenheit* that also calls for a guarding/sheltering or a reminiscing, the '*il y a*' is the formulation of freedom, of the abandonment of beings to the *y*, to the spacing of a place.[18]

In the releasement of beings into the clearing of Being, nothing is properly held back or 'withdrawn'. This means, according to Nancy, that the ontological difference is annulled. We know that for Heidegger the ontological difference is the way in which Beyng comes to pass as the forgetting of Being. Metaphysics thinks Being always from out of beings and in view of beings as that which is different from beings. Being is the answer to the question: What are beings qua beings? This way of questioning beings sets Being apart from beings and thought as their ground. Hence the ontological difference is invoked by metaphysics, but it is not thought as such, the focus being on the two different elements, the relation between which is one of grounding. The ontological difference is overcome in a leap into *Ereignis*, where the difference is thought as *Unter-schied* and *Austrag*.[19] What is so thought is not Being as the different, but rather the inbetween that perdures and out of which Being and beings differentiate themselves. The co-belonging of Being and beings is now thought transitively as overwhelming and arrival: Being comes over beings and unconceals them; beings arrive and abide in sheltering the overcoming that unconceals them. Here, beings are not expropriated or abandoned by Being; rather they shelter the truth of Being.

When Nancy speaks of the annulment of the ontological difference, he seems to think something similar to the Heideggerian step back into the domain where Being and beings can be experienced from out of the difference in which they are held apart and toward each other. Nancy comes to think of the ontological difference, of the fact that Being is not a being, by looking back to the Latin etymology of the word '*rien*'. As Nancy points out, 'nothing' [*rien*] does not mean 'not a thing at all' but rather the thing itself, *res*, insofar as it is no thing, that is, in so far as it empties itself out of its essence, its whatness.[20] Here Nancy differentiates between *le néant* (nothingness, *das Nichts*) and *le rien* (nothing, *rem*, the thing). Nothingness is what Being turns into as soon as it is posited in its difference from beings, as the universal and the highest. Nothing, on the other hand, is the thing taken in its existence (and not in its essence, as this or that): 'Nothing is the thing tending towards its pure and simple being of a thing, consequently also towards the most common being of something and thus towards the vanishing, momentary quality of the smallest amount of beingness [*étantité*].'[21] The difference is cancelled as a difference between two realities, Being and being, the ground and the grounded, but also as the abandonment of beings by Being, the withdrawal and reserve of Being. There are only beings, nothing behind, beneath or beyond them. Or, in other words: There is no difference between existence and the existent, the existent's 'reality' is nothing other than the putting into play of its own existence. Hence, the annulment of the ontological difference has nothing to do with the confusion between Being and beings, a forgetting of their difference. Rather Nancy writes: 'This step back [from the ontological difference into the dif-ference] is the *identity of being and beings*: existence. Or more precisely: freedom. Freedom: *the withdrawal of every positing of being, including its being posited as differing from beings*.'[22]

If existence is equated with freedom, it is because there can only be existence where the essence or the signification of this existence is not given. Nancy writes

> once existence clearly offers itself ... as a factuality that contains in itself and as such, *hic and nunc*, the reason for its presence and the presence of its reason, we must ... think its 'fact' as a 'freedom'. This means that we must think what gives existence back to itself and only to itself, or what makes it available as an *existence* that is neither an essence nor a sheer given [in the sense of a brute, meaningless fact].[23]

The annulment of the ontological difference, the move from 'Being is not a being' to 'Being is nothing but that there is being [*qu'il y a l'étant*]' does not mean that we can no longer make any distinction between Being and entities, that there is brute meaningless given. On the contrary, it means that the difference is itself active or praxical, in the technical sense that opposes *praxis* to *poiesis*. It is 'the reality of Dasein insofar as it is, in and of itself, open and called to an essential and "active" relation to the proper fact of being'.[24] To make this difference is to make sense, but it is not to produce something else above existence itself, a transcendent signification. But this non-givenness of such a signification does not mean that it is projected into an inaccessible realm from which the existent would be cut off. Rather than the 'powerlessness to fix the sense of existence, this non-givenness has to be thought positively as "the power to leave it open"'.[25] Sense is non-givable: it is not what awaits us at the end of a long process, it is not what existence strives for or desires as if it aimed at some object or some ideal above existence itself. The non-givenness of sense makes up the entire act of existing itself. We could also say that existence aims at and desires nothing but the non-givenness of its sense, that is, it aims at and desires nothing but its freedom.[26] Does that not contradict what was said at the beginning, namely, that existence is the position of essence? Not if we recognise that the positioning of essence is an offering, an exposition so that the essence is not posited in-itself, in pure self-presence, but 'handed over to itself [*remis à soi*]',[27] 'exposed to being *of* itself, *for* itself, and *unto* itself what it is *in* itself'.[28] As Nancy says:

> To exist does not mean simply 'to be'. On the contrary: to exist means *not* to be in the immediate presence or in the immanency of a 'being-thing'. To exist is not to be immanent, or not to be present to oneself, and not to be sent forth *by* oneself. To exist, therefore, is to hold one's 'selfness' as an 'otherness', and in such a way that no essence, no subject, no place can present *this otherness in itself* – either as the proper selfness of an other, or an 'Other', or a common being (life or substance).[29]

The whole point is to understand this self-relation as something else than a self-determining (Kant: to be free is to give oneself the law of one's own action without any relation to what is outside oneself as rational being) or self-making (Sartre: to be free is to be the origin of one's own life-project or of one's own meaning, to be able to negate what one is and make oneself into the self one wants to be). In both cases, the self becomes a self-founding entity absolved from any relation with exteriority. The self closes itself upon itself in the infinite circle of self-relation.

To think of the givenness of the self as relation is to think the self as opening or spacing, or as différance. Différance is not a relation between two things that would exist prior to their being put into relation, a relation that would first let them appear as different from each other, but only insofar as each would remain identical to itself. Rather, différance is the openness or spacing that first allows something like a self to identify itself. What both Derrida and Nancy emphasise is the irreducibility or absolute exteriority of the 'spacing' that allows for something to exist.[30] This 'spacing' *is* not, but it allows that there be things. Following this logic, existence lies not in the immediacy of self-presence but rather in the 'movement' of being-unto-self or being-toward-self. This means that there is nothing given at the origin of this 'movement' or this 'exposition'. Rather, existence is an 'effect' of the spacing that rends the immediate presence of the self and turns it inside-out, exposing it to itself and others.

We started by saying that for Nancy, being means positioning: *that* a thing is rather than *what* it is. In speaking in this way, we seemed to repeat the *essentia/existentia* distinction that Heidegger diagnoses as the key feature of metaphysical thinking (*existentia* is the actual presence or givenness of some 'what'). Later, we said that nothing (or being) is the thing tending towards the simple and most common being of a thing. This seemed again to reaffirm Being as *existentia* and remain within the metaphysical thinking of Being as essence and existence. Yet Nancy's positioning is not metaphysical: neither essentialist nor existentialist, neither the position of an essence, nor the pure position of an existent that would have to make its own essence. Rather, if what exists has the structure of Différance, then this means that the existent does stand there within its essence but is fully engaged in existence, in an active relation with its Being.

2. The *Ethos* and *Praxis* of Existence as Decision

We are now in a position to understand how the 'freedom' of existence, the 'non-givenness' of its essence makes of existence an *ethos* and a *praxis*. While Nancy writes that his ontology is both an *ethos* and a *praxis*, I think it is important to understand that the *ethos* is itself a *praxis* and vice versa, since this exemplifies the same shift from Heidegger's insistence on the gift towards Nancy's emphasis of freedom outlined above.

In his essay on Heidegger's 'Letter on Humanism', Nancy comes to the conclusion that when existence is understood as self-relation, as opening for and to sense, then 'ethics becomes the ontology of ontology itself'.[31] We could take this affirmation to mean that ethics is metontology. Indeed, this thought is not far from the position Heidegger held in the 1928 lecture course, *The Metaphysical Foundations of Logic*. There, Heidegger speaks of a metontology, which is the domain of the metaphysics of existence, as the domain where the question of ethics may be raised properly for the first time.³² The universalisation and radicalisation of fundamental ontology, which consists in the analytic of Dasein and of the temporality of Being (and hence which is descriptive in its approach), leads to a turn or swerve into a metontology: a reflection on beings as whole or of the totality of beings in the light of the Being brought to light in fundamental ontology. Ontology depends on the factical existence of Dasein, which depends on the factical presence of nature. Hence fundamental ontology leads back to a metontology or a metaphysical ontic, even though the latter still depends on Dasein's understanding of Being. The metaphysics of existence, which clarifies the role of existing Dasein in the totality of beings is housed in metontology and builds the bridge to, or consists in the metaphysical foundations of, ethics. Yet, Heidegger puts into question such an understanding of the relation between ontology and ethics in the *Letter on Humanism*, not because it is mistaken, but because we do not know what is meant by the two terms, ontology and ethics, let along how they relate, until we think them in relation to the truth of Being. Here's what Heidegger says in the *Letter*:

> If the name 'ethics', in keeping with the basic meaning of the word *ēthos*, should now say that ethics ponders the abode of the human being, then that thinking which thinks the truth of being as the primordial element of the human being, as one who eksists, is in itself originary ethics. However, this thinking is not ethics in the first instance because it is ontology. For ontology always thinks solely the being (on) in its being. But as long as the truth of being is not thought all ontology remains without its foundation.³³

Hence the 'ontology of ontology' here is not the metontology of 1928, but the thinking that ponders the truth of being as the abode (*Aufenthalt*) of the human being. This thinking of the truth of Being, or more precisely the thought of the human being in its relation to the truth of Being, is the thought of a leaping into and a steadfastness in *Da*-sein, in the there.

But while Heidegger has, according to Nancy, a tendency to think the *Aufenthalt* of the human being in the open region as an abiding and the place of this *Aufenthalt* as abode (*demeure*, house), Nancy himself thinks it more actively as conduct. Or, for Nancy, it is essential to remember that to 'remain in the opening', to abide, is to act. Indeed, we should remember that Heidegger's 'Letter on Humanism' is a reflection on *'l'agir'*, das *Handeln*. If Heidegger has defined Dasein in *Being and Time* as the entity for whom 'in its very Being that Being is an *issue* for it', this issue is for Nancy an action or conduct: The translation of *'es geht um das Sein'* by *'il s'agit de l'être'* lets 'the issue' appear clearly in relation to an *agir*: an action or a conduct. Nancy understands this conduct as decision. To 'decide to exist' means to let existence come to itself. The whole point is to understand this movement of 'owning' at the heart of existence that Nancy calls 'decision'. Here, we must turn to essay 'The Decision of Existence' and the insightful reading of the concept of authenticity (*Eigentlichkeit*: ownness or the proper) in *Being and Time* it proposes.[34]

In *Being and Time*, it can seem as though authenticity and inauthenticity are two possibilities of being between which Dasein is free to choose, while its existence as such remains indifferent to this choice. Indeed Heidegger does say that existence, as a potentiality-for-Being (*Seinkönnen*) which is in each case mine, 'is free either for authenticity or for inauthenticity or for a mode in which neither of these has been differentiated [*frei für Eigentlichkeit oder Uneigentlichkeit oder die modale Indifferenz ihrer*]'.[35] Of course, Heidegger also says that 'possibility, as an *existentiale*, does not signify a free-floating potentiality-for-Being in the sense of the "liberty of indifference" *(libertas indifferentiae)*. In every case Dasein ... has already got itself into definite possibilities.'[36] Dasein is always already involved in existing, and this means that it has always already 'lost itself', or that thrown Dasein is always already falling, entangled in what is of concern, so that it has not taken hold of its own existing. But Dasein can be freed for its ownmost potentiality-for-Being so that it can choose itself.[37] At the same time, we know that whatever this choice consists of, authenticity is only an 'existentiell modification' or a 'modified way of grasping' falling everydayness.[38]

Based on this textual evidence, Nancy will make two claims: 1) the decision of authentic existence is made right at inauthenticity or indecision itself, and 2) this decision does not concern two distinct alternatives that would float in front of Dasein and between which Dasein would have to choose. Nancy defends this reading of *Entschlossenheit*, that is, of disclosedness in the proper mode of resoluteness or decidedness,[39] by going back to the sections on idle talk and ambiguity in *Being and Time*. In these sections, Heidegger maintains that inauthenticity is the inability to distinguish between what is originary and what is not, what is properly understood and what is not. For Nancy, this situation of indistinction or undecidability is the *proper* situation of the opening: it is disclosedness or existence itself. If Dasein were able to decide on what is originary it would appropriate its own origin, it would open the opening for itself, or would open itself to the opening from itself. Nancy explains:

> thus mastered and appropriated, that opening up, that disclosedness, would no longer exactly be the opening that it *is*. What is to be decided is disclosedness's difference from itself, by reason of which (a reason with neither fundament nor reason) *disclosedness cannot be made one's own* and thus is what it is, in its ownness: to exist. Therefore, 'to decide' means not to cut through to this or that 'truth', to this or that 'meaning' of existence – but to expose oneself to the undecidability of meaning that existence *is*.[40]

Proper (or decided) existence is not another kind of existence. In a sense, the existent does not decide or resolve itself for anything else than what it already is. Rather, in the decision, the existent lets existence relate to itself. If this decision must be a decision *in favour of* existence, not because existence would be absolutely good, but because only in existence can there be a decision as that which cuts/decides. Existence is always the arche-decision: a decision for decision, that is, a decision not to decide in advance on what the existent must decide, a decision for in-decision in which alone there can be decision.[41] Again, if existence reaches itself or touches itself, it is always as something that is 'without-ground' or 'without-essence', essentially in suspension. The opening is 'properly' received as such when it decides (itself), that is, when it decides to hold itself firmly to the opening that it is. This holding (*tenue*: ethos or habitus) is without assurance or stability. As we said above, to abide or remain in the opening is to act, and this act is a decision, a decision in which suspended existence received a certain firmness or steadfastness, but one that has an essentially different character than a ground or soil.

3. 'Our' Responsibility for the Freedom of the World

I started by quoting the passages where Nancy speaks of his ontology as *ethos* and *praxis*, of existence as an exigency, a demand to become what we are. In all of these passages, Nancy was clear that the ontology in question is the ontology of being-with or being-in-common. Yet, in focusing on the texts where Nancy engages directly with Heidegger in order to clarify Nancy's understanding of existence, I seem to have turned the existent into a self that is entirely focused on its ontological relation to existence, distorting Nancy's focus on community and world. Indeed, while I have underlined the active dimension of existence as conduct and decision, it does seem that any activity implied by existence is purely internal and does not involve any external actions. Hence, it seems that despite its active dimension, the 'praxis' of existing is not political, if by that we mean that it leads to being engaged in the world with others in a certain way. Yet, such a separation between inside and outside, between an internal conduct and an external action is exactly what Nancy's ontology seeks to undo. In order to overcome the suspicion of a divide between the inside and the outside, it is now necessary to outline the way in which other beings are essentially implicated in existence, and in doing so distance Nancy further from Heidegger.

It is true that for Heidegger, Dasein is essentially Being-with. But at the same time, what singles Dasein out? – this Dasein that is in each case mine, is its existence, its essential, active relation to Being, which is always at issue for it. Of course, existence means, insofar as its structure is ecstatic, that Dasein is exposed to beings, always already entering into meaningful relation with them. But this exposure is always a function of existence, of the co-appropriation of the human being to Being, and vice versa. Hence, Heidegger's originary ethics ponders the belonging of Dasein to Being and not Dasein's relation to Others and to the totality of beings. In speaking of the necessary exposition of what exists, Nancy will emphasise the exteriority that is needed for the existent to be exposed or open. For Nancy, the thought of existence requires that we think being as singular plural, while in Heidegger one can get the impression that Dasein is an isolated self that is open and responsive to an impersonal Being.

For Nancy, there is no opening (no disclosedness or no 'self-relation') without an outside, and hence the spacing at the heart of self-relation requires a plurality of existents, a plurality and sharing-out of the 'there'. If the *ethos* and *praxis* of existence – opening up the opening by holding oneself to indecision – makes the closure of a Subject (I or We) impossible, then the existent is necessarily from the start implicated in the world, exposed to others. Hence, while it ponders existence as *ethos* and *praxis*, Nancy's originary ethics is responsive not only to existence, but also to the existents in the concrete materiality. In Heidegger, on the contrary,

> always, and in the final analysis, it is *existence* as such that puts at stake freedom and the openness in which beings present themselves. However, in this coming into presence, beings themselves in general also *exist* in a certain way, and singularly. We could say: because existence is in the world, the world as such itself also exists – it exists because of the proper existence of existence, which is outside of itself: *this* tree exists in its singularity and in its free space where it singularly grows and branches out. It is not a question of subjectivism, the tree does not appear to me thus, it is a question of the material reality . . .[42]

Of course, Heidegger also says that the world exists but this is because world is the where-in of Dasein's factical existence or the space of intelligibility in which Dasein finds itself. For Nancy, the world is also neither the totality of what is nor a big container, but it is also not the coherent space of understanding in which Dasein finds itself. Rather, the world is the totality of all the expositions and being-toward of all that exists, the play of the existents' articulations. Nancy explains the concept of articulation or juncture in relation to community in the following way:

> By itself, articulation is only a juncture, or more exactly the play of the juncture: what takes place where different pieces touch each other without fusing together, where they slide, pivot, or tumble over one another, one at the limit of the other without the mutual *play* – which always remains, at the same time, a play *between* them – ever forming into the substance or the higher power of a Whole.[43]

The mutual play between existents, their coexistence or coexposition, gives form and coherence to the world, but without subsuming the *cum* of the *ex* into a One.[44] While I have linked existence to the verbs 'remaining', 'abiding', 'acting' and 'deciding', here

Nancy links this praxis of existence to the way in which we inhabit the world.

The question of the existence of the world, not as the context of the existence of Dasein, but as the proliferation of differences among beings, is, Nancy recognises, a difficult question. It is not so much a question of extending the kind of being of Dasein to all other beings. Rather, it is a question of understanding how other beings also display modes of existence that are not reducible to their being available for Dasein, there to be taken up into the circuit of its existence and illuminated by it. Does this mean that all other beings exist as this decision of existence that was discussed above? In a fragment at the end of *The Experience of Freedom*, Nancy wonders whether he should claim that all beings are free and replies candidly: 'Yes, if I knew how to understand this.'[45] If freedom is not anymore the property of a self-legislating subject but the withdrawal of the cause or ground of what exists or is abandoned, then the freedom of the world, of all that exists in its singularity and plurality, is essentially equivalent to its creation *ex nihilo*. The rose grows and the stone rolls without 'why', but this absence of ground does not enclose them within themselves. If this were the case, the rose or the stone would find in this absence of ground all the reason of the world. Rather, the stone or the rose is without ground because it grows or rolls outside of itself, 'with the reseda, the eglantine, and the thistle – as well as with crystals, seahorses, humans, and their inventions'.[46] This freedom of the world forces us to rethink the relation between the human being and the rest of beings differently than as the technological exploitation of an essentially unfree nature in free, human production. Nancy is clear that the point is not to demonise technology and appeal to human beings to protect nature against exploitation – such a reversal would not undermine the free subject/unfree nature dichotomy. At the same time, he is less than explicit, at least in this fragment, about the way in which such relation ought to be conceptualised. What we do learn from him is that we exist to or towards this freedom of the world and that this makes us responsible for it.

In *Being Singular Plural*, Nancy explains the relation between the human being and other beings in the following way: Humans are 'those who expose *as such* sharing and circulation by saying "we", by *saying we to themselves* in all possible senses of that expression, and by saying we for the totality of all being'.[47] World is existence, freedom, exposition; the human existent is exposed to and also exposes this exposition in saying 'we' for all beings and for each one, one by one. Nancy explains this redoubling of exposition in the following terms:

> Humans are the exposer [*l'exposant*, the exponent] of the world; they are neither its end nor its ground – the world [that is, the exposing of singularities to themselves and each other] is what is exposed by and to humans [*l'exposé de l'homme*]; it is neither their environment, nor their representation.[48]

This exponential characteristic of human beings also means that humans, and humans alone, are also potentially the unexposer of the exposing. If human existing takes on the active connotation of 'deciding to exist', it is because it is always possible for the existents that we are to close off exposition. Hence, when Nancy ends the second section of *The Creation of the World* by affirming that 'it is for us to decide for *ourselves* [*c'est à nous de nous décider*]',[49] the 'us' in favour of which we are to decide cannot be the self-enclosed human subject, individual or collective. Our existence as decision is the responsibility for the freedom of the world, understood as the ungrounded diffraction of beings (*Ent-scheidung, Auseinandertreten*) that make up the world.

The decision of existence is the decision to inhabit the world in such a way that the world can really form a world: an ungrounded, untotalisable plurality of existences, co-existing and co-appearing to themselves and each other. Inhabiting the world for Nancy requires that we stop seeking to totalise the world in a representation or ground it in a principle. In both cases, we posit a place outside of the world (the place of the principle or of the onlooker) from which the world appears as a totality or unity. At the same time, inhabiting the world insofar as it requires that we relinquish all transcendent meaning of the world (this is what Nancy calls the process of world-becoming or *mondanisation*[50]) cannot merely lead to endless circulation and exchange between existences. Such circulation and exchange arise from the general equivalence between all existences, a general equivalence that erases all differences, and hence all meaningful *co*-existence and *ex*-position. To learn to inhabit the world is to learn to stand within a world that has no firm ground, but the consistency of which resides only in the mutual articulation and play of all existences. In *The Creation of the World*, Nancy is very clear that this inhabiting, which is the true creation of the world (*mondialisation*), is a struggle.

In *The Truth of Democracy*, Nancy will be more careful to differentiate between what belongs to existence and its sense, and what belongs to politics. Politics, Nancy claims, ought not to take over the sense of existence or to prefigure the good that makes up a good life. If it does so, then we have a metaphysical politics, one in which existence is referred to a good outside of itself that the *polis* aims to realise. Rather, politics ought to open a space for the affirmation of existence, an existence that is, as I showed in this chapter, always without essence and without guarantee, always plural and shared, always exposed to itself and the world. In this sense, the 'struggle for the world' encountered in *The Creation of the World* is political insofar as it aims to open a space where 'there is room for all the world and for everyone [*pour tout le monde*], but a genuine place, one in which things can genuinely *take place* (in this world)'.[51] For those who would too quickly find in this call to struggle for the world a justification of political actions, of protests, revolts and revolutions, violent or non-violent, it should be pointed out that in both texts Nancy describes this struggle first and foremost as a 'struggle of thought'. It seems that for Nancy the struggle to enter into the thought of existence *alone* can 'dislodg[e] the very foundation of general equivalence' and put into question 'its false infinity'.[52] While Nancy's emphasis on thought might suggest quiescence or passivism to some, it should be underlined that this thought is not merely theoretical or abstract, but 'very precisely concrete and demanding'.[53] It is a thought at work in the world, a transformative praxis, creative of a sense in excess of all produced meaning or measurable value. Just as existence unsettles the opposition between being and acting, Nancy's politics unsettles the opposition between thinking and acting.

Notes

1. Jean-Luc Nancy, *Being Singular Plural*, trans. R. D. Richardson and A. E. O'Byrne (Stanford: Stanford University Press, 2000), pp. 7, 71, 99.
2. Ibid., p. 99.
3. Jean-Luc Nancy, *The Truth of Democracy*, trans. P.-A. Brault and M. Naas (New York: Fordham University Press, 2010), p. 54, n.6.

4. Jean-Luc Nancy, *The Inoperative Community*, ed. P. Connor (Minneapolis: University of Minnesota Press, 1991), p. 35.
 5. Nancy, *Being Singular Plural*, pp. 22–3.
 6. Ibid., p. 25.
 7. Immanuel Kant, *Critique of Pure Reason*, trans. P. Guyer and A. W. Wood (Cambridge: Cambridge University Press, 1998), A592/B620–A603/B631. Martin Heidegger, *Basic Problems of Phenomenology*, trans. A. Hofstadter, rev. edn (Bloomington: Indiana University Press, 1988), §7.
 8. Jean-Luc Nancy, 'Of Being-in-Common', in The Miami Theory Collective (ed.), *Community at Loose Ends* (Minneapolis: University of Minnesota Press, 1991), p. 2.
 9. Jean-Luc Nancy, *The Birth to Presence*, trans. B. Holmes et al. (Stanford: Stanford University Press, 1993), p. 43. For a reading of the abandonment of being as it relates to the imperative of being, see François Raffoul, 'Abandonment and the Categorical Imperative of Being', in B. C. Hutchens (ed.), *Jean-Luc Nancy: Justice, Legality and World* (London and New York: Continuum, 2012), pp. 65–81.
10. Jean-Luc Nancy, *Dis-Enclosure: The Deconstruction of Christianity*, trans. B. Bergo, G. Malenfant and M. B. Smith (New York: Fordham University Press, 2008), p. 24. See also *Being Singular Plural*, p. 16.
11. By revealing itself in what is [*in das Seiende*], being withdraws. In this way being, with its truth, keeps to itself. This keeping to itself [*Ansichhalten*] is the way it discloses itself early on ... By bringing the unconcealment of what is [*Un-Verborgenheit des Seienden*], it founds, for the first time, the concealment of being. Concealment remains, however, the characteristic of the refusal that keeps to itself [*des an sich haltenden Verweigerns*]. Martin Heidegger, 'Anaximander's Saying', in *Off the Beaten Track*, trans. J. Young and K. Haynes (Cambridge: Cambridge University Press, 2002), p. 254; translation modified.
12. See Nancy, *The Birth to Presence*, pp. 36–7.
13. See Jean-Luc Nancy, *The Experience of Freedom*, trans. B. McDonald (Stanford: Stanford University Press, 1993), §12. See also Patrick Roney, 'Evil and the Experience of Freedom: Nancy on Schelling and Heidegger', *Research in Phenomenology*, 9:3, 2009, pp. 374–400.
14. Martin Heidegger, *The Question Concerning Technology and Other Essays*, trans. W. Lovitt (New York: HarperCollins, 1977), pp. 28–34, here 32.
15. Ibid., p. 31, n.24.

16. Martin Heidegger, *Pathmarks*, ed. William McNeill (Cambridge: Cambridge University Press, 1998), pp. 252 and 260.
17. Jean-Luc Nancy, *A Finite Thinking*, ed. Simon Sparks (Stanford: Stanford University Press, 2003), p. 184.
18. Jean-Luc Nancy, *L'impératif catégorique* (Paris: Flammarion, 1983), p. 145. An abridged version of the chapter from which I am quoting is translated as 'Abandoned Being' in *The Birth to Presence*, but the paragraph I am referring to is omitted. See *The Birth to Presence*, p. 40.
19. Martin Heidegger, *Identity and Difference*, trans. J. Stambaugh (Chicago: The University of Chicago Press, 2002), p. 65. See also the translator's introduction, p. 17, n.3.
20. As Littré explains, the literal meaning of the word *rien*, which goes back to its etymological root in the Latin *rem* (accusative of *res*), is something. Only when the negative particle *ne* or *ni* is added to form the locution *ne . . . rien* or *ni . . . rien* does it mean nothing. In this way, the sentence '*Il serait dangereux de rien entreprendre*' means 'it would be dangerous to undertake something' while the sentence '*il serait dangereux de ne rien entreprendre*' means the exact opposite, namely that it would be dangerous to undertake nothing or not to undertake something. As a noun, *un rien* means a very little thing, something that is almost nothing at all, as in the phrase '*pleurer pour un rien*', 'to burst into tears for a trifle'.
21. Jean-Luc Nancy, *The Creation of the World, or Globalization*, trans. F. Raffoul and D. Pettigrew (Albany: SUNY Press, 2007), p. 103.
22. Nancy, *The Experience of Freedom*, p. 167; emphasis in the original. Here, Nancy seems to be thinking of existence more in terms of Heidegger's *Ereignis* and not as the human being's insertion [*Einrückung*] in the there. See Martin Heidegger, *Contributions to Philosophy (Of the Event)*, trans. R. Rojcewicz and D. Vallega-Neu (Bloomington: Indiana University Press, 2012), §179.
23. Nancy, *The Experience of Freedom*, pp. 9–10.
24. Nancy, *A Finite Thinking*, p. 175. In the French version published in *La pensée dérobée* (Paris: Galilée, 2001), Nancy adds an explication of the kind of praxis that the ontological difference is: '*À savoir, la* praxis *selon laquelle l'être* fait *l'étant (ou l'existant): il ne le fait pas comme un produit, il le fait en tant qu'il se fait être en ex-istant dans l'existant ou comme existant* [The *praxis* according to which being *makes* the being (or the existent): Being does not make it as a product, but it makes it insofar as it makes *itself be in ex-isting in the existent and as the existent*].' See also *The Birth to Presence*, p. 103.

25. Nancy, *A Finite Thinking*, p. 178.
26. Nancy, 'La liberté vient du dehors', in *La pensée dérobée*, p. 133.
27. Ibid., p. 130.
28. Nancy, 'Of Being-in-Common', p. 3.
29. Nancy, *The Birth to Presence*, pp. 154–5; translation modified, emphasis in the original. In the language of *Being and Time*, this thought was expressed by saying that to exist is have one's own being (one's own self) as possibility, but such that the self I have to be is not something (some ideal image of myself) that I can represent to myself, hold in front of me and appropriate for myself. The relation is not between a present self and a future possible self. Rather, what the existent (Dasein) has as its ownmost possibility is its Being, its existence itself, which can never be fully its own since it is exposed to limits that are not (birth, death) and hence cannot be appropriated.
30. Nancy, *Being Singular Plural*, p. 30.
31. Nancy, *A Finite Thinking*, p. 187.
32. Martin Heidegger, *The Metaphysical Foundations of Logic*, trans. M. Heim (Bloomington: Indiana University Press, 1984), §10 Appendix, pp. 154–9.
33. Heidegger, *Pathmarks*, p. 271.
34. For a reading of 'The Decision of Existence' in relation to Heidegger and Kierkegaard, see Werner Hamacher, 'Ou, séance, touche de Nancy, ici', in D. Sheppard, S. Sparks and C. Thomas (eds), *On Jean-Luc Nancy: The Sense of Philosophy* (London: Routledge, 1997), pp. 40–63.
35. Martin Heidegger, *Being and Time*, trans. J. Macquarrie and E. Robinson (New York: Harper & Row, 1962), H. 232, see also H. 53.
36. Ibid., H. 144, see also H. 12.
37. See ibid., H. 42.
38. See ibid., H. 103 and 179.
39. *Entschlossenheit* is rendered in the Macquarrie and Robinson translation by resoluteness and *Entschluß* by resolution. In French, Martineau translates the former with *résolution* and the latter with *décision*. Nancy, for his part, uses 'ouverture décidante/décidé', deciding/decided opening or decisive opening for Entschlossenheit, which the English translator renders as decisiveness, losing the connection with the opening (Erschlossenheit, disclosedness). See Nancy, *The Birth to Presence*, pp. 87–8. For the French original, see *Une pensée finie* (Paris: Galilée, 1990), pp. 117–18.

40. Nancy, *The Birth to Presence*, p. 97; emphasis in the original.
41. See Nancy, *The Experience of Freedom*, §12, especially pp. 138–40.
42. Nancy, *The Experience of Freedom*, p. 172, n.2; emphasis in the original.
43. Nancy, *The Inoperative Community*, p. 76; emphasis in the original.
44. Nancy, *The Creation of the World, or Globalization*, p. 73.
45. Nancy, *The Experience of Freedom*, p. 160.
46. Nancy, *Being Singular Plural*, p. 86.
47. Nancy, *Being Singular Plural*, p. 3; translation modified, emphasis in the original.
48. Ibid., p. 18; translation modified.
49. Nancy, *The Creation of the World, or Globalization*, p. 74; emphasis in the original.
50. Ibid., p. 44.
51. Ibid., p. 42; translation modified, emphasis in the original.
52. Nancy, *The Truth of Democracy*, p. 31.
53. Nancy, *The Creation of the World, or Globalization*, p. 53.

2

Badiou and Nancy: Political Animals
Christopher Watkin

This chapter explores the way in which Nancy seeks to elaborate a non-anthropocentric politics that nevertheless acknowledges a distinctive human capacity for language. It sets up what is at stake for such a politics via a brief sketch of the way in which Alain Badiou treats the difference between the human animal and the immortal subject. Whereas Badiou's appeal to the human capacity for thought seems to relegate his concern for the animal, Nancy's appeal to the capacity for language widens politics beyond the human and, far from providing a basis for human exceptionalism, is the means by which Nancy argues for an equal dignity between human and non-human beings. The assertion of equality in Nancy's politics of all beings is not complete, however, without an appeal to a secularised version of Christian love not simply for all people but for all beings, human and non-human.

1. Badiou, the *Zoon Politikon* and 'Animal Humanism'

For Badiou, the decisive distinction in political anthropology is not between the human and the animal, but between the human animal and the immortal. To understand what is at stake in this all-important difference, and where it becomes problematic, we need to begin with his reading of Aristotle, both in his published work and in the augmented accounts given in his seminars at the Ecole Normale Supérieure.[1] In the seminar 'Qu'est-ce que vivre ?' ('What is it to live?') from 2003–4,[2] Badiou frames his discussion of Aristotle in terms of the passage from a 'two' to a 'three', the passage that marks the distinction expressed in *Logics of Worlds* between democratic materialism (for which there are only two elements: bodies and languages), and Badiou's own materialist dialectics (for which there are three: bodies, languages and truths).

He frames the distinction between the human animal and the immortal in relation to two quotations from Aristotle. The first situates Aristotle firmly as the philosopher of 'life' and therefore also of the animal as a living being. It is the famous claim, at the beginning of the *Politics*, that the human is the political animal. Badiou understands this to mean that, for Aristotle, the human is political *as an animal*, not in a way that transcends the animal, and one answer to the question 'What is it to live?' is that to live is to engage in politics in the Greek sense, participating constructively in the affairs of the city and finding one's harmony there, rather than seeking any truth beyond the circulation of ideas and opinions within the city. The human is not an animal that contingently happens to engage in politics, but an animal whose singular life is in its essence political; for humanity (for Aristotle, it would be more accurate to say 'for certain male humans'), to live is to live in the *polis*, and to live the good life is to live politically. In the light of the *zoon politikon*, Aristotle's politics for Badiou is all about finding an adequate language for the political being of the human animal.

Badiou's second quotation from Aristotle stands in contrast to the claim that humans are political animals. In the *Nicomachean Ethics* (X, 7) Aristotle writes:

> If the intellect, then, is something divine compared with the human being, the life in accordance with it will also be divine compared with human life. But we ought not to listen to those who exhort us, because we are human, to think of human things, or because we are mortal, to think of mortal things. We ought rather to take on immortality as much as possible, and do all that we can to live in accordance with the highest element within us; for even if its bulk is small, in its power and value it far exceeds everything.[3]

In the 2003–4 'What is it to live?' seminar, Badiou argues that, as divine or immortal, the human is no longer rightly described as a political animal. Why not? Because if there is one thing the immortals care precious little about, it is politics understood as the circulation of opinions within the city. To live as an immortal in this way is to live with a certain essential immobility, like Aristotle's divine Unmoved Mover. Whereas the political animal circulates within society exchanging language and opinions, Aristotle's human who 'takes on immortality as much as possible' moves all things while itself remaining unmoved and unmoving. Badiou calls these unmoving exceptions to the circulation of bodies and languages 'truths', and truths mark the difference between the democratic materialism he rejects and his own materialist dialectics.

The key to understanding Badiou's materialist dialectics is that the third term after bodies and languages (which in this 2003–4 seminar he calls 'principles', before later settling on 'truths' in *Logics of Worlds*) is not reducible to the first two: the immortal cannot be contained in, or explained by, the animal because the immortal lives with principles, lives as a prince (Latin: *princeps*). Badiou concludes that, from Aristotle onwards, we must each decide whether to live according to the Two (bodies and languages) or the Three (bodies, languages and truths). This Aristotelian scaffolding helps Badiou set the scene for showing the task that faces the modern era. We have seen that Aristotle's immortal bears a strong resemblance to his divine Unmoved Mover. He argues for a similar complicity in his critique of modern Western humanism's reliance upon God, arguing that the human-more-than-animal is complicit with the divine. Classic humanism is the knotting together of God and Humanity,[4] and we have no right to continue deploying 'humanity', classically understood, without God. So in fact the death of God leads first not to the (humanist) exaltation of humanity, but to the discovery of an essential animality which engulfs and overpowers the human: 'the odour of the animal suffocates him'[5] says Badiou, quoting Pierre Guyotat. In the first instance, classic humanism without God yields nothing but the human animal (*l'homme animal*), the human bereft of its immortality and having only body and language.

In *The Century*, Badiou argues that this necessity to abandon the Human after abandoning God led, in the twentieth century, to two opposite reactions: Sartre's radical humanism and Foucault's radical anti-humanism. For Sartre, humanity is the historical creator of its own absolute essence, while for Foucault, humanity is on the limit of a coming inhumanity that Foucault's own thought anticipates.[6] Today, however, at the beginning of the twenty-first century, both radical humanism and radical anti-humanism have withered on the vine of popular opinion. All that we are now offered, according to Badiou, is a lily-livered return to a regime of bodies and languages, eviscerated of the divine and in which what is left is nothing but species-humanity, an animal body.[7]

Badiou's verdict on this species-humanity is not flattering. Even allowing for a splash of rhetorical colour, if we were to say that he has little time for the human animal that succeeds the death of God, we need be in no fear of having overstated the case. This 'systematic killer' pursues 'interests of survival and satisfaction neither more nor less estimable than those of moles or tiger beetles',[8] while being among all the animals 'the most obstinately dedicated to the cruel desires of his own power'. Described by Badiou as a 'featherless biped' whose charms are not obvious',[9] humanity is a 'crafty, cruel and obstinate animal'[10] who, in 'the simple reality of his living being', is 'contemptible'.[11]

This contemporary species-humanity comes hand in hand with an 'animal humanism' that extends rights and protection to animals and sees the wretched, suffering human body as worthy only of pity.[12] Faced with the cynical impotence of this animal humanism in the context of what he sees as the failed attempt to resurrect classical humanism without God, Badiou turns his attention to the need to overcome this godless animality in some way: 'Let us call our philosophical task, on the shores of the new century, and against the animal humanism that besieges us, that of a *formalized in-humanism*.'[13] In this call for a new in-humanism, Badiou is taking an explicitly Nietzschean line – Nietzsche, who defined the human as that which must be overcome:

> 'God is dead' means that man is dead too. Man, the last man, the dead man, is what must be overcome for the sake of the overman. What is the overman? Quite simply man without God. Man as he is thinkable outside of any relation to the divine. The overman decides undecidability, thus fracturing the humanist predicate.[14]

In Badiou's own language the choice is between animality and communism,[15] a 'communism of the idea' that, like Aristotle's immortal, adds a third term, unmoved and unmoving, to the ever-changing circulation of bodies and languages. This third term locates Badiouian immortality as a peculiarly human affair because it relies on a specifically human capacity for thought. Badiou defines the human and the political in terms of this capacity for thought:

> Thought is the one and only uniquely human capacity, and thought, strictly speaking, is simply that act through which the human animal is seized and traversed by the trajectory of a truth. Thus a politics

worthy of being interrogated by philosophy under the idea of justice is one whose unique general axiom is: people think, people are capable of truth.[16]

This routing of the materialist dialectic through the uniquely human capacity for thought introduces an irreducible anthropocentrism into Badiou's thought, echoed in his dismissive account of 'animal humanism', and his description of the human animal in particularly unflattering terms. Politics for Badiou is a matter of truths, and incorporation into a truth relies on the uniquely human capacity for thought. Politics is, therefore, a human matter. Given Badiou's appeal to the uniquely human capacity for thought, is such an anthropocentrism inevitable, and must the political be thus circumscribed? Might it be possible to acknowledge a uniquely human capacity and yet not privilege the human politically? It is in the spirit of exploring this question that we now turn to the thought of Jean-Luc Nancy, who seeks to understand politics in a non-anthropocentric way not by denying any uniquely human capacity, but as a concomitant of the human capacity for language.

2. Nancy and the 'With' of all Beings

We have seen that Badiou understands the limit between the human animal and the immortal in terms of the specifically human capacity for thought, and also that this goes together with a dismissal of 'animal humanism' and of the dignity of the human animal. The animal is excluded from an account of political subjectivity that relies on the human capacity for thought. Nancy approaches the question of the animal with a determination to avoid the sorts of limits and exclusions that Badiou's politics allows. In the first instance he wishes to exclude from his account of the political any reliance on determinate human capacities, but this leads to difficulties when it comes to the role played in Nancy's politics by the notion of sense. Nancy is forced to reintroduce some minimal notion of the capacity for language into his account, but in doing so he works hard to mitigate a return to anthropocentrism. Much of the work of this mitigation is done by an appeal to a non-theological hyperbole of Christian love, which is not without its own problems for Nancy's thought. After sketching Nancy's politics of all beings, and the way in which he introduces capacity without anthropocentrism, I shall draw out this problematic account of love through an engagement with the second volume of his deconstruction of Christianity, *Adoration*, and a recent published interview with Philip Armstrong and Jason Smith entitled *Politique et au-delà* ('Politics and beyond').[17]

The death of God for Nancy leads not to a desire to overcome human animality, as it does for Badiou, but to a need to disrupt the human/animal distinction. In *Dans quels mondes vivons-nous?* ('What worlds do we live in?')[18] he holds that the death of God entails not only the death of 'man' but also of 'material', 'life', 'nature' and 'history' insofar as all of these are 'substance-subjects' given with predetermined ends and not liable to essential transformation. The need to rethink the human comes about because the death of God not only wipes away final ends such as the meaning of life and the reason for the world's existence, but also disrupts any determinate reason, sense or essence of the 'common'.[19] Whereas previously the common was thought to have been grounded in a determinate land, blood, family, tribe or totem, in lacking ground it now simply presents itself as a problem.

In the same way that, for Badiou, the death of God led to the dichotomy of a Sartrean humanism and Foucauldian anti-humanism, both of which he rejected, so also for Nancy the death of God causes a bifurcation in accounts of the human. The first response to this problem of the common, and the one that pre-dates the death of God, seeks to sustain the relation of the common to a divine and unchanging purpose that transcends it and brings it resolution, balance or harmony. A prime example of this is Aristotle's attempt to explain *why* the human is the *zoon politikon*: so that humans can debate the just and unjust in the *polis* as a means of enabling them to live a 'good life'. In this way, humanity re-appropriates as its own product the meaning of its own essence. In this first picture, there is a fixed *telos* of the common.

Nancy describes the second response to the question of the essence of the common, and the response that is properly subsequent to the death of God, through the examples of Rancière and Deleuze (and Nancy's description also fits Badiou's thought) who refuse the resolutions and harmonies of the first response, focusing instead on 'the tipping point of the event, the rarity of its intervention, the almost exclusive value accorded to the moment of insurrection'.[20] Nancy finds both of these responses inadequate. The common is to be thought neither as having a transcendent *telos*, nor as being contingent on the tipping point of an event. It is also notable here that Nancy rejects the Aristotelian *zoon politikon* for reasons quite opposite to those of Badiou. For Nancy the political animal is rejected because it is in thrall to a determinate and unchangeable understanding of the good life; for Badiou the problem is the lack of any clear horizon for the political animal, lost as it is in the interminable circulation of opinions in its democratic materialism.

The reason Nancy persists in arguing that neither existing approach addresses the essence of the common is that, on his account, this essence is not political at all as both approaches presume, but metaphysical.[21] In an essay entitled 'The Centre: Opening Address' published in English in the volume *Retreating the Political*, Nancy and Lacoue-Labarthe insist that there is

> a disjunction or a disruption more essential to the political than the political itself, and which, moreover, seems to us to provide the stake, on several different accounts, for more than one contemporary interpretation. A stake which, for now, we will sum up in the following way: the transcendental of the *polis* is not an organicism, whether that of a harmony or of a communion, nor that of a distribution of functions and differences. But no more is it an anarchy. It is the an-archy of the *arche* itself (assuming that the demonstrative pronoun 'it' can still apply in the lexicon of the 'transcendental').[22]

Nancy's critique here is that the *zoon politikon* is secondary to a prior ontological sociality that overflows the motif of humanity as the social animal and 'that in its principle extends far beyond the simple theme of humanity as a social being (the *zoon politikon* is secondary to this community)'.[23] This more than human basis of sociality is what in *The Experience of Freedom* Nancy calls the archi-originary ethicity 'without which there would be neither Plato's Good, nor Kant's good will, nor Spinozistic joy, nor Marxian revolution, nor Aristotle's *zoon politikon*'.[24] It is also what, in *The Sense of the World*, he calls the 'archi-constitution of the political animal'.[25] The politics of the political animal only ever supervenes on a prior an-archic condition of all being, not just of human being.

This metaphysical condition prior to the Aristotelian *zoon politikon* is not simply a community of thinking or speaking beings but of all beings, human, animal, vegetal, mineral and ideal: an ontological condition which Nancy evokes as singular plural being, or as 'the with' (*l'avec*). The ontological condition of the singular plural is prior to any politics in the Aristotelian sense, and this anteriority is crucial for understanding how Nancy thinks about the relation between the human and the animal. To begin with, it means that we ought no longer to speak of 'relation' at all, nor of 'the human' and 'the animal'. In *Being Singular Plural*, Nancy insists that if we are to think the 'with' as the essential trait of being then 'what is at stake is no longer thinking: – beginning from the one, or from the other, – beginning from their togetherness, understood now as One, now as the Other, but thinking, absolutely and without reserve, beginning from the "with"',[26] which includes but is not limited to an animal-and-human 'with'. From the moment we realise the radical nature of Nancy's claim here, namely that the 'with' is constitutive of and equiprimordial with all beings, we understand that the way he navigates the question of the human and the animal will necessarily be very different to Badiou's approach. There is no 'limit', 'relation' or 'link' between the human and animal for Nancy, 'especially if such a bond presupposes the pre-existence of the terms upon which it relies',[27] and no equivalent of Badiou's transition from the human animal to the immortal. The *with* is the exact contemporary of the two terms 'human' and 'animal', not an adjunct that supervenes on their prior individuality.

From the 1980s onwards, Nancy is emphatic that we cannot think the being-together of humans and animals without at the same time thinking the being-together of all beings. The unworked community is not the community of humanity but of the 'ends of man', understood not as *telos* or completion but as the limit at which the human ceases to be simply human or the animal simply animal:

> man, animal, or god have been up to now the diverse names for this limit, which is itself diverse. By definition, the fact of being exposed at this limit leads to the risk – or the chance – of changing identity in it.[28]

There is a second reason why it is reductive to try to speak in terms of a 'relation between' human and animal in Nancy's ontological account of the common, namely that the human is always also already animal: 'The difference between humanity and the rest of being (which is not a concern to be denied, but the nature of which is, nevertheless, not a given' is 'itself inseparable from other differences within being (since man is "also" animal, "also" living, "also" physico-chemical etc.)'.[29] To say that the human is 'also' animal is not to say that the human is partly animal. On the contrary, it is wholly animal, and wholly living, wholly physico-chemical. Once more, there is no limit between human and animal, but a constitutive overlapping.

It follows that to ask after the relation between humans and animals in Nancy is to commit the same error as seeking the essence of the common in a politics that is only ever derived from a prior metaphysics: it is to assume that the 'with' is secondary, not constitutive. As he says, 'we would not be "humans" if there were not "dogs" and "stones"'.[30] Once more, this is not to say, after the fashion of some ontologised Saussurean differentialism, that the human is human inasmuch as it is not animal and not stone. It is rather to say that the human only is, only exists, in mutual exposition with the animal and the mineral, which is a different and complementary claim to saying that it is 'also' animal and 'also' mineral. This understanding the human and the animal in the wider context of being-together does not take the meaning of the human as a given, and Nancy calls its general excess of sense beyond the given 'technique'.[31] In this condition of 'technique', individual and collective ends (*finalitiés*) mix, contradict, overlap quicken or slow each other in the suspension of essence and *telos*. Technique names peoples, nations, religions, languages, cultures, hierarchies and governments,[32] all that in a determinate anthropology would be called 'culture' in excess of, or in the place of, the 'natural'. What is more, technique is not restricted to the province of human beings. Readers of Nancy will be familiar with his 'ecotechnics', the idea that 'our world is the world of the "technical", the world whose cosmos, nature, gods, whose system, complete in its intimate jointure, is exposed as "technical"'.[33] In *The Creation of the World*, Nancy describes the condition of ecotechnicity in the following terms: natural life in all its forms (human, animal, vegetal, viral) is now inseparable from a set of conditions out of which everything that we call 'nature' develops.[34] For Badiou, it is the immortal as opposed to the human animal who becomes the subject of politics; for Nancy, the relation between politics and the human/animal distinction is to be traced through ecotechnics. It now remains to explore the politics of Nancean ecotechnics, and why that politics is problematic.

We have seen that Nancy rejects the political determination of the essence of the common, but this does not mean that the common is apolitical. On the contrary, technique provides the basis for a particular politics, namely communism. First of all, communism names the fact that 'reality is the real of this intrication which weaves and combines, in addition to human beings, all the beings of the world'.[35] In the second place, communism also names the demand to do the right thing by (*faire droit à*) this reality, where to do the right thing is to resist the temptation to search for foundations or ends outside this interweaving. Communism names the fact and the demand into which humanity has come. So communism for Nancy is not an ideal of life or an ideal organisation of society, and in this it is not an alternative to Aristotle's *zoon politikon* which, as we have seen, serves the determinate end of living the good life. It is in this sense that we must understand the animal (human or non-human) for Nancy as political. The animal, along with the human, along with all other beings, is technical. The name for this technique is 'communism', understood both as a fact and as a demand, and it is the response to that demand which is 'political' in the non-metaphysical sense.

3. Capacity without Exclusivity: The Human as *Animal Monstrans*

Nevertheless, in addition to this embrace of all beings in ontological communism, Nancy does acknowledge a unique place for the human as a being of language and the 'being of sense',[36] the being that exposes the being of all beings. Whereas it might be thought that the reintroduction of a human capacity into his account of the condition of the political would bring with it an anthropocentric division between the human and the animal, Nancy works hard to prevent his appeal to language from leading to any anthropological exceptionalism. He does this by rethinking the Heideggerian trope of humanity as the shepherd of being in terms of a mutual collaboration between the human and the non-human in the exposition of being, and by deconstructing the separation between humanity as the subject of language and the non-human as its object.

While for the Heidegger of the 'Letter on Humanism' humanity is the shepherd of being, Nancy argues that we should not understand this to mean that humanity produces being as being's master. Humanity does not decide if and how being will appear.

That there is something (rather than nothing), and that there are such and such things (i.e. the world) is not a human decision. The world is simply (a) given in its eventhood, its surging forth (*surgissement*).[37] Nevertheless, what is not given, nor can it be, is this surging forth itself, which for Nancy is 'the being of beings as the desire/ability of sense'.[38] In other words, the event of being gives itself as the-to-be-made-sense-of ('l'avoir-à-faire-sens'). It is this event, and not being itself, that humanity, as part of that same being, is responsible for, but not as its 'shepherd'. Nancy draws a clear distinction between the Heideggerian position and his own, so as to reject Heidegger's image of *Dasein* 'guarding' being.[39] Nancy insists it is less a case of mounting a guard, and more of 'letting be'.

This move from a humanity that alone ek-sists and that shepherds the world to a humanity that surges forth along with the rest of the world, and is responsive to that world's nascent sense, entails a change in the notion of human dignity. The dignity of humanity is not in its possession or use of language, but in being exposed to the 'essence of sense' in the surging forth of the world.[40] Human dignity is not something possessed, something isolable within the atomised human being. It is something experienced in the irreducible and mutual exposition of all beings, human and non-human.

The idea that the specificity of the human resides in *showing* the surging-forth of the world in concert with the world is further developed in Nancy's reflections on cave art, where we witness a shift from humanity as the *animal loquens* or *animal intelligens* to Nancy's own *animal monstrans*, the 'showing animal', or rather more accurately but more clumsily to modern ears, the 'monstrating animal'; a term explained at some length in the essay 'Painting in the Grotto'.[41] In this essay, Nancy invites his reader to imagine the unimaginable: the moment of the first cave painting, the first act of monstration. This complex moment is not simply the beginning of painting but also 'the monstration of the commencement of being'.[42] But what does it mean to show the commencement of being? It means to show the surging forth, the there-ness of the world that remains 'forever a stranger in the world, nowhere taken up in the world in no place, but at the same time it is spread everywhere over the surface of the world as the most immediate taking-place of this world'.[43] It is not that this strangeness begins to exist with the first cave art: the first human does not create the world. Rather, it is that the strangeness of the world for the first time becomes present in the absence, opened in the world by the first mimetic hand print on a cave wall.

Nancy does not set human consciousness, language or monstration over against the world, but understands them as part of the world which is to-be-exposed and monstrated. The first cave art is not only the monstration of the commencement of being, but also the birth of the *animal monstrans* which in showing the world, shows itself showing. Humanity is indivisibly both *animal monstrans* and *animal monstrum*, exposed in its mimetic absence to the incorporeal outside of the world that opens at the very heart of the world.[44] In showing the world, humanity also shows itself as an entity within the world, just like all other entities. To borrow a Merleau-Pontean turn of phrase (and Merleau-Ponty is never too far away from Nancy as he rethinks the relation of the human and language), the *homo monstrans* is 'of' the world both an entity within it and an exposer of it.[45] There is no rigorous dichotomy between the status of the human and the non-human: the human is never 'showing' without being also, and at the same time, 'shown'. Both showing and shown, the *animal monstrans* shows the strangeness of the world and itself as a stranger in the world.[46]

If the *animal monstrans* is never 'showing' without also being 'shown', then it is also true that entities in the world are never 'shown' without at the same time participating in their showing. Existence writes, speaks and shows itself not as a subject in opposition to an object (it is only on the mistaken basis of continuing to assume the subject/object dichotomy that this Nancean position can be thought to flirt with animism) but as an entity surging forth in the world among other entities. In seeking to explain how and to what extent the world is showing as well as shown, Nancy pushes the analysis further to arrive at something structurally similar, though of course in a very different register, to the theological doctrine of double inspiration according to which the words of the Christian Bible are both fully human, reflecting the various personalities and linguistic proclivities of their individual writers, while at the same time being fully divine.[47] For Nancy, a similarly double authorship is expressed in the following terms: 'The simplest way to put this into language would be to say that humanity speaks existence, but what speaks through its speech says the whole of being [l'étant]'.[48] Beings do not ventriloquise human speech any more than human speech ventriloquises the non-human, and just because 'the whole of being' speaks it does not cease to be the case that 'man speaks existence'. To the contrary, the speaking is double or it is not at all.

It does not follow from the fact that human language is the means through which being exposes itself, that the human itself enjoys any particular privilege:

> There is not, on the one side, an originary singularity and then, on the other, a simple being-there of things, more or less given for our use. On the contrary, in exposing itself as singularity, existence exposes the singularity of Being as such in all being [*en tout étant*].[49]

In terms of the exposition of the world, the whole of being passes through the human ('passe par l'homme'), but in the exposition of being humanity itself is exposed, along with all other beings, outside the human and to the sense of the world. Again, humanity does not give sense to the world but exposes it.[50] There is, to be sure, a difference between humanity and the rest of the world, but this distinction is not qualitatively different to other distinctions within being because, as we have seen, 'man is "also" animal, "also" living, "also" physico-chemical etc.'.[51] In other words, the difference is not a dichotomy; it does not set humanity over against the world as subject to its object, but rather sets it resolutely within the world and its circulations of sense.

Before we can leave this account of human language it remains to be shown that language is not an exclusively human preserve for Nancy, or rather that language is not qualified by the definite article. Rather than Language there are tongues, words and voices, an originary sharing of voices without which there would be no voice.[52] In *Adoration*, Nancy claims his account of the relation between the human, language and the world by evoking human language not to argue for the privilege of the human but, quite to the contrary, for the equality of the human with non-human existents. It is humans who are beings of language, but language exposes the infinite excess of sense of all beings, not just of human being. While language is traditionally appealed to as the guarantor of the unique status and dignity of the human being as opposed to all non-human existence, for Nancy it functions in quite the opposite way. It shows that the human is equally exposed, equally in an infinite excess of sense[53] with all other existents. Rather than being over against the world, human beings are *of* the world, and they are that which within the world opens as to its outside without which there would be no world.⁵⁴ The world is only 'the human world' to the extent that it is the non-human to which the human is exposed. Nancy concludes that 'Humanity is the exposing [*l'exposant*] of the world; it is neither the end nor the ground of the world; the world is the exposure [*l'exposé*] of humanity; it is neither the environment nor the representation of humanity.'⁵⁵

It is in this way that Nancy seeks to introduce the human capacity for language into his account of the 'with' of beings, without having that capacity drive a wedge between the human and the non-human and thereby undercut his insistence on the extension of the 'with'. This is in contrast to Badiou's privileging of the capacity to think in his account of subjectivisation, his concomitant rejection of 'animal humanism', and his downplaying of the rights of non-human life in relation to the human. Nevertheless, Nancy's ontological communism, and the way in which human language serves not to raise the human above the animal but to expose the equality of all beings, has some problems of its own. It is to these that we now turn.

4. Nancy's 'Christian' Love for all Beings

Two critiques can be raised to Nancy's way of understanding politics in relation to the human/animal distinction. The first is that it leaves itself unable to make what are argued to be necessary political distinctions between different beings (between humans, animals and stones, for example); and the second is that ecotechnics reintroduces the theological after the death of God. In what follows, we shall see that the two critiques are related. But first, we shall treat them separately.

The first critique argues that, in refusing the sort of discrimination between animal and immortal that Badiou employs in his restriction of political subjectivity to those with the capacity for thought, Nancy forecloses the possibility of making ontologically grounded discriminating judgements between different beings. In *Adoration*, for example, we see a systematic refusal to retrench the ambit of adoration in a way that would introduce a distinction between the animal and the human. When Nancy evokes the dignity, price or value of each existence, he insists that it apply to all beings: 'Only at this price, this priceless price, will we be able to honour the stakes of relation: the stakes of being in the world, shared among men and among all beings.'⁵⁶ Anything less than the incommensurable priceless price of all beings falls short of what singular plural ontology warrants, and Nancy is adamant in maintaining this incommensurability and ontological indiscrimination. In the light of this Nancean insistence on the non-discrimination of adoration, the first critique asks the following question: Can Nancy's position provide a way of discriminating, politically, between the human and human, or between human, animal, plant and inanimate object? What is at stake in this question is framed by Badiou, though not in relation to Nancy, in his lecture course from 2004–5, 'S'orienter dans la pensée, s'orienter dans l'existence' ('Orienting oneself in thought; orienting oneself in existence').[57] Here, Badiou evokes a 'democracy without borders' that includes the rights of each one – man, woman, child, animal, even plant – and condemns the uncontrollable tendency to extend humanism to all life. In other words, the position Badiou is critiquing is unable to set limits on its notion of rights, an inability which leads to the sort of anomaly (in Badiou's thinking) where we expend more time and effort saving the orang-utans and whales than we do helping some human beings. Whether or not we agree with Badiou's example of humans and whales, it is very hard to hold the position that all beings (humans, animals, fauna, inanimate objects) should be viewed as flatly incommensurable and of equal dignity.

The same dilemma is sketched in a more extreme form by John Llewelyn when he rehearses the familiar dilemma of the conflicting interests of the human host and the living cancer cell,[58] or again by John Mullarkey in *Post-Continental Philosophy*, who adds the case of the foetus and the mother.[59] The problem is that if Nancy's radical incommensurability of all beings leaves him no basis on which to distinguish, politically, between different beings, then the universality of being-with is politically useless. Coming from a very different starting point, and considering the singular plural exclusively in terms of the human, a similar concern is voiced by Ian James when he inquires in *The New French Philosophy* whether Nancy's thinking of sense as being-with 'account[s] for the fact that some bodies will be born into and as an unequal share of material existence', say into poverty or slavery.[60] It is unclear whether Nancy's radical incommensurability can account for the fact that 'bodies are always born into different sites of material existence that are shaped unequally'. If it cannot, then it will be ill-equipped to address such inequalities in a political frame, and

Nancy's attempt to elaborate a politics on the basis of a metaphysics of the common will be an inadequate basis upon which to make political decisions. We shall return to this critique after setting it alongside the second objection to Nancy's position.

The second critique is that ecotechnics and Nancy's ontological communism are Christian, thinking the human/non-human relation as a sort of incarnation. In 'Flesh and Body in the Deconstruction of Christianity', Roberto Esposito makes the specific claim that in Nancean ecotechnics we see 'the semantics of incarnation as place, form, and symbol of the union between human and non-human'.[61] He goes on to write, 'I would go so far as to say ... that technology is the non-Christian, even post-Christian, figure of the incarnation.'[62] This is problematic in a number of ways. First, Esposito's analysis is elaborated in the first instance in relation to Nancy's *The Intruder*, rather than to ecotechnics in general. This narrowness explains claims like the following:

> It matters little whether or not ... the non-human that penetrates mankind is divine, since today a prosthetic or implanted organ could be inanimate or from another human. What matters is that the inanimate, divinely so to speak, allows mankind or a single human to continue to live.[63]

This is neither what is meant by incarnation in Christianity, nor by ecotechnics in Nancy. In the case of the orthodox (Chalcedonian) doctrine of the hypostatic union, the word does not become flesh in order to allow flesh to continue to live in any temporal or immediate sense that might be analogous to a heart transplant. Christ is not 'fully God and fully man' in order that he may live temporally, but so that others might live eternally. In the case of ecotechnics, when Nancy says that the human is 'also' animal, 'also' living, 'also' physico-chemical, he does not mean that the non-human has 'penetrated' humankind as Esposito suggests, but that the non-human is irreducibly constitutive of the humankind that, without it, would not be human at all. Once more, 'with' is coeval with 'being'.

Secondly, even if there is a homology between incarnation and technology, it does not necessarily follow that technology is a form of incarnation. In other words, similarity does not prove influence. It might equally be, and indeed there is a good Nancean case for making this argument, that incarnation is the Christian figure of ecotechnics. There is just as much ground, if we accept the similarity, to claim that Christianity is ecotechnical as to claim that ecotechnics is Christian.

Despite the doubtful theological overtones of Nancy's heart transplant, however, there is a Christian influence in ecotechnics, and one about which Nancy is quite open. It comes not in terms of incarnation but in terms of love, and it helps us to see how Nancy responds to the first of the two critiques sketched above. Nancy's ecotechnics recognises a radical ontological incommensurability of all beings, material and immaterial. In *Adoration*, he locates the ethos appropriate to this ontological non-discrimination in what he names 'the love called "Christian"', which is 'strictly indissociable from equality'.[64] Nancy describes this love through a quotation from Kierkegaard's *Works of Love*:

> Since the neighbour is every human being, unconditionally every human being, all dissimilarities are indeed removed from the object, and therefore this love is recognisable precisely by this, that its object is without any of the more precise specifications of dissimilarity, which means that this love is recognizable only by love.[65]

In the light of this Kierkegaardian insistence that love be blind to determinate qualities, what Nancy is doing in his ecotechnics is taking the Christian command of universal love and simply making the 'universal' more universal, widening it from all people to all beings in his account of adoration. This also helps us see why Nancy leaves his thought open to the sort of critique formulated by Badiou, and suspected by James: it is of the very nature of this love to be for all without distinction, and so when this love is universalised to all beings its lack of discrimination is not incidental but constitutive.

If we compare two passages separated by almost twenty-five years, one from 'Of Divine Places' (1987),[66] and one from *Adoration* (2010), we can see that Nancy's thought in relation to the love he elaborates in *Adoration* follows a trajectory from a more explicit to a more implicit theological register. In 'Of Divine Places', Nancy evokes the divine as clearly manifest:

> The god may very well be made manifest selfsame with the heavens, or with the sea, or with the skin of man or the animal's gaze; it may be

that he is manifest selfsame with everything that is open and offered and in which he has dispatched himself.[67]

Five pages further on, Nancy once more lists the places of divine manifestation, this time including 'an animal, a person, a stone, a word, a thought'.[68] Twenty-three years later, in *Adoration*, Nancy discusses in very similar terms the 'salut!', the address that accompanies and makes possible all speech, in terms of which sense is circulated among beings:

> This existence makes sense or *is* sense, and with it the whole world can make sense, from 'salut!' to 'salut!', the whole world can make sense. Do not the morning sun, the plant pushing out of the soil, address a 'salut!' to us? Or the gaze of an animal?[69]

It becomes clear from this juxtaposition of passages that Nancy's ecotechnics does indeed draw on theological influences. So whereas ecotechnics really does not follow any incarnational paradigm that is recognisably Christian at all, its radical equality does bear comparison with 'the love called "Christian"', and the 'priceless price' of each being in *Adoration* is homologous to Nancy's earlier meditation on the manifestation of God.

We should be careful at this point, however. It is one thing to recognise this resonance with theology, and quite another to say that Nancy's thought is 'theological' in any wider sense. This one case of influence is one chapter in a longer story towards which Nancy gestures in *Adoration*:

> the civilization that for a time called itself 'Christian' called for a commandment of universal love in response to a demand come from further away than a religion, come from a mutation of civilization itself.[70]

Although Christianity has an influence on ecotechnics, Nancy's position is that it does not necessarily have a claim on it. Ecotechnics is Christian only in a weak sense, to the extent that it takes the shape of its universal concern from Christian love. To claim that ecotechnics (and therefore Nancean politics) is Christian in a strong sense, or in other words to claim that ecotechnics is a form of covert Christianity, we would also have to prove that this universality is not merely manifested primarily in the Christian tradition, but also that it does not precede or exceed this tradition in a way that cannot be recuperated by it. We are otherwise left with the more modest claim that both Christianity and ecotechnics partake of the same universality. It is with the weaker of the two senses of influence that I want to argue that Nancy's ecotechnics is a generalised, non-anthropocentric inflection of Christian love; the secularisation of which takes its universality beyond the human to embrace all beings.

This excursus via Nancy's borrowing from Christian love also allows us to respond to the critique that Nancy's ontological communism is unable make political discriminations between the human and the non-human. It will be remembered that such discriminations cannot be made for Nancy on the basis of any exclusively human capacity. Indeed, in 'Painting in the Grotto', Nancy uses the capacity for language in the cause of establishing an equality between human and non-human beings, rather than a qualitative difference, and in *Adoration* he insists on the 'priceless price' of all beings. The excursus via love has helped us to see, not that Nancy does after all introduce a discrimination between the human and the animal to act as an equivalent for Badiou's qualitative distinction between the immortal and the human animal, but that his principled indiscrimination is necessary, despite the problems it brings. Just as 'the love called "Christian"' embraces all with no respect to determinate qualities, Nancy's ontological communism and the politics to which it gives rise cannot but retain the ineradicable problems that flow from its refusal to introduce an ontological discrimination between the 'priceless price' of all beings.

Notes

1. The transcription of the seminars is freely available online. While not reviewed by Badiou, and therefore 'not committing him' as the URL's disclaimer has it, they are nevertheless full prose transcriptions of the seminars providing valuable further information on ideas sometimes covered more briefly in the published works. See <http://www.entretemps.asso.fr/Badiou/seminaire.htm>. All translations from the seminars are my own.
2. Badiou, 'Qu'est-ce que vivre?', seminar 2003–4. <http://www.entretemps.asso.fr/Badiou/03-04.3.htm>.
3. *Aristotle: Nicomachean Ethics*, ed. and trans. R. Crisp (Cambridge: Cambridge University Press, 2000), p. 196.

4. Alain Badiou, *Le Siècle* (Paris: Seuil, 2005), p. 246. *The Century*, trans. A. Toscano (Cambridge: Polity Press, 2007), p. 168. For more detail, see Badiou's seminar from 2000–1 entitled 'Le Siècle'. <http://www.entretemps.asso.fr/Badiou/00-01.1.htm>.
5. See Badiou's 2001–2 seminar 'Images du temps présent (1)'. <http://www.entretemps.asso.fr/Badiou/01-02.3.htm>; C. W.'s translation.
6. Badiou, *Le Siècle*, pp. 246–7. *The Century*, p. 172.
7. Badiou, *Le Siècle*, p. 247. *The Century*, p. 173.
8. Alain Badiou, *L'Ethique* (Caen: Nous, 2003), pp. 80–1. *Ethics: An Essay on the Understanding of Evil*, trans. P. Hallward (London: Verso, 2002), p. 58.
9. Badiou, *L'Ethique*, pp. 27–8. *Ethics*, p. 12; translation altered.
10. Alain Badiou, 'Afterword: some replies to a demanding friend', in Peter Hallward (ed.), *Think Again* (London and New York: Continuum, 2004), p. 237.
11. Badiou, *L'Ethique*, p. 28. *Ethics*, p. 12.
12. Badiou, *Le Siècle*, p. 247. *The Century*, p. 175.
13. Badiou, *Le Siècle*, p. 251. *The Century*, p. 178.
14. Badiou, *Le Siècle*, p. 238. *The Century*, p. 168.
15. Alain Badiou, *Circonstances 4: de quoi Sarkozy est-il le nom?* (Paris: Lignes, 2007), p. 133. *The Meaning of Sarkozy*, trans. D. Fernbach (London: Verso, 2009), p. 74.
16. Alain Badiou, *Abrégé de métapolitique* (Paris: Editions du Seuil, 1998), p. 111. *Metapolitics*, trans. J. Barker (London: Verso, 2005), pp. 97–8.
17. Jean-Luc Nancy, *L'Adoration: déconstruction du christianisme 2* (Paris: Galilée, 2010). Jean-Luc Nancy, Philip Armstrong and Jason E. Smith, *Politique et au-delà* (Paris: Galilée, 2011). All translations from *Politique et au-delà* are my own.
18. Aurélien Barru and Jean-Luc Nancy, *Dans quels mondes vivons-nous?* (Paris: Galilée, 2011).
19. Nancy et al., *Politique et au-delà*, p. 40.
20. Nancy et al., *Politique et au-delà*, p. 41.
21. Nancy et al., *Politique et au-delà*, pp. 41–2.
22. Jean-Luc Nancy and Philippe Lacoue-Labarthe, *Rejouer le politique* (Paris: Galilée, 1981), p. 25. Simon Sparks (ed.), *Retreating the Political* (London: Routledge, 1997), p. 114.
23. Jean-Luc Nancy, *La communauté désœuvrée* (Paris: Christian Bourgeois, 2004), pp. 71–2. *The Inoperative Community*, trans. C. Fynsk (Minneapolis: University Of Minnesota Press, 1991), p. 28.
24. Jean-Luc Nancy, *L'Expérience de la liberté* (Paris: Galilée, 1988),

p. 200. *The Experience of Freedom* (Stanford: Stanford University Press, 1993), p. 163.
25. Jean-Luc Nancy, *Le Sens du monde* (Paris: Galilée, 1993), p. 147. *The Sense of the World* (Minneapolis: University of Minnesota Press, 1998), p. 93.
26. Jean-Luc Nancy, *Être singulier pluriel* (Paris: Galilée, 1996), p. 55. *Being Singular Plural*, trans. R. D. Richardson and A. E. O'Byrne (Stanford: Stanford University Press, 2000), p. 34.
27. Nancy, *Être singulier pluriel*, p. 55. *Being Singular Plural*, p. 34.
28. Nancy, *La communauté désœuvrée*, p. 191. *The Inoperative Community*, p. 78.
29. Nancy, *Être singulier pluriel*, pp. 36–7. *Being Singular Plural*, p. 18.
30. Nancy, *Être singulier pluriel*, p. 37. *Being Singular Plural*, p. 18.
31. Nancy et al., *Politique et au-delà*, pp. 443–4.
32. Nancy et al., *Politique et au-delà*, p. 45.
33. Jean-Luc Nancy, *Corpus* (Paris: Métailié, 1992), p. 78. *Corpus*, trans. R. A. Rand (New York: Fordham University Press, 2008), p. 78.
34. Jean-Luc Nancy, *La Création du monde, ou, la mondialisation* (Paris: Galilée, 2002), p. 140. *The Creation of the World, or Globalization*, trans. F. Raffoul and D. Pettigrew (New York: SUNY Press, 2007), p. 94.
35. Nancy et al., *Politique et au-delà*, p. 44.
36. Nancy, *L'Adoration*, pp. 114–15. Jean-Luc Nancy, *Adoration: The Deconstruction of Christianity II*, trans. J. McKeane (New York: Fordham University Press, 2013), p. 78.
37. Jean-Luc Nancy, *La Pensée dérobée* (Paris: Galilée, 2001), p. 100. François Raffoul and David Pettigrew (eds), *Heidegger and Practical Philosophy* (Albany: SUNY Press, 2002), p. 75. The French 'Cela, donc, est donné' can be equally well translated as 'that, then, is a given' or, in a phenomenological register, as 'That, then, is given'.
38. Nancy, *La Pensée dérobée*, p. 100. *Heidegger and Practical Philosophy*, p. 75.
39. Nancy, *La Pensée dérobée*, p. 112. *Heidegger and Practical Philosophy*, p. 84.
40. Nancy, *La Pensée dérobée*, pp. 102–3. *Heidegger and Practical Philosophy*, p. 77.
41. Jean-Luc Nancy, 'La peinture dans la grotte', in *Les Muses* (Paris: Galilée, 1994), pp. 117–32. 'Painting in the grotto', in *The Muses*, trans. P. Kamuf (Stanford: Stanford University Press, 1996), pp. 69–79. In this essay, Nancy plays on the resonance between

monstration, the monster and the monstrous. Nancy intends, by these latter two terms, to show that the introduction of mimesis and absence into the world is a making-strange, and thus that 'Man began with the strangeness of his own humanity' ('La peinture dans la grotte', p. 121. 'Painting in the Grotto', p. 6). It is this strangeness – of the human and of the world as they are monstrated – that is monstrous.

42. Jean-Luc Nancy, *Les Muses* (Paris: Galilée, 1994), 122. *The Muses*, trans. P. Kamuf (Stanford: Stanford University Press, 1996), p. 70.
43. Nancy, *Les Muses*, p. 129. *The Muses*, p. 76.
44. Nancy, *Être singulier pluriel*, p. 109. *Being Singular Plural*, p. 85.
45. Nancy, *L'Adoration*, p. 90. *Adoration*, p. 60.
46. Nancy, *Les Muses*, p. 122. *The Muses*, p. 70.
47. The doctrine of double inspiration is extrapolated from such verses as: 'no prophecy was ever produced by the will of man, but men spoke from God as they were carried along by the Holy Spirit.' 2 Peter 1: 21 (ESV).
48. Nancy, *Être singulier pluriel*, p. 36. *Being Singular Plural*, p. 17.
49. Nancy, *Être singulier pluriel*, p. 36. *Being Singular Plural*, p. 17.
50. Nancy, *Être singulier pluriel*, p. 109. *Being Singular Plural*, p. 85.
51. Nancy, *Être singulier pluriel*, p. 36. *Being Singular Plural*, p. 18; translation altered.
52. Nancy, *Être singulier pluriel*, p. 109. *Being Singular Plural*, p. 85.
53. Nancy, *L'Adoration*, p. 23. *Adoration*, p. 14.
54. Nancy, *L'Adoration*, p. 90. *Adoration*, p. 60.
55. Nancy, *Être singulier pluriel*, p. 37. *Being Singular Plural*, p. 18.
56. Nancy, *L'Adoration*, p. 89. *Adoration*, p. 59.
57. <http://www.entretemps.asso.fr/Badiou/04-05.htm>.
58. John Llewelyn, *The Middle Voice of Ecological Conscience: A Chiasmic Reading of Responsibility in the Neighbourhood of Levinas, Heidegger and Others* (Basingstoke: Macmillan, 1991), p. 263.
59. John Mullarkey, *Post-Continental Philosophy* (London: Continuum, 2006), p. 118.
60. Ian James, *The New French Philosophy* (Cambridge: Polity Press, 2012), p. 50.
61. Roberto Esposito, 'Flesh and Body in the Deconstruction of Christianity', *Minnesota Review*, 75, 2010, p. 96.
62. Esposito, 'Flesh and Body', p. 96.
63. Esposito, 'Flesh and Body', p. 96.
64. Nancy, *L'Adoration*, p. 88. *Adoration*, p. 59.

65. Nancy, *L'Adoration*, pp. 88–9. *Adoration*, p. 59; C. W.'s emphasis.
66. Jean-Luc Nancy, *Des lieux divins* (Mauvezin: TER, 1987).
67. Nancy, *Des lieux divins*, p. 17. *The Inoperative Community*, p. 123.
68. Nancy, *Des lieux divins*, p. 22. *The Inoperative Community*, p. 127.
69. Nancy, *L'Adoration*, p. 29. *Adoration*, p. 18; translation altered.
70. Nancy, *L'Adoration*, p. 88. *Adoration*, p. 58.

3

Nancy and Hegel: Freedom, Democracy and the Loss of the Power to Signify
Emilia Angelova

In this chapter I argue that for Nancy, the political and the pre-political are bound by a mutual constitutive principle, what Nancy calls the 'sense'[1] of democracy. This sense is the source of democracy's meaning – and for Nancy, it is not anything stable. Nancy submits that we are coming to the end of an age in which meaning has been supported by given, traditional principles. Today meaning can no longer be referred to a beyond – for instance, the familiar principles of God, Man, History, Science, Law, Value.[2] The destruction of the community's relation to this beyond leads to shock and disappointment, but for Nancy, in the midst of this shock, democracy as politics and government nonetheless remains as a source of meaning. However, the principle of democracy undergoes a mutation and needs to be rethought. Democracy can no longer rely on the traditional beyond for its ideals, even its ideal of freedom. This is because the modern subject continually affirms the unlimited freedom of what Nancy calls an extremity, a freedom that even exceeds our own-most uniqueness of difference, that forges invention, creates new ideals and dreams, that cannot be tied to a given principle. Behind new ideals there is, then, a threat of destruction of such ideals: it is the loss of the beyond that opens the way for forging ideals, and positing new ideals that seem to be fixed or given, threatens to return us to a beyond that removes freedom. In the midst of shock, in the freedom of democracy, meaning comes back to us only in the 'loss of the power to signify'.[3]

Nancy's reflection on the political value of freedom depends upon understanding not so much whether or not there is freedom that belongs to some verifiable order, but rather how and why we can say that meaning comes back to us in the freedom of democracy, despite the loss of the power to signify. Since the freedom of democracy cannot refer to any traditional beyond, and thus cannot be part of any axiomatic ontology, meaning must come back through something evental that, by its very occurrence, haunts the political and returns as the political's own pre-political condition. As Nancy puts it, the 'possible meaning or sense of democracy' stems from 'little more than a minimal argument or schematic protocol' that neither requires nor allows an axiomatic ontology.[4] For Nancy, this 'minimal' 'sense of democracy', what gives democracy meaning, springs from recognition of the essential finitude of the human being, which constrains human being to present, in sensible form, what would otherwise be abstract ideas (of, e.g., humanism). The sense of democracy thus arises, for Nancy, through a repetition without number, which Nancy calls *iteration*.[5] This is precisely because the sense of democracy cannot refer to an abstract idea or transcendent beyond, it cannot refer back to an already given, *a priori* origin of sense, that sense would repeat for a second or third time. Rather, sense derives from a past that it makes originally. What this requires is 'that the *always already* be thought otherwise than as an *a priori*'.[6] The iteration of sense is therefore not delimitation of an epoch, and it does not erupt out of a previous stage in history that can be well defined or stationed in time. In sense, then, the idea of origin effaces itself, and sense opens onto a more originary (non)origin. This is why the political, the body politic that has a sense of democracy, must open onto a pre-political that is not tied to or defined by already given stages or ideals, but can only anticipate, as its referent and meaning, an always perfectible democracy, what Nancy calls the 'truth' of democracy.

As iterative, the sense of democracy precisely bars access to the stable beyond of the tradition. The 'sense' we are left with thus both extends beyond itself and disrupts itself, it is the 'experience' of our making sense of our finite 'being in common'.[7] Democracy depends upon being open, since democracy must open frontier to the other. Yet the sense of democracy arises from the iteration of the indeterminacy of our being in common, and to this extent is constricted by this 'origin' of iteration. This is why Nancy charges that modern democracies have above all proven 'incapable of *experiencing the intrusion of the stranger*'. To substantiate this, Nancy appeals to Nietzsche's principle of the uncertainty of meaning: 'since moral correctness assumes that one receives the stranger by effacing his strangeness at the threshold, it would thus never have us receive him'.[8]

I will attempt to explain below why the principle of uncertainty of sense, or meaning, matters to thinking the political, and where it originates, where and how it comes to appear. My focus is Nancy's Hegel, specifically on the structural and phenomenological openness of the principle of negation, sublation, Hegel's own formulation of this openness as 'problematics of textuality' (a term that Nancy coins), and the implications for 'sense'. In contextualising Nancy on Hegel, I draw on Kant, especially on the idea of freedom shared between them. Nancy learns a lesson from Hegel on the negativity of spirit and what 'loss' would mean under negativity's condition. This complicates the modern heritage and what is meant by freedom, monarchy, the nation-state, violence and the subject.

I begin Part 1 with Nancy's view on the restlessness of negation, and how it furnishes a commentary on negativity in Hegel. In Parts 2 and 3 I give accounts of restlessness in two further contexts that I will develop and examine as consequences of the preliminary view below, showing how this account of restlessness leads to Nancy's view of the sense of democracy.

1. The Problematics of Textuality and Loss in Nancy's Hegel

In both *The Speculative Remark* (1973/2001) and *Hegel: The Restlessness of the Negative* (1997/2002), Nancy takes up Hegel as the 'inaugural thinker of the contemporary world'.[9] Nancy's Hegel is a thinker of a community confronted with loss, a lost community, that gives way to contemporary society – the *Sittliche Substanz* (ethical substance) that gives way to the *Bürgerliche Gesellschaft* (bourgeois society). This Hegel, who is haunted by the loss of community, inaugurates a discourse of philosophy where life and immediate sensibility are dialectically 'lost.' For Nancy's Hegel, loss as such cannot be abandoned to an archaic past, to a principle, *arché,* given in and by the past; rather loss is a function of and within 'experience'.[10] Specifically, the loss that opens the freedom of the modern functions both as ground and inoperative ground of 'experience'. In an unorthodox Hegel, for whom the system does not complete itself in the present, because it depends on loss as its inoperative ground, Nancy reads loss and the negativity of spirit as mutually co-constitutive, co-ontological, and thus as an 'unrest [*Unruhe*]',[11] since it can never close itself.

The word 'unrest' functions as a vehicle to introduce a wholly new problematic in Hegel. Nancy argues that from the outset Hegel begins with a co-ontology, a co-implication of loss and negativity as the operative principle which alone brings into trembling motion the whole of the speculative system. At the foundation of Hegel's system, Nancy argues, there lies the critical force of this co-ontology. This critical force and its trembling reveals where and how traditional metaphysics opens both to politics and to aesthetics. Hegel sets out to overcome the abstractly rational reason of Kant's dogmatic idealism. By opening his system to unrest, it is this Hegel that is disturbed by Nancy. 'Unrest' is formulated in this way by Hegel, in the *Philosophy of Mind: Being Part Three of the Encyclopedia of the Philosophical Sciences* (1830):

> Spirit [*der Geist*] is not an inert being, but on the contrary, absolutely restless (*unruhig*, troubled, agitated, restless) being, pure activity, the negativity or ideality of every fixed category of the abstractive intellect; not abstractly simple but in its simplicity, at the same time a distinguishing of itself from itself; not an essence, that is already finished and complete before its manifestation, hiding itself behind its appearances, but an essence which is truly actual only through the determinate forms of its necessary self-manifestation.[12]

This basic formulation of Spirit's unrest or disquiet is found in *The Phenomenology of Spirit* and as well in *The Science of Logic*, amongst other writings. In the space of twenty years Nancy twice revisits this problematic and, as I show in this part, his writings on aesthetics and politics derive from it. This is because attention to unrest is precisely what lets Nancy access the principle of negation in Hegel as he does.

The spirit's unrest is the central theme in Nancy's first text, *The Speculative Remark*, although this term does not appear in the book's title, as it does with the second Hegel book. The speculative remark, mentioned in the title, is on the meaning of negation and the principle of negativity, which Hegel appended to the second edition of *The Science of Logic*, in 1831. In the remark, Hegel insists on the twofold meaning [*sens*] of sublation [*aufheben*] as suppressing, yet preserving. This is what Nancy, in the subtitle, calls *one of Hegel's bons mots*. This remark, Nancy proposes, will have influenced the entire preface of the *Logic*, which was being prepared for the edition. The remark is, incidentally, Hegel's last text: Hegel signs it seven days before his death.

Nancy's term 'problematics of textuality' is actively formulated a year after the *Speculative Remark* appeared, and applies to Hegel's speculative remark itself. By Nancy's own phrasing, problematics of textuality appear precisely where a unifying principle of a logical representation of the rationality of the concept, as unity of the sensible and the rational, is claimed, yet cannot be delimited in the present. This is what we find in sublation as suppressing the sensible in the name of the rationality of the concept, yet precisely also needing to preserve the sensible as unified with the rational. 'Problematics of textuality' are 'problematics in the plural'. The problematic of being in Hegel's *Science of Logic* illustrates this. We try to grasp the concept of 'being' as a unity of the sensible and the rational, as comprehending all of sensible being under the category 'being'. But to do this, our category 'being' must be void of all determinate sensibility. The category of being thus breaks up; indeed Hegel's text breaks up at this point, for what is really at issue is a nothing that comes to be in becoming. The problematic of being is thus really a problematics in the plural (of being, nothing, becoming), and something sensible, becoming, breaks into the text. The problematics of textuality are thus defined by the 'indefinite somewhere', in a place and time which 'cannot be assigned by the discourse of philosophy': 'in the very movement of foundation, something which inaugurates philosophy occurs in a sort of jolt, of throb or a pulsation'. These are problematics that are other-inflected, they are literally 'in the plural': 'their [these problematics] very rigour makes of them ... unrests [*inquiétudes*]'.[13] (Looking ahead, it is precisely this sort of exposure to unrest that is at issue in the sense of democracy.)

Nancy understands this unrest as opened by an 'interrogative'[14] principle, through which philosophy inaugurates itself by turning on itself and its starting point (in the manner of Heidegger's *Dasein* questioning its own existence). This is what he finds in the speculative remark and the problematics of textuality. The interrogative structure, though, concerns repetition and how the *aufheben* already operates in the text. The reason for this is apparent in Nancy's restatement of Hegel's own remark, 'To sublate [*aufheben*] and the sublated [*das Aufgehobene*] ... constitute one of the most important concepts: a plural works as a singular.'[15] A plural works as a singular because the suppressive work of *auf-*

heben must preserve *das Aufgehobene*: *aufheben* must repeat yet transform *das Aufgehobene*; for *aufheben* to operate, it must come back to *das Aufgehobene* as already operating in the text, and yet no longer operate that way. Nancy thus urges that the task of thinking, which is marked by the interrogative structure, concerns a 'plasticity'[16] of understanding that corresponds with this complication of the very meaning or movement of the proposition. This is what he is concerned with when he says of the speculative remark: 'one must therefore understand both the truth of the *aufgehoben* through the already-past of becoming [*le déjà-passé du devenir*] and the becoming already-past through (or 'as') truth that exposes itself by *aufheben* [by sublating]'.[17] This reversibility of the already-past of becoming and the becoming already-past through exposure leads Nancy to detect an other-inflected, or alterity-inflected, ontological-epistemological framework (to 'read Hegel *otherwise*' with respect to truth, 'read or write *otherwise* the *Aufhebung*') in the problematics of textuality.[18] This is because there is *nothing* external to the system in which the *aufheben* arises, and yet the system, in turning back upon itself, must be open to something more than is given in it as claiming to be present.

Kant's transcendental philosophy separates the ideas of nature and freedom, he encloses a metaphysics of subjectivity in its own sphere. For Nancy, Hegel's speculative remark undermines this separation, via the interrogative structure above. But, for Nancy, Hegel's system had the ambition of enclosing this interrogative iteration within the present. Nancy shows this is not possible: if we attend to the problematics of the text, we find that the iteration goes back to something before the system (the nothing, the other, the loss), out of which meaning arises (which will be the pre-political of the sense of democracy). For Nancy, then, there is a more radical exposure at work, because of the temporality of the operations in question. We can better grasp what is stake in this shift from Kant to Hegel to Nancy by turning to Heidegger's view of Kant (which inspires Nancy), first in relation to the temporality of being, and second, in relation to the image.

a) First Relation to Heidegger

Nancy approaches Hegel as a philosopher for whom negativity and the idea of freedom are central. To do this, Nancy reintroduces into Hegel an idea of alternative temporality from Heidegger's

Kant. As a result, Nancy approaches aesthetics (sensibility) as the clue to metaphysics of nature, and politics as the clue to metaphysics of freedom.

The connection to sensibility arises through Kant's critique of the paralogism of substantiality (his critique of the *ego cogito*), which is crucial to his new grounding of ontology. On the way to retrieval of ground, as Heidegger puts it, we come 'to a decision regarding the "temporality" of or rather the timelessness of the I'.[19] Nancy takes seriously in Kant (and in Hegel as consequence), that in this retrieval of the more original essence of time, time as 'self-affection' must be taken as guide. The context for clarifying sensibility's self-affection is the fourth critical question posed by Kant, a rethinking of *humanitas* which Nancy will then develop as central to his own view.

That is, in *Kant and the Problem of Metaphysics*, Heidegger clarifies that the 'I' of the correlation between I and being, expressed in Kant's unity 'I think', grasps (*verstehen*) something other than within-timely beings. Kant uses the term time (*Zeit*) for the ego. And as Heidegger puts it, for the time of entities present at hand, Kant uses the term *das Zugleich* (since, e.g., when Kant formulates the law of logic of the excluded middle, he speaks of this as a condition that excludes an A and ~A being present at hand 'at the same time').

Drawing on Heidegger's diction, Nancy offers that where Kant asks 'What is man [*der Mensch*]?', he is not asking for a definition by *genus* and *differentia specifica*. Such a difference operates according to the principle of contradiction (that defines man as rational animal and not non-rational), and as such appeals to a non-original essence of time, that could be given all at once, in the manner of *das Zugleich*. In contrast, for Nancy, the question of man as the question of a free being must have an interrogative structure, in which 'man' relates to her/ his condition to overcome its inauthenticity. Man relates to her/his self in the mode of comprehending a relation with something incomprehensible, which is not an 'I' that is fixed as a within-timely being.

For Nancy, the ground of the question 'What is man?' is thus the alternative temporality, the futurity, upon which ontological access to the essence of freedom depends. From Heidegger, Nancy takes it that the ground of both the possibility and the impossibility of contradiction is arrived at from out of the orientation towards man *of* the future as connecting up with one's self, in the mode of her/ his own becoming, making a decision 'for' freedom.[20] Nancy's critical force lies with the insight that Kant must deny the temporal character of the 'principle of contradiction', and simultaneously posit this negation in its temporal character as the becoming past of the future to-come, the hidden and open ground, to which man's questioning activity is profoundly open, exposed, and vulnerable. It is this point about negation and its temporality that Nancy brings to his reading of Hegel's speculative remark and the problematics of textuality.

Nancy thereby derives consequences from Heidegger about a minimal ontological-political foundation in Hegel. For Heidegger, negating the principle of contradiction (when the philosopher Kant thinks of being and non-being, being and thinking, as holding together) 'expresses that temporal character which, as preliminary "recognition" ("pre-paration"), originally belongs to all identification as such'.[21] This alternative temporality is what we find in Hegelian negation as well. It follows that the problematics of textuality (which unify conceptual reason with what it is thinking about, the nothing outside the system), concerns the way in which reason is caught in a double bind between pursuing its own denegation and finding itself depending on a preliminary 'recognition' that is not its own doing. This double bind emphasises a constitutive vulnerability in question, a referral to that 'which makes possible' (condition of possibility), the 'finitude of human subjectivity in its wholeness'.[22]

Kantian limit as *humanitas* thus presents us with an interrogative structure of being 'more finite than man'.[23] As Nancy's own work shows, Heidegger's 'Letter on Humanism' reiterates the same proposal for a 'humanity without a humanism', it deposes from ontology the morally autonomous rational Subject and Enlightenment's normativity approaches to ethics, and gives us, as Nancy claims, the task of thinking an other-inflected ontology. Actively engaging temporality as open interrogative structure in Hegel and Heidegger unmistakably concerns us with an inherent heteronomy or responsibility towards alterity. For Nancy, this involves active understanding of that which makes 'action [*l'agir*] as such'.[24] This requires, as per Nancy's Hegel, understanding (*faßen*)[25] what it is to experience/ to think freedom, actively retracing a condition of possibility that is a constitutive outside of Enlightenment's morality of reason, namely, a Greek *praxis* of making sense.[26]

b) Second Relation to Heidegger

In *The Muses*, Nancy again stresses that, since Kant, the duality of relation between freedom and nature is the operative principle of, as per Nancy's coinage, a problematics of textuality.[27] However, Kant divided freedom from nature, the interiority of the subject's powers from what is beyond. Nancy does not do so, and the reason for this adds to our point about exposure above. This is because, in Nancy's view, the sensible unity of experience, the making of sense, is supported by a space where truth neither inheres in an interiority (the subject's powers), nor derives from an external beyond in a place and time outside.

Alison Ross argues in this direction. For Kant, in and through art, 'the centrality of a cognitive relation to nature is suspended at the same time that an insight into the subject's powers is won through that suspension'.[28] The dissolution of reference to a ground beyond, in a time and a space other than the space-time of the here and now, incurs loss of a reference to nature as independent object via a merely cognitive relation. Simultaneous with the loss incurred, a second motion is set to work, that displaces reference to a nature independent from human purposes, to freedom's unlimited idea (since we become aware that we are constituting nature as object). Displacement precisely shifts focus away from the thing (outside) and to interiority's constitutive power (the subject), as if nature is reason's own sublime offering. There is thus the 'opportunity to make of it [nature] an articulate vehicle for the presentation, by analogy, of reason's ideas'.[29] (To anticipate, for Nancy, the politics of the beyond us (e.g., 'beyond' this world which is in Kant) is transformed into a trans-immanent punctuating of sense, auto-reflexivity without a self, 'between us'.[30])

Kant's move, transformed in Nancy, is well documented in 'The Vestige of Art', as announcing the occurrence of interrogative, creative, structure in the image (copy and original).[31] Again, Hegel and Kant are both invoked later by Nancy, but as thinkers anticipating what Heidegger will make of them, especially in the *Vorbild*, fore-image, the model of a being yet to be created: a 'mimetic triplicity of portrait-reconstruction-model', as Nancy calls it.[32]

To clarify this, prior to showing, reproducing or representing something else, each thing shows itself. It gives an image of itself. It *shows itself*, while re-producing something else. In Kant's sublime offering, which posits aesthetics as the clue to metaphysics, nature 'shows itself' insofar as it gives ontological access to nature: the image acts simultaneously as impartation of knowledge. Heidegger writes: 'a photograph ... immediately offers a look. It is image in the first sense. But while it shows itself, it wants to show precisely that from which it has taken its likeness.'[33] Nancy describes what emerges here as an inversion 'of mimetic values', an inversion of the relation between the original and the derived. It is a confusion or an exchange of place between what shows itself, actively, and what shows something else, passively, derivatively. This reversibility, whereby the one (the gaze) becomes the object of the other (what op-poses or stands against it); this ambiguity, whereby the one transforms and is transformed into the other, defines the act of seeing and the look of every image. However, defined in this duplicitous way, the identity of the image, as that of the gaze, is unstable and uncertain. The identity of a thing constitutes what it is in itself in distinction from what it is not, from its other. Yet the image seems to lack precisely this, insofar as it reverts into its other, at the very moment when it is defined as itself; a reproduction which in turn *presents itself* as the original thing itself. By virtue of the confusion of the original and the derived, the identity of each thing, its original self-image, divides into an infinite multiplicity of reproductions, images and images of images, as in a hallway of mirrors. Overcoming this confusion of image and reality, wherein thought vacillates uncertainly between contradictory impressions of being, philosophy, or the tradition of metaphysics, requires the idea of a purely intelligible reality.[34] But this idea cannot be secured. The having of images is thus inherently a trembling that exposes the one having the image to something beyond.

2. Hegel, and Nancy: Implications for the Political and Politics

It is not enough for Nancy to remain with Heidegger. Nancy's politics of community is influenced via his turn to Heidegger, but more recent work moves past it as well. Nancy rejects a vision of community as the sharing of a common property, activity or substance. Community, rather than being predicated on having something in common, is defined by *existing* in common. Indeed, we do not possess our existence: we are ('in') our existence. And as exposure and openness, our being-together is characterised by the shifting and yet shared border at which our different existences touch one another. Again, in Nancy's view, it is important to emphasise that existence does not precede this contact, but is defined by it. (If our existence did precede this contact, then we would be able to answer the question 'What is man?' by appeal to an essence of *humanitas*, vs. interrogation of ourselves.) The condition of possibility *par excellence* for our existence is our exposure to others, and this exposure implies a relation with alterity that is radically different despite existing within the world.[35]

The trans-immanent relations to alterity, which define being-singular-plural, are thus also the basis of community. Such is our pre-political existing in common. The open question is: just where does existing, sense making as *praxis* of sense, arise?

On Hegel's trajectory, it is community that provides knowledge with its concretely historical context, so the break-up of the community is the break-up of knowledge. This means that knowledge is no longer organised around instrumental and totalisable objects as ends in themselves; rather, knowledge 'completes' itself on the model of the speculative or the infinite proposition. By its constitution or 'form', the infinite proposition excludes understanding, says Hegel in the *Phenomenology of Spirit*, of the 'usual way of relating the parts of a proposition':

> The sublation of the form of the proposition must not happen only in an immediate manner, through the mere content of the proposition. On the contrary, the opposite movement must find its explicit expression [*ausgesprochen*] . . . This alone is the speculative in act [*das wirkliche Speculative*], and only the expression of this movement is a speculative exposition [*Darstellung*].[36]

For Nancy's Hegel, the 'loss' of the personal other implies that progression is no longer determined by the set steps of a necessary logic. There is not a law-like necessity that historically determines an epoch of understanding. Instead, understanding arises via a sublation, *Aufhebung*, that is not grounded in already set determinations. '[A]ll determinations are missing; every determination had to be missing in virtue of the law of the beginning.'[37] To grasp this speculative movement in terms other than epochal understanding (which precisely wants to delimit the beginning of the movement in the determinations of a prior epoch) demands thinking of a co-constitutive and other-inflected co-ontology. In terms of politics and freedom, this means thinking the political together with the pre-political, thinking that freedom as action and a decision 'for' (re-cognitive) identification as such is neither already constituted, nor constituted by an autonomous self that would already be there, outside, like a given nature – but rather freedom is co-ontological (equiprimordial) with the pre-political. (Part three, on Antigone, will clarify what is meant by the pre-political here.)

Nancy leads us to reconsidering the transformation of the question (of the interrogative structure), such that the question can no longer constitute its ground, but finds this co-constituted with something prior to the question. As Heidegger put it, 'metaphysics stabs itself in the back', not to terminate the life of thought, rather so as to transform our relation to it. Giving up the metaphysical way is an urgency 'if the truth of Being is to be experienced as the history which even metaphysics bears without knowing it'.[38] Nancy's transformation of the question of 'what' or 'essence' is a transformation of our relation to it. And the transformation demands thinking togetherness through, and in, thinking otherness.

When Nancy conceives the question of freedom as the 'leap into groundlessness', that is, an opening up of the 'essential province of freedom', this means that the pre-political (praxis of) 'sense' (experience of freedom) must be thought together with loss of reference from a (substantive) beyond. The pre-political more originally understood in Hegel *via* Nancy, has nothing in common with knowledge as object-historical understanding [*Seinsverständnis*]. Nancy thus insists that the political must face up to its own condition of possibility as one of iterability, as that which simultaneously suppresses and preserves being and nothing in their difference.

a) Freedom, We, and the State in Nancy's Hegel

Jason Smith writes of the very minimal definition of the 'political' that we are left with in Nancy: the political is defined as the 'union as such' as its own end.[39] This also reduces to a minimum adherence to the political in its familiar moments (e.g., the moments we find in Hegel on constitution, sovereignty, war), for where Nancy adheres to these moments, it is to them in their 'most abstract' form.⁴⁰ The last chapter of *The Restlessness of the Negative* titled 'We' is therefore 'not to be identified with' any reference to the theory of the State, or any explicit reference to the 'entire problematic of *Sittlichkeit* and its triadically implicated moments' of family, bourgeois society, and the state.⁴¹ The translator's introduction tells us that it is as though 'from the moment the name "state" is removed [in *The Restlessness of the Negative*], the name Hegel itself seems eclipsed'.⁴² A footnote to the book, Nancy's own, refers to this moment in Hegel:

> Love is said to be 'essential principle of the State'. This does not define an amorous politics, and it supposes that Hegel thinks 'the State' as the *sublation* (or upheaval) [*relève*] of the apparatus of separated power that we designate with this name. In other words, he exposes what will become into our time the primary political theme: no longer the institution and nature of government, but the contradiction of the separation and non-separation of the 'common' considered for itself – and also, consequently, the contradiction of separation and non-separation within being-with-the-other itself. Consequently, through his incontestably naïve and dated confidence in a certain model of the State, Hegel also provides the lineaments of a thought of the contradiction of every philosophical *foundation* of the political.⁴³

From Hegel's *Philosophy of Right*, the 'union as such', which Nancy has in mind, is defined this way:

> If the state is confused with civil society and its determination is equated with the security and protection of property and personal freedom, the interest of individuals [*der Einzelnen*] as such becomes the ultimate end for which they are united; it also follows from this that membership of the state is an optional matter. But the relationship of the state to the individual [*Individuum*] is of quite a different kind ... Union as such is itself the true content and need, and the vocation [*Bestimmung*] of individuals [*Individuen*] is to lead a universal life.⁴⁴

Below I discuss this dismantling of the political in light of the context of Nancy's first book on Hegel. In the *Phenomenology of Spirit*, Hegel's model of the State is established by the French Revolution, and the 'State' is a 'shape', a figure to be left behind and sublated – i.e., a difference to be suppressed and self-preserved – and so a moment whose becoming what it is ought to be dropped from Objective Spirit. I discuss this in light of what interests us in the problematics of textuality of Hegel's text: the problem is that figure appears as that by means of which the concept figures itself – and so figuring necessarily occludes the conceptuality of the concept. Nancy intervenes in the textuality of the *Aufhebung*, in order to expose the reversibility or iterability of an unheard of history of the violence of relation, calling on and for 'the thought of the common "for itself"'.[45]

In the first place, I suggest, Nancy's intervention aims at the limit of unity behind Hegel's renewal of the three absolutes of the philosopher's ideal: the good, the true and the beautiful. The counter-violence of the reading gesture aims at exposing to a more originary interpretation the existential questions, including, what is truth and what is being, as to 'the good, the absolute good' that 'fulfils itself eternally in the world ... and is already fulfilled in and for itself and does not need to wait upon us for this to happen'.[46] The good as always-already fulfilled, even in Hegel, is not the presence of the *parousia*, of redemption through absolute knowledge. For Nancy, it 'means that the True and the Good are *already there*, already accomplished ... the *Unruhe* itself ... of the effort of thought that is its own meaning [*qui est à lui-même son sens*]'.[47] In Nancy's Hegel, violence is a 'death that has no inner signification', a loss of inner signification of the death of the individual – the reader bears witness to the 'effectuation' of a displacement of suffering, loss, mourning, upon a subjectivity that is not representational. To suffer the pain of loss is to relate simultaneously to the image of death, the figuring of subjectivity as a self-relating without a relation, the exposition of thought as a position in knowledge without access to representation. On the one hand, we have lost the very possibility of a higher signification, the death of signification itself. But the text, and we, the reader, bear witness to the trace of otherness in every identity and in every subject. On the other hand, displacement and the plural senses of death, warn against the difficulties of isolating philosophical discourse – isolating plural thinking – from the 'difficulties of being'. The thought of being-in-as-common as such (as being 'for itself'), what is neither ethics nor ontology, depends upon the iterability of its own action as it sets out to constitute itself as a possibility for being. With the aid of the trope, indeed language as conceptual system, the speculative philosophy sets itself up as moving along, advancing from shape to shape, through the unfolding conceptuality of the sublated concept. Nancy's intervention into the phenomenological progression of shapes is a claim to a more originary understanding of this advancement, such as would reveal the driving force behind the absolute systematicity of the movement as practically impossible to articulate around problems of the law, sovereignty, and the juridical sphere (concepts represented in Objective Spirit). There is something about temporality (and shapes in the phenomenology the abbreviated chronological succession into a logical necessity, but now with the insistence on the 'between us' of appearing) in Nancy's move – and this is where the political and pre-political are constitutively brought together.[48] Problematics in the plural, the exposure of singularity as constitutive element of the sublation, does not pass on the model of transition to/ from but in becoming, the passage to the 'determinate being [*Dasein*]'[49] – relationality, of that which cannot come to pass is a withdrawal in a being-with: in Nancy's words, 'that produces the being-already-past in determinate being'.[50]

In Hegel, Nancy locates the political as constitutively together with its pre-political co-ontological other: the community of being-in-common, but as experience of in-experience/ decision *for* freedom as creative idea, sublime offering. The 'self' [*das Selbst*] is a moment always-already sublated: 'in a higher movement of reason in which such seemingly [*solche Scheinende*] utterly separate terms pass over into each other spontaneously, through that which they are . . . the dialectically immanent nature of being and nothing themselves [is] to manifest their unity, that is, becoming their truth'.[51] Nancy's Hegel is pressed upon, disturbed in this retracing of the modality of the speculative as that which enables the textuality of form, the instant of rest of restlessness in its accessibility (ground's abandonment) – transcendence as simultaneously ground and un-ground, 'in' existence.[52] Nancy articulates this precisely pre-reflective relationality with being-in-common (omnipotence, resoluteness, explosivity) of the concept: 'spirit spiritually anticipates itself and relates to itself as there-being in the not-being of the concept'. In *Truth of Democracy*, Nancy proposes an explanation: '[D]emocracy is first of all a metaphysics and only afterwards a politics. But the latter is not founded on the former . . . it is but the condition whereby it is exercised.'[53] When elaborating on the 'infinite in the common', he similarly says that 'democracy . . . must also, in some way be "communist"', 'democracy *is spirit* before being a political and social form, institution, or regime', for otherwise it would be 'but the management of necessities and expediencies, lacking in desire'.[54]

b) Loss is Loss 'for Us'

Sharing with Adorno the view that loss is 'for us' (rather than an absolute past, as Adorno objects to Benjamin), Nancy intervenes specifically in Adorno's reading of Hegel (*via* Marx, in Adorno's *Minima Moralia*), that Hegel 'assigns to individuation ... an inferior status in the construction of the whole', and that thereby Hegel aims 'with serene indifference ... for liquidation of the particular'. Hegel approaches the classical political (e.g., techniques of power, as Foucault, and Althusser have noted) through the trope of the State (*Staat*), and in Nancy this adds a necessary layer of legibility, a problematics of textuality. In Nancy, with the onset of the speculative philosophy at the 'end' of the text and at the 'end' of history itself, the 'state' retreats, it 'subtracts' itself in a more originary mode of violence from the negativity of the 'nothing', from the ontological-political, and revealing a more originary opening of space, a bare, denuded space resisting appropriation, an un-instrumentalisable pre-political. This pre-political is that which was to be 'thought through it and in its stead'.[55] The question of performative violence ought to be posed as concerned with the 'speculative philosophy', and concerned with philosophy as 'completing' the 'task' of thinking, *Denken*, as 'form', this latter referring to a time as 'time-form' always implicating a 'before' as in sequential time, the known 'history' of Being as that which is a constituted product, a concern with the extent to which the 'science', *Wissenschaft* of philosophy 'is' the difference of form (irreducible plurality). To speak with Nancy, the 'being-different' of 'the' form, is the 'being of "being" in its difference (identity, then)'.[56]

Nancy then drops the Subject – i.e., the State – the 'it' itself (Being) in 'it gives' (the 'there is', to speak with Heidegger). And this same operation applied to the movement of the State, from Hegel's *Philosophy of Right*, a movement in Objective Spirit, that is, a movement that is instrumentally grounded in the *Technik* (political apparatus) of Spirit, and in Enframing or *Gestell*, grounds against a framed grasp of essentia-existentia, and a foreign framework of reference – 'reference' supporting in a beyond (interiority) of representational thinking. In other words, he drops what Adorno calls, a 'fantasmatic correlate of the subject of *a proprietary and securitary individualism*'.[57]

3. The 'Sense' of Action, Having Something Done

What follows from this as we part with the indifference that marks essential being? I want to elaborate on this consequence for this 'parting with': following Nancy on Hegel's point 'having something done'. At the opening of the chapter on Objective Spirit in the *Phenomenology of Spirit*, 'The Ethical Order', Nancy notes that Hegel anticipates Heidegger: that with the appearing of the linguisticity of affirmation of the difference of Substance, the concretisation of the actual universal shall be in the form of 'something done'[58] – recalling here a certain corruption, *Verwesung*, of the figure of man (that is, the entropic tendency to self-destruction for its own sake, substance's negativity for its own sake). Hegel found this insufficiency in the figure of Antigone: 'Action' (the case of Antigone's deed of burial from M470 recounted by Nancy in the *Speculative Remark*) as imposing a law of sovereignty upon a space that is not-yet political (i.e., not-yet self-conscious), is not sufficient.

In Nancy's sharpening of this point in the *Speculative Remark*, in Hegel, we attend to the social-communal orientation aiming towards language as limit of a rationality that is the real as self-transcendence. Hegel's *Begriff* dialectically occludes the enigma of the genetic condition of possibility: already in Hegel, Nancy shows, *Begriff* self-constitutes itself as a possibility of being for-itself, and so loses its 'innocence'.[59] This invisible act of occlusion abandons knowledge to the unknowability of its condition, and abandons it to the thought that is unknown, or to its 'un-condition'. Even, more importantly, the invisibility of occlusion is a mode of elision: what Antigone does, acts on, forces Substance out of inherent relation to itself; it makes arise the plasticity of Substance as that law of 'Law', which cannot in itself be known, but only is affirmed as a fore-knowledge (fore-grasping), the Unconscious knowledge of the Law.

Hegel addresses agency and the experience of action as marks of tragedy's trajectory in the *Phenomenology of Spirit*. The prehistory to how Antigone enters into Hegel from Sophocles' trilogy is worth briefly recounting. For the poet Hölderlin, Sophocles' *Antigone* comes to be the exemplary case of the appropriation of a divine position, for she positions herself against Creon and the rules of the city, thus presupposing the 'appropriation of the right to institute difference by oneself'.[60] Antigone transgresses the human limit in the manner typical for the tragic hero – one who 'desires difference and exclusion excludes himself, and suffers, to the point of irreversible loss'.[61] As tragedy is about 'expulsion' and thus about transgression generally, the question that Hölderlin ponders in his 'return'[62] to Sophocles of *Antigone*, however, stands out, since what takes on the form of transgression here is not concerned as such with the particularities of instituting the difference by oneself, as is the case with the decidedly 'modern'[63] tragic personality of Oedipus that 'goes into particulars', offering up a religious and sacrificial interpretation of the social ill.

For the poet Hölderlin, the 'fable' of Oedipus is set as a 'trial of heresy', the tragic fault falling with the individual who 'interprets too infinitely the word of the oracle and in which he is *tempted in the direction of the nefas*. [The transgression, the sacrilege, is thus the excess of interpretation.]'[64] With transgression in *Antigone*, however, the topic changes: for Hölderlin, Sophocles pursues a 'denegation' of Aristotelian mimetology of original, copy and catharsis, the experience of guilt as purification as per the spectacular (performative theatrical, imitative) relation to the subject. The very case of Antigone is different. Thus the 'guilt' that associates with Antigone in Hegel's chapter six, though singular, paradoxically belongs to two sets of values at once, two cultural-historical epochs at once, the Modern Romantic theory of individuality, the 'speculative suicide' or sacrifice and at the same time, the Ancient Mimetic theory of catharsis, the purification of passion, tragic effect or guilt. But it also belongs to neither.

Nancy presents us with the injunction to think co-constitutively together otherness (togetherness 'as' otherness): political with the pre-political – an Oedipus co-constitutively together with Antigone. We have seen above that with the later Heidegger of reversibility a crucial insight enters. With this later Heidegger in mind, Nancy pursues, in his claim of being-toward-death, a more originary 'locus' as the place of what 'gives' the given, is simultaneously a location of thinking 'in another place', namely, a touching-on, and so a place other than succession of economies and the transcendental-ontological tradition. In Nancy's words, this is 'where the impossible itself cannot be touched, even though one *touches its limit*'.[65] In this location, a displacement, the 'essence of thinking' and presencing (that which is presencing-absencing is deprived of any principle, an *archē* or *telos*) understood as an 'event', arise together. But such an arising together gives rise, as we have seen above, to an *ethos* in movement that is lost 'on the limit of all language' and so a more originary origin, not an *ethos* that can be represented. It is 'because' of the subjective im-possibility/ inconceivability that the formalism and abstraction of such *ethos* might not 'exist', that insistence – the return to 'identity' and its 'tremble' (affirming difference first, and arriving at identity, then) emerges as *praxis* of sense, action, something done, to be thought. In a more 'originary ethics', as Nancy coins this term developing it out of the later Heidegger, 'origination [*Ursprung*]' connects the way the human complies with unconcealment as presencing: 'in' this other place, a touching-on, or 'origination', *praxis*, action, its sense, 'harks back to unconcealment as the identical trait of both *phusis* and the human, to their freedom as one and the same opening'.[66]

Notes

1. For the use of sense in the plural, see Nancy, 'The Senses of Democracy', in Jean-Luc Nancy, *The Truth of Democracy* (New York: Fordham University Press, 2010), pp. 37–45.
2. B. C. Hutchens, *Jean-Luc Nancy and the Future of Philosophy* (Kingston: McGill-Queen's Press, 2005), p. 161.
3. Giorgio Agamben et al., *Democracy in What State? New Directions in Critical Theory* (New York: Columbia University Press, 2011), p. 58.
4. Jean-Luc Nancy, *The Truth of Democracy* (New York: Fordham University Press, 2010), p. 38.
5. Jean-Luc Nancy, *The Speculative Remark*, trans. C. Surprenant, (Stanford: Stanford University Press, 2001), pp. 16–17.
6. John Sallis, *Logic of Imagination* (Bloomington: Indiana University Press, 2012), p. 185.
7. Jean-Luc Nancy, *Hegel: The Restlessness of the Negative*, trans. J. Smith and S. Miller (Minneapolis: Minnesota University Press, 2002), p. xxiv.
8. Jean-Luc Nancy, *Corpus*, trans. R. A. Rand (New York: Fordham University Press, 2008), p. 162; translation modified.
9. Nancy, *Hegel: The Restlessness of the Negative*, p. 3.
10. Nancy's use of the term experience is underwritten by the impli-

cation that we are exposed to the non-experience of experience. See Peter Fenves's Foreword to *Experience of Freedom* (Stanford: Stanford University Press, 1993), esp. p. xviii.
11. Nancy, *The Speculative Remark*, p. 86.
12. G. W. F. Hegel, *Philosophy of Mind Being Part Three of the Encyclopedia of the Philosophical Sciences* (1830), trans. W. Wallace (Oxford: Clarendon Press, 1971). Sec. 378, Zusatz, p. 3; translation modified. Cited in Nancy, *Hegel: The Restlessness of the Negative*, p. 6.
13. Nancy, *The Speculative Remark*, pp. xviii, 86.
14. Ibid., p. 15.
15. Ibid., p. 29.
16. Ibid., p. 15.
17. Ibid., p. 29.
18. Ibid., p. 19.
19. Martin Heidegger, *Kant and the Problem of Metaphysics*, trans. R. Taft (Bloomington: Indiana University Press, 1990), pp. 133, 132.
20. Jean-Luc Nancy, *The Experience of Freedom* (Stanford: Stanford University Press, 1993), pp. 82–3, cf. Martin Heidegger, 'Vom Wesen des Grundes'.
21. Heidegger, *Kant and the Problem of Metaphysics*, p. 133.
22. Ibid., p. 133.
23. Ibid., p. 133.
24. Jean-Luc Nancy, 'Heidegger's "Originary Ethics"', in François Raffoul and David Pettigrew (eds), *Heidegger and Practical Philosophy* (Albany: SUNY Press, 2002), p. 83.
25. Nancy, *The Speculative Remark*, p. 16.
26. Martin Heidegger, *Basic Writings*, ed. D. Farrell Krell (Harper SanFrancisco: HarperCollins, 1993), pp. 241, 252–3, 256.
27. Cf. Jean-Luc Nancy, *The Muses* (Stanford: Stanford University Press, 1996), pp. 2–3. We are referred to a problematics of textuality, in the question formulated in the first essay in *The Muses*: 'Why are There Several Arts and Not Just One?' Nancy formulates such a problematics of textuality in relation to Hegel, when he says, e.g., 'Assuming at least, as one must, that our question itself can be maintained in its uniqueness and in its unity of question. What might one mean by a principle (or a reason or an essence) that would not be a principle of plurality, but the plural itself as principle? And in what way must this properly belong to the essence of art?'
28. Alison Ross, *The Aesthetic Paths of Philosophy: Presentation in*

Kant, Heidegger, Lacoue-Labarthe, and Nancy (Stanford: Stanford University Press, 2007), p. 5.
29. Ibid.
30. Heidegger, *Basic Writings*, p. 252.
31. Nancy, *The Muses*, p. 89.
32. 'Masked Imagination', in Jean-Luc Nancy, *The Ground of the Image* (New York: Fordham University Press, 2005), p. 85. Nancy continues: 'He [Heidegger] says that Kant uses all three senses without formally distinguishing them, and he expresses a doubt that these distinctions alone will be able to clarify the schematism. But of course this is precisely what he sets out to do.'
33. Nancy, *The Ground of the Image*, p. 66.
34. Cf. Sallis, *Logic of Imagination*, pp. 154–60, 170–8. I owe this thought to ideas expressed by Jacob Potempski, unpublished paper.
35. Jean-Luc Nancy, Avital Ronell and Wolfgang Schirmacher, 'Love and Community: A Round Table Discussion' <http://www.egs.edu/faculty/jean-luc-nancy/articles/love-and-community/> Accessed: 19–09–2013. Discussion held at the European Graduate School in August 2001.
36. G. W. F. Hegel, *Phenomenology of Spirit*, trans. A. V. Miller (Oxford: Oxford University Press, 1977), M65.
37. Nancy, *The Speculative Remark*, p. 40.
38. Citation is taken from Heidegger, *The Question of Being*, 1956, E.T. p. 94, by Otto Pöggeler. In Thomas Sheehan (ed.), *Heidegger the Man and the Thinker* (New Brunswick: Transaction Publishers, 2010), p. 180.
39. Nancy, *Hegel: The Restlessness of the Negative*, p. xxii.
40. Ibid., p. xxiii
41. Ibid., p. xxi.
42. Ibid., p. xxiii.
43. Ibid., p. 119, n.11. Nancy here means 'Love' in reference from Hegel, *Philosophy of Mind*, sec. 535.
44. G. W. F. Hegel, *Elements of the Philosophy of Right*, trans. H. B. Nisset (Cambridge: Cambridge University Press, 1991), sec. 258, Addition. This text is cited in Nancy, *Hegel: The Restlessness of the Negative*, p. xx.
45. Nancy, *Hegel: The Restlessness of the Negative*, p. xxiv.
46. G. W. F. Hegel, *The Encyclopedia Logic*, trans. T. F. Geraets, W. A. Suchting, and H. S. Harris (Indianapolis: Hackett, 1991), Addition para 212:286.
47. Nancy, *The Speculative Remark*, p. 149.

48. Nancy engages in similar fashion in two other essays, 'Finite History' and 'The Jurisdiction of the Hegelian Monarch'. See Lean-Luc Nancy, *The Birth to Presence* (Stanford: Stanford University Press, 1993).
49. Nancy, *The Speculative Remark*, p. 106.
50. Ibid., p. 41.
51. Ibid., p. 105.
52. Peter Fenves helpfully introduces this in *Experience of Freedom*, p. xxiii. Fenves says this: 'For Nancy, subjectivity is not simply impotent; if power implies causality, which it surely does, then the shipwreck of subjectivity means it has *none*, and this marks the end of subjectivity altogether [contrasting this with Sartre's fragile humanity of being "condemned to be free"]. But in this end there is *finite* freedom, a freedom that does not amount to a limited space of action but is, rather, the opening – in thought, in experience – onto the limit, onto groundlessness, onto "existence" without essence.'
53. Nancy, *The Truth of Democracy*, p. 34.
54. Ibid., p. 14.
55. Nancy, *Hegel: The Restlessness of the Negative*, p. xxv.
56. Nancy, *The Speculative Remark*, p. 193, n.6.
57. Nancy, *Hegel: The Restlessness of the Negative*, p. 76; cf. xxi.
58. Hegel, *Phenomenology of Spirit*, M474, M477.
59. Ibid., M468.
60. Philippe Lacoue-Labarthe, *Typography*, trans. C. Fynsk (Stanford: Stanford University Press, 1989), p. 233.
61. Lacoue-Labarthe, *Typography*, p. 233. To this extent even Oedipus or Creon are not 'positive' heroes; their essential defining characteristic is that they are expelled from the normative.
62. Ibid., p. 229. 'Return to Sophocles' is in Hölderlin's words. This is to say, Hegel disagreed with Aristotle-Schelling interpretation of Antigone.
63. Ibid., p. 228.
64. Ibid., p. 233; Hölderlin's words.
65. Jean-Luc Nancy, *A Finite Thinking*, ed. Simon Sparks (Stanford: Stanford University Press, 2003), pp. 110–11.
66. Reiner Schürmann, *Heidegger on Being and Acting: From Principles To Anarchy*, trans. from the French by Christine-Marie Gros (Bloomington: Indiana University Press, 1987), p. 125.

4

The Event of Democracy
François Raffoul

Jean-Luc Nancy's rethinking of democracy unfolds from a twofold conviction: first, from the belief that the term itself has become somewhat of a common place, and to such an extent that the word itself has effectively dissolved any problematic character and possibility of an authentic questioning as to its senses. 'When it is taken for granted in every discourse that "democracy" is the only kind of political regime deemed acceptable by a humanity that has come of age, that has been emancipated, and that has no other end than itself then the very idea of democracy loses its luster, becomes murky, and leaves us perplexed.'[1] Nancy reminds us that the totalitarianisms of the twentieth century have come out of such democracy, and that one should therefore not ignore the 'traps' or 'monsters' that lurk behind this murkiness; further, he claims that democracy has lost most of its power of signification. With respect to this 'nonsignifying word *democracy*', Nancy explains: 'Is it at all meaningful to call oneself a "democrat"? Manifestly, one may and should answer both "no, it's quite meaningless, since it is no longer possible to call oneself anything else", and "yes, of course, given that equality, justice, and liberty are under threat from plutocracies, technocracies, and mafiocracies wherever we look". *Democracy* has become an exemplary case of the loss of the power to signify.' Incapable of 'generating any problematic or serving any heuristic purpose', democracy then 'means everything – politics, ethics, law, civilization – and nothing'.[2] This loss of significance gives a task for thought, namely, 'to stop letting common sense pullulate with free-floating incoherencies the way it does now and force democratic nonsignificance to stand trial in the court of reason'.[3] It thus becomes a matter of rethinking the senses of democracy, and of re-engaging what is at stake with this term.

The second conviction pursued by Nancy is that it is not a matter of simply understanding democracy in its traditional exhausted sense, as a political regime among others, but first and foremost as an *ontological fact*. Nancy insists principally on this point: democracy is not, first and foremost, a political form. It must rather be approached in its ontological scope – Nancy even uses the term 'metaphysical' – and not primarily as a political reality. As he states in *The Truth of Democracy*: 'Democracy is first of all a metaphysics and only afterwards a politics.'[4] In the title there lies no doubt the significance of the expression chosen by Nancy, the 'truth' of democracy: democracy must be approached in its ultimate significance or truth, and not as a given political reality. 'The truth of democracy is the following: it is not, as it was for the ancients, one political form among others. It is not a political form at all, or else, at the very least, it is not *first of all* a political form.'[5] In the pages that follow I will attempt to explore this double conviction in Nancy's rethinking of democracy, and how the twisting free of democracy from the political opens the possibility of grasping democracy as an event.

1. The Inadequacy of Democracy

The twisting free of democracy from the political would require us to re-engage the senses of the political [*le politique*] as such (which becomes rethought as co-existence as such, while 'politics' [*la politique*] refers to the forms of the state). It also indicates straight away that democracy, as Nancy put it in a recent interview, 'is at once political and more than political, or better ultra-political (*outre-politique*)',[6] if not archi-political. It is, in any case, 'more' than politics. Everything goes through politics, but does not originate or end there. The expression 'everything is political', with its implicit reference to totality, is for Nancy a fascistic or totalitarian formulation. That is because the 'with' at the basis of democracy unfolds first, not in a politics, but as an ontology or a metaphysics.

What Nancy gestures towards here – in addition to a delimitation of the political through which, precisely, 'not everything is political'[7] – is what he attempted to develop in *The Truth of Democracy*, namely to approach democracy, not as a political form or regime, but as an *event*. Indeed, democracy becomes a power of imagining, of invention, without subject, mastery, and even identity in a given form, which allows Nancy to draw a contrast between democracy and the political.[8] Democracy represents 'a sort of principial going beyond of the political'[9] (even though this going beyond can only occur by starting from the polis and its institutions). In turn, the political can then be re-engaged for itself from this excess, so that 'politics as a whole must be remobilized from elsewhere'.[10] Indeed, democracy is not only in excess of the political, it is also in excess *of itself*, that is, of its own idea, form or concept, precisely to the extent that democracy is first of all an event, and as event can only exceed its own definition. This is why democracy is not a political form: as an event, it necessarily exceeds any established form or figure.

There lies what Nancy refers to as the 'inadequacy' of democracy, an inadequacy to itself that Nancy saw manifested in the disappointment expressed in May '68 about the shortcomings of democracy. May '68 revealed such ontological inadequacy or incompletion, the fact that democracy always falls short of itself and of its possibilities, opening the space and perspective of a perfectibility. In a 2007 interview, Nancy referred to Derrida's 'democracy to come' in a perspective that combines the eventful character of democracy with its incompleteness and perfectibility: 'In Derrida the to come, the *à venir*, is always strictly opposed to the future, to *l'avenir*, that is, to the present-future that is projected, represented, given in advance as an aim and as a possible occurrence.'[11] The 'to come' or *à venir* designates what 'is essentially and always in the coming, of what has never come or come about, come down and made itself available'. Therefore, if democracy is already given,

> made, confected [*faite*], established, then one will no longer be able to say that democracy is to be improved; but if one says that it has not been perfected [*parfaite*], then it must be understood that its essence perhaps eludes all representable, anticipatable, and realizable perfection – not because it would be a utopia but because its essence is the very tension of an exigency that is not related to a realization. And yet it is not a question here of renouncing real struggles or actual transformations, far from it!

Derrida had indeed stressed in *Rogues* that democracy is 'a concept that is inadequate to itself'.[12] The fact that democracy is inadequate to its concept, that it is irreducible to a conceptual form, indeed *to its own idea*, is referred by Derrida to a self-*différance* at play.[13] I will argue that such incompletion and inadequation –

indeed *différance* – must be thought from the eventful character of democracy. Democracy is inadequate to itself because in its very happening, in its very coming, it is always other than itself. It is always incomplete and inadequate to itself in the sense of the incalculability of the event. Seeing that it is incalculable in its happening, democracy 'cannot be, by essence, determined or defined'.[14] In fact, the form itself always presupposes the event of its *formation (and deformation)*, as the form 'only draws its force and its form to the dynamics of formation-deformation that always include the risks of monstrosities, of translations'.[15]

2. Democracy as Event

Taken as power and as sovereignty of the *demos*, democracy must in fact be rethought *in its truth* from the ontological condition of being-with and in terms of it: as we noted above, Nancy seeks to understand democracy first as an ontological fact. This is why, as he explains in *Être-avec et Démocratie*, 'in order to truly understand the nature of this power and therefore of the political nature of democracy, it is necessary first to consider its existential or ontological stakes'.[16] What are those ontological stakes? Democracy corresponds to an 'anthropological and metaphysical mutation: it promotes the "with", which is not a simple equality but the sharing out of sense'.[17] If the 'people', the *demos*, is sovereign, it is in the sense that it shares out sense, and that there is no principle above or outside of this 'with'. To that extent, the power of the people becomes rethought as sharing out of being, as disposition of singular beings.

Democracy as power of the people signifies the power of all insofar as they are together, that is to say, with one another (*les uns avec les autres*). It is not the power of all as power of anyone or of the whole mass over a simple juxtaposition of dispersed individuals. It is a power that presupposes, not a dispersion held under the authority of a principle or of a gathering force, but the dis-position of juxta-position. That means both a disposition that does not include any hierarchy or subordination, and a juxtaposition in an existential sense as a sharing of the sense of being.[18] Democracy is hence ultimately the sharing of sense, or the event of co-existence, an existence that is not ruled from above by some transcendent principle, and not based on any nature. It expresses the immanence of sense to itself: it 'names a regime of immanence of sense – immanence to the people, immanence to the totality of beings, immanence to the world'.[19] Modern democracy is much more than just another political regime. It is an anthropological and metaphysical mutation, and a genuine revolution in the being of humanity.

> We are talking here about a mutation of culture and civilization so profound that it attains the same anthropological proportions as the technological and economic mutations that have come along with it. That's why Rousseau's contract doesn't just institute a body politic, it produces mankind *itself*, the humanity of mankind.[20]

This is also in part because democracy, as Nancy puts it, engages not only the human being as a political figure, as 'citizen', but the human being as such and as a whole: 'modern democracy does engage, absolutely and ontologically the human being and not just the 'citizen'.[21] It is to that extent democracy is not simply a political *form*, but rather an *event*, the event of co-existence.

Never has this irreducibility of what Nancy calls the '*spirit* of democracy' ('democracy' is *spirit* before being a political and social form, institution, or regime'[22]), to any order, form or political regime, indeed political party or ideology, been as patent as during the events of May '68, the celebration of which was the occasion for Nancy's short but dense essay, *The Truth of Democracy*. It is significant that it was a reflection on such events – indeed on their very eventfulness – that gave Nancy the occasion to develop an original analysis of democracy, of what democracy means, and of what remains to be thought with that term. Nancy situates his reflection in the context of the 2008 celebration in France of the fortieth year anniversary of the events of May '68. More precisely, his essay arose out of a polemic with an (in)famous statement by then newly elected French President Nicolas Sarkozy, who had declared that one should 'liquidate the heritage of May '68', to be done with May '68, and bury it along with other misfortunes of history. Against such a declared intent, Nancy on the contrary sought to understand May '68 as that moment when the very essence – or *truth* – of democracy came to light and began to be articulated. As he writes in his introductory comments, it 'was a questioning of the very truth of democracy that was ventured there [in the movement of May '68]'.[23] Nancy then describes the ambition of this book as an attempt to 'clarify and help develop that first venture'.²⁴ Instead of a 'liquidation' of the legacy of May '68 (perhaps the effort to close what was opened there), we have here an attempt to approach this event as still to come, a democracy to come in excess of its traditional forms, and perhaps as the very incalculable event of the future.

As I suggested above, the very title, the *truth* of democracy, already indicates that Nancy attempts to think democracy away from received representations, and indeed, away from the very regime of representation, approaching it as an event exceeding norms, laws, and established or given forms. He argues that, in its truth, democracy cannot be enframed within the horizon of the possibilities that remain 'linked to an organized if not organic action, to a planning process or prospective'²⁵ characteristic of the very form of the state. Democracy exceeds the representations of the predictions of an organised world, precisely to the extent that, as 'to come', it exceeds representation: 'the future is precisely what exceeds representation', wrote Nancy in *The Creation of the World*.²⁶ It is such an excess of the 'to come' of the future that manifested itself in May '68, revealing that democracy, in an essential way, demands to be *invented*. 'Sixty-eight was the first irruption of the demand for such a reinvention.'²⁷ Nancy further situates his reflections explicitly within the opening of Nietzsche's task of a transvaluation of all values, and he makes the claim that what is at stake in his rethinking of democracy as invention is an exit out of nihilism. For him, overcoming nihilism is tantamount to overcoming the regime of representation, of 'world-views' or 'word pictures', and of 'the theoretical paradigm' that implies the closure of a horizon. According to Nancy, as we have begun to 'clear a path for the way out of nihilism', we have also exited the regime of representation:

> In truth, we were in the process of displacing the entire regime of thought that allowed for the confrontation of opinions. For we were exiting not only the time of 'conceptions', 'visions', or 'images' of the world (*Weltbilder*) but the general regime in which a vision understood as a theoretical paradigm implied the sketching out of certain horizons, the determination of goals [*visées*] and an operative foresight [*pré-vision*].²⁸

To the paradigm of the establishment of pre-given forms (such as the motifs of progress, rights, reason, etc.), Nancy opposes the notion of an exposure to an incalculable, that of the event. All these notions, 'man', 'humanism', but also 'community', 'communism', 'sense', etc., must be exposed to what Nancy calls the 'going beyond' of an excess: exposed 'to a going beyond in principle: to that which no prediction or foresight [*prévision*] is able to exhaust insofar as it engages an infinity in actuality'.[29] This is what May '68 revealed. It revealed the subversive character of the event with respect to any posited forms of the state, or even ideologies or political organisations. 'Instead of developing and advancing visions and previsions, predictions and forecasts, models and forms', May '68 was 'given to greeting the present of an irruption or disruption that introduced no new figure, no agency, or authority'.[30] Indeed, democracy as exposure and event supposes as well that there is no subject that masters such a process. One cannot 'presuppose . . . a subject that is master of its representations, volitions, and decisions'.[31] The event exceeds the mastery of the subject, which finds itself, as subject, 'already surpassed by events [*dépassé par les événements*]'.[32] This is the sense of Nancy's often-repeated references to Pascal's saying, 'Man infinitely transcends man' [*l'homme passe infiniment l'homme*]. The figure of the human is not given, and cannot be encapsulated in a form. The subject, instead of being assured of itself in a self-enclosure, is instead open to that excess of itself.

3. Groundless Democracy

Understood as co-existence or the being-in-common of singular existences, democracy cannot be grounded in the form of pre-given subjectivity. In fact, democracy cannot be grounded: it manifests a radical lack of foundation. The ontological *fact* of democracy (and the truth of democracy is, first, precisely, that democracy is a *fact*) is without foundation or substrate. This must be understood from the perspective of Nancy's understanding of being and of world: they are pure facts, rather than derived from any prior principle or substance. One finds this elaborated for instance in *Being Singular Plural*, where we read: 'Being absolutely does not preexist; nothing preexists; only what exists exists.'[33] Nothing pre-exists existence, there is no a prior being, no substrate; instead, it is 'from an abandonment that being comes forth: we can say no more. There is no going back prior; being conveys nothing older than its abandonment.'[34] And 'it is not permitted us to ask by whom'! It is important, Nancy argues, to approach this 'fact-ness' of being without referring it to any founding cause. The fact of existence is without ground, without reason. 'The world is such a fact: it may well be that it is the only fact of this kind . . . It is a fact without reason or end, and it is our fact. To think it is to think this factuality, which implies not referring it to a meaning capable of appropriating it, but to placing in it, in its truth as a fact, all possible meaning.'[35]

The existence of the world as shared must be distinguished from the motif of representation and instead approached as an excess, in 'a stance by which the worlds stands by itself, configures itself and exposes itself in itself, relates to itself without referring to any given principle or to any determined end'.[36] An absence of principle affects existence. This is why Nancy would speak of an 'an-archic' democracy: there is no model and no principle for it, as it is no longer reduced to or adjusted to a representation or to a principle. The very word *democracy* for Nancy seems to contain an internal barrier to the possibility of a foundational principle.

> Indeed, I would go so far as to say that democracy essentially implies an element of *anarchy* . . . There is no 'demarchy', no principle of foundation in 'the people', only the oxymoron or paradox of a principle lacking a principate. That is why the *right* or *law* the democratic institution generates has no real existence other than its own unceasing and active relationship to its own lack of foundation.[37]

One must speak then of the 'without-reason' or groundlessness of democratic existence. Without reason, or including entirely its own reason within itself, away from any request from a principle of sufficient reason, democratic existence is utterly groundless.

This is how Nancy understands Plato's supposed mistrust of democracy, as a critique of its groundlessness: 'Plato blames democracy for not being grounded in truth and therefore illegitimate from the very beginning.'[38] This opens the following alternative: either one seeks to establish democracy on a foundation, or else assume its groundlessness as such: 'From then on, our history has two alternatives: either politics (with law) is ungrounded and should stay that way or else it seeks to endow itself with a ground or foundation, a "sufficient reason" à la Leibniz.'[39] For Nancy, the latter option can only lead to violence and oppression, and 'unfailingly turns the shared heavenly assumption it proclaims into domination and oppression'.[40] This absence of ground also implies that there is no human nature. 'Democracy, as a species to the genus politics, is incapable of being grounded in a transcendent principle. So the only thing that grounds or founds democracy is an absence: the absence of any human nature.'[41] There is thus no reason, no substrate, and no subject that subtends democracy as the event of co-existence.

4. What Sovereignty?

Paradoxically, it is in the very absence of a masterful subject that would direct its process that the sovereignty of democracy is affirmed. Indeed, Nancy wants to think a sovereignty that is essentially different from mastery and power. The sovereignty that Nancy speaks about is not another form of domination by which a masterful subject posits its law, not a self-founding sovereignty, 'since it is no longer a matter of founding', but rather 'the only form of possible "auto"-nomy which precisely no longer has recourse to any heretofore possible forms of a politics'.[42] The 'power' of the people arises not out of mastery and agency, but out of a singular withdrawal of essence and principle. In other words,

> the same condition that insures that sovereignty receive its concept also deprives it of its power: that is, the absence of superior or foundational authority. For the sovereign authority must be essentially occupied with founding itself or with overcoming itself in order to legislate prior to or in excess of any law.[43]

What does sovereignty mean? 'Sovereignty designates, first, the summit.'[44] As summit, it is also 'the most high': 'As summit (*summum, supremus*), the sovereign is not only elevated: it is the highest. Its name is a *superlative*: literally what raises itself above from below, and what is no longer comparable or relative. It is no longer in relation, it is *absolutum*.'[45] This implies that nothing, no authority or instituting force, is above it: 'nothing either precedes it or supercedes it', so that henceforth, 'Sovereignty is the end of any political theology',[46] and instead 'the creation of an atheological assumption'.[47] Sovereignty, Nancy explains, is grounded 'neither in *logos* nor in *mythos*. From birth, democracy, Rousseau's democracy, knew itself to be without foundation.'[48] Sovereignty is never founded. 'It would rather be defined by the absence of foundation or presupposition.'[49]

Thus, sovereignty is groundless, subjectless and unsubstantial, and therein lies its sovereignty, a 'negative' or anti-sovereignty, as it were, even a 'sovereignty without sovereignty',[50] outlined 'around a hollow'.[51] Marked from the nothing from which, *ex nihilo*, it creates itself, sovereignty must institute itself. 'If sovereignty is not a substance that is given, it is because it is the *reality* that the people must give themselves, insofar as it is not, itself, a substance or a given subject.'[52] Recalling Derrida's analyses in 'Force of Law' on the groundless performativity of the law, Nancy stresses that on that basis, 'if the sovereign exercises its power, it is entirely on the condition of the "state of exception" where laws are suspended. The fundamental illegitimacy that is in this case the condition of legitimacy must legitimize itself.'[53] Sovereignty has no foundation and yet must exercise itself from such groundlessness.

This is why what is at issue is the *exercise* of sovereignty, an exercise that is not ruled from above or founded in principle. This is the radical sense of auto-nomy at work in democracy: sovereignty is rigorously identical to its exercise, for it 'has no outside to precede, found, or duplicate'.[54] The sovereignty of democracy is thus the relation to itself of the sovereign, i.e., the people: 'the self of a relation to self cannot be given prior to this relation itself, since it is the relation that makes the self (*self* means *to self* and there is no case in which there is a subject of *self*). The sovereign does not find a sovereignty that is given: he must constitute it and thus constitute himself as sovereign.'[55] The sovereignty of democracy is subjectless, precisely to the extent that the people are the subject of itself, a sheer relation-to-itself, and an invention of itself:

> A people are always their own invention. But it can also invent itself by giving itself a sovereign and by giving itself *to* a sovereign or even by giving the sovereignty to itself. In each case the people determine themselves differently, and determine the very sense of the word *people* differently: assembled people, subjected people, insurgent people – or rather: people as a body, people as a group, people in secession. Constituting sovereignty, alienating sovereignty, revolutionary sovereignty.[56]

Ultimately, sovereignty points to a 'nothing', and not to a substrate. 'Sovereignty turns out strictly to be that *nothing* itself',[57] writes Nancy (referring to Bataille's expression that 'sovereignty is NOTHING'), indicating that sovereignty is nothing but its very exercise. It is also the condition of its self-relation. The sovereign is the existent who depends on nothing, either on finality or on subjection. 'Dependent on nothing, it is entirely delivered over to itself, insofar as precisely, the "itself" neither precedes nor founds it, but is the *nothing*, the very thing from which it is suspended.'[58] In any case, democracy must be assigned to this post or a-theological nothing, and 'requires ... that the *nothing* – since there is no other world – be taken absolutely seriously'.[59] That nothing is what we have in-common, it is nothing that is a matter of sharing in democratic existence. This is why Nancy explains that if the people are sovereign, it is in the sense of taking responsibility for that nothing and lack of foundation,[60] and insisting on the absence of transcendent author or subject in co-existence, on the withdrawal of all idols. 'Sovereignty is not located in any person; it has no figure, no contour; it cannot be erected into any monument. It is simply the supreme. With nothing above. Neither God nor master. In this sense, democracy equals anarchy.'[61] The power of the people becomes the nothing shared by all (and each).

What then is the all-powerfulness of the people? This is the question. And perhaps it is absolutely necessary for democracy to be able to envisage this question while maintaining the principle of the *nothing* of sovereignty. Being nothing, or being founded on nothing, does not mean being powerless [*ne rien pouvoir*]. It means to found and measure power by that *nothing* which is *the very thing* of *the reality* of the people; its nature as non-foundational, non-transcendent (at least in the usual sense), non-sacred, non-natural etc. *Res publica, summa res – nihil*.[62]

5. The Time of Democracy

Democracy understood as an ungrounded event and exercise of self-position, supposes a specific modality of temporalisation. Nancy describes such an event as 'disjunction rather than continuity, as secession rather than succession',[63] a time that is less *chronos* than *kairos*, 'less duration and succession than opportunity and encounter, an advening without advent'.[64] Derrida had connected the event as such with the revolutionary,[65] and, as Marie-Eve Morin rightly notes, Nancy assumes the Derridean understanding of the event as break, rupture, disruption, and interruption of an absolute unpredictable arrival.[66] For the event, and the event of democracy, breaks the very thread of the possible, the continuous fabric of time itself, interrupts linear time and succession (the *order* of time) in an accidental arrival, from which hiatus, in turns, another time happens. Such is the time of democracy, the revolutionary moment itself as interruption/production of temporality. In fact, the very groundlessness of democracy calls for revolution, a 'permanent revolution', as it were, Nancy engaging democracy in terms of what he calls a 'politics without foundation', even a 'politics in a State of permanent revolution'!.[67] 'Democracy comes right out and demands a *revolution*: a shift in the very basis of politics, frank acceptance of the absence of foundation.'[68] At the same time, it suspends revolution in an oscillation between the insurrectional moment, and 'the hardening into place of the revolutionary State'. (The word 'state', Nancy reminds us, literally means: that which is established, guaranteed, and thus supposedly grounded in truth.) Democracy reveals the excess of a pure event, founded on nothing, outside representation, escaping all horizons of calculability (in opposition to the logic of economic and technological globalisation). The event is given nowhere in advance, but instead 'constitutes the eruption of the new', that is unpredictable because it is without face, and thus the 'beginning of a series of appearances' by which Kant defines freedom in its relation to the world.[69] According to the very structure of the event, it happens in the incalculable, in the mode of what Derrida refers to as the possibility of the impossible. For Derrida, the impossible, which he writes as im-possible to mark the excess with prior conditions of possibility, is possible and takes place as im-possible. In fact, the im-possible is according to Derrida the very structure of the event.[70] As Nancy puts it, the event 'must not be the object of a programmatic and certain calculation ... It must be the possibility of the impossible (according to a logic used often by Derrida), it must know itself as such, that is to say, know that it happens also in the incalculable and the unassignable.'[71] The impossible, in this context, does not mean that which is not simply possible, and therefore without effects. The impossible, or the im-possible, means that which happens outside the conditions of possibility offered in advance by a subject of representation, outside the transcendental conditions of possibility, which, for Nancy, actually render impossible the subject of this experience of the world. The transcendental makes experience impossible; the im-possible is the possibility of the experience. Derrida often writes that an event or an invention is only possible as im-possible. In Nancy's words:

'Our question thus becomes clearly question of the impossible experience or the experience of the impossible: an experience removed from the conditions of possibility of a finite experience, and which is nevertheless an experience.'[72] Democracy thus takes place in the excess of the im-possible as the structure of the event.

In its truth or spirit ('spirit' in the literal sense of a breath and an inspiration), democracy is not a form or a regime but an exposure, a shared exposure: 'Democracy means that neither death nor life has any value in and of itself, but that value comes only from shared existence insofar as it exposes itself to its absence of ultimate of sense as its true – and infinite – sense of being.'[73] That spirit or truth of democracy is the presence of the incalculable, which prevents the closure of a project of mastery – Nancy calls this Capital – that interrupts the demands for a full and complete technological exploitation of all resources.

6. Democracy without Figure

Giving thought to this unpredictable arrival, rather than a messianism, even without a Messiah, Nancy speaks of a moment of 'messianic inspiration' in the events of May '68, in the sense in which, instead of proposing new visions, directions and objectives, it welcomed the irruption of the new, still without a figure. Indeed, as Nancy stresses, 'democracy has no figure. Better, it is by essence not figural.'[74] No (given) figure – that is, also, with no identity – but the opening of a proliferation of figures, 'figures affirmed, invented, created, imagined, and so on';[75] in short, the renouncing of Identification for the sake of a multiplicity of identities: a proliferation of identities shared out in the world. No figure, but the task of sketching a configuration of a common space. Here, it would be necessary to leave the One, identity, for the singular plurality of identities. The renunciation of the One opens the plurality of singularities:

> The renunciation of every principal form of identification – whether it be borne by the image of a King, a Father, a God, a Nation, a republic, a People, a Man, or a Humanity, or even a Democracy – does not contradict, indeed quite the contrary, the exigency of identification in the sense of the possibility for each and every one to identify him or herself (or as people like to say today 'to take up a subject position') as

having a place, a role, and a value – and inestimable value – in being together.[76]

To that extent, what is called 'the good life' consists precisely in not being determined 'in any way by any figure or under any concept',[77] not even by the concept of the *polis*, but in a certain exposed and non-figural being-with.

Indeed, what democracy manifests, beyond any figures, is the exposure to the incalculable event of our being-in-common. In chapter VII of *The Truth of Democracy*, titled 'The Sharing (Out) of the Incalculable', democracy is described as the very opening of our being-in-common, that is, once again, not an established political form ('the share of the sharing (out) of the incalculable ... exceeds politics'),[78] but as an event, and also as the very condition of our existence in-common. This is the reason why, as Nancy reminds us, it was no accident if in May '68, the desire for democracy took the form of a call to community, to being-together, indeed to communism, if it is the case that communism means that we are in common. What was at stake was the 'true possibility of being *all together, all and each one of among all*'.[79] This is why Nancy insists: 'It has to be repeated yet again: it is not by chance that the words *communism* and *socialism* came to bear, after undergoing all kinds of distortions, the exigency and fervor that the word *democracy* itself was unable or was no longer able to nourish.'[80] Indeed, in 'Finite and Infinite Democracy', Nancy goes as far as to state that the deepest desire of democracy *is* communism, a word that became used at the end of the eighteen century,[81] and thus contemporary with Rousseau's work: 'In this sense, the true name that democracy desires, the one it has in fact engendered and borne as its horizon for some one hundred and fifty years, is the name communism.'[82] For Nancy, communism carries the desire for community, against the state (the very term 'soviet' – council – implied a contestation of the state), and it is the

> expression of society's drive to be more than a society – to be a *community* with a symbolic truth of its own. That was the idea behind the word, if you can even call it an idea; it certainly wasn't a concept in the strict sense, more of an urge or impulse of thought impelling democracy to interrogate its own essence and ultimate purpose.[83]

7. The Non-Equivalence of Democracy

This being-together cannot however, be taken as commonality under some regime of equivalence. We saw how, for Nancy, democracy is not tantamount to a principle of equality (or then equality but in the sense of an equality of singularities, the equality of the 'each' in their exposure to one another: each one unique, each one equally in his or her absolute singular exception, each one incommensurable, so that 'strict equality is the regime where these incommensurables are shared out'),[84] but rather must be determined in terms of a sharing, and that means a sharing of plurality and differences. It is matter of thinking the common and co-existence while giving its rights to the singular event of difference, that is, to *non-equivalence* (in turn, such non-equivalence is not tantamount to inequality!).[85]

The sphere of the common is not unique. It comprises multiple approaches to the order of meaning – each of them itself multiple, as in the diversity of the arts, thought, desire, the affects, and so on. What 'democracy' signifies here is the admission – without any heavenly assumption – of all these diversities to a 'community' which does not unify them, but, on the contrary, deploys their multiplicity, and with it the infinite of which they constitute the numberless and unfinalisable forms.[86]

For Nancy, the space of sharing is never equivalent to the common or the identical, but rather the co-exposure of singularities. It is thus the space of singularities and differences. In an important gesture, Nancy breaks with this understanding of democracy in terms of what Marx called 'general equivalence'. Democracy itself can even become, Nancy warns us, 'the name of an equivalence even more general than the one Marx spoke of', namely, a regime in which 'ends, means, values, senses, actions, works, persons'[87] are all interchangeable. This is why, against such regime of 'general equivalence', he proposes a democracy of non-equivalence. In fact, Nancy insists, democracy is assigned to 'what must remain diverse, indeed divergent, multiple, even heterogeneous'.[88] Against a democratism of indistinction, where 'everything and everyone would be on the same footing and at the same level', he proclaims that 'the democratic exigency confronts us with the task of distinction'.[89] This is what would constitute a way out of nihilism, if it is the case that nihilism represents a 'nullification of distinctions, that is, the nullification of senses or values'.[90] In fact, sense is constituted from distinctions, from the distinction of one sense from the other, so that 'one value is essentially non-equivalent to any other'.[91]

General equivalence is the symptom of a globalised and unified complex in which no local events can avoid being propagated to the rest of the world. For Nancy, this interconnection of phenomena is governed by a logic of economic profit, that is, by *money*. 'Money', he writes, 'is what Marx called general equivalence.'[92] Nancy's thesis is that this system of equivalence – with its convergence of global capitalism and technological development – absorbs all domains of existence and practices: 'the value of any value is equivalence'.[93] In the end, for Nancy, it is that very equivalence 'which is catastrophic'![94] Far from any possibility of other-worldly salvation, we are, in Nancy's words, abandoned or 'exposed to a catastrophe of sense'.[95] It is thus a matter of thinking this exposure, and what happens to us from it, or 'after' it. To escape this destruction, one should not project another future, but remain with and attend to a *present*. As Nancy makes clear, this is not the present of immediacy, but the present of an approach, of a coming into presence, and in this sense the *exact opposite* of general equivalence.[96] It would be a present that welcomes and makes room for the non-equivalence of all singularities.

It is matter of an attention and respect for singularity as such, an esteem that would be the contrary of an 'estimation', an esteem that would go towards the priceless, the *inestimable*. 'Thus we propose a hypothesis with respect to an internal displacement of technology and capital that would make an inversion of signs possible: the insignificant equivalence reversed into an egalitarian, singular and common significance. The "production of value" becomes the "creation of meaning".'[97] This creation of meaning is what Nancy refers to as the creation of the world; and to create the world means,

> immediately, without delay, reopening each possible struggle for a world, that is, for what must form the contrary of a global injustice against the background of general equivalence. But this means to conduct this struggle precisely in the name of the fact that this *world* is coming out of nothing, that there is nothing before it and that it is without models, without principle and without given end, and that it is precisely *what* forms the justice and the meaning of a world.[98]

At the same time, this struggle cannot be the object of a programmatic calculation but, once again, it must happen as a possibility of the impossible, 'it must know itself as such, that is to say, know that it happens also in the incalculable and the unassignable'.[99]

Such a democracy of the 'singular plural', echoing Nancy's previous work on *Being Singular Plural*, would allow for an overcoming of nihilism, which is always a negation of differences, values and sense. This is why Nancy, admitting the oxymoronic nature of the expression, calls for a Nietzschean democracy, that is, a democracy wed to difference and singularity, and not to the reign of the common and the indistinct.[100] Another Nietzschean resonance in this thinking of democracy lies in how Nancy understands democracy as a space devoid of any reference to a supra-sensible or supra-historical authority: 'Democracy means the conditions under which government and organisation are de facto possible in the absence of any transcendent regulating principle', he writes in 'Finite and Infinite Democracy'.[101] In *The Truth of Democracy*, Nancy reiterates that democracy stands for 'the name of a regime of sense whose truth cannot be subsumed under any ordering agency, whether religious, political, scientific, or aesthetic'.[102] An 'an-archic' democracy, as it were, which Nancy again refers to Nietzsche, insofar as democracy is 'that which wholly engages "man" at the risk and chance of "himself", as "dancer over the abyss", to put it in a paradoxically and deliberately Nietzschean way'.[103]

8. The People, Being-with, Democracy

As we saw, Nancy insists that democracy is not first and foremost a political form, but an ontological and anthropological fact. That is because the *demos* of democracy, the people, are precisely not first a political notion, but an ontological reality. As he explains in *Être-avec et Démocratie*, 'The people is thus not first a political entity. It is an anthropological (or ontological) reality that answers to the demand of giving meaning to areas of formation and circulation (what we call "languages", "cultures", all these forms of sharing of that insensible infinite which we give ourselves to feel).'[104] What kind of reality is 'the people'? Nancy clearly seeks to separate the term from any reference to a unity, a unified totality. At the beginning of *The Confronted Community*, Nancy recalled how in 1983, Jean-Christophe Bailly had suggested as a title for an issue of a forthcoming journal: 'Community, number'. Nancy described

The Event of Democracy 105

how struck he was by the elliptic elegance, precision and aptness of such title, and how the very notion of 'number' opened the reflection onto the thematics of plurality and consequently onto another understanding of the people. 'Number', he explained,

> served as a sudden reminder of the obviousness not only of the substantial multiplication of the world's population, but, along with that plain fact – as its effect or as its qualitative corollary – of the obviousness of a *multiplicity escaping unitary assumptions*, of a multiplicity multiplying its differences, dispersing itself in small groups, indeed in individuals, in multitudes or in populations.[105]

'People' would no longer point to the group or the whole, but to an irreducible plurality. 'Number' here transforms and displaces the traditional references to 'crowds', 'masses' and 'people'. Away from the totalitarian appeals to such crowds or classes, Bailly's formulation allowed to grasp the problem of the people no longer as a question of good governance, no longer as a political issue, but as an ontological question, bearing on the sense of community and being-with: 'what, then, is community if number becomes the unique phenomenon by which it is known – even the thing in itself – and if there remains no "communism" or "socialism" of any kind, either national or international, underpinning the least figure of community nor even the least form, the slightest identifiable schema of community?'[106] Ultimately, 'number' shifts the emphasis from the common or the One to the plural, and 'people(s)' now designate an irreducible plurality rather than one unified entity. 'And what, then, is number if its multiplicity no longer counts as a mass awaiting its *mise en forme* (formation, conformation, information), but rather counts, all in all, for its own sake, within a dispersal we wouldn't know whether to name dissemination (seminal exuberance) or crumbling (sterile pulverisation)?'[107] Between the motifs of the common, the together, and the numerous, Nancy seeks to reveal a sense of the people that preserves a certain plurality, and therefore also singularity as well (since singularities are what is plural), which implies that it preserves a certain resistance of singularity to plurality and of plurality to singularity: 'neither communion nor atomisation, just the sharing and sharing out of a space, at most a contact: a being-together without assemblage'.[108]

Such being-together without assemblage can best be expressed by the French plural *les gens*, rather than by the singular *le peuple*. One sense of the people gives way to another, one that retains the plurality of singular beings. In *Being Singular Plural*, Nancy refers to the expression '*les gens sont bizarres*' ('people are strange') to convey the singularities of *les gens*, rather than the anonymity of a unified group, *le peuple*. This is why he takes issue with Heidegger's description of *das Man*, 'the They' or 'the One', for such a conception of being-with misses the singularity of peoples. 'The people is not the Heideggerian "One". The word "people" does not say exactly the same thing as the Heideggerian "one", even if it is partly a mode of it', he explains.[109] Indeed, the 'one' designates an anonymity, in which there is no distinction. Certainly, for Heidegger, the 'one' responds to the question who, but it is not clear precisely 'who' gives this response, and who in that way distinguishes him or herself from the One:

> Heidegger understood that 'one' would only be said as a response to the question 'who?' put to the subject of *Dasein*, but he does not pose the other inevitable question that must be asked in order to discover *who* gives this response and who, in responding like this, removes himself or has a tendency to remove himself. As a result, he risks neglecting the fact that there is no pure and simple 'one', no 'one' in which 'properly existing' existence [*l'existant 'proprement existant'*] is, from the start, purely and simply immersed.[110]

For Nancy there is never a pure and simple 'one', and people 'clearly designates the mode of "one" by which "I" remove myself, to the point of appearing to forget or neglect the fact that I myself am part of "people"'. Yet, Nancy insists, 'this setting apart [*mise à l'écart*] does not occur without the recognition of identity'.[111] 'People' designates an existence that is only as numerous, dispersed, and as disseminated singularities: it is always these peoples, this particular person, etc. . . . Peoples are always singular, never an anonymous indistinction:

> 'People' clearly states that we are all precisely *people*, that is, indistinctly persons, humans, all of a common 'kind', but of a kind that has its existence only as numerous, dispersed, and indeterminate in its generality. This existence can only be grasped in the paradoxical simultaneity of togetherness (anonymous, confused, and indeed massive) and disseminated singularity (these or those 'people(s)', or 'a guy', 'a girl', 'a kid').[112]

In other words, peoples are 'silhouettes', always singularised, 'outlines of voices, patterns of comportment, sketches of affects, not the anonymous chatter of the 'public domain'.[113] Typical or general types, such as ethnic, cultural, social, generational, and others 'do not abolish singular differences; instead, they bring them into relief'.[114] Further, at the level of singular differences, they are, Nancy writes, not only individual but infra-individual, for it is 'never the case that I have met Pierre or Marie per se, but I have met him or her in such and such a "form", in such and such a "state", in such and such a "mood", and so on'.[115] Existence is always singular, and never happens generally.

The expression 'people are strange' thus reveals this singularity of existence. To be a self, to be oneself, is to be a singularity. 'From faces to voices, gestures, attitudes, dress, and conduct, whatever the "typical" traits are, everyone distinguishes himself by a sort of sudden and headlong precipitation where the strangeness of a singularity is concentrated. Without this precipitation there would be, quite simply, no "someone".'[116] Such singularity is, by itself, plural: 'someone' designates the singularity of the person, that is, his or her difference with everybody else. This is why Nancy also takes issue with Heidegger's negative characterisation of the everyday, and the conflation of the everyday with the 'One'. Nancy explains that Hegel was the first to have seen that thinking must attend to the 'grayness of the world'. And the Heideggerian 'one' still 'assumes an absent, lost, or far away "grandeur"'.[117] However, truth cannot be the truth of some other-worldly domain, but 'can be nothing if not the truth of being in totality, that is, the totality of its "ordinariness", just as meaning can only be right at [à même] existence and nowhere else'. This is why, as Nancy concludes, 'the "ordinary" is always exceptional', not because it is other than ordinary, but because in its very ordinariness, it remains *singular* and thus exceptional, so that, therefore, the exception is the rule: 'What we receive most communally as "strange" is that the ordinary itself is originary. With existence laid open in this way and the meaning of the world being what it is, the exception is the rule.'[118] This is what the themes of 'wonder' of being reveal: not some extraordinary state of existence, but the world itself in its singular plurality. 'Themes of "wonder" and the "marvel of Being" are suspect if they refer to an ecstatic mysticism that pretends to escape the world. The theme of scientific curiosity is no less suspect if it boils down to a collector's preoccupation with rarities. In both cases, desire for the exception presupposes disdain for the ordinary.'[119]

If the world 'always appears [*surgit*] each time according to a decidedly local turn [of events]', if its 'unity, its uniqueness, and its totality consist in a combination of this reticulated multiplicity',[120] then the everyday must be heard literally as every day, each singular day. Now, 'Heidegger confuses the everyday with the undifferentiated, the anonymous, and the statistical.' These exist only in reference to differentiated singularity, the singularity 'that the everyday already is by itself: each day, each time, day to day'. The everyday manifests a generalised differentiation, a 'constantly renewed rupture', with its 'intimate discord, its polymorphy and its polyphony, its relief and its variety'.[121] Even the repetitiveness of the everyday can only take place because there is first the each day, and thus difference as such. Similarly, continues Nancy, peoples (more than 'the people') can be merged only on the basis of a prior distinction and difference: 'Likewise "people", or rather "peoples", given the irreducible strangeness that constitutes them as such, are themselves primarily the exposing of the singularity according to which existence exists, irreducibly and primarily – and an exposition of singularity.'[122]

Let us stress that this exposition of singularities is such that it cannot be enframed in a merely 'human' world. The world is not anthropocentric. Nature, Nancy writes, is also strange:

> we exist in it in the mode of a constantly renewed singularity, whether the singularity of the diversity and disparity of our senses or that of the disconcerting profusion of nature's species or its various metamorphoses into 'technology'. Then again, we say 'strange', 'odd', 'curious', 'disconcerting' *about* all of being.[123]

Peoples testify to this plurality of singularities, not to a unified human whole, not to a given signified, but consist in a being of exposure.

Conclusion: The Invention of Democracy

As we saw, Nancy claims that democracy is not a political regime among others, and that its 'exact' or 'correct' form cannot be determined, or even achieved: democracy is an openness, always inadequate to its concept or to any form, as it happens, outside conceptuality, and thus remains to be *invented through* an originary praxis. It is thus not insignificant that Nancy defines democracy, in 'Finite and Infinite Democracy', as the 'conditions of possible *practices* of government and organisation [*les conditions des pratiques possibles de gouvernement et d'organisation*], in the absence of any transcendent regulating principle'.[124] Because of its radical lack of foundation, democracy can only become a matter for praxis.[125] As Jacques Rancière emphasised in *Hatred of Democracy*, democracy only consist in its practice, what Nancy calls its exercise: 'Democracy is as bare in its relation to the power of wealth as it is to the power of kinship that today comes to assist and to rival it. It is not based on any nature of things nor guaranteed by any institutional form. It is not borne along by any historical necessity and does not bear any. It is only entrusted to the constancy of its specific acts.'[126] Democracy is a taking responsibility for that very lack of foundation, and a *decision* for being-in-common. 'That is why the *right* or *law* the democratic institution generates has no real existence other than its own unceasing and active relationship to its own lack of foundation.'[127] In fact, democracy names our condition as that of an existence without basis or subject, and which must take upon itself its own lack of basis. It is a kind of sovereignty without support, resting on nothing, 'a dance upon the abyss'. There lies its eventful character.

The senses of democracy are not given *a priori*, just as the sense of our co-existence in the world is not given, or founded in some substrate. The world rests upon nothing, and that is how it makes and creates sense. Because it is not given, democracy is a matter of invention and decision. Democratic sovereignty rests on nothing (given), and as such is an exercise of itself, in an original *praxis* of meaning: 'meaning is always in *praxis*', writes Nancy.[128] To that extent, democracy is the name for this invention of itself, against the background of an absence of foundation and principle, an atheological existence: 'Prior to anything else, democracy is theocracy's "other". That makes it the "other" of law dispensed from on high as well. Law is something it has to invent. It has to invent itself.'[129] Never established as a given, never fulfilled, achieved, or adequate to itself, democracy is to be made and enacted.

Nancy thus attempts to rethink democracy in terms of an analysis of our being-in-common, and not from some pre-given and inadequate theoretical models; no longer as a particular political system, but as an event, and indeed as the very condition of our existence as each time in-common. This element of sharing is never, for Nancy, the space of the common or the identical, but rather of our sharing our singularities and differences. Nancy stresses that what we share is our singularities, that is, our differences. Ultimately, democracy is the sharing of the incalculable event that we are, and names the event of a humanity whose being lies only in its exposure, without given ends or principles. '*Democracy* is then the appellation, the utterly inadequate appellation of a humanity that finds itself exposed to the absence of any given end – a heaven, a future – but not less exposed to the infinite for that. Exposed, existing.'[130]

Notes

1. Jean-Luc Nancy, *The Truth of Democracy*, trans. P.-A. Brault and M. Naas (New York: Fordham University Press, 2010), p. 37.
2. Jean-Luc Nancy, 'Finite and Infinite Democracy', in *Democracy in What State?*, trans. from the French by William McCuaig (New York: Columbia University Press, 2011), p. 58.
3. Nancy, 'Finite and Infinite Democracy', p. 59.
4. Nancy, *The Truth of Democracy*, p. 34.
5. Ibid., p. 32.
6. Peter Gratton and Marie-Eve Morin (eds), *Jean-Luc Nancy and Plural Thinking: Expositions of World, Ontology, Politics, and Sense* (Albany: SUNY Press, 2012), p. 236.
7. Nancy, *The Truth of Democracy*, p. 50.
8. Ibid., pp. 29–30
9. Ibid., p. 29.
10. Ibid., p. 29.
11. 'Philosophy as Chance: An Interview with Jean-Luc Nancy', with Lorenzo Fabbri, trans. P.-A. Brault and M. Naas, *Critical Inquiry*, Winter 2007, p. 431.
12. Jacques Derrida, *Rogues: Two Essays on Reason*, trans. P.-A. Brault and M. Naas (Stanford: Stanford University Press, 2005), p. 72. Hereafter cited as R, followed by page number.
13. 'Democracy is what it is only in the différance by which it defers itself and differs from itself. It is what it is only by spacing itself beyond being and even beyond ontological difference; it is (without being) equal and proper to itself only insofar as it is inadequate and improper, at the same time behind and ahead of itself, behind and ahead of the Sameness and Oneness of itself.' Derrida continues

that passage by pointing out that democracy 'is thus interminable in its incompletion beyond all determinate forms of incompletion.' Derrida, *Rogues*, p. 38.
14. Nancy, *The Truth of Democracy*, p. 16.
15. Martine Meskel-Cresta, '(Les) dehors (de) la démocratie?', in Gisèle Berkman and Danielle Cohen-Levinas (eds), *Figures du dehors: Autour de Jean-Luc Nancy* (Paris: Cécile Defaut, 2012), pp. 138–9.
16. Jean-Luc Nancy, 'Etre-avec et Démocratie', at: <http://strassde-laphilosophie.blogspot.fr/2013/02/etre-avec-et-democratie-jean-luc-nancy.html>.
17. Ibid.
18. Ibid.
19. Ibid.
20. Nancy, 'Finite and Infinite Democracy', p. 60.
21. Ibid., p. 60.
22. Nancy, *The Truth of Democracy*, p. 15.
23. Ibid., preface.
24. Ibid.
25. Ibid., pp. 5–6.
26. Jean-Luc Nancy, *The Creation of the World, or Globalization*, trans. F. Raffoul and D. Pettigrew (Albany: SUNY Press, 2007), p. 50.
27. Nancy, *The Truth of Democracy*, p. 8.
28. Ibid., p. 9.
29. Ibid., p. 11.
30. Ibid., p. 14.
31. Ibid., p. 11.
32. Ibid., p. 11.
33. Jean-Luc Nancy, *Being Singular Plural*, trans. R. D. Richardson and A. O'Byrne (Stanford: Stanford University Press, 2000), p. 29. Hereafter cited as BSP, followed by page number.
34. Jean-Luc Nancy, *The Birth to Presence*, trans. B. Holmes et al. (Stanford: Stanford University Press, 1993), p. 43; translation modified.
35. Nancy, *The Creation of the World, or Globalization*, p. 45. However, this without-reason is not tantamount to the nondifferentiation of capitalistic exchange: 'This does not at all mean that anything makes sense in just any way; that would be precisely the capitalist version of the without-reason, which establishes the general equivalence of all forms of meaning in an infinite uniformity.' Ibid, p. 52. We will return to this nonequivalence later.

36. Nancy, *The Creation of the World, or Globalization*, p. 47.
37. Nancy, 'Finite and Infinite Democracy', pp. 65–6.
38. Ibid., p. 63.
39. Ibid., p. 63.
40. Ibid., p. 63.
41. Nancy, 'Finite and Infinite Democracy', p. 66. One should instead speak of *denaturation*: 'There is something we really should get straight once and for all, since its theoretical basis and consequences are well known: not only is there no such thing as "human nature", but "humankind" *(l'homme) is* virtually incommensurable with anything you could call a "nature" (an autonomous and self-finalised order), because the only characteristics it has are those of a subject without a "nature" or one that far outstrips anything we could call "natural" – in a certain sense (either pernicious or felicitous depending on one's point of view) the subject of a *denaturation*.' ('Finite and Infinite Democracy', p. 66.)
42. Nancy, *The Creation of the World, or Globalization*, p. 93.
43. Ibid., p. 103.
44. Ibid., p. 99.
45. Ibid., p. 97.
46. Ibid., p. 99.
47. Ibid., p. 106.
48. Nancy, 'Finite and Infinite Democracy', p. 62.
49. Nancy, *The Creation of the World, or Globalization*, p. 103.
50. Ibid., p. 107.
51. One recalls here Claude Lefort's analyses of democratic power as organised around a central void – a *lieu vide* or empty place – a site of power that no one can claim to embody and which thus remains empty. See, for instance, Claude Lefort, *The Political Forms of Modern Society: Bureaucracy, Democracy, Totalitarianism*, ed. John B. Thomson (Cambridge, MA: MIT Press, 1986), pp. 199, 279, 285, 303. 'Power' is then assigned to a void.
52. Nancy, *The Creation of the World, or Globalization*, p. 104.
53. Ibid., p. 103.
54. Ibid., p. 99.
55. Ibid., pp. 99–100.
56. Ibid., p. 104.
57. Ibid., p. 102.
58. Ibid., p. 103.
59. Nancy, *The Truth of Democracy*, p. 55, n.10.
60. 'The democratic *kratein*, the power of the people, is first of all the

power to foil the *archē* and then to take responsibility, all together and each individually, for the infinite opening that is thereby brought to light.' (Nancy, *The Truth of Democracy*, p. 31.)
61. Nancy, *The Truth of Democracy*, p. 31.
62. Nancy, *The Creation of the World, or Globalization*, p. 104.
63. Nancy, *The Truth of Democracy*, p. 13.
64. Ibid., p. 16.
65. Jacques Derrida and Elisabeth Roudinesco, *For What Tomorrow... A Dialogue*, trans. J. Fort (Stanford: Stanford University Press, 2004), p. 83.
66. Marie-Eve Morin, *Jean-Luc Nancy* (Cambridge: Polity Press, 2012), p. 114. 'For Nancy, May '68 was an event in the strong sense: a "break" with "History", a breach or opening in the thought of time as succession and progression where potentialities were encountered outside of or beyond the question of feasibility and realization.' (Morin, *Jean-Luc Nancy*, p. 114.)
67. Nancy, 'Finite and Infinite Democracy', p. 64.
68. Ibid., p. 63.
69. Nancy, *The Creation of the World, or Globalization*, p. 59.
70. On this, see my 'Derrida and the Ethics of the Im-possible', in *Research in Phenomenology*, vol. 38, 2008.
71. Nancy, *The Creation of the World, or Globalization*, p. 49.
72. Ibid., p. 65.
73. Nancy, *The Truth of Democracy*, p. 31.
74. Ibid., p. 27; modified.
75. Ibid., p. 26.
76. Ibid., p. 27.
77. Ibid, p. 27.
78. Ibid., p. 17.
79. Ibid., p. 14.
80. Ibid., p. 14.
81. Although Nancy traces its first appearance to the fourteenth century, 'with the meaning of "people" having in common a property belonging to the category of "main morte" – that is, not being submitted to the law of heritage'. It then appeared in a significant way in the eighteenth century, 'in a text written by Victor d'Hupay de Fuveau in 1785 – four years before the French Revolution. It designates the project or the dream to found a community of life – which precisely is supposed to replace that of the Monks.' See Jean-Luc Nancy, 'On Communism', *Critical Legal Thoughts*, 26 July 2009.

82. Nancy, 'Finite and Infinite Democracy', p. 87.
83. Ibid., p. 68.
84. Nancy, *The Truth of Democracy*, p. 25.
85. As Nancy clarifies, 'the challenge is thus to introduce a new non-equivalence that would have nothing to do, of course, with the nonequivalence of economic domination . . .' (Nancy, *The Truth of Democracy*, p. 24).
86. Nancy, 'Finite and Infinite Democracy', p. 72.
87. Nancy, *The Truth of Democracy*, p. 24.
88. Ibid., p. 21.
89. Ibid., p. 22.
90. Ibid.
91. Ibid.
92. Jean-Luc Nancy, *L'équivalence des catastrophes (après Fukushima)* (Paris: Galilée, 2012), p. 16.
93. Ibid.
94. Ibid., p. 17.
95. Ibid., p. 20.
96. Ibid., p. 64.
97. Nancy, *The Creation of the World, or Globalization*, p. 49.
98. Ibid., p. 55.
99. Ibid., p. 49.
100. Nancy, *The Truth of Democracy*, p. 22; also on p. 33, where Nancy suggests another oxymoron, that of 'egalitarian aristocracy'.
101. Nancy, 'Finite and Infinite Democracy', p. 59.
102. Nancy, *The Truth of Democracy*, p. 33.
103. Ibid., p. 33.
104. Nancy, 'Etre-avec et Démocratie'.
105. Jean-Luc Nancy, 'The Confronted Community', trans. A. Macdonald, *Postcolonial Studies*, 6:1, 2003, p. 28; my emphasis.
106. Ibid., p. 28.
107. Ibid., p. 28.
108. Ibid., p. 32.
109. Nancy, *Being Singular Plural*, p. 6.
110. Ibid., p. 7.
111. Ibid., p. 7.
112. Ibid., p. 7.
113. Ibid., p. 7.
114. Ibid., p. 8.
115. Ibid., p. 8; slightly modified.
116. Ibid., p. 8.

117. Ibid., p. 10.
118. Ibid., p. 10.
119. Ibid., p. 10.
120. Ibid., p. 9.
121. Ibid., p. 9.
122. Ibid., p. 9.
123. Ibid., p. 10.
124. Nancy, 'Finite and Infinite Democracy', p. 59; translation modified, my emphasis.
125. On this original praxis of democracy, one that might engage a 'dislodging of the very foundation of general equivalence'; see Nancy, *The Truth of Democracy*, p. 31.
126. Jacques Rancière, *Hatred of Democracy*, trans. S. Corcoran (Brooklyn: Verso, 2006), p. 97.
127. Nancy, 'Finite and Infinite Democracy', p. 66.
128. Nancy, *The Creation of the World, or Globalization*, p. 54.
129. Nancy, 'Finite and Infinite Democracy', p. 61; translation modified.
130. Ibid., pp. 74–5.

5

Thinking Nancy's 'Political Philosophy'
Ignaas Devisch

Do we have anything to say?

A volume on *Nancy and the Political* presupposes a relationship between these two signifiers. Nancy scholars, it seems, would be left behind with one final question: what kind of relationship? Naturally, the only true philosophical stance is to refuse this presupposition and start thinking it: does the oeuvre of Nancy have any relationship with the political at all? Only once this question has been unravelled, we can start thinking about 'Nancy and the Political'. My central thesis is that, though interesting and fascinating, Nancy's social ontology does not lead to a breakthrough in thinking the political. Moreover, his gesture away from the political to the social, results into a conceptual vacuum when it comes down to the political. More than Nancy, the oeuvre of Claude Lefort and Michel Foucault, two philosophers Nancy hardly refers to when thinking the political, is well equipped to think the political today.

First of all, I analyse how Nancy develops two central concepts of the political, justice and power. Next to that, I will sketch his shift towards the social and conclude this with an analysis of his regained attention to the political in recent writings. Secondly, I investigate the way Nancy refers to Lefort and Foucault in a minor way and question this lack of attention by a brief sketch of the concept of power in both their oeuvre, in order to argue that Nancy is not only mistaken in not paying attention to their analyses, but also why their oeuvre can be of help in thinking the political today, with or without Nancy.

1. About 'The Political'

Obviously, Nancy has written on the political. In several of his books and articles, he has written on the retracement of the political, on democracy, on sovereignty, on justice or on globalisation; and also on sacrifice, terror, theodicy, suffering, destruction, violence, sovereignty or totalitarianism.[1] Above, I put Nancy's 'political philosophy' between brackets, because Nancy has never put forward a new political philosophy or a new form of politics. Rather than fading interest in the political as such, his interest lies in seeking another way of thinking the political. His aim is to investigate what politics can still mean today. The disappearance of most of our political foundations, of politics as foundation, demands that we go in search of the horizon that this absence reveals. We are revealed as a naked existence, an existence without essence, without foundation or fixity and, as Nancy writes in several texts, this has significant political consequences as well.

In the 1980s, along with Philippe Lacoue-Labarthe, Nancy started to write about the question of the political. Together, and contrary to the mainstream analysis of deconstruction at that point, they understood Jacques Derrida's deconstruction as an explicit political gesture. A first hint of this was given at the famous conference 'Les fins de l'homme' in Cérisy-La-Salle in 1980, on the potential political and ethical implications of Derrida's work. That same year, Lacoue-Labarthe and Nancy organised a forum for re-evaluating philosophical reflections on the political. The activities of the *Centre de recherches philosophiques sur le politique* resulted in two publications: *Rejouer le politique* and *Le retrait du politique*.[2] The latter (the retreat of politics) sums up the centre's intentions. The title can be read as a subjective genitive: politics has retracted and been forced off the stage because its foundations have fallen away. The form of politics that has in fact disappeared is what Nancy later calls 'la politique de la destination', the politics of destination: a politics that aims to realise a sovereign goal or preordained destiny of a people.[3] This form of politics has largely disappeared, and has been replaced by an international politics of human rights. Politics therefore exists precisely in the traces of the disappearance of the old politics; traces that must be retraced. According to the gesture of deconstruction, Nancy is also convinced that 'old school thought' does not disappear by simply overcoming it, but by retracing the meaning in order to dismantle them.

Despite the announcement of a third volume, only two volumes were published. In 1984, Nancy and Lacoue-Labarthe definitively closed the centre, giving multiple reasons for this act. The primary reason was that the centre, as a site for philosophical research into politics, had possessed a certain function and benefit, but that it had become more of a meeting place instead of a space for research and collaboration. The result was that the centre was no longer fulfilling the role its founders had envisaged.

Nancy and Lacoue-Labarthe did not close the centre because of banal organisational reasons, but for philosophical reasons; and their final declaration sheds a light on the absence of a coherent political philosophy in Nancy's oeuvre. Looking back, Nancy states at length in *La comparution/The compearance*:

> We were becoming aware of the weight of a growing consensus which concerned 'in the end the political itself', designated as 'the absolute danger of the definite impasse of thought and praxis'. To this we added: The end of marxism, curiously and modestly baptised the 'end of ideologies' has been insidiously transformed to deny any consideration or transaction having to do with the identity of the collectivity, its destination, the nature and exercise of sovereignty. A slowly accredited intellectual attitude privileges ethics or the esthetic, even the religious (and sometimes the social) over and against the political. Two consequences seemed to us to follow: the suspending of any questioning of that which we were then calling the 'essence of the political' and the suspension of any necessity, indeed any legitimacy, of effective political choices. One sees that nothing has changed in any essential matter.[4]

In more than one way, this extensive quote from *The Compearance* sheds light on Nancy's relationship with the political: as a consequence of the end of ideologies, the political is suspended. What we first of all need to think is therefore not the political but the social, namely the question of the ontological condition in which we find ourselves and the implications of this ontology for every form of being-with. Nancy's questioning of our living together is far broader than the question of politics in the strict sense of the word, and also precedes everyday politics. In an interview with Francis Fisher, he distances himself from the 'politics to come' which still functioned as the subtitle of *The Compearance*:

> I am afraid that it is a little too easy to say: 'this is another politics'. I myself have written that phrase more than once: 'another politics'.

> But I'm not entirely sure what politics means. Perhaps we should be clear and say that politics means being-in-common (although this is precisely too broad a meaning).[5]

Later in that interview, Nancy points to the problem in even more general terms:

> I think that one of the big problems for philosophers and intellectuals today is that we have nothing more to say on the political level . . . I am ashamed sometimes when, like many other people, I say that politically we must be against this and for that, because I am immediately aware that this doesn't get us very far. When Socialism was a viable alternative, we had a certain representation of a communitarian way of life. We have nothing like that now.[6]

When it comes down to the political, Nancy seems to be hesitate in defining philosophy's role in it: he says that today we have no substantial political alternative to common regimes, since socialism has disappeared; the only thing left, so it seems, is what Nancy calls 'being-in-common'. In this sense, Nancy is a true philosopher who would certainly hesitate to answer the question of this volume: what about 'Nancy' and the political? To him, far from being evidence given, 'Nancy and the political' is surrounded by questions and hesitations. Nancy's focus on the social comes partially from his uneasiness with the fact that, now that the political has (to be) retreated, contemporary politics has become limited to a purely moral defence of human rights in the context of an international community.[7] Rather than acquiescing with the status quo, our contemporary living together demands more profound reflection. It is not another politics, a new political philosophy or a reinvented public space that Nancy has in mind. Rather he proposes a profound ontological analysis of our pre-political condition which he calls being-with, singular plural being or coexistence.

2. The Haunting of the Political

Despite Nancy's dedicated focus on the social for years now, in recent writings, the political arises again, as if Nancy himself is urged to return to his early writings. Recently, time and again, he reminds us of these early political writings in interviews or conference talks.[8] It appears Nancy only now acknowledges the need to return to this early work, as if 'Nancy and the political' is still ahead of us. Let me therefore start our analysis of Nancy and the political with a return to these writings and 'retrace' his political thought.

Since we are after 'Nancy and the political', it seems logical and apodictic to follow Nancy's path of political thinking, or to look after the political consequences of his social ontology. As the ontological condition of our being-with or singular plural being has already been commented by many scholars, I won't sketch this anew.[9] Let me therefore take a closer look at one of the political concepts, prominently present in his oeuvre from the very beginning, namely justice,[10] and use Nancy's analysis of justice as a topical example of his struggle with the political.[11] Themes such as right, justice, judgement or law appear in various places in his work and form an important cluster of questions. In a number of other places in Nancy's work, juridical questions pop up, such as the Day of Judgement, being judged and judging, being summoned, the law, covenant, right and justice, or being responsible in a way that enables him to demonstrate the pre-political conditions of right and justice.[12] For Nancy, justice is, in the first place, bound up with the fact of our co-existence, with what is unique about every existence in its co-existence with other creations.[13]

The most coherent explanation of justice is to be found in Nancy's 'Cosmos Basileus'. There, Nancy discusses this question through a reflection on the unity of the world. The unity of the world is nothing other than the diversity and, hence, the world's non-unity. A world is always a plurality of worlds. Existing begins with the exposure to plurality, and to the sharing of this plurality. The sharing of the world or co-existence is, according to Nancy, thus also the 'law of the world'. The world has no other law than this; it is not subject to a sovereign authority such as God or other supreme causes. The world always means co-existing, being shared and divided, and is never a unity or a totality. Therefore the law of the world cannot be equated with the accomplishment of one or the other, unity or totality. On the contrary, already in the opening sentences of his essay, Nancy describes the nomos of the world as the dissemination, the division and the allocation of sharing of world.[14] Nancy's explanation of this nomos is just as brief as the description of it. Things to be disseminated can be places, but just as well portions of food or rights and duties. To the question of the just measure (of such a distribution), Nancy answers that the measure of covenant of the law or of absolute justice lies nowhere other than in this sharing itself, and in the exceptional singularity of everyone with everyone else in that this sharing offers.[15] Let me try to unpack this sequence: because the world is not given once for all, there is no fixed place for none of us. On the contrary, because the world arises in and through the taking place of every singular plural appearance, its division and its divide are at stake time and time again, that is within every one of us, with each appearance, and each time something or someone appears. Sharing or division [partage] is thus precisely that which connects the theme of the world or existence and that of justice: the covenant is also 'nothing other' than co-existence. Co-existence is not something added to existence, as a phenomenon in itself. Co-existence is existence, existing as dividing-sharing. As a consequence, justice means therefore doing justice done, what must be given, what belongs to 'every unique, singular creation in its coexistence with other creations'.[16] Justice is not in the first place a matter of a singularity, and only later the relation of this singularity to others. That which makes the singular unique is at once that which puts it into relation: there is no singularity without plurality. Therefore, to do justice to the singular absoluteness of one's proper being is, thus, simultaneously to do justice to the plurality of the singular.

As Nancy notes in 'Cosmos Basileus', the demand of this justice is infinite. How this demand is implemented is far from clear, since it seems to unfold, ultimately, as an unbearable injustice. There are natural disasters, deadly viruses, crimes, and so forth. These things 'do injustice' to existence; they make us suffer and there is no answer to the question of why there would be such injustice. The theological justifications have disappeared. Justice no longer enters from outside the world to recuperate the world's injustice or to sublate it, but is a given with the world, as the law of its act of donation. The world is itself the supreme law of justice. Not the world as it is but that the world is, that it always surges forth again, always plural singular.

As we can see, Nancy's deconstructive strategy in his discussion of justice is no different than the way he approaches other (political) concepts or questions. He takes a number of already existing motifs, and gradually unpacks them so as to introduce them into his own vocabulary with new meanings, or changes in their meaning.[17] Time and again, Nancy expands political issues to existential matters, to the ontological conditions of possibility of existence. These conditions are central to his oeuvre in its entirety. Nancy's emphasis in the context of justice as in all the other cases is on the real multiplicity in which our existence takes place. Existing, he emphasises, is not only being open, but also being responsible. To be responsible means we always are in relation to something. We are always already thrown into existence and must always be able to answer for our existence. In this responsibility, we are judged because our appearance is in the sharing that we are with and in respect to others.[18]

3. No Justice but Power

When it comes down to a political translation of this analysis of justice, it remains highly unclear how Nancy's oeuvre can be of help here. What does 'sharing of our co-existence' mean politically? How does the 'world as the supreme law of justice' open up towards the political? It is a call for democracy. What kind of democracy, however? These questions remain unanswered in Nancy's writings. If justice does not illuminate Nancy's 'political philosophy', can power? Power is another key concept in political philosophy and Nancy's stance towards. Can it help us to better grasp his 'political philosophy'? Although Nancy is very attentive to the political dangers of the lament over lost communality, and the shadow of totalitarianism, he never translated this attention into a discussion of the power or political struggle in democracy; neither did he dedicate an at length article or book chapter on the question of power, a crucial concept of thinking the political. He only wrote a few fragments here and there, and most recently, nearly one page in answer to a question posed by Philip Armstrong and Jason E. Smith.[19] Apparently Nancy does not need the concept of power in his 'political philosophy'. According to his theoretical stance, the non-necessity to think political power is indeed intentional: for Nancy, our political problems today lay bare that in our analysis of them, the ontological horizon is what matters. In a number of places in his work, he emphasises that our ontological condition – the in-common, the singular plural, the being-with – is a fundamental social condition; as a singular plural entity, man can only comprehend himself from the standpoint of the social: the singularity of being is plural in its being and any plural being is always singular.[20] Nancy thinks the political and democracy from the horizon of a shared existence that is opened or exposed to its absence of sense and the ultimate sense of existence.[21] Sense, being that which matters, is not a political but a metaphysical issue.[22]

If power plays a role in Nancy's philosophy, it is only to dissolve the current (political) use of it and to go beyond it. Democracy, Nancy writes, 'is the exceeding of power – but in its truth and greatness (or even its majesty!), not in its nullification' or 'in power, there is no longer the necessity of government'.[23] In this case, 'exceeding' means without foundation or undetermined.[24] For Nancy, power needs to be reinvented, as is the case with democracy. This reinvention seems to be quite radical, because Nancy calls for a revolution and a complete retracement of the question of power. For Nancy, we only understand power as 'domination, privatised of sense': 'we need a revolution, not a political one, but *of* politics or in relation to it. We need, quite simply another "civilisation", which means, above all, of course, another way of recognizing sense.'[25,26]

Can one be more radical? A revolution, another civilisation, a new definition of politics, a complete renewed understanding of sense; it appears new times will come upon us. In recent small papers and interviews Nancy often repeats his revolutionary statements, but he does not elaborate; they are unelaborated statements, no more, and make his thinking of the political to be surrounded with a sort of apocalyptic tone. This tone was completely absent in his early work in which Nancy announced the contours of a political philosophy. At that time, Nancy repeatedly wrote on politics and the need to *retrace* it, a focus which disappeared once he started to elaborate on the social ontology of the singular plural. It was waiting until now, until he explicitly referred to what he wrote back then.

But even when Nancy talks about democracy in his most recent work, he again elaborates on the ontology of the singular plural,[27] but does not analyse democracy or power in an extensive way; he keeps on referring to the closure of a horizon, the insignificance of the word and the necessity for a reinvention or a radical gesture. In *The Truth of Democracy*, he argues that the truth of democracy is 'an unworking or an inoperativity' and 'central to the work of existence'.[28] For Nancy, the sharing of existence exceeds the political order, although politics 'must make possible the existence of this share' and 'maintain an opening for it'.[29] We would remain prisoners of a vision of politics as the putting to work and activation of an absolute sharing (out): the destiny of a nation or a republic, the destiny of humanity, the truth of relation, the identity of the common. In short, everything that might have seemed robe subsumed by the glories of monarchy and that various 'totalitarianisms' wanted to replace with a literally democratic glory: the absolute power of a people identified in its essence and in its living body, an indigenous people or a people of workers, the self-production and autochthony of a principle substituted for the princes of yesteryear.[30]

In turn, to Nancy it is crucial to understand how the sharing of existence follows a line of thought that prohibits us from the seduction of an absolute power of a people, enclosed upon itself. The sharing is always to share and to divide, and because it is a pre-political structure, we need to think the pre-political instead of the political:

This implies that politics must be distinguished in both senses of the term – keeping it distinct and granting it the distinctions it is due: in particular, by ceasing to dilute the exercise of power and the symbols of power through a democratism of indistinction where everything and everyone would be on the same footing and at the same level. One of the most glaring signs of the democratic malaise is our inability to think power as anything other than an adversarial or malevolent agency, as the enemy of the people, or else as the indefinitely multiplied and dispersed reality of all possible relations of force. In the name of taking these 'micro powers' into account, one forges the specificity of (political) power *itself*, along with its proper and distinct destination.[31]

Being one of the few times when Nancy talks about power, this passage tells us a lot. For Nancy, we are unable to think power as anything other than a malevolent agency, as the enemy of the people even, or as the dispersed reality of all possible relations of force. The latter refers to Michel Foucault's conception of power, to which I will come back. It is most surprising that Nancy does not refer to Claude Lefort, whose work he is very familiar with and which demonstrates quite the solution to Nancy's complaint. While Nancy concludes that we still need a way out of nihilism, Lefort analysed how it is possible to organise a democratic political form, constituted as an ever-undetermined regime based on a non-foundation called 'the empty place of power'. To analyse

Lefort's thesis, let me move away from Nancy to Lefort and see if he thinks power 'as anything other than a malevolent agency, as the enemy of the people even or as the dispersed reality of all possible relations of force'.

4. From the Pre-political to the Political: Claude Lefort

It is surprising that Nancy hardly refers to the work of one of the fellows of the *Centre for Philosophical Research on the Political*, Claude Lefort, who has made of democracy and power the central topics of his texts.[32] Different from Nancy, Lefort has not stopped warning us against the dangers of totalitarianism, explicitly starting from an analysis of power as the crucial notion to understand the political. For Lefort, one cannot understand the political without understanding the way power is (re-)presented in a society. He starts from the idea that it is important to discriminate several political regimes. Since democracy and totalitarianism are particular political regimes with different representations of power, Lefort argues that it all comes down to understanding their distinct characteristics. In the whole of his oeuvre, Lefort articulated in a subtle way the formal differences between totalitarianism and democracy, starting from the distinct way they deal with the 'place of power'. In a democracy, the place of power becomes 'infigurable' according to Lefort. In other words, in democracy the place of power is 'empty'.[33]

This 'empty place of power' or 'void' is one of the central theses in Lefort's work: the idea that political regimes can be distinguished from one another by the way in which the place of power is (re-)presented in them. The essence of power, Lefort writes, is 'to present and make visible a model of social organisation'.[34] In democracy – as a political regime distinct from absolute monarchy and totalitarianism – the place of power is 'symbolically empty'. With the disappearance of the absolute monarchy during the French Revolution, the king is murdered and what is left is his empty place. Since this 'birth of democracy', no one has been consubstantial with power, as the king used to be. In a democracy, no single person owns power or *is* power; we can only *re*present power and are therefore never really present in it. This is why Lefort writes that, in democracy, 'the place of power, as such, is symbolically empty'.[35] It is not really empty as long as there are people governing, but no single governor coincides with what he represents; he is only temporarily mandated to represent the people. I quote:

> The legitimacy of power is based on the people; but the image of popular sovereignty is linked to the image of an empty place, impossible to occupy, such that those who exercise public authority can never claim to appropriate it. Democracy combines these two apparently contradictory principles: on the one hand, power emanates from the people; on the other, it is the power of nobody. And democracy thrives on this contradiction. Whenever the latter risks being resolved or is resolved, democracy is either close to destruction or is already destroyed.[36]

Every democracy is inherently characterised by a divergence at the heart of its regime. The empty place of power installs an exteriority at the heart of the modern political order that prevents it from foreclosing itself. The specific 'form' of democracy is that it never obtains an accomplished and fulfilled form. In a way, the only 'form' of democracy is its formlessness, a form without form. With this formlessness, we seem to have arrived at the most characteristic aspect of democracy: its indeterminacy, its indefinite, provisional character. Although the source of legitimacy in a democratic regime is *the* people, 'the people' remains indeterminate. This indeterminacy, and thus also vulnerability, is a core principle of democracy in Lefort's theory. Ultimately, the particularity of democracy lies in its vulnerability. Because its order is never definite, it can always be perverted from within.

A second key feature of democracy, for Lefort, is the separation of the principle of power, of law and of knowledge. Right and knowledge turn into spheres that are not entirely under political control. In a democracy, there is no longer a totality which transcends its parts. A democratic society is characterised by different spheres, none of which dominates all other spheres. This internal dissension within a democratic regime allows people to be legitimately opposed to a regime without being expelled or excluded from it. Think about the ongoing presence of media which inscribe at the heart of society the possibility of criticising the current political regime.

The opportunity for criticism and disagreement is constitutive of democracy. It makes democracy a questionable regime in every sense of the word. Bernard Flynn agrees with that, quoting Lefort in his book of the French philosopher: 'the identity of modern society, and of modern humanity as well, is not one of loss but rather one that is continually called into question. Who we are, and who speaks in our name, is given in modernity not as a fact but as a question.'[37] With democracy, the political order has become a questionable, and, thus, an indefinite matter. Who we are, what the conditions are of our being together, turn out to be the political questions par excellence in contemporary society.

Here, we considered one of the most remarkable starting points of Lefort's reflection on political modernity: the collapse of the traditional political markers and foundations does not put us into an unbearable situation. On the contrary, the questionability of the political framework is a constitutive condition of our being together. Democracy, as Lefort conceives of it, institutionalises conflict at the heart of its functioning. It is because we can quarrel or debate with each other at an institutional level – a parliament, a public debate, etc. – that there is democracy.

Democracy is defined by the intertwining of this indeterminacy. The empty place of power is of crucial importance, and is completely absent in the regime that Lefort calls 'totalitarianism'. Since, for Lefort, totalitarianism is a response to the failure of democracy, the danger of a 'refiguration' of power is always a latent possibility within democracy. If the empty place of power is 'filled' again, the danger of totalitarianism is already around the corner:

> But if the image of the people is actualized, if a party claims to identify with it and to appropriate power under the cover of this identification, then it is the very principle of the distinction between the state and society, the principle of the difference between the norms that govern the various types of relations between individuals, ways of life, beliefs and opinions, which is denied; and, at a deeper level, it is the very principle of a distinction between what belongs to the order of power, to the order of law and to the order of knowledge which is negated. The economic, legal and cultural dimensions are, as it were, interwoven into the political. This phenomenon is characteristic of totalitarianism.[38]

Lefort's analysis of power demonstrates that an understanding of our being together cannot be separated from an understanding of society as a whole. The way we are related to each other is connected, or even determined, by the political contours of society and the power relationships we are embedded in. Lefort's analysis is therefore crucial to distinguish the place of power in democracy from the one in totalitarianism. What we have learned from his analysis is the absolute necessity to reflect upon the place of power as it enables us to discriminate democracy from totalitarianism. In a democracy, power is a struggle but not a battle scene. The empty place of power makes of us all representatives of power, while none of us are really present in it, a formal but crucial difference from totalitarianism. As the regime that institutionalised conflict, democracy involves the ongoing interplay of consensus and dissensus, strife and struggle.

Nancy's complaint that we are unable to think of power as anything other than a malevolent agency, as the enemy of the people even, does not seem to be applicable to Lefort. For Lefort, the emptied power is the condition of every democracy, of existence even, and this far from a mere negative signifier. It is highly remarkable that Nancy did not even acknowledge Lefort's analysis when it comes down to this point: Lefort clearly distinguishes power from other political concepts. He thinks power and struggle as a positive condition of living together, while Nancy claims that there is a lack of thinking on the topic.

5. Power within Democracy: Michel Foucault

Next to the complaint about power as a malevolent agency, Nancy also referred to power as the dispersed reality of all possible relations of force, which would forge the specificity of (political) power, along with its proper and distinct destination.[39] As said, this is a reference to Michel Foucault. Maybe even more than Lefort, Foucault has made of power a central topic of his entire oeuvre. Foucault believed the question of power is crucial in understanding our society. In a lecture from 7 January 1976, he wrote:

> Power, if we do not take too distant a view of it, is not that which makes the difference between those who exclusively possess and retain it, and those who do have it and submit to it. Power must be analysed as something which only functions in the form of a chain. It is never localised here or there, never in anybody's hands, never appropriated as a commodity or piece of wealth. Power is employed and exercised

through a net-like organisation. And not only do individuals circulate between its threads; they are always in the position of simultaneously undergoing and exercising this power. They are not only its inert or consenting target; they are always also the elements of its articulation.[40]

For many contemporary readers, such talk of a pervasive power seems counterintuitive in relation to modern Western democracies: surely the sceptres of powerful dictators and monarchies are consigned to history. Foucault would certainly agree that the traditional sovereign power has collapsed: the powerful sovereign, whose prime interest is to secure the territory of the nation, is no more. According to him, a more subtle form of power pervades modern democratic societies nonetheless. Consequently, his analysis focuses on the presence of power in contemporary society 'after' the collapse of traditional figures of power; he searches for the micro-mechanisms of power in today's society.

In order to explain the micro-mechanisms of today's power, Foucault contrasts the contemporary use of power with the way Niccoló Machiavelli explained it in *The Prince*, as the classic and most famous example of the traditional concept of power in political theory. The main occupation of the prince is to maintain or even augment his territory. He is not concerned with the interests of his subjects – subject in the meaning of 'to be subjected' – but with his territory and how to defend it. This traditional function of (sovereign) power, Foucault writes, is put under pressure from the sixteenth century on, and is finally subject to change during the eighteenth century. He notices two general tendencies or movements underlying the rise of the question of government: state centralisation on the one hand, and dispersion and religious dissidence on the other.[41] While Machiavelli speaks of sovereignty, territory and subjects, Guillaume de La Perrière, for instance, defines government, in *Le miroir politique*, as 'the right disposition of things'.[42] For de La Perrière and many others of this period in Western Europe, government is no longer concerned with territory but with people in relation to their goods, their environment, and their conditions of life. Foucault stresses the fact that with the rise of this 'new art of governing', both the scope and nature of governing has shifted. Because of the collapse of traditional sovereignty, Foucault stresses that power is present in a far more subtle way, and therefore rather difficult to localise. As he writes in 'Governmentality': 'Consequently, sovereignty is far from being eliminated by the emergence of a new art of government, even by one which has passed the threshold of political science; on the contrary, the problem of sovereignty is made more acute than ever.'[43]

In his course of 1977–8, Foucault focuses on the question of power, and how it is operational within the area of health and fitness. His course is an extended exploration of how our preoccupation with health and fitness has to do with the use of a particular form of power. The key term to understanding this new form of power is what Foucault describes as *governmentality*.[44,45] This new form of power differs substantially from the traditional power of the sovereign. The power of the sovereign in political society manifests itself primarily with the threat of death; a monarch defends his power and territory with the threat of death to intruders as well as to citizens who disobey the law; as long as the monarch is able to keep his power, or even expand it, his political task is fulfilled. How citizens behave, what they eat or how they live, is not his concern. In the shift identified by Foucault, the focus of power changes from maintaining the sovereign territory to querying for the interests of the nation's subjects. It is the passage from a 'state of territory' to a 'state of population'.

Governmentality then takes charge of life rather than of death; it is the use of power to manage the lives of the people of the nation. Power understood as governmentality is interested in the way subjects live, work or eat, and how they take care of their health or personal hygiene. In general, it is the absorption of everyday life, of the economy or 'household' (see the traditional Greek meaning of '*oikonomia*'), into politics.[46] Since the eighteenth century, Foucault writes, political economy occupies the centre of the political scene. In addition to defending its territory against exterior forces, a nation and its people also have to be strengthened from the inside. Consequently, economy and rationality are replacing the traditional virtues which governed Feudal society (wisdom, justice, and prudence). Governmentality is characterised by a series of techniques, procedures, institutions or calculations, through which the state manages the population in this new political and economical context. The result of this management is called *discipline*[47] or *biopower* in Foucault's earlier work. One by one, Foucault developed these theoretical concepts to explain how our lives (our '*bios*') are increasingly captured by dispositives or apparatuses determining our behaviour and self-understanding.

Lois McNay rightly accentuates the fact that 'the notion of government does not replace the theory of disciplinary biopower; rather modern societies are characterized by a triangular power complex: sovereignty-discipline-government or *governmentality*'.⁴⁸

Looking at Foucault's analysis of power, political power is never simply dispersed or indefinitely multiplied. It is analysed from its contemporary representation, different indeed from the centralised power of Machiavelli's *Prince*, simply because power operates differently today. Biopower does not demonstrate the domination of force in all of our relations. It makes explicit how we are less forced to things than we used to be, but this does not make our lives free from power and influence from outside. If Foucault analyses how power within democracy should not be understood as centralised, but rather as an omnipresent network of imperatives, mechanisms, and instructions that we should obey.

Conclusion: 'Nancy and the Political'

We have explored Lefort's and Foucault's respective philosophies of power. Both philosophers offer an analysis of the precariousness of democracy, but their analysis does not necessary achieve or foreclose our political horizon, neither does it make of power a distinct concept. How then must we understand Nancy's criticism?

Nancy's 'non-necessity' to think power and the non-evidential character of 'Nancy and the political', lays bare an ambivalent stance towards the political. Thinking the political implies more than (righteously) postulating the need to open up the horizon of sense. Several of Nancy's phrases on power or democracy end up here. Democracy, he writes, is 'the name of a regime whose truth cannot be subsumed under any ordering agency, whether religious, political, scientific, or aesthetic; it is, rather, that which wholly engages "man" at the risk and chance of "himself" ... then, the duty to invent a politics *not of the ends* of the dance over the abyss, but of the means to open the spaces of their being put to work'.⁴⁹ Claiming that power does not need to be analysed because 'the political' should be reinvented, is at least ambivalent: even if power is a concept to be reinvented, in the meantime, we are living in the midst of its use and abuse. In the French philosopher's oeuvre, one finds a remarkable silence regarding both the individual-state relation and the bureaucracy of the (social struggle for) power. Consequently, for Simon Critchley, Nancy is simply unable to think politics because of his diagnosis of the withdrawal of the political, which, he argues 'leads to an exclusion of politics, understood as a field of antagonism, struggle, dissension, contestation, critique and questioning'.[50] Indeed, all Nancy offers are small indications of what his thought about the political might be; that is to say, a note here and there. Although one can easily point to his reflection on justice, sovereignty and freedom among other political key concepts, Nancy's very minor reflections on power seems more than a footnote. Precisely because he fails (or refuses) to analyse the place of power and social struggle, his work seems to fit into a political order in which power and economics no longer seem to be a matter in an ideological struggle, the order of liberal democracy.

Nancy, however, is very aware of the risk of implicit legitimation of the current state of things, and his thought cannot support liberal democracy; one should certainly not seek his political orientation in the direction of liberalism. Not only social ontology and its emphasis on being-with is a radical undermining of atomistic liberalism; on closer inspection of Nancy's work, it can also be of much help to analyse political decisions in a critical way, be it in liberal democracy or another political regime. Nancy regards the liberal order with the requisite critical reserve, but the order as such remains outside of his consideration. Despite his explicit reservations about liberalism and the atomisation of society, despite his call for a retreating of the political, and despite his claim that political decisions are still made, all in all Nancy's narrative seems to relate all too easily to the model of liberal democracy. In his refusal to analyse social struggle and the place of power, Nancy does not appear to offer any immediate help on this shortcoming.

Though interesting and fascinating, Nancy's gesture away from the political to the social, results into a conceptual vacuum when it comes down to the political, with a whole world between the political analysis of power and ending up in foreclosing our political horizon. Do we actually need a revolution to think power? Lefort and Foucault demonstrated the opposite. By not analysing power because 'the political' should be reinvented, or because 'we need a revolution or simply another civilisation', Nancy seems to postpone his 'thinking of the political' time and again: 'If we first think the being of our being together in the world, we will see which politics gives this thought a chance.'[51]

In a quoted passage from *The Truth of Democracy* (we remain 'prisoners of a vision of politics as the putting to work and activation of an absolute sharing (out)', Nancy seems to predict that if we expect that much from democracy, it can only lead to disappointment. More and more, the question appears to be: Does Nancy not expect too much from democracy?[52]

Notes

1. Ignaas Devisch, *Jean-Luc Nancy and the Question of Community* (London: Continuum - Bloomsbury, 2012).
2. Jean-Luc Nancy, e.a., *Rejouer le politique* (Paris: Galilée, 1981); Jean-Luc Nancy, *L'impératif catégorique* (Paris: Flammarion, 1983); Jean-Luc Nancy, *Thinking Better of Capital. An Interview: Studies in Practical philosophy* (Paris: Flammarion, 1999); Jean-Luc Nancy, *Le retrait du politique* (Paris: Galilée, 1983).
3. Jean-Luc Nancy, 'Changement de monde', *Lignes*, 35, 1998, pp. 42–52.
4. Jean-Luc Nancy, 'La comparution/ The compearence from the existence of "communism" to the community of "existence"', *Political Theory*, 20:3, 1992, p. 27.
5. Nancy, 'Thinking Better of Capital. An Interview', *Studies in Practical Philosophy*, 1:2, 1999, p. 220.
6. Ibid., pp. 220–1.
7. See especially the interview '*Thinking Better of Capital*' and a conference talk at the University of Toulouse: <http://www.canalu.tv/video/universite_toulouse_ii_le_mirail/interroger_la_politique_interroger_le_commun_jean_luc_nancy.8842>.
8. See the conference talk at the University of Toulouse: <http://www.canal-u.tv/video/universite_toulouse_ii_le_mirail/interroger_la_politique_interroger_le_commun_jean_luc_nancy.8842>; Alena Alexandrova, Ignaas Devisch, Laurens ten Kate and Aukje van Rooden (eds), *Re-treating Religion: Deconstructing Christianity with Jean-Luc Nancy* (New York: Fordham University Press, 2012). See also a radio interview: <http://laviemanifeste.com/archives/5791>.
9. See, among others: Devisch, *Jean-Luc Nancy and the Question of Community*; B. C. Hutchens, *Jean-Luc Nancy and the Future of Philosophy* (Chesham: Acumen, 2005); Ian James, 'Jean-Luc Nancy and the Future of Philosophy', *French Studies*, 61:1, 2007, pp. 126–7; M.-E. Morin, *Jean-Luc Nancy* (Cambridge: Polity Press, 2012).

10. Jean-Luc Nancy, 'Lapsus judicii', *Communications*, 26, 1977, pp. 82–97; Nancy, *L'impératif catégorique*.
11. In earlier writings, I already sketched the importance of 'freedom' and 'sovereignty' for Nancy's political thought. Ignaas Devisch, 'Nancian virtual doubts about 'Leformal' democracy: Or how to deal with contemporary political configuration in an uneasy way?', *Philosophy & Social Criticism*, 37:9, 2011, pp. 999–1010; Devisch, *Jean-Luc Nancy and the Question of Community*.
12. The texts 'Lapsus judicii' and 'Dies irae' are a discussion with Lyotard's work. The latter reacts to 'Lapsus judicii' in his *L'enthousiasme*: Jean-François Lyotard, *L'enthousiasme: La critique kantienne de l'histoire* (1986), p. 17, n.13. Nancy, in his turn, reacts to Lyotard in a postscript to the second version of 'Lapsus judicii'. Jean-Luc Nancy, *A Finite Thinking*, ed. Simon Sparks (Stanford: Stanford University Press, 2003), pp. 170–1. Nancy wants to make clear that the law feeds off proclaiming justice, of its juris-diction, and that the law thus always presupposes 'the particular case', a lapsus (fall, faulty). The law needs to 'fictionalise' (from the Latin fictio: forming, manufacturing, and from fictum: lie, fantasy) its fall in order to install its universality. In this way, jurisdiction is always and already juris-fiction: 'Law and case come before right only if they are modeled, shaped, fashioned – fictioned – in and through one another. The implications of this necessity are quite radical, however: the installation or inauguration of right must of itself be fictioned.' Nancy, *A Finite Thinking*, p. 157. Such a juris-fiction can, according to Nancy, be found especially in Kant's work.
13. Jean-Luc Nancy, *Being Singular Plural* (Stanford: Stanford University Press, 2001), pp. 185–9.
14. Ibid.
15. Ibid., pp. 188–9.
16. Ibid., p. 188.
17. Devisch, *Jean-Luc Nancy and the Question of Community*.
18. Jean-Luc Nancy, 'Lignes de sens. Dossier Jean-Luc Nancy', *Spirale*, 239, 2012, pp. 31–55.
19. Pierre-Philippe Jandin, *Jean-Luc Nancy: Retracer le politique* (Paris: Michalon, 2012); Jean-Luc Nancy, *Politique et au-delà: Entretien avec Philip Armstrong and Jason E. Smith* (Paris: Galilée, 2011), p. 28.
20. Jean-Luc Nancy, *The Creation of the World, or Globalization*, trans. F. Raffoul and D. Pettigrew (Albany: SUNY Press, 2007); Nancy, *A Finite Thinking*; Nancy, *Being Singular Plural*.

21. Jean-Luc Nancy, 'Démocratie finie et infinie', in L. Fabrique (ed.), *Démocratie, dans quel état?* (Paris: La Fabrique, 2009), pp. 77–94; Jean-Luc Nancy, *The Truth of Democracy*, trans. P.-A. Brault and M. Naas (New York: Fordham University Press, 2010); Nancy, 'Lignes de sens. Dossier Jean-Luc Nancy'; Jean-Luc Nancy, *Vérité de la démocratie* (Paris: Galilée, 2008).
22. Nancy, *Politique et au-delà*, pp. 41–2.
23. Nancy, 'Démocratie finie et infinie', pp. 80, 90.
24. Ioan Alexandru Tofan, 'Sur la légitimité théologique de la démocratie', *Meta: Research in Hermeneutics, Phenomenology, and Practical Philosophy*, 3:1, 2011, p. 202.
25. Nancy, *Politique et au-delà*, p. 36. I quoted from the (not yet published) translation of the text. Thanks to Philip Armstrong for allowing me to use his translation.
26. Graham Burchell, Colin Gordon and Peter Miller, *The Foucault Effect: Studies in Governmentality with Two Lectures by and an Interview with Michel Foucault* (Hemel Hempstead: Harvester Wheatsheaf, 1991).
27. Nancy, *The Truth of Democracy*, p. 17.
28. Ibid., p. 17.
29. Ibid., p. 17.
30. Ibid., pp. 17–18.
31. Ibid., p. 22.
32. Devisch, 'Nancian Virtual Doubts about "Leformal" democracy'.
33. Nancy, *Le retrait du politique*, p. 72.
34. C. Lefort, *The Political Forms of Modern Society* (Cambridge: Polity Press, 1986), p. 282.
35. Ibid., p. 279.
36. Ibid., p. 279.
37. Flynn, *The Philosophy of Claude Lefort: Interpreting the Political*, p. 159.
38. Lefort, *The Political Forms of Modern Society*, pp. 279–80.
39. Nancy, *The Truth of Democracy*, p. 22.
40. M. Foucault and C. Gordon, *Power/Knowledge: Selected Interviews and Other Writings 1972–1977* (Hemel Hempstead: Harvester Press, 1980), p. 80.
41. M. Foucault, *Security, Territory, Population: Lectures at the Collège de France, 1977–1978* (Basingstoke: Palgrave Macmillan, 2007), p. 88.
42. Ibid., p. 92.
43. Burchell et al., *The Foucault Effect*, p. 101.

44. Ibid., p. 101.
45. I am of course aware that the notion of 'disciplinary power' and the process of 'normalization' used by Foucault in the first volume of the *History of Sexuality* are an important step in Foucault's reconceptualisation of power. But discussing it here would lead us too far.
46. Foucault describes economy as 'the government of the family' (Foucault, *Security, Territory, Population*, p. 107).
47. 'La discipline est, au fond, le mécanisme de pouvoir par lequel nous arrivons à contrôler dans le corps social jusqu'aux éléments les plus ténus, par lesquels nous arrivons à atteindre les atomes sociaux eux-mêmes, c'est-à-dire les individus. Techniques de l'individualisation du pouvoir. Comment surveiller quelqu'un, comment contrôler sa conduite, son comportement, ses aptitudes, comment intensifier sa performance, multiplier ses capacités, comment le mettre à la place où il sera plus utile: voilà ce qu'est, à mon sens, la discipline' (M. Foucault, *Entretien avec Michel Foucault Dits et écrits 1954–1988* (Vol. II), pp. 140–60 (Paris: Gallimard, 1994), p. 191).
48. L. McNay, *Foucault: A Critical Introduction* (Cambridge: Polity Press, 1994), p. 117. Although these two concepts describe apparently the same phenomenon, there are nevertheless important differences between biopower and governmentality. Governmentality, for example, is far more indirect in its intervention than biopower is. For a detailed analysis see McNay, *Foucault: A Critical Introduction*, pp. 122–3.
49. Nancy, *The Truth of Democracy*, p. 33.
50. S. Critchley, 'Re-tracing the Political: Politics and Community in the Work of Philippe Lacoue-Labarthe and Jean-Luc Nancy', in D. Campbell and M. Dillon (eds), *The Political Subject of Violence*, pp. 73–93 (Manchester: Manchester University Press, 1993). For a discussion on this passage: Morin, *Jean-Luc Nancy*.
51. See also: Jandin, *Jean-Luc Nancy: Retracer le politique*, p. 118; Nancy, *The Truth of Democracy*, p. 34.
52. Many thanks to Dr Aukje van Rooden for reminding me of this passage and for her thoughtful comments on my chapter.

Everything is Not Political

6

Image-Politics: Jean-Luc Nancy's Ontological Rehabilitation of the Image
Alison Ross

Nancy's writing on the image may be understood as a critical engagement with the traditions of modern aesthetics and classical theories of art. However, the starting point for his approach to the image indicates that his writing on this topic has much wider ambitions than the treatment of a regional aesthetic topic. Nancy defines the image as a mode of access to sense. He clarifies the stakes of this position when he emphasises that the 'access' to sense that the image provides is neither comprehensible in the terms of traditional mimetic theories of the image (Plato), nor in those of the idiom of representation (Christian icons). It is clear that he wants to contest the view that the image is merely some sensuous version or presentation of a prior and primary intelligible idea. The traditional conception of the image is not able, in Nancy's view, to comprehend the access to sense that the image provides. Hence Nancy attempts an ontological rehabilitation of the image, which reiterates the precepts of his conception of being as 'co-presence'.

The point of departure for Nancy's ontology is the absence of any compelling existential regime of meaning for existence. His philosophy acknowledges the exigencies of this situation, by taking the question of ontology raised at the 'end' of Western metaphysics, to be the 'question of social Being'. 'Being-with' is, for him, the collective, interstitial network of its occurrence, meaning that there is no single node or term that grounds being. He articulates the co-presence of being in terms of the category of sense or meaning. Being, he argues, does not 'have' meaning; rather 'the phenomenon of Being ... is meaning', and this meaning is 'in turn, its own circulation – and *we* are this circulation'.[1] He writes: 'Being cannot *be* anything but being-with-one-another, circulating in the *with* and as the *with* of this singularly plural coexistence'.² The articulation of this conception of being as co-presence is one that is enabled by a series of historical shifts on the question of intelligible forms. These shifts, which can be seen in exemplary form in the way modern aesthetic theory treats the topic of the image, culminate in the unravelling of the coherence of the dualism between intelligibility and materiality. This dualism, which I will explain in further detail below, is the presumption that intelligible ideas are 'prior' to the 'secondary' material forms that attempt to 'imitate', 'embody' or 'represent' them. Because in modern aesthetics attention is paid to the meaning of sensible form per se, the dualist conception that understands such form as derivative of an original, intelligible idea unravels.

The stakes of the ontology of co-presence can be explained in relation to two of Nancy's key formulations, which respectively stage the positive and negative thesis of his ontology: first of all, Nancy argues in the context of referring to the image, that 'sense is its own withdrawal'.³ This statement can be explained in a provisional way in the following terms: instead of sense being like a truth that could be presented in an image, Nancy defines sense as a praxis that is always in the process of taking shape. The implications of this point can also be seen in the critical target of his conception of sense, which we can present as the negative thesis of his ontology. Nancy takes a critical stance on the presumption that 'ideas' have a shaping role over 'materiality'. Such a presumption depends on the presupposition of the coherence of the dualism between intelligibility and sensibility, or an intelligible 'model' and its sensible 'imitation'. This postulated coherence in which sensible presentation in an image can be considered to be the secondary manifestation 'of' an intelligible or presentable idea, he argues, is false.⁴ In his criticisms of those projects that rely on the dualism of intelligibility and sensibility, Nancy shows that actually accounting for what the image 'is' and 'does' in such projects requires something like his conception of 'being singular plural', that is, the positive thesis of his ontology.

Nancy argues that the emergence of sense is each time a singular occurrence. Sense does not emerge from the container of an originating 'idea', but from the plural, interstitial network of sensible and affective relations. This position draws heavily on the example of sense making in art works for its elucidation and defence. This can be seen in Nancy's targetted discussion of the image in classical aesthetics. But it is also evident in the frequent references Nancy makes to the dualist ontology that underpins those attempts to separate out 'authentic' sociality, from the 'false' theatrical spectacles and images identified in classical (Plato) and modern (Rousseau) political theory.[5] Such dualism separates the proper mode of social being from improper distortions of sociality. The implication of this critique of dualist ontology in political theory is that misconceptions concerning the image support a false account of what is involved in sociality. According to Nancy, the posture of this position is sustained in recent post Marxist projects of social criticism, such as de Bord's Situationism. This point regarding the false conception of sociality in political theory can also be related to Nancy's criticisms of the presumed capacity of ideas to have a shaping role over material forces. Nancy, in effect, uses his conception of being as co-presence and the re-working of the notion of the image that it entails, to criticise as programmatic those conceptions of politics organised around an idea of authentic sociality. Just as 'truth' is not 'represented' with finality in an image, but is a praxis that is always at work, so too sociality cannot be instituted nor regulated by the idea of an authentic society. Furthermore, sociality is not a regional 'social' ontology. Rather, being 'is' being-with. If being-with is a hybrid, dynamic making of sense, Nancy's ontology takes a critical perspective on models of identity based politics. Such politics is out of tune with the way things 'are': it relies on a version of the dualism that sets up an idea of an 'essence' that would be both separate from the field of materiality and that would be able to regulate its forms. I will try to specify the precise implications of this point in the third part of this chapter. Despite his use of the category of 'first philosophy' or 'ontology' as the reference point for his discussion of the image, Nancy in fact draws on the precise understanding of materiality in the history of modern aesthetics, so as to articulate and frame the principles of his ontology. His references to modern aesthetics can thus be used to clarify the position his ontology of the image implies for politics. This is the hypothesis I will pursue here.

This chapter is divided into four parts. In the first two parts I set out the general terms of Nancy's ontology and then I consider his ontological approach to the topic of the image. Next, I examine the detail of his references to the image in his treatment of politics. In particular, I analyse the way that Nancy's treatment of politics combines two of the main features of his relational ontology: his conception of the quasi-historical 'withdrawal' of sense, and his related criticism of the ontological priority of 'ideas' over materiality in traditional conceptions of the image. Finally, I set out some of the implications for Nancy's discussion of political topics and themes of the aesthetic context that, in my view, frames his attempt to provide an ontological rehabilitation of the image.

1. Nancy's Ontology

The point of departure for Nancy's philosophy is the absence of any compelling transcendent regime of meaning for existence. He takes this situation as a condition that must be understood, both, in its occurrence and in its implications. Accordingly, he proposes to carry out an ontological inquiry into the 'end' of metaphysics, a seemingly paradoxical 'first philosophy'. He resolves this paradox by recasting the question of being as 'a "question of social Being"'.[6] In terms of the structure he gives to this ontology, as well as the terminology he uses to articulate it, Nancy draws on two different trajectories: on one hand, there is his account of philosophy as articulating regimes of meaning and his view that the history of philosophy presents the exhaustion of all regimes of signification; on the other, there is his political-economic diagnosis of the impact of capitalism on social being. These two trajectories converge in Nancy's contrasting of History (as a system that gives a sense, or direction, to existence) and what he terms the 'historiality of history'.[7] The passing of given or prior significations such as 'democracy', 'art for art's sake' or the 'total man' in Western metaphysics and the disappropriating operations of the exchange system of global capital, are taken by Nancy to expose the 'event-character' or 'historiality' of history, the emergence into view of the contingency of the 'sense of the world'.[8] This opposition of historiality and History informs Nancy's discussion of works from the history of philosophy, which can be seen especially in his view that these works are structurally incomplete as concerns their meaning and direction.[9]

Nancy argues that there are three formal structures of sense, which are constitutively oriented to: 1) observance of a pre-given all-encompassing order (i.e., the ancient philosophy); 2) salvation (i.e., recovery from alienation, the Christian Fall, or the expropriation of labour); and 3) existence with no guiding and justificatory foundation, but in accordance with an ethics of praxis of sense-making, which is an ethics of the sensibility or 'affectability' (the ability or 'aptitude' of the senses to be affected). In *The Sense of the World*, he states that: 'The sensible or the aesthetic is the outside-of-itself through which and *as* which there is the relation to itself of a sense in general or through which there is the *toward* of sense.'[10]

To unpack these rather obtuse formulations we can characterise Nancy's position in the following way: he neither wants to dispense with the intelligibility of material existence nor to ground this in a primordial source, be it the ideal forms, divine fate or destiny, or even, like Heidegger, an epochal opening of an ingenious questioning. Is it possible to grasp intelligible meaning as it emerges from sensibility, from the affectability of the senses? Where could we look for this process? How might we set it out? The combination of these constraints gives rise to the problem of finding suitable contexts able to adequately stage his position. In effect, he looks to a few privileged contexts in order to develop a language able to articulate, conjure, and explain the functioning of sense beyond dualism.

Most recently, the history of Christianity has become a testing ground for the rehearsal of his ideas. In his writing on Christianity he wants to see if he can present the sense of certain moments in that history differently, but still do so in a way that holds onto the experience of the divine. In other words, the so-called 'deconstruction of Christianity' does not seek to expunge the existential dimension of spiritual sense, but to locate and describe it without recourse to an 'other-worldly' reference:

> 'What is an opening that would not sink into its own openness? What is an infinite sense that nonetheless makes sense, an empty truth that yet has the weight of truth? How can one take on afresh the task of delineating a *delimited* opening, a figure, therefore, that still would not be a figurative capturing of sense (that would not be God)?'[11]

In his earlier writings, where he is concerned with articulating the experience of meaning as this arises from sensible existence, Nancy singles out the context of eroticism and sexual curiosity as the praxis that stages the genesis of sense from the materiality of the body. The sense of existence is 'right at' (*même à*) the surface of the sensible body where its material exposure to other bodies is structured with the syntax of pleasure and pain. Nancy uses pleasure and pain to describe the exposure to meaning in the contact of bodies: bodies are not indifferent to one another. The erotics of the body better 'expose', or 'perforate' the supposed interiority of meaning, bringing out the 'forgotten' origins of sense in the exteriority of sensible contact. Pleasure and pain do not belong to the 'body', nor do they have their origin in the 'outside world', but right at the surface where contact occurs. The syntax they give is not able to restore a structure of signification capable of grounding meaning; rather, it is used by Nancy to provide a glimpse of the *coming* of meaning, 'at the very point where pain and joy mixed together compose the non-signifying origin of significance itself'.[12] With this position, Nancy defends the idea that affectability rather than 'the subject' is the locus and condition of the practice of sense-making.

Nancy uses eroticism to stage how it is that patterns of meaning are determined in each case and at each moment. It is clear, moreover, that he wants to re-conceive the erotics of the body away from privatised conceptions of pleasure so that the registers of joy and pain have more general implications. His use of the vocabulary of the circuitry of touch aims to underline this group of themes: touch is Nancy's way of placing meaning 'at' the surface, not as the surface, but as what emerges from the circuit of relations *between* the surfaces of bodies. It is worth noting that this treatment of eroticism and his deconstruction of Christianity often rely on the same vocabulary and themes, a confluence that can be explained in terms of Nancy's repeated emphasis on the status of Christianity as a religion of incarnation.[13]

Nancy's approach has important implications for the understanding of the image in projects of social criticism. He is critical of the separation forged in post-Marxist critical theory between the mere spectacle of the image and the 'real' field of capitalism, as this is disclosed through the activity of critique.[14] Post-Marxist critical theorists like Guy de Bord endorse the dualist perspective that denounces the 'surface' materiality of images in comparison to the 'depth' of ideas, because they assume that the incisive way of understanding things is to separate out the superficiality of the image from the 'insights' of discursively founded critique. Nancy sees in this move a basic incomprehension of the materiality of the image. Against it, he argues that the making sense of things cannot be divorced from the processes of meaning making at the level of materiality, which is the level of the image. There is a discipline of the senses to meaning in the way things are presented, and the dualist position that looks behind the presentation of things for their true meaning obscures and mystifies the perceptible, tangible being-with of sense.

He makes a similar point regarding the uses of aesthetic reflection in modern aesthetics. The category of symbolic meaning in the history of modern aesthetics overlooks the way in which the image brings together the relational properties of meaning. The symbol of the flower in nature, which is one of the key examples of beauty as the symbol of morality in Kant's *Critique of Judgement*, is not a symbolisation in an image of some idea or property that is different in kind to what it presents; such as the Kantian idea of moral value. Instead, Nancy might say: one way of experiencing the moral idea of freedom, is to be in the presence of this flower, reflecting (in a Kantian fashion) on its organised form. The real meaningfulness of that experience of the moral idea is owed to this flower for its coming to pass.[15] It is the symbolic presentation of the moral idea that brings together in material forms the relevant aspects able to show the meaning of morality. The materiality of the existence and communication of meaning requires a new understanding of the symbolic, not as a separate form that displays an otherwise self-subsistent idea, but as the process of making sense that brings things or aspects together *in concreto*.

In *Au fond des images*, Nancy uses this way of defining the symbol to describe the work of the image as that which shows 'that' and 'how' something exists.[16] Nancy takes this vocabulary from Heidegger's discussion of the 'work' of the 'work of art' in his 'Origin of the Work of Art' lectures. Nancy's use of this vocabulary is intended to emphasise the process of making (or, 'work') that goes into the experience of meaning as a working *relation*, rather than an imprisonment in moments of sense-perception.[17]

2. Nancy's Ontological Rehabilitation of the Image

In line with his general perspective on the breakdown of 'ideas' as orientating schemas of meaning, Nancy refuses to treat the image as a signifier of an interiority or depth, as if images were material 'symbols' of prior and primary ideas. In particular, he wishes to consider the image apart from what he refers to as the *doxa* of mimesis and its framework of representation. Thus he refers to the image as 'what takes the thing out of its simple presence and brings it to pres-ence, to *praes-entia*, to being-out-in-front-of-itself'.[18] In his view, the image opens up a certain way of looking at sensibility that is not destitute of sense. The pertinent question to ask is why Nancy thinks that the image is able to do this. This question is especially pressing because, in some of his texts such as *Les Muses*, he argues that we must dispense with the concept of the 'image'. Nancy is interested in the topic because of the way it crystallises the problem of how something 'unpresentable' can be visible in the sensible. In this respect, it is clear that Nancy's comments on the image, and especially his provocative position that we need to do away with it, rely on an understanding of the historical relation between image and idea. If we consult his work on Christianity, such as *Dis-enclosure: the Deconstruction of Christianity*, it seems that the motivation for this position comes from his view that, in the Western tradition, the dualist structure of sense has been grounded in the notion of an invisible core driving and giving force to material sense.[19]

By and large, Western philosophy has inherited its understanding of the relation between image and idea from Plato, which has been partly transformed by Christian theology. Image is here understood as representation in sensible or material form of an originally immaterial archetype. The exigency of this relation in Plato is grounded in the Idea itself, as a call to embodiment. The Idea carries this demiurgic index in itself and thereby refers to its appearance, its copy in the material world. The perceptible presentation is, thus, justified by the Idea's ontological demand, but at the same time it exhausts that justificatory ground. Any further representation is illusory because ontologically groundless. The 'secondary' copies of the arts, for instance, are detached from the participatory relation to ideas that perceptible presentations claim. We see that in Plato the lack of authentication by ideal forms does not just make art's productions worthless from the perspective of cognition, but it actually turns them into dangerous illusions.[20]

In Christian theology, the problems that were raised under the topic of Christology adopted many of the features of neo-Platonic metaphysics. The question was asked anew: How and why was the intelligible or the divine related to or embodied in the sensible? What was the exigency and what was the mode of this relation? In the case of Christology, the divine takes the form of visual semblance, but this semblance is restricted to the mode of embodiment in human form. Further, the question of the exigency of this relation is taken up in the frame of the history of redemption: it is because human resources are unequal to the task and goal of salvation that the divine takes sensible form in the world.

Here too the status of artistic representation is a significant marker for the perspective of Nancy's ontology. In terms of the degree of removal from the origin, the secondary copies of art in the Platonic tradition have their parallel in the Christian icon, which is taken to represent, rather than incarnate, the divine. In both of these traditions the image is defined in the terms of degrees of resemblance, and this entails a further complexity in conceptions of the image. In the primary copies of perceptible forms that participate in the idea, or in the human form that incarnates God, the image has a resemblance to the idea. In the secondary copies of art the relation of resemblance is lost, and in the representations of the religious icon the relation of the image to the idea is strictly symbolic.

In *Les Muses*, Nancy recasts this traditional positioning of the image as a shadow, symbol, or fallen distortion, of a primary idea in light of his thesis regarding the obsolescence of the dualism of ideas and sensuous forms. He argues that the motif of the sensible visibility ('la visibilité sensible') of the intelligible is the crux of all grand theories of imitation.[21] These theories

> have never been anything but theories of the imitation, or the image, of the Idea (which is itself, you understand, but the *self-imitation* of being, its transcendent or transcendental miming) – and reciprocally, all thinking about the Idea is thinking about the image or imitation. Including, and especially, when it detaches itself from the imitation of external forms or from 'nature' understood in this way. All this thinking is thus theological, turning obstinately around the great motif of *'the visible image of the invisible God'*, which for Origen is the definition of Christ. Therefore, all of modernity that speaks of the invisible or the unpresentable is always at least on the verge of renewing this motif.[22]

If the dualist frame of reference for thinking the relation between the intelligible and the sensible is no longer tenable, as Nancy has it, then the image, insofar as it too belongs to the sensible realm, has to be re-thought in a new conceptual constellation. The paradox of an imitation of the invisible or (only) intelligible, which has been, according to Nancy, the cornerstone of the onto-theological doctrines of the image, now appears as an absurdity. How are we to understand the image (what it is or what it does) in this new situation without crudely reducing its aura or depth to 'mere' illusions, and without confining experience of art to an appreciation of technical achievement or a historical knowledge? Here Nancy's idiom of making sense out of material forms intends to provide a workable language; and it does so, notably, by systematic reference to the experience of the arts. In essence, this idiom allows one to give up the transcendent or the transcendental without liquidating the spiritual experience of the image. Sense, he says, 'is its own withdrawal'.[23] Sense is ever given to us ahead of us, always only in its process of taking shape, and never as a (final) truth capable of being presented in an 'image'. In its being a sensible form, the image shares in the potency of organised material relations. Its withdrawal is a 'trace' of spiritual depths, an invitation to understanding, to intellectual striving for meaning. But it is also inescapably an imitation of truth. One cannot simply shake off its metaphysical stamp. It is what it is for us, namely, a religious icon or a philosophical topic, because of that stamp. And what is this stamp? It is, according to Nancy, the 'idea', that 'truth', is essentially visual, which is why it can be imitated in visual representation.[24]

For Nancy, what becomes clear in our historical epoch is the absurdity of imitating something that is not there in the way it was supposed to be. The coherence of the image in its 'meaning' as an imitation of what is otherwise unpresentable is now lost:

> The image withdraws as phantom or phantasm of the Idea, destined to vanish in ideal presence itself. It withdraws therefore as image *of*, image of something or someone that, itself or himself or herself, would not be an image. It effaces itself as simulacrum or as face of being, as shroud or as glory of God, as imprint of a matrix or as expression of something unimaginable. (Note in passing, because we will return to this, that it is perhaps first of all a very precise image that gets effaced: man as the image of God.)[25]

When the image is considered in its historico-philosophical designation, it jars with Nancy's general position on sense. In his words, the dialectical operation of the image-idea demands an 'identification of the model or the cause, even if it is a negative one'.[26] In contrast, the trace of the sensible does not articulate the couple of the presenting sensible and the presented ideal ('sensible présentant et de l'idéal présenté'):

Image-Politics   149

> We are dealing with this: the form-idea withdraws and the vestigial form of this withdrawal is what our platonising lexicon makes us call 'sensible'. *Aesthetics* as domain and as thinking of the sensible does not mean anything other than that. Here by contrast the trace is not the sensible trace of an insensible, one which would put us on its path or trail (which would indicate the way [*sens*] toward a Sense): it is (of) the sensible (the) *traced* or *tracing*, as its very *sense*.[27]

It is no exaggeration to claim that the image is the test case for Nancy's relational ontology. If his ontology works in the case of the image, in the case of what is stamped as the sensible form of the idea, then it works tout court. The articulation of Nancy's ontology in the case of the 'image' is also significant, because it underscores how reliant the articulation of this ontology is on the language and concepts of art and aesthetics. For him, the historical process of the withdrawal of the form-idea couple is a process that the field of modern philosophical aesthetics describes. He writes, 'aesthetics' deals with what our 'platonizing lexicon' makes us call 'sensible'. But the trace that aesthetics treats 'is not the sensible trace of an insensible, one which would put us on its path or trail (which would indicate the way [*sens*] toward a Sense): it is (of) the sensible (the) *traced* or *tracing*, as its very *sense*'.[28] If the tradition of aesthetics is crucial for developing these implications of the conception of the image-idea (the sensible intelligible), so too the praxis of the arts are crucial for explicating the idea of a sense that is always ahead of itself. They are the material sites in which, even according to the canonical texts from the tradition of philosophical aesthetics, sense is made rather than 'given'. Hence the category of the symbol, as Nancy shows in the case of Kantian aesthetics, is the material site where the idea is experienced rather than, as Kant would hold, a material form that evokes in analogical form an already given idea.

3. Nancy's Image-politics

Nancy's ontology is an exercise in describing the most fundamental features of existence. The praxis of sense making that defines existence with no guiding frame of meaning is not really a contention or a thesis, so much as it is intended as a description of the way things are primarily: '"Ontology" does not occur at a level reserved for principles, a level that is withdrawn, speculative, and altogether abstract. Its name means the thinking of existence.'[29] As Nancy presents it, 'the thinking of existence' is a difficult exercise in so far as it requires a rigorous thinking through of the question of what it means to live today. For Nancy, the contemporary exigency that most requires thought is 'the stripping bare of being-in-common'.[30] The operations of market capital, he claims, raise the question of existence in an unavoidable way. Capital 'exposes the stripping bare of the *with* as a mark of Being, or as a mark of meaning'.[31] In his view, capital exposes the 'with' because it exteriorises meaning in relations of exchange, and it does so in a totalising and inescapable way. Capital has an ambivalent significance for the contemporary ontology of existence. It both intensifies the exigencies of the contemporary situation in its comprehensive stripping bare of being-with, but also nullifies the consequences of this situation in its presentation of being-with as being-of-market-value. The consequences of this contemporary situation still need to be thought through. Ontology, Nancy claims, as an exercise in thinking, is neither otiose, nor an indolent refusal of action.[32] In fact, this exercise in thinking distinguishes the question of the sense of existence (ontology), from contemporary attempts to provide a 'final' answer to it. Such attempts only accentuate the question of sense. Capital, for instance, in Nancy's view, *raises* the question of the origins of sense in putting forward market value as a totalising regime of sense. Similarly, when politics is conceived of as a total schema of value and signification it only raises the question of the origins of the sense of being-with more insistently.[33] He cites in this regard 'nationalism, fundamentalism, and fascism in all their various forms' each of which, he says, react against the 'misery' of capitalism.[34]

Nancy calls his ontological investigation into the presuppositions of 'politics' [*la politique*] 'the political' [*le politique*].[35] The presuppositions he identifies are organised around the two extremities his ontology of sense describes: at one end, is the 'history of the representation-of-self as the determining element of an originary concept of society'.[36] At the other, is the 'co-appearing' that is not 'appearing', 'or some other concept of becoming-visible'. The latter alone can retain the question of how to live in a condition with no guiding regime of sense.[37] This polar schema of evaluation of the political draws on the notion of the 'invisible' origin that becomes 'visible' and it shares therefore the conceptual vocabulary and concerns that we identified in Nancy's analysis of the

Image-Politics 151

image. I would now like to briefly consider the significance of this overlap. In my comments I will focus on the important role that the terminology of aesthetics has in Nancy's treatment of 'image-politics'. Aesthetics models the primacy that Nancy allocates to sensible forms for the experience of meaning. In the final section I will consider whether Nancy's tacit reliance on the vocabulary and concepts of aesthetics impairs the 'generality' of his ontology.

In a recent defence of May '68, Nancy describes the activism of this era as part of the post-War climate of a reinvention of democracy. His discussion of the events of May is important, since it allows him to consider a period in which what he calls the 'withdrawal of sense' was acutely felt. 'We were exiting', he writes:

> not only the time of 'conceptions', 'visions', or 'images' of the world (*Weltbilder*), but the general regime in which a vision understood as a theoretical paradigm implied the sketching out of certain horizons, the determination of goals [*visées*] and an operative fore-sight [*pré-vision*].[38]

This statement can usefully be considered in relation to his critical comments, in the context of his reflection on the topic of the image, that invocations of the 'unpresentable' are always 'on the verge of renewing' the motif of the visual imitation of the idea. In Nancy's view, references to the 'unpresentable' reinstate the theological motif of the 'identification of the model or the cause, even if it is a negative one'.[39] Taking into account this background, it seems that Nancy's reference above to an 'exit' from the 'time of "images" of the world' specifically intends to scrutinise how modes of 'identification' (what his work on the image describes as the 'imitation of ideas') have lost their coherence. Accordingly, appeals to them can be seen as ways of stifling the contemporary exigency for indeterminate and plural practices of being-with. In other words, modes of 'identification' are out of step with the contemporary uncovering of 'being' as 'being-with', which it is the purpose of ontology to think. As we saw in our earlier discussion of the status of the image in Christology, Nancy argues that the form-idea couple brings along with it the logic of identification with a model. For him, this logic suppresses the possibilities of the plural origins of sense that follow from the ontology of being as co-appearing. Instead such conceptions of the image contain sense to an intelligible model that is separated from sensible forms.

When Nancy refers to the absence of a figure or sensible presentation of the 'truth of the common'[40] he has in mind the conception of the 'origin' as 'irreducibly plural':

> If the origin is irreducibly plural, if it is the indefinitely unfolding and variously multiplied intimacy of the world, then *not gaining access to the origin takes on another meaning.* Its negativity is neither that of the abyss, nor of the forbidden, nor of the veiled or the concealed, nor of the secret, nor that of the *unpresentable*.[41]

If the 'truth of the common' cannot be presented, then, in his view, this supports the plurality of practices of sense making; and it does so, because the meaning of its negativity *is* sense-making praxis. The unravelling of the coherence of the dualism between ideas and sensibility, as if an 'idea' could anchor 'sensibility', means, for Nancy, that the experience of intelligibility is a work in progress that, moreover, is made out of dynamic relations with material sources of sensibility. The point is native to aesthetic practices of meaning, but Nancy here extends its logic to 'democracy': 'Democratic politics renounces giving itself a figure' and in doing so 'it allows for a proliferation of figures'.[42] For Nancy this logic of the 'proliferation of figures' also tells us how the attributes of such politics can be met: 'the "common" ... can be sovereign only under a condition that distinguishes it from the sovereign assumption of the state and from any political configuration whatsoever'.[43] We can understand that the reference to 'democracy' is not a reference to a type of state or other kind of political configuration, but a practice of meaning, which does not regulate where and how meaning can be made.

In this context, Nancy's remarks regarding the renunciation of a politics of the figure must also be distinguished from those references to an image of community that is yet to be installed, and which would be carried by the figure of (the identification of) a negative image. For him, such a thinking of the common falls into the category of the referential ideality of the unpresentable. What is sought in the negative image is 'precisely the exalted and over-exalted mode of the *propriety of what is proper*, which persists and consists in the "somewhere" of a "nowhere" and in the "sometime" of a "no time", that is, in the *punctum aeternum* outside the world'.[44]

The aspiration to propriety is what Nancy intends the vocabulary of society as subject, or society as 'representation as subject' to indicate. He takes Rousseau's account of the festival of the people as a key example of this type of thinking of society in which authentic sociality is represented in a spectacle. For Nancy, Rousseau's very fusion of authentic sociality with representation in the image of the spectacle undoes the premise that 'authenticity' can be distinguished from illusory sociality, and leaves him instead with the less weighty distinction between a good and bad spectacle. Further, the coming to presence of society in this spectacle means that the togetherness of the people needs to be defined in terms of 'acts' rather than an 'essence', of being-in-common rather than a given 'togetherness'. Rousseau shows that 'we are' the staging of ourselves as exposed-to rather than bearing a predetermined meaning. Nancy shows that Rousseau's thinking of community on a model of propriety is self-deconstructive with respect to his use of the onto-theological model of the image-idea.[45]

Nancy's critical treatment of Rousseau has general applicability for political theory. Nancy identifies the reliance on the distinction between the false and true image, and the false (illusory) and true (authentic) spectacle in classical and modern political theory (Plato and Rousseau), and in recent projects of social criticism (de Bord's Situationism). Nancy uses these case studies for two different purposes. First, he wants to show how deeply political thinking invests in the presuppositions of the ontology of the image as the sensible form of intelligible ideas. Second, he wants to show that such approaches to politics miss the implications that follow from a rigorous analysis of this traditional ontology. In each case these approaches to politics can be shown to presuppose the precepts of Nancy's ontology. The unacknowledged presupposition is that the 'exteriority' of the image *is* in fact the 'interiority' of the idea. Accordingly, the aspiration for a distinction between the false and true image, is shown to be the mere split between the reversible designations of the 'bad' and 'good' image:

(For the Situationists, then, a certain idea of 'art' almost always plays the role of the good spectacle, and it is no accident that the [bad] 'spectacle' for them is first and foremost the falsification of art.) In the bad spectacle, the social being imagines [*se représente*] the exteriority of interests and appetites, of egotistic passions and the false glory of ostentation. At the most basic level, this Manichean division not only supposes a distinction between the represented objects, but it also supposes an opposition within the status of the representation: it is what is now in interiority (as manifestation, expression of the proper), now in exteriority (as image, reproduction). As such, *the fact that these are intertwined is ignored:* there is no 'expression' that is not [already] given in an 'image', no 'presentation' not already given in 'representation'; there is no 'presence' that is not presence to one another.[46]

In this passage, he emphasises, against the Situationists, that the exteriority of the visible 'image' *is* already the expression of invisible 'interiority'. Nancy's discussion of other conceptions of the 'good spectacle', such as Rousseau's festival, emphasise the theological logic of an invisible core that drives a visible presentation: in the good spectacle, 'the social or communitarian being presents its proper interiority to itself, its origin *(which is itself invisible)*, the foundation of its rights, the life of its body, and the splendour of its fulfilment'.[47] In these conceptions:

It must be said that 'intelligible reality' can only be the reality of *the sensible* as such – and that the 'intelligible reality' of the community can only be the reality *of being-in-common* as such. This is why reduction to or subsumption in intelligibility (Idea, Concept, Subject) regularly comes into tension with *its own* requirement that it provide an intelligibility of the sensible that occurs within sensibility, for it and right at [*à meme*] it; this is often so forceful an opposition that it leads to a rupture, where sensible intelligibility either breaks apart or dissolves itself altogether.[48]

In this ontological treatment of 'being-in-common' in political theory, it is again striking how much Nancy's thinking of the image relies on the grammar of philosophical aesthetics and its distinctive way of re-conceiving the arrangement of 'sensible intelligibility'. Just as the distinction between intelligible reality and the sensible is a distinction that is undone through the logic of the trace of the sensible, so too the insistence on such an opposition, as in the Kantian notion of beauty as the symbol of morality, can force it to 'break . . . apart or dissolve . . . itself altogether'. As we saw, this occurs in Kant because it is the experience of the flower that puts the very idea of morality into meaningful 'relation', as an idea that can be experienced at all.

Nancy, as we have seen, wants to maintain that in the retreat of the political 'co-appearing' is not 'appearing', or some other

Image-Politics 155

concept that would be compatible with the logic of 'becoming-visible'. He argues that this insight entails shifting the presupposition 'of the whole politico-philosophical order, which is always an ontological presupposition'. Just as in the analysis of the image, so too in his treatment of politics, he insists that sense is made and not given, the locus of sense occurs 'at' the interstices of relations of exteriority rather than 'in' the interior plenitude of an 'idea'. The project of rethinking politics as 'co-appearing' focuses specifically on the logic of propriety in traditional dualism. He writes:

> Today, when thinking moves too quickly, when it is fearful and reactionary, it declares that the most commonly recognised forms of identification are indispensable and claim that the destinies proper to them are used up or perverted, whether it be: 'people', 'nation', 'church', or 'culture', not to mention the confused 'ethnicity' or the tortuous 'roots'. There is a whole panorama of membership and property, here, whose political and philosophical history has yet to be written: it is the history of the representation-of-self as the determining element of an originary concept of society.[49]

The conception of 'representation-of-self' is the logic of identity as model or cause. This logic underpins different regulating 'images' of community (whether this be ethnic belonging, membership of a nation, or the identity of a people). What changes in the age of the 'retreat' of the political and makes such images of community self-deconstructive is that there is no 'space' 'onto which a figure of community could be projected'. But this does not mean that there are no figures of community. Indeed, if we put to one side the pernicious way that claims to political membership work, and which Nancy's ontology intends to lay bare, it is still important to ask whether, 'being-together' 'can do without a figure and, as a result, without an identification'? As we saw, the ontological critique of the image culminates in its rehabilitation. So too, in the case of politics, Nancy argues that if we grasp 'the full extent of the withdrawal of . . . [the] figure and identity' of the 'figure of community', then it would be 'appropriate' to ask whether '"substance" consists only in its spacing'.[50] This comment is significant. As in the case of his treatment of the image, Nancy here opens up the idea that there is an exigency to figuration. His ontology implies that the 'figures' of 'being-together' will be those whose meaning does not reside in the 'representation-of-self', but in the exterior, plural practices of sense making.

4. The Aesthetic Context of Nancy's Ontology

Nancy's approach to image-politics is ontological: that is, it aims to think through the logic and presuppositions of the 'political', rather than advance a 'politics' of its own. On the other hand, Nancy's relational ontology of 'being-with' attempts to describe existence as it is; in doing so, he not only uses 'co-appearing' as the measure for his critical approach to the tradition, but also draws on it to provide a positive conception of the conditions under which relational being can flourish. What Nancy can't do is draw any imperative connection from the former description of how things are, to the latter dimension of what we should do. The connections, as we saw above, are implied. Were the connections any stronger, Nancy's ontology would lose its claim to account for the presuppositions underpinning different practices of being-with. The generality of the ontology is fundamental to its claim to treat the variety of practices of being-with. In the way he rehabilitates the ontology of the image and uses this topic to lay bare the situation of being-with that underpins the 'retreat of the political', Nancy must see himself to be privy to an insight that has hitherto been obscured from the philosophical tradition. What resources does he draw on to found this insight? And do they compromise the 'generality' of his ontology?

On his account, the resources of the philosophical tradition alone are insufficient to raise the full dimensions of the question of 'being-with', or to overturn the presuppositions of this tradition. It is capital, he claims, that raises this question in a comprehensive and inescapable way. If we look closely at the way Nancy stages the implications of his ontology it seems to me that neither of the frameworks he puts forward – that is, neither the self-deconstructive presuppositions of the philosophical tradition nor the market operations of capital – really capture the motives and form his ontology takes. We need, I think, to look carefully at the pivotal status of aesthetics for the articulation and defence of Nancy's ontology, in order to really gauge why the 'image' would even be a topic of importance for him. This topic, I have argued, also structures his approach to 'politics' and the ontology of 'being-with' in terms of the 'spectacle' (as in his treatments of

Rousseau and the Situationists). The presumed coherence of the position Nancy defends in each of these cases rests on the features it borrows from the aesthetic tradition, which he characterises as if they were general characteristics of 'being-with'. For instance, the idea that the 'origin' of democratic practice is not a 'figure', nor a 'negative figure' but the praxis of plural figures is not an insight into the history and institutions of democratic practices from the perspective of 'ontology' so much as it is an application of his account of what is distinctive about modern 'art' practice, once it is released from its pre-modern role in church and state patronage. The following question thus arises: what cogency is lent to his ontology of the image and his approach to image-politics of its aesthetic mode of articulation? Two examples can briefly indicate the stakes and pertinence of this question.

First, in his recent discussion of democracy Nancy argues that there is no 'truth of the common', no 'figure' of democracy, but that democracy still imposes a 'common space'. In this common space that is without a figure, democracy 'opens up the greatest possible proliferation of forms that the infinite can take, figures of our affirmations and declarations of our desires'. The case for this position is elucidated through reference to the proliferating practices of sense-making in the arts:

> What has been happening in art over the last fifty years demonstrates in a striking way just how real this exigency is. The more the democratic city renounces giving itself a figure, the more it abandons its symbols and its icons in a no doubt risky fashion, the more it witnesses the emergence of all possible aspirations towards new and unprecedented forms. Art turns every which way in an attempt to give birth to forms that it would wish to be in excess of all the forms of what is called 'art', and in excess of the very form or idea of 'art'.[51]

It is clear that the retreat of a governing 'idea' of art has historically freed 'art' for the exploration of new forms. Can the process of sense making in art be transferred to the sense-making practices of the 'democratic city'? In 'Being Singular Plural', both 'art' and 'democracy' are described by Nancy as significations whose meaning is waning. The question is: Does Nancy generalise the experience of sense making in the case of 'art' to characterise the possibilities of sense making in other fields? If so, is his description of the possibilities of the 'democratic city' really a description of art practice whose precepts are transferred, without appropriate qualification, to the city?

Second, the structure of market equivalency that characterises capital is derided by Nancy as a type of nihilism in which all sense of distinction is lost. He dispenses with the nihilistic vocabulary of 'equivalence' in favour of the singularities of the measure of the 'incommensurable'.[52] The ontological notion of dynamic singular plural access to sense is modelled on the experience of artworks in which sense is made each time in the singular circumstances of a particular work. Such 'sense' is not imprisoned in an isolated moment of sense perception, however. And here too, Nancy draws on the experience of sense that the sheer variety of practices associated with contemporary art support to expound on his claim regarding the deficiencies of 'equivalence' in market capital.

Like any exercise in 'first philosophy', Nancy's needs a vehicle of articulation. His characterisation of being as 'being-with' and sense as 'coming to presence' keeps politics separate from substantive accounts of 'being' and 'being-in-common' as an 'essence'. 'We do not have access to a thing or a state, but only to a coming. We have access to an access.'[53] The claim that his ontology describes the fundamental relatedness and dynamic mode of sense of being also implies that neither is it a cipher for 'ethics' or 'aesthetics', since it would fairly be said as 'first philosophy' to precede these regional fields of activity. However, it is the experience of art that provides the exemplary mode of truth as a 'coming to presence', rather than the essence of a 'thing' and it is aesthetics that uncovers the logic whereby the intelligible does not underpin the sensible but arises from contact with it. His 'first philosophy' thus generalises the categories of modern aesthetic discourse and the aesthetic attitude as this is cultivated in the modern experience of art.

His ontology can only describe the way it contends things are, and furthermore the mode of Nancy's description of how things are, relies on the exemplary, but restrictive model, of sense making practices in the arts. Nancy's 'general' ontology is developed from a regional ontology of the arts. This regional ontology determines the topics and approach he takes towards image-politics. Looked at critically, the intended gap between what the ontology describes and the imperative form of what we should do thus intervenes from another angle: the ontology is too regional for general applicability. In his concern to articulate the 'ontological' structure of 'being-with', Nancy lays bare the troubling presuppositions of the practice of such ontological inquiry: whether it is too 'general' or, as I have suggested, too 'regional', the characteristics that organise his ontology are in either case too distant from the institutional practices they purport to understand. The gap between 'ontology' and 'politics' that Nancy insists on can, in this way, be sharpened and reformulated: there is an inescapable limitation that conditions any 'ontological' analysis of 'politics'.

Notes

1. Jean-Luc Nancy, *Being Singular Plural* (Stanford: Stanford University Press, 2000), p. 2. I would like to thank Sanja Dejanovic for her comments on an earlier version of this chapter.
2. Ibid., p. 3.
3. Jean-Luc Nancy, *The Muses*, trans. P. Kamuf (Stanford: Stanford University Press, 1996), p. 92.
4. Ibid., p. 97.
5. Nancy, *Being Singular Plural*, p. 68.
6. Ibid., p. 57. I have treated some of the aspects of Nancy's discussion of the image in A. Ross, 'Jean-Luc Nancy: Der Sinn des Bildes', in Simone Neuber and Roman Veressov (eds), *Das Bild als Denkfigur* (Munich: Wilhelm Fink, 2010), pp. 315–30.
7. Jean-Luc Nancy, *The Sense of the World* (Minneapolis: University of Minnesota Press, 1997), p. 77.
8. Nancy, *The Sense of the World*, pp. 24, 77.
9. Jean-Luc Nancy, 'Philosophy without Conditions', in Peter Hallward (ed.), *Think Again: Alain Badiou and the Future of Philosophy* (London: Continuum, 2004), pp. 39–50, 45. In his recent work on the deconstruction of Christianity, Nancy considers the implications of Christianity for the articulation and presentation of this view of the 'end' of certain traditional regimes of meaning. Nancy is strongly influenced by Nietzsche's view that the significance of Christianity is that it marks its own 'end' in incarnating God in the image of man and sacrificing him. The end of Christianity is the staging of the death of God in man's, corporeal, 'image'. This deconstruction of the meaning of Christianity is best seen as an attempt to render its meaning differently, but to do so in such a way that the question of spiritual depth is not simply extinguished. Jean-Luc Nancy, *Dis-Enclosure: The Deconstruction of Christianity*, trans. B. Bergo, G. Malenfant and M. B.Smith (New York: Fordham University Press, 2008), p. 141.

10. Nancy, *The Sense of the World*, p. 129.
11. Nancy, *Dis-Enclosure*, p. 157.
12. Nancy, *The Sense of the World*, p. 146.
13. See, for instance, his discussion of Mary Magdalene and Christ in Jean-Luc Nancy, *Noli me tangere* (New York: Fordham University Press, 2008), pp. 37 and 61.
14. Nancy, *Being Singular Plural*, p. 72.
15. See Nancy, *Being Singular Plural*, p. 58. It is worth consulting Nancy's essay on the sublime in this connection. Here he talks about moral ideas in terms of an access to sense and an offering. Once again the material genesis of sense is emphasised: 'There is – in poetry at least – an *elevation* (that is, a sublime motion: Kant uses the verb, *erheben* here) to the "Ideas" which, even though it is an elevation, remains aesthetic, that is, sensible. Would one have to conclude from this that there could be another form or mode of sublime presentation in art, that of moral feeling, which would be distinct from the first mode? But in truth, it is in art and as art that the sublime offering happens. There is no opposition between an aesthetics of form and an ethical meta-aesthetics of the formless. The aesthetic always concerns form; the totality always concerns the formless. The sublime is their mutual offering. It is neither simply the formation nor formalisation of the formless nor the infinitisation of form (which are both philosophical procedures). It is how the limit offers itself to the border of the unlimited, or how the limit makes itself felt: exactly on the cutting edge of the figure the work of art cuts.' Jean-Luc Nancy, 'The Sublime Offering', in *Of the Sublime: Presence in Question*, trans. J. S. Librett (Albany: SUNY, 1993), pp. 25–55, 50.
16. The corollary of this perspective on meaning is that the social relations of capital cannot be adequately analysed when these relations are understood as a fall that happens to some authentic and primary subject or when the 'false' materiality of the capitalist market becomes the target of authentic critique. Nancy tries to think the image in line with his view that sense or meaning emerges out of contact with material forms, rather than belonging to things as an essential property or value. To put this in the language of his ontology, we might say that the image is not a container of meaning, but opens a relation of affectability to the senses, a series of circuits that charge meaning. Thus, his recent analyses of Christian paintings and the status of icons in the tradition of Christianity exploit the opening in meaning that characterises the inescapability of the question of meaning now that the finitude of meaning is in full view.

17. The genesis of sense is a praxis in so far as it is a working relation with materiality that is, in Heidegger's terms, attentive to the wonder 'that there is' being [*es gibt*]. I discuss Heidegger's 'Origin of the Work of Art' essay and the connections between Nancy and Heidegger in A. Ross, *The Aesthetic Paths of Philosophy: Presentation in Kant, Heidegger, Lacoue-Labarthe, and Nancy* (Stanford: Stanford University Press, 2007), pp. 95–9 and 138–42.
18. Jean-Luc Nancy, *Ground of the Image*, trans. J. Fort (New York: Fordham University Press, 2005), p. 21: 'what takes the thing out of its simple presence and brings it to pres-ence, to *praes-entia* to being-out-in-front-of-itself'. The French word '*fond*', used in the title and discussion of the collection *Au fond des images*, suggests 'bottom' as in depth, as well as the 'back' of a stage or room, and pictorial 'background', as in a painting, emphasises the role of the arts in articulating this position.
19. There are numerous passages in Nancy's work that may be cited to corroborate this position. Some of these passages I will cite later in the text. For recent formulations of this point, see Nancy's discussion of Origen in *Dis-Enclosure*, p. 157.
20. See Hans Blumenberg's discussion of the 'index' of ideas in Plato in Hans Blumenberg, *The Legitimacy of the Modern Age*, trans. R. M. Wallace (Cambridge, MA: MIT Press, 1993), pp. 71–2.
21. Nancy, *The Muses*, p. 89.
22. Ibid., p. 89.
23. Ibid., p. 92.
24. Cast this way, Nancy's position can be compared with Heidegger's commentary on Plato's *eidos* in his essay 'Plato's Doctrine of Truth', in *Pathmarks*, ed. William McNeill (Cambridge: Cambridge University Press, 1998); see especially p. 164.
25. Nancy, *The Muses*, p. 93. See, too, *Being Singular Plural*: 'It is necessary ... to understand the theme of the "image of God" and/or the "trace of God" not according to the logic of a secondary imitation, but according to this other logic where "God" is itself the singular appearance of the image or trace, or the disposition of its exposition: place as divine place, the divine as strictly *local*. As a consequence, this is no longer "divine", but is the dislocation and dis-position of the world (what Spinoza calls "the divine extension") as that opening and possibility [*ressource*] which comes from further away and goes further, infinitely further, than any god.' (Nancy, *Being Singular Plural*, p. 17.)
26. Nancy, *The Muses*, p. 96.

27. Ibid., p. 97; Nancy's emphasis.
28. Ibid., p. 97.
29. Nancy, *Being Singular Plural*, pp. 46–7.
30. Ibid., p. 63.
31. Ibid., p. 64.
32. 'To enter into ... thought is already to act. It is to be engaged in the praxis whereby what is produced is a transformed subject rather than a preformed product, an infinite subject rather than a finite object.' Jean-Luc Nancy, *The Truth of Democracy*, trans. P.-A. Brault and M. Naas (New York: Fordham University Press, 2010), p. 31.
33. Nancy, *The Truth of Democracy*, p. 26.
34. Nancy, *Being Singular Plural*, p. 64.
35. See Philippe Lacoue-Labarthe and Jean-Luc Nancy, *Retreating the Political*, ed. Simon Sparks (London and New York: Routledge, 1997).
36. Nancy, *Being Singular Plural*, p. 47.
37. Ibid., p. 68.
38. Nancy, *The Truth of Democracy*, p. 7.
39. Nancy, *The Muses*, p. 96. Nancy's emphasis. In *The Truth of Democracy*, Nancy writes: 'Democratic politics renounces giving itself a figure; it allows for a proliferation of figures – figures affirmed, invented, created, imagined, and so on. That is why the renunciation of Identification is not a pure asceticism and why it has nothing to do with courage or virtuous abstinence, both of which would continue to be thought on the basis of resignation or loss. Democratic politics opens the space for multiple identities and for their sharing (out), but it is not up to it to give itself a figure. That is what political courage today must learn to acknowledge' (pp. 26–7).
40. Nancy, *The Truth of Democracy*, p. 27.
41. Nancy, *Being Singular Plural*, p. 13; emphasis added.
42. Nancy, *The Truth of Democracy*, p. 26.
43. Ibid., p. 2.
44. Nancy, *Being Singular Plural*, p. 13. This comment is made in the context of his criticisms of the use of the 'capitalized "Other"' to designate the ethical relation.
45. Ibid., pp. 68–9.
46. Ibid., p. 68; emphasis added.
47. Ibid., p. 68; emphasis added.
48. Ibid., p. 55.
49. Ibid., p. 47.

50. All citations in this paragraph are from Nancy, *Being Singular Plural*, p. 47.
51. Nancy, *The Truth of Democracy*, p. 27.
52. Ibid., p. 50.
53. Nancy, *Being Singular Plural*, p. 14.

7

Immanent Surface: Art and the Demand for Signification
Jonathan Lahey Dronsfield

Question

There appear to be three ways in which art today is contemporary for Jean-Luc Nancy: conceptual non-identity with itself, being in tune with its own questioning, above all a political signification:

> 'The contemporary question may well be that of the conceptual nonidentity of art, which gives rise to (or manifests itself as) the difficult-to-identify identity of "art in general".'[1]
>
> 'The most manifest sense of this expression, "contemporary art", is to designate an art constantly in tune with its own debate, contemporary with its own questioning or its own suspension; in short, contemporary with this distancing from itself.'[2]
>
> 'The idea of art as directly, immediately, as such, political, is truly an entirely contemporary idea, it's an idea that is even remote from the idea of the engagement of the artist.'[3]

Nancy is in agreement with the first two; the third he disclaims. Art's conceptual non-identity is consonant with its self-questioning, for the question which art unfolds is the ontological one of what it is; a question which makes art different from itself in itself. According to this twofold conception, art is before anything else the exposition of the question 'What is art?' This is established in 'Art Today', the most recent of the above texts, a lecture at the Accademia di Brera in which is also discussed the third way in which art is contemporary – namely its being political. But that art be political is at odds with its being a question as to what it is. Art today, then, for Nancy, is riven by two basic but contradictory ideas: the 'contemporary idea' that art can and should be political, and the idea that art is contemporary in virtue of being a question as to what it is. While the first states that art is the production of political signification, the second implies that art goes beyond any signification whatsoever. 'Beyond signification' is the point of departure for Nancy's conception of art:

> without doubt art can be defined in no other way, in the first instance, than as a transgression and a being carried away beyond signs ... It exceeds signs but without revealing anything other than this excess, like an announcement, an indication, an omen – of groundless unity.[4]

The question of signification hinges on a distinction of sense, one which distinguishes between sense as signification, and sense as that which exceeds signification. Sense was once termed by Nancy our 'existential/transcendental condition' within which signification and non-signification is possible.[5] What he was after was a way of saying that we are not simply our immediate and present signification. It is clear from Nancy's work since that time that art is the realm which best demonstrates this. Art is our 'disengagement' from signification, our 'suspension' from it; it 'isolates what we call a "sense", or a part or feature of this sense ... so as to force it to be only what it is outside of signifying'.[6] Sense as signification is the presentation of signifiers whose signifieds are ordered, closed and knowable.

Sense beyond signification is the abandonment of the signifier and the forswearing of the appropriation of signifieds in favour of opening: opening the world to its sense, opening the world to its possibilities, opening sense to possibility. If an artwork knows its place in a pre-given network of signification it reinforces an order of signs; if it refers to a pre-constituted discourse it reduces to illustration. Art which presents itself as assessable in terms of political 'language' is one which forecloses art's disclosing and dis-enclosing the sense of the world as possibility, because it sees art as essentially a means of communicating a political message, ordered by an already-decided political discourse, or as a means to a political end, where at its basest art becomes a way of doing politics. Indeed, the 'usual' signification of art today is political.[7] But political art is possible only if art is assured of the continuity of movement from signifier to signified and the causal link between them. Such is the extent to which art today declares itself to be political, that an artwork which eschews any overt political signification 'appears suspect in being *only* aesthetic'.[8] Against this political conception of art, Nancy wishes to say that it is only in *not* being signification that art can open up the closure of political signification. In this sense, art opens up the possibility of world. If art opens on to possibility then it opens on to the world's political possibilities, the possibility of the political, the world as a political possibility, and the politics of the possible.

Economy

Part of what politics does, for Nancy, is to make an opening for a share of that which is without value, that which is not exchangeable or reducible to exchange – indeed, strictly speaking, that which is unshareable. But the sharing itself is not for politics to do. Politics brings about the conditions of access to it. But the sharing is carried out elsewhere than in politics; it is carried out by 'love, friendship or thought, knowledge or emotion' – or art.[9] To think that politics, democratic politics, can share out the unshareable can only lead to a disappointment with democracy. Instead, democracy is that which separates what is shareable from what is not shareable. Or, as Nancy has put it recently, democracy 'can only organize the *possibility* that a sense or a plurality of senses might commence in several ways (in art, in life, in and as bodies)'.[10] But in what way is it for art to 'share the unshareable'? It can only be in giving a sense of the unshareable. The unshareable is a sense of the world 'outside' of the world, but sensed within it, a sense beyond the world sensed inside the world. This is the sense that art can share, but not by making it sensible in the form of a signification. Signification cannot but reduce everything to the level of that which can be shared in the form of that which is exchangeable; it has no room for the unshareable; it is closed to it.

If art is to share the unshareable then it must do so without reducing itself to signification, and without allowing itself to be fixed in value according to an order of signification. It must in some way take a stance against the economy of signification. Then we might say it intervenes by introducing into political economy what we might call the an-economic, where the privative 'an' does not designate something that art lacks, but on the contrary a privation that it has, that is part of it, and that is constitutive of its sense. Art *has* non-signification. But if we appeal to this term, the an-economic, we must not forget that art is no less 'economic', no less exchangeable, than any other economic commodity; modernity has shown us that even the greatest works which are not determined by signification are an intrinsic part of the economy of art. But no good artist will allow the economy of art to determine his *praxis*. If art shares, along with thought, in the sharing of the unshareable, then it is because the task of both is not to allow the economic to dictate what is an- to economy, not to allow signification to be the arbiter of the an-economic, not to allow economy to signify what it is not. There is no signification of what is an- to economy; the an-economic is outside the economy of signification.

It is a fallacy to think that art which is explicitly 'political' in what it signifies – 'oppositional', 'revolutionary', etc. – is *therefore* outside or oppositional to the capital economy of art. On the contrary, the more signifying the artwork, the more secure and exchangeable is its place in that economy. For this reason it is not enough to claim for the artwork an 'antiaesthetic' for instance, since the 'anti' of antiaesthetic is no less a signification than the aesthetic. More so, because in signification resides opposition to the value of beauty. In the antiaesthetic the 'without why' of the beautiful – Angelus Silesius' 'The rose is without why, it blooms because it blooms'[11] – is displaced or superseded by the 'with why' of the political – 'Everything is political'. To say that 'everything is political' is to say one of two things: that art is not art unless its 'why', its reason, is political; or, the reason why art is of value is because it is political. Equally, if works which are 'beyond' signification circulate in the economy of art no less than those which signify, it is because the economy of art cannot master what is an-economic to it. If it could, then such works would be excluded from that economy by the economy itself – precisely by being given a signification determinant of their non-belonging, their being outside, 'beyond'.

When Nancy states that democracy is not figurable it is because the common space that it imposes, its space of the common, is in fact open – open to the proliferation of all possible forms that this 'beyond' signification might take.[12] This is precisely what art since the late 1950s demonstrates, for Nancy. He does not give examples, but we would have to include installation art which takes over the entire space of presentation of art such that we cannot say with surety where the art begins or ends, or early video art where the body is constitutive of the medium in which it is made, or forms of conceptual art which question the readability of text. The more that democracy 'renounces giving itself a figure' – or, in other words, the more its significations, its symbols and icons, are not reducible to one figure, or indeed its significations to symbols and icons – the more artists seek to produce forms which exceed or escape those of art and the idea of art hitherto. This is why democracy, according to Nancy, cannot take responsibility for these forms, for they exceed its space – we might say they space democracy – in the sense that they create hitherto unseen or unheard places, places not determined politically or by political discourse, where democracy can be played out as if for the first time; but neither can it not take responsibility for them, for they are its space, a space 'outside' it but internal to it. And this spacing is what separates democracy from politics. It is not for art to produce 'figures' of the political or to achieve political aims. Art is political if it assists in maintaining the separateness of the political sphere, and it can only do this by resisting the demands of the 'real' social world insofar as these are expressed as the need for signification. Art is political to the extent that it maintains a certain distance between itself and the world to which it nonetheless addresses itself and any political discourse readable in the present.

Those who charge artworks which cannot be said to be 'political' with being '*only* aesthetic' are those for whom 'everything is political'.[13] But the declaration 'everything is (or should be) political' is, for Nancy, totalitarian, in that every sphere of existence is politically absorbed or assumed by it. One of the consequences of this is that the specificity of the spheres in which such absorption does happen is lost. If there is no separate sphere of the political, then, for Nancy, there are no separate instances of communal existence. There is a suppression at work in the claim that 'everything is political', of the separateness of politics as a sphere of existence. Those who suppress the separateness of politics are 'often', for Nancy, those for whom democracy is not an end in itself, those for whom the overriding question is to what end democracy should be directed. If we agree with Nancy that politics in the form of democracy can be the end of art, then at the same time we must accept that this entails the end being not a closure but an opening, and therefore not politically determinate. And accepting this is to commit to it. Whatever the end might be for politics, it is necessarily incommensurable with the end of art as opening beyond signification. It may be that art aims for democracy as its *telos*, but were it to attain to that end democracy could not be allowed to become a limit to it. So if politics were the end of art it would come at the price of its non-closure and a separation from itself. But this separation, so troublesome for those for whom 'everything is political', is precisely what allows for a visibility, a specific point of view otherwise not granted to the political, of what the political might be. The political face-to-face with itself in the form of art at its end senses itself unable to grasp itself fully, and remains exposed to an end which is not its own – the 'political' work of art works against itself. This is anyway and always the case with art. The end of a work of art is non-coincident with any given meaning of it, and the end of a work of art is always at work beyond the work. Such, in my view, is how art in the form of its end stands as a lesson to politics.

Spectacle

One example, discussed by Nancy, of an art which purports to be 'political' in virtue of its signification, is that of the Situationists and their critique of the 'society of the spectacle'. The problem, for Nancy, is not the spectacle, but its being construed as either good or bad – the bad being the falsification of art, while 'a certain idea of "art"' can provide the good.[14] That 'certain idea' was, for Guy Debord, 'a movement of negation in pursuit of its own transcendence', where art would appear as part of the 'real' history until now covered over by the spectacle.[15] But such a negation cannot be achieved without counterpoising to 'false' appearances – signs of commodity and symbols of capitalist abundance – the signified of the 'real' hidden beneath them.[16] The intuition of situationism is correct for Nancy: a society which exposes itself to itself in the form of the spectacle has no horizon with which to make sense of being-with, thus leaving untouched the ontological presupposition of the common in what it is to be-in-common. But because the Situationists' intuition understands the spectacle simply as 'mere appearance' or 'false appearance', and authenticity as something hidden beneath or more originary than or opposed to appearance, their critique of alienation remains no less beholden to metaphysical signification than the spectacle. Sensible appearance, or rather the sensibility of exteriority, is disregarded in favour of a 'real' defined as the opposite of mere appearance, and hidden by it. Appearance is reduced to the 'same', and what it hides is made 'other'. An art that seeks to produce signifieds so as to oppose alienation in the name of a critique which remains beholden to an ontology of 'same/other' can only commit its own symmetrical alienation – in the case of the Situationists in the form of the signification 'genius artist', a supposedly originary 'creativity' 'hidden' by the 'mere appearance' of the spectacle. Such 'Romanticism' is egoistic, and remains shielded from the exteriority of the social and the contingency of the 'outside world' 'without which it is impossible to expose it *as ego*'.[17]

The point here is that the Situationist critique does not escape the economy of signification it seeks to negate. There is nothing an-economic to it. Situationism amounts to one more signification striving to replace another that it claims to be false. Even if it seeks to contest dominant politico-institutional norms of signification, it is not a suspension of, or a disengagement from, signification. What the Situationist critique is incapable of thinking, for Nancy, is man as something to be produced and created and made, rather than man as a given or a 'real' to be uncovered beneath his appearance or defined in terms of a more 'real' signification. It would be helpful here to turn to what I think is an important, but relatively undeveloped, notion in Nancy's work – that of *'poiepraxic* or *praxipoietic* thought'. It occurs when Nancy asks (in *The Sense of the World*) whether in Marx there is such a thing as non-alienated labour, and replies with an extraordinarily enfolded question:

> What does 'self-production' mean? Does it mean *poiesis, praxis*, or some other, un-heard of thing? Could it be that one has to surmount (?) the distinction and manage a *poiepraxic* or *praxipoietic* thought?[18]

Praxipoietic thought would overcome the distinction between *praxis* and *poiesis* by facilitating excess of sense, an-economising on sense, by not reducing or tying sense to signification, by resisting the demand, the political demand, for signification 'more real' or more historically efficacious. It would be a thought which is *neither praxis nor poiesis*, because to achieve it involves opening production to pleasure, the sensuous pleasure of touch.[19] We will shortly come to this. And what 'self-production' means, therefore, is the production of a self out of an excess to oneself – out of an excess to the significations with which we might 'ordinarily' normatively and politically make sense of ourselves, and be made sense of. But at the same time it is an excess which makes possible one's appropriation; precisely because of the indeterminacy of this excess, and therefore the indeterminacy of its value, it can be converted to exchange value. Here is the imperative for a renewed 'ontological' questioning of the economic that I began addressing above.[20] But what can be retrieved from the Situationists' critique is the affirmation of society '*as* exposed itself to itself and only to itself'.[21] It is the sensibility, rather than simply the intelligibility of this exposition of the social with respect to itself, that must be thought. Nancy shifts the question away from the appropriation of 'society' in appearance (the Situationists), and the opposite but complementary question regarding the essence of being in which the social does not figure (which would be Heidegger's question), to the matter of being-in-common and man's experience of the exteriority of that common without recourse to an interiority or a proper opposed to it. If we put it in terms of the everyday, then the task is to think the everyday of the social in such a way that its truth is neither divested of everydayness through hyper-signifying its proper as something 'hidden' by history (the Situationists), nor reduced to an insignificant 'everydayness' in favour of an authentic history of the people proper (Heidegger).[22] If art is to be critical, politically critical, it will need to accord with an ontology not of negation or of being, but of being-with, the common of a world taken to be a totality and a plurality, a singular plurality, where the 'with' of being-with is not divided by metaphysical oppositions of the sort 'same/other', 'appearance/real', but is singularised as that which plurality has in common.

World

Art provides the 'most telling examples' of what a world is. This is because a world, for Nancy, 'perhaps always, at least potentially, shares the unity proper to the work of art'.[23] As soon as I feel myself to be part of a world, I am already sharing in it. But this does not mean that whatever it is in which I share makes immediate sense or that it is common sense, at least not simply in the everyday sense in which we tend to use that phrase. Whatever the common means has in each case to be made and produced. This is why we must attend to the specific works in which a world is given. But can we say that there is a unity given by 'each one of the arts', by painting, video, installation art, and so on? Nancy appears to think so. He writes that 'each one of the arts exposes in its way the unity of "art"'.[24] But the 'one' of each one is not the same with each iteration of the medium; there is every time another unity given by the 'one' of each one of the arts, and by the one of each work within each one of the arts. It may be the case that 'the unity of a single art is ex-posed . . . only in its works one by one', but what is singular about each one of these arts is put into question by each work.[25] The one of each work must pose a question to each and every one of the 'single' arts, whether or not it is in or of any particular 'one' of those arts. If, as Nancy argues, it must be the case that each art, each style, each genre exposes the unity of a world, then they do so only on condition that no hierarchy pertains between them, such that no one work is 'in' or 'of' a single art – or that each single art is no less 'in' or 'of' each one work.

We must insist on this point given that the question we are raising here is that of signification and art's resistance to and excess over it. If, as Nancy maintains, there is no greater signification in art today than that of the political, then we must address the question of the medium in which that signification is made, not just because of the supposed determinate connection between mediums and specific senses (painting to seeing for example), which we examine below, but because mediums can be made to circulate in the political economy as an intrinsic way of commodifying artworks for the art market or objectifying them as 'cultural' capital – and we include in political economy those philosophical discourses about art ('aesthetics') which propound medium-specific distinctions. Is the signification 'painting' any the less forceful and vested with these interests today than it was in the 1950s and the era of medium specificity? Equally, those works which seek the 'disappearance' of their medium in the social, which we might say that situationism is an instance of, are they not just as subject to and objective of certain forceful vested interests, precisely for their politicised opposition to the former? We state, then, that each artwork divides and disperses any general signification we can give of the world which it shows, including the status, value, function and utility of the medium by which it shows it.

The unity of each work of art as world is an enclosed space, but one which, as Nancy puts it, dis-encloses its meaning. The unity of a work is not one which is fixed or final. All works point beyond themselves to that non-exchangeable value, that excess, that indeterminacy, that immateriality out of which the work materialises itself not for multiple interpretations, which will come, but for unheard unseen possibilities of senses of the world to come. This 'to come' is the sense that the unity of art lacks – lacks not as if it could be made good by the addition of something yet to be seen or heard (by, say, an interpretation), but a necessary senselessness, an an-economic sense, the lack of sense which is the very excess and irrecuperable feeling we experience, we sense, when confronted by art. For Nancy this lack satisfies a desire 'to give ourselves the sense or the feeling – together and each by himself – of an overflow of meaning ... to sense and to feel according to a truth that no meaning can saturate ... and that no unity can sublimate'.[26]

But this desire is not simply a desire to feel; it is a desire for a feeling quite determinate in its effect, 'a desire to experience oneself as irreducible to a signification'.[27] To be without signification, without fixed sign, is not to be ascribed an identity, a place, an intention, a meaning. A desire for none of these, or none fixed or final, is a desire detached from any specific objectification. Nancy understands it as 'the desire for the sense of desire itself'.[28] But the implications of such desire are political, for what it embodies is a rejection of the imposition of signification. A desire for sense over signification is the gathering and focusing of a force of resistance to any sense given in advance as something to be read off from the work or understood by it or communicated through it as the sign of something else. Yet the desire to experience oneself 'as irreducible to a signification' can at the same time be a desire nonetheless to signify. A desire not to be reduced to a signification may be a desire to signify indeterminately, to multi-signify or un-signify, or to be insignificant, or it may be a desire not to be reduced to a signification of one's 'own'. But to be 'irreducible to a signification' is not itself reducible to a-signification, to be 'irreducible to a signification' does not mean in each case being without signification. To make oneself out of an excess to signification can at the same time be to transform signification, to transgress or undo signification, or to dis-own signification, but none of these is possible without the force of a *felt* resistance to signification risking in turn a certain signification.

Moreover, why does Nancy construe such a desire as a 'silent protest',[29] a kind of reduction to silence? Silence is not the beyond of signification. Silence is as much a signification as is noise. The protest may be against the imposition of a 'last word', but the absence of a last or final word is not silence. The protest may be against the assigned signification of silence. Or if the protest is silent then it is neither the absence of words, nor what follows after 'last word'; silence is itself made up of words, and as well is constitutive of them. Artists write silences, they compose silences, they reveal silences – in words they disclose silences between words – in words silences rhythm the work of words through the way artists space them. A desire for a feeling beyond signification is not the desire for silence without word, it is a desire for the feeling of how words themselves, or noise or silence, can undo the fixity of signification, can disperse the meaning of signs, can open up, from within the unity of a work, the possibility of world.

Gesture

'... and Babel is unified at last by gestures'[30]

Works which are political through their signification can be saved from themselves, and saved for art, through their artistic gesture. In the aforementioned 'Art Today', Nancy gives the example of just such a piece, by Sylvie Blocher.[31] All artworks – and this goes as much for an overtly political work as for one in which it is difficult to discern any signification at all – consist of an artistic gesture. It is what remains beyond any signification, a sign without signification. A gesture is the 'sensible sense' of an intention, but which cannot be reduced to that intention. It may accompany the intention, but at the same time lend a sense to that intention at odds with it, because the gesture has a sensibility which is not one of signification. More than that, the gesture cannot be understood in terms of reason at all. If the gesture gives a sign it is one which signals rather than signifies – a wink in the Heideggerian sense.[32] What it signals is not some meaning of the gesture but a beyond of it, beyond a reason for it, beyond an intention for it, a beyond in which is to be found only possibilities. This is art's dis-enclosure: 'Although there are closures in art, as in politics, the principle of art as a gesture in itself, if you like, in its own work, is that it is in dis-enclosure: it doesn't close, it opens.'[33]

A work is a work not because it closes in on itself, but because it opens out beyond itself to a possibility, even if at the same time it alone has glimpsed this possibility. A work of art is not for itself, in its gesture it sees beyond itself as an enclosed thing to the possibility of world that it disencloses, beyond any 'end', finality or closure to which the work may wish to be put by artist, by critic, or by philosophy. Art is always in a state of dis-enclosure because it is always to a greater or lesser extent gesture.

Not only does the artistic gesture point beyond signification, it serves to separate the signification from the artwork's form. It is a gesture of 'form for its own sake, the liberation of a form in its own right'.[34] The gesture of form 'in itself' is the artwork's outside, but not, *pace* Nancy, a 'pure' outside. The artwork in its 'own right' is not some interiority closed off from what lies outside of it, it is art's outside inasmuch as the work is dis-enclosed from itself to an outside that no signification can determine. Art's outside is the chance afforded it to form possibilities which may even oppose any meaning it might be claimed to signify. This 'own right' of art gives nothing back to art, nothing is owed the work because the work could not 'state' such a right without signification, and without staking its right in the form of reason. The work has already dis-owned whatever might come of it by separating signification from form through its gesture as art. This is the seriousness of the fact that any one artwork can give rise to multiple 'interpretations', none of which, including the artist's own and those of any constituency in whose 'voice' or 'interest' or 'desired outcome' the artist speaks or is made to speak, can claim sovereignty over others. The stronger the artistic gesture, the more work we must do to understand it. Standing outside of that which it seems to accompany, the gesture receives a sensibility foreign to what it would otherwise assume in the world to which the artwork addresses itself. Artists take the gesture back to a point prior to which it appears natural, to somewhere before it becomes fixed in the oppositions natural/constructed, and action/product. In this way the gestures of the artist appear as signals for a language beyond signification.

Touch

There is a 'limit' gesture, and it is touch. To touch is to be 'at the limit', touching is '*being at* the limit'.[35] Touch is at the limit because at the very moment one touches something, one feels oneself touched by touch. Touch only touches because it is touched by what it touches. This makes it for Nancy the 'proper moment of sensuous exteriority'.[36] We will of course hesitate at this 'proper'. Exteriority is presented 'as such', and yet as sensuous, something sensed somewhere, at some location. Sensuousness is essential for touch, yet is what divides touch from any 'as such', divides touch from itself. We agree with Derrida: there is no proper touch, strictly speaking; it is lost 'at the proper moment of touching upon it'.[37] And this constitutes an interruption. There is no proper touch without its interruption. Touch is touched by what it touches. And in touching, touch feels itself (touches itself) touching. When one touches (anything) one at the same time self-touches. When one touches (something outside) at that moment one touches touching (from the inside). Touching is interrupted in itself, while the one touching is dis-located. Inherent to touch is the interruption of touch, because intrinsic to touch is self-touching. This is what it is to *be* at the limit, to touch the limit of oneself, and at the same time – but a time spaced – be touched by a limit. The self-touching given in touch is the immanence of touch – yet for which an outside is necessary. The interruption of immanence is the transcendence of touch, but transcendence happens nowhere else than where immanence forces it to.

Nancy finds with art the most productive way of thinking the relation between immanence and transcendence, because artworks in their way are the limit of the gesture of touch. There is a movement in art, for Nancy, akin to that in touch. By their gestures artworks touch us. It is in the singular touch of this particular artwork – 'the singular difference of a *touch* and a zone of touch' – that the sense of world, or in other words the sense of something unified and whole, is given, but not something to which significations in the form of generalities could be ascribed or prior significations provided.[38] Art is the most productive way of thinking the relation between immanence and transcendence because artworks do not reduce that relation to the fixity of an opposition, and they do not resolve its difficulty in dialectic. Indeed, such is the 'originary' sense given by the touch of art, that there is a 'trace' of art every time the 'dialectical complicity' of immanence and transcendence (for instance, in the form of ecstasy) is interrupted. The touch of art would precede the sense of 'self' given by the experience of such complicity.[39] Artworks think transcendence from within immanence, from within nowhere but that work, there. Yet they do so by transcending any specific signification the work might bear. It is as if an artwork's immanence is divided by the transcendence of its exteriority, but at that moment both transcendence and immanence lose their sense. Neither term is sufficient to account for the work of art, neither can be grasped 'as such'. The finite existence that is each artwork is not possible without the simultaneous yet spaced coming into play and withdrawal of immanence and transcendence.

Art touches us, touches itself, touches the sense of touch itself, and sends us to a beyond of signification. Artworks are gestures touching us from a there where they are, in the right-here where we are, to an out-there beyond signification. In this way do artworks through their touch spatialise the world for us – make it discontinuous, interrupt the continuity of its present and disrupt the 'flow' of its signification. Nothing would ever take place were the world purely continuous and fully present to itself. Taking his point of departure from Heidegger – 'Der Raum räumt', space spaces – Nancy argues that artworks are the taking place of world in space.[40] The world is not simply external to art; the world is not simply an exteriority to art's interiority. In creating a world, art brings us face-to-face with the world, but not as if the work were separate from the world. The exteriority of the world is inside the work of art, and the exteriority of the artwork is inside the world. Art exteriorises the world, displaces it as if we are outside of it, or dislocates us to another place inside the world, away from the 'common sense' of the world. Art exposes us to world – and exposes the world as world – from the inside of art, right-here, to an out-there, beyond or outside signification. This sense of the world can only be given by disrupting the world's sense and interrupting our senses, the world's sense in the form of its general significations and its common sense, and our senses in their ordering and function.

But at this point we are obliged to interrupt this discourse of interruption, to consider a disruptive intervention of Derrida's: that we cannot do away with 'the continuistic and immanentist postulation' challenged by Nancy.[41] 'It can also happen, it can moreover *always* happen – we have to insist on it – that the intuitionistic-continuistic logic of immediacy shows itself to be as irrepressible as desire itself.'[42] Derrida's point here is that we can never do away with the logic of immediacy, even if experience tells us that immediacy 'itself' nowhere happens. And this goes as much for Nancy's writings on touch and the sharing of sense as it does for the 'haptical' discourses they seek to break from, or at least distance themselves from. It is a logic the symptoms of which show themselves in Nancy's texts as elsewhere. Without this logic we would forever be assured of the opposite of the 'continuistic' postulation: and where do we find a figure that would embody such an absolute separateness? If artworks proffer figures of separateness, what separates them is given through the artwork's touch.

Were there no logic of immediacy there would be no problematic of touch in the first place. But I think that this is why art takes on such importance for Nancy. It reveals the presence of touch elsewhere than the world so present unto us that we cannot touch it. Because the experience of artworks is so often one of displacement and deferment, and at the same time one in which we find our senses addressed, the sense of immediacy given is spaced. Were it not for art we would not *sense* the problematic of touch, it would be covered over by the immediacy of the world.

Zones

Artworks are zones of many senses, where the distinctions between them are blurred and where touch traverses all of them. This is partly why each artwork is a singular plural, and why no one 'type' or 'medium' of art is reducible to any one sense. Nancy argues in a paragraph absent from the first English presentation of 'Why Are There Several Arts And Not Just One?'[43] that in any act of sensing, 'there are other zones of sensing, overlooked by the zone that is sensing at this moment, or else on which this zone touches on all sides but only at the limit where it ceases being the zone that it is'.[44]

Thus begins the 'long detour' glimpsed in 'Laughter, Presence', on Baudelaire's 'The Desire to Paint':[45] 'What of the sharing of the senses?'.[46] Either a sense senses, but cannot sense the other senses – 'sight does not see sound and does not hear it' – or it senses the other senses but is no longer its own sense – '[sight] touches on this nonseeing and is touched by it'.[47] Sight touches other senses, and is touched by its own non-seeing of those other senses. Sight is interrupted in its seeing by its not being able to see the other senses it touches and which touch it. But it is precisely this interrupted sensing and spacing of sensing, and the co-touching and co-responding of senses one to the other, which give the touching of any one thing and the world in which it is given, the world in which it is, there, in this world, here. There would be no experience of the discreteness of the world without it. Any sensing of the world by the senses, any *aesthesis*, gains its unity in this heterogeneity of the senses. The very principle of touch is heterogeneous. The heterogeneity of the senses forms one body sensing. Nancy calls this heterogeneity the *corpus*. In touch all five senses are touched, and in any one of the (other) senses the body is touched.

In touching there are other zones of touching felt. This is both the dislocation of sense and an opening for another sense, and it is not difficult to see it as the possibility of other signification, or signifying otherwise. By this I mean that each sense is not in control of its sensing, and each corpus of senses is not master of its senses or the principle of their order (this is where Nancy's corpus, a body of nothing but sense organs, comes close to Deleuze's body without organs, for which art is also the most exemplary of examples).

If each sense can touch upon and be touched by another, then the co-interruption of the senses can give rise to possibilities of signification where what is meant by that which offers itself to be sensed is disordered in the sensing. A colour can be disorganised in the sensing of it such that it can disorder re-order and put out of order both the body sensing and the sense of the world. Think of the colour red in Barnett Newman's *Vir Heroicus Sublimis*, the colour red in Jean-Luc Godard's *La Chinoise*, the colour red in Anne Carson's *Autobiography of Red,* the colour red in Orhan Pamuk's *My Name is Red*.[48] In each of these singular works, the sight of the colour red is interrupted by its being sensed otherwise, and the act of seeing it is shown to be co-constituted by senses other than that of seeing. The world presented by each of these works is one in which the colour red is rhythmed, resonanced and given significations until then unheard. It is the interruption of each sense by the other senses which gives rise to this possibility. In these artworks what we mean by possibility is transformed. 'Red' in these works cannot be reduced to an interpretation of it; nor can appeal be made to the purity or the 'as such' of the colour. In other words we are moved beyond any signification given by the world from which and at the very moment at which the colour red is drawn; and the mediums of painting, film, poetry and fiction are displaced from the senses normatively associated with them.

Transimmanence

There is no pure immanence – from sense to sense. And no pure transcendence – from a sign to the beyond of what it signifies. We must not understand the intervals in the continuity of sense as something brought to bear on the world simply from the outside, and we must not construe the interruptions of signification as occurrences simply in the world. Sense is neither an elsewhere than this world, nor a predicate of world, but 'the constitutive "signifyingness" or "significance" of the world itself. That is, the constitutive *sense* of the fact that there is world'.[49] The sense of this 'there is' is what artworks help make explicit. Artworks are the site at which is shown the transcendence of the world's immanence, and the immanence of the world's transcendence. The sense of both must be suspended. Again we see that the concepts of immanence and transcendence do not seem adequate to the task of naming the relation between them – precisely because of the plural movement of their singular relation. How not to immanentise transcendence, but to 'inscribe' transcendence '*along the edge of immanence*', at once both a concession to the insufficiency of the concepts, and an imagising of the relation between them?[50] Nancy notes that this is 'the greatest difficulty':

> Quite simply, that the sense of the world is this world here as the place of existence. This 'quite simply' contains the most formidable stake, the one that requires of us, in order to say this absolutely simple thing, a completely different style or, rather, an interminable alteration of style.[51]

Yet Nancy names the relation, this sense of the world, this 'absolutely simple' (not italicised) thing, *transimmanence*. We should not be surprised to find that he will later come to see the inaptness of doing so. Nancy has recently admitted that this neologism, which he says is a paleonym in the Derridian sense, 'lacks the intuitive form for the linguistic sentiment', and he has ceased using it.[52] The inaptness of the neologism is its not having been taken up by the world it names, its sense not enough of the world in order to be moved by it. But when from the mid-1990s on he began devoting much of his writing to the philosophy of art, the term transimmanence struck Nancy as especially apt for the sense of the world formed by the work of art. Indeed, art is the decisive turning twisting spiralling in and of the transcendence/immanence couple, to the extent that transimmanence 'takes place' as art:

> One might say: [art] touches on the immanence and the transcendence of touch. Or in still other terms: it touches on the transimmanence of being-in-the-world. Art does not deal with the 'world' understood as simple exteriority, milieu, or nature. It deals with being-in-the-world in its very springing forth.[53]

Art is the transcendence of immanence as such, the transcendence of an immanence that does not go outside itself in transcending, which is not ex-static but ek-sistant. A 'transimmanence'. Art exposes this. Once again, it does not 'represent' this. Art is its ex-position.[54]

> It is only possible to bring this work [of art] into the medium of sense, first of all into the medium of an eventual 'sense of art' as such (and of a 'sense' of the word 'art'), by interrupting the hold of the discourse (in conformity with the law of touch) through this 'hermeticism' whereby the work touches only itself, or is to itself its own transimmanence. And this is not valid only for the work of an artist, for a style, for a genre, for each of the arts and for new 'arts' to come: it is valid for the singular plural of the essence of the arts.[55]

I cite these instances of Nancy's use of the term transimmanence to emphasise its intimate proximity to art. Does the fact that Nancy later stops using the term indicate a rescinding of the importance of art in staging and revealing the displacement of signification? This is not the case. Throughout Nancy's writings on art what we might call 'the transimmanence problem' does not go away; on the contrary it impinges all the time, and his writings constantly attempt to deal with it, even if they no longer name it. Instead, Nancy seeks ways of articulating transcendence and immanence spatially, together in their separation, apart and a part. There is no letting up on the stress placed on art as the space in which the coupling and de-coupling of these terms is played out. It is a space in which any sense of the purity of either immanence or transcendence withdraws, where neither can be seen to be in opposition to the other, where one can take place in the other, and where no possibility of dialectic between them exists. That space is a surface; one of the other names for the transimmanence problem is surface.

Surface

'Surface' is how the world happens. It is the event of the 'there is' of world, a *purus actus* happening everywhere, where everywhere is surface: 'the surface of the world as the most immediate taking-place of this world, its "continued creation": an immediacy such that it right away spurts outside of itself, completely turned inside out into the exterior manifestation of forms'.[56]

If the exteriorisation of 'there is' world is nothing but the forms the world takes, then there can be nothing between the world's forms other than surface. The inside of art too is nothing but surface. The 'ontological content' of the artwork is, as Nancy puts it, 'sur-face'.[57] Art's surface is the exposure of an inside to an endless outside, endless because there is no limit to finitude. This exposure entails an interval between the surface and possibility. Art's opening to the world is spaced by this interval. The practice of art is making 'possibility' for the world by interrupting the surface of the world with other forms, interrupting surface through sur-facing. Part of the difficulty here is in making sense of ground and surface as a distinction transformed by rethinking surface. 'Bring the ground forward as if it were surface',[58] 'in coming to the surface, everything has passed through the ground',[59] 'what is to be seen is entirely in the ground and entirely at the surface'.[60] If there is nothing but surface, then what distinguishes surface from superficiality is that whatever is gathered to the surface is grounded, but grounded in the surface, and grounded as the surface. Ground as ground withdraws – or rather there never was ground – or better still 'there is' ground nowhere than at the world's surface. Hence the affirmation: 'the world, moreover, is but surfaces on surfaces'.[61]

One could see the entire history of art as the bringing to the surface this matter of the world being 'but surfaces on surfaces'. The surface of an artwork is not the surface of something which has a 'beneath', nor is it the top of a depth; there is nothing under the surface of art. Whatever can be said to be 'beneath', 'depth', 'under' is all part of the surface of a work. The surface is where all of these linear dimensions or measured spaces emerge into and arise out of; the surface is their gathering into a 'where' they can be sensed. It is where all that is immanent to the work is made available for sensing, where what is immanent does not appear from somewhere other than surface, and where whatever might be transcendent about the work does not go elsewhere.[62] Whatever the work conceives comes out of its surface – the two are self-same.[63] Immanence is brought to the surface in art, puts itself on display there.[64] One or more than one of the world's 'multiple immanences' are spread over its surface.[65] If the work of art is a surface where immanence touches transcendence, it is not to face a beyond of the world, but to sur-face a possibility in it; not to promise some other world or 'other-worldly' world, but to bring immanence into proximity with what is beyond signification. Such is what we name here art's *immanent surface*.

'The'

Nancy writes that 'art in general cannot not *touch*, in all the senses of the word',[66] and that the 'concern' of '"art" in general' is that there is no art that is not the art of a clear touch on the obscure threshold of sense'.[67] In other words, that all arts touch is what is 'general' about art. Yet, 'there is no "art" in general'. Why? Precisely because all arts touch each other, and in so doing affirm the limits of each art, and become the threshold of the other. If all art touches and cannot not touch, then there is no specific art of touching properly speaking. There is no 'the' art at all. This is one of Nancy's typical gestures according to Derrida: 'there is no "the"'.[68] And it applies to touching. There is no 'the' touch, no touch 'in general'. Touch is what interrupts all sense. And all touch is shared across the senses and between the touching and the touched. As soon as there is sharing of touch there is no longer any definitely articled touch, no 'the touch'. Each touch is singular, and the singularity of each touch is plural. If there is no the 'to touch' and no 'the' to touch how could there be any 'the' of anything, given the primacy and originarity of touch for Nancy? But that there is no 'the touch' does not mean a return to what might be supposed to threaten such discourse here, namely (as Derrida puts it) 'the most irresponsible empiricism'.[69] For without the 'the' there is no empiricism to speak of, no 'the' empiricism in the sense of a theory of it, and no isolated untouched instances of touching to which it would want to point. The deconstructive gesture of 'there is no "the"' accounts for the sharing of touch by attending to the act of touching (and pointing), the sense of touching, and the way that touching spaces the sense of anything, including all and any 'the's'.[70]

There is no 'art in general'. But this does not stop Nancy facing art in general with *its* responsibility, and he uses the example of a certain touch in doing so, the touch of physical violence, the touch of a blow. Art's violence is not that of a real blow, but not because it is a mere semblance of a blow, but because, on the contrary, it touches the real and the real has no ground, whereas a blow is its own ground. A real blow is not simply violent; its violence is that its effect is indissociable from its signification, in that there is no interval between its sign and what it signifies. In this sense a physical blow is both its own sign, and as if that sign were a pure sign. And at the same time a blow collapses the distinction between signification and sense, it reduces signification to the sense of pure physicality. It is the responsibility of art to discern the one from the other: in terms of, say, images of political violence, to discern a groundless image from an image which is nothing but a blow; in terms of 'art in general', to discern a groundless touching of the real from the 'nothing but ground', which in this case would be the 'nothing but blow', of over-determined political signification.[71] But art must distinguish in this way without appeal to ground. This is impossible for political art made political through its signification. The touch of art is precisely that 'there is' ground nowhere than at the surface. The blow that art strikes is against the demand that its blow be real, that it have direct, immediate and readable political impact in the 'given' social world, a world 'given' in advance of art by its significations and their order and fixity in the social and political realms. This is the demand for signification as such, in the form of a figure grounded on an unquestioned surface/ground distinction; and whether that figure be taking the blows or dispensing them he would be insensible to the fact that at the level of the real there is no difference. Against this, the task of art seeking to touch on real political situations is how to do so without taking one's stance on the ground which would make sense of that situation simply through political signification.

Question

If art goes beyond any signification it follows that art which signifies the political must entail the forgetting of the question of what art is. If art involves an essential questioning, then art which declares itself to be political claims an identity to itself through what it is not; an identity gained at the expense of what art is. In becoming political, art gives up the questioning which, in suspending it from itself, would bring about the separation necessary for exposing it to the matter of its own identity. In giving up this questioning art loses the means by which to see its internal difference to itself – and thereby the space in which to open the possibility of the political – a difference which exceeds any signification it might bear.

If touch is the limit of gesture and the gesture of art the limit of touch, then in an important sense the problematic of touch cannot go beyond art, art becomes the limit of touch. Yet this is intolerable for political art. Political art seeks its end in the political, it is nothing if it does not touch the political, and its touch must be real. Whereas for Nancy art attains itself, its end as possibility, in the retreat of the political and in the withdrawal of the ground of signification on which to distinguish the real, and that end is an opening in which signification is not determinate. It is not that we cannot touch art (although it is bad enough that it is forbidden to touch what we see in the gallery and museum, on stage and screen), it is that we cannot negate 'untouchable' art in favour of art with a real blow; this is what political artists cannot bear. It is why so many strive for the 'disappearance' of the work into the social, why the 'anti-aesthetic' aimed for the negation of the artwork as object, and why the Situationists saw in art the means to reveal a 'real' and newly historicised signification. Against which we say that we are only exposed face-to-face with the problem of political art when touch is no longer able to grasp fully, and therefore to cover over with its hand, the problematic of touch precisely through its insistence on touch, on presence, on the presence of touch in the form of the determinate impact of a real blow.

Alain Badiou believes Nancy to be seeking 'another figure for the labor of thought that is politics'. Perhaps this is indeed what Nancy sets out to achieve. But he does not do so by passing, as Badiou maintains, 'from the poem into prose' or by conceiving 'the poem itself as prose'. Nancy does not leave *poiesis* behind. Rather, he spatialises his prose with it. Neither *praxis* nor *poiesis*, Nancy's *praxipoiesis* is a labour of thought en-joying its interruption by *poiesis*. For Badiou, the unfortunate consequence of what he calls Nancy's 'de-sublimation' of politics is that it 'remains by and large prophetic'.[72] However, I would argue that Nancy's *praxipoietic* thought, his *poietic praxis* of thought, is not at all prophetic, it is indeterminate. It foreswears *pre*-figuring any determinate outcome in the form of a signification we can hold before ourselves as a desired political outcome. It foreswears the determinate reality of a blow, the over-determined political signification of a strike, in favour of a more originary touch. If a figure should emerge it will do so through a labour of thinking which does not carry with it the pre-given already decided meaning of this or that signification, and which disarms itself in advance of the force of political signification, and which risks its appropriation by the forces to which it might otherwise be opposed. And if it is to be a figure of a philosophical labour of thought it will be one which both opens itself to the touch of art, and is opened by, made possible by, the touch of art.

The work of Nancy puts into practice the question of touch, and it does so by not simply philosophising about it but by producing philosophy out of the way in which art touches it. Nancy is one of the few philosophers today prepared to let art touch his philosophy by philosophising right at artworks contemporary with his practice as a philosopher. His work rhythms itself with art, and by 'with' I mean for and against, in and out, to the extent that art is one of the syncopations by which it breathes. Nancy knows that it is not for philosophy to answer the question of what art is; its task rather is to assist art in unfolding the question of what it is.[73] Art is separated from itself by the question that it is. One modality of this is played out through the movement of its touch. By sharing in the problematic of touch, touching artworks right there in their intimate disassociation from themselves, philosophy commits to its co-appearing with art. Or in other words, philosophy takes responsibility for the fact that it cannot answer the question of what it, philosophy, is – not without the assistance of art. I would go so far as to say that this is an important way in which Nancy's philosophy can be experienced politically, for it requires thinking the limits of philosophy 'outside' of philosophy. If art today is political, it is because it is creating spaces for the political in the wake of the retreat of the political. Art today can only create such spaces by going beyond signification. If philosophy is to have political import, then it needs to follow Nancy's lead and assist art in this going beyond, only then will philosophy become contemporary with itself.

Notes

1. Jean-Luc Nancy, *The Muses*, trans. P. Kamuf (Stanford: Stanford University Press, [1994] 1996), p. 101, n.1.
2. Jean-Luc Nancy, *Philosophical Chronicles*, trans. F. Manjali (New York: Fordham University Press, [2004] 2008), p. 59.
3. Jean-Luc Nancy, 'Art Today', trans. C. Mandell, *Journal of Visual Culture*, 9:1, [2006] 2010, pp. 95–6.
4. Jean-Luc Nancy, *The Ground of the Image*, trans. J. Fort (New York: Fordham University Press, [1999–2004] 2005), p. 26.

5. Jean-Luc Nancy, *The Birth to Presence*, trans. B. Holmes et al. (Stanford: Stanford University Press, [1976–93] 1993), p. 153.
6. Nancy, *The Muses*, pp. 21–2.
7. Nancy, *The Ground of the Image*, pp. 95–6.
8. Nancy, *Philosophical Chronicles*, p. 24.
9. Jean-Luc Nancy, *The Truth of Democracy*, trans. P.-A. Brault and M. Naas (New York: Fordham University Press, [2008] 2010), p. 17.
10. Jean-Luc Nancy, 'The Commerce of Plural Thinking', interview with Peter Gratton and Marie-Eve Morin, in Peter Gratton and Marie-Eve Morin (eds), *Jean-Luc Nancy and Plural Thinking: Expositions of World, Ontology, Politics, and Sense* (Albany: SUNY Press, 2012), p. 236.
11. Angelus Silesius, *The Cherubinic Wanderer*, trans. M. Shrady (Mahwah, NJ: Paulist Press, [1657] 1986), p. 54; translation modified.
12. Nancy, *The Truth of Democracy*, p. 27.
13. Nancy, *Philosophical Chronicles*, p. 24.
14. Jean-Luc Nancy, *Being Singular Plural*, trans. R. D. Richardson and A. E. O'Byrne (Stanford: Stanford University Press, [1996] 2000), p. 68.
15. Guy Debord, *The Society of the Spectacle*, trans. D. Nicholson Smith (New York: Zone Books, [1967] 1994), paragraph 190.
16. Nancy, *Being Singular Plural*, p. 52.
17. Ibid., p. 53.
18. Jean-Luc Nancy, *The Sense of the World*, trans. J. S. Librett (Minneapolis: University of Minnesota Press, [1993] 1997), p. 100.
19. Ibid., p. 134.
20. Jean-Luc Nancy, 'Nothing but the World: An Interview with *Vacarme*', trans. J. Smith, *Rethinking Marxism*, 19:4, [2000] 2007, pp. 529–30.
21. Nancy, *Being Singular Plural*, p. 54.
22. Nancy, *Philosophical Chronicles*, p. 38.
23. Jean-Luc Nancy, *The Creation of the World, or Globalization*, trans. F. Raffoul and D. Pettigrew (Albany: SUNY Press, [2002] 2007), p. 42.
24. Nancy, *The Muses*, p. 31.
25. Ibid., p. 31.
26. Nancy, *Philosophical Chronicles*, p. 61.
27. Ibid., p. 62.
28. Ibid., p. 63.

29. Ibid., p. 63.
30. José Saramago, *The Year of the Death of Ricardo Reis*, trans. G. Pontiero (London: The Harvill Press, [1984] 1992), p. 342.
31. In my view Nancy is mistaken to contend that this work is 'over-determined' in its signification. Nancy is not sure of its title, but seems to think that it could be *Rape in Bosnia*. It is in fact *Été 93*. If this is not extraordinary enough for a piece supposedly 'over-determined' in its signification – or perhaps such nominalism is the inevitable outcome of the work's determinism – Nancy then goes on to offer a description of the work so at odds with the one given by the artist herself that she believes *Été 93* to have aroused in Nancy the fantasy of another piece altogether. As a consequence, Blocher is publishing a response to Nancy in a forthcoming issue of the journal in which Nancy's article appears, *Journal of Visual Culture* (also included is my discussion of the work in question). Nancy, 'Art Today', pp. 95–7.
32. Nancy, 'The Commerce of Plural Thinking', p. 237. For more on Nancy's interpretation of Heidegger's *Wink*, see Jean-Luc Nancy, 'On a Divine *Wink*', trans. M. B. Smith, in David Pettigrew and François Raffoul (eds), *French Interpretations of Heidegger: An Exceptional Reception* (Albany: SUNY Press, [2003] 2008), pp. 167–86. Heidegger appeals to the notion in his writings on Hölderlin and elsewhere, notably in the late 1930s texts (published posthumously) *Besinnung, Gesamtausgabe*, Band 66, ed. Friedrich-Wilhelm von Herrmann (Frankfurt am Main: Vittorio Klostermann, [1939] 1997); and *Beiträge zur Philosophie (vom Ereignis), Gesamtausgabe*, Band 65, ed. Friedrich-Wilhelm von Herrmann (Frankfurt am Main: Vittorio Klostermann, [1938] 1989).
33. Jean-Luc Nancy, 'On Dis-enclosure and its Gesture, Adoration', trans. J. McKeane, in Alena Alexandrova, Ignaas Devisch, Laurens ten Kate and Aukje van Rooden (eds), *Re-treating Religion: Deconstructing Christianity with Jean-Luc Nancy* (New York: Fordham University Press, [2009] 2012), p. 336.
34. Ibid., p. 336.
35. Nancy, *The Birth to Presence*, p. 206.
36. Nancy, *The Muses*, p. 17.
37. Jacques Derrida, '*Le Toucher*: Touch/to Touch Him', trans. P. Kamuf, *Paragraph*, 16:2, 1993, p. 127.
38. Nancy, *The Muses*, p. 19.
39. Nancy, *The Sense of the World*, p. 135.
40. Martin Heidegger, *Bemerkungen zu Kunst–Plastik–Raum* (St Gallen: Erker Verlag, [1964] 1996), p. 13

41. Derrida introduces the 'continuistic postulation' in his discussion of Deleuze and Guattari's conception of the haptic and their insistence that it takes place in what they call 'smooth', as opposed to 'striated', space. The haptic then, for Derrida, is identified with proximity. He quotes from *A Thousand Plateaus*, just after it has been established that the eye fulfils a 'non-optical function': 'The first aspect of the haptic, smooth space of close vision is that its orientations, landmarks, and linkages are in *continuous* variation.' Gilles Deleuze and Félix Guattari, *A Thousand Plateaus: Capitalism and Schizophrenia*, trans. B. Massumi (Minneapolis: University of Minnesota Press, [1980] 1987), p. 493; Derrida's emphasis. To which Derrida: 'What makes the haptical, thus interpreted, cling to closeness; what identifies it with the approach of the proximate (not only with "close vision" but any approach, in every sense and for all the senses, and beyond touch); what makes it keep up with the appropriation of the proximate, is a continuistic postulation ... I said continuistic *postulation*–for the continuous is never given. *There is never any pure, immediate* experience of the continuous, nor of closeness, nor of absolute proximity, nor of pure indifferentiation.' Jacques Derrida, *On Touching – Jean-Luc Nancy*, trans. C. Irizarry (Stanford: Stanford University Press, [2000] 2005), pp. 124–5.
42. Derrida, *On Touching*, p. 129.
43. Jean-Luc Nancy, 'The Muses (Why are there several arts and not just one? A discussion of the plurality of worlds)', trans. I. Hamilton Grant, University of Warwick, 28 April 1994.
44. Nancy, *The Muses*, p. 17.
45. Charles Baudelaire, 'The Desire to Paint', in *Paris Spleen*, trans. L. Varése (New York: New Directions Books, [1869] 1978), p. 78.
46. Nancy, *The Birth to Presence*, p. 389.
47. Nancy, *The Muses*, p. 17.
48. Jean-Luc Godard (dir.), *La Chinoise*, Anouchka Films/Les Productions de la Guéville/Athos Films/Parc Film/Simar Films, France, 1967. Barnett Newman, *Vir Heroicus Sublimis*, oil on canvas, Museum of Modern Art, New York, 1950–1. Anne Carson, *Autobiography of Red: A Novel in Verse* (New York: Vintage Books, 1998). Orhan Pamuk, *My Name is Red*, trans. E. M. Göknar (London: Faber & Faber, [1998] 2001).
49. Nancy, *The Sense of the World*, p. 55.
50. Ibid., p. 183, n.48.
51. Ibid., p. 56; in italics – yet parentheses – in the original.
52. Jean-Luc Nancy, *Adoration: The Deconstruction of Christianity II*,

trans. J. McKeane (New York: Fordham University Press, [2010] 2013), p. 106, n.9.
53. Nancy, *The Muses*, p. 18.
54. Ibid., pp. 34–5.
55. Ibid., p. 35.
56. Ibid., p. 76.
57. Nancy, *The Ground of the Image*, p. 9.
58. Jean-Luc Nancy, *Multiple Arts: The Muses II*, trans. Simon Sparks et al. (Stanford: Stanford University Press, [1980–2000] 2006), p. 203.
59. Nancy, *The Ground of the Image*, p. 121.
60. Ibid., p. 118.
61. Nancy, *The Muses*, p. 76.
62. Nancy, *The Birth to Presence*, p. 356.
63. Nancy, *The Ground of the Image*, p. 118.
64. Nancy, *Multiple Arts*, p. 168.
65. Jean-Luc Nancy, 'Chromatic atheology', trans. B. Belay and V. Rehberg, *Journal of Visual Culture*, 4:1, 2006, p. 124.
66. Nancy, *The Muses*, p. 11.
67. Ibid., p. 83.
68. Derrida, *On Touching*, p. 287.
69. Ibid., p. 287.
70. If there is no 'the' to touch then can we say that touch is 'the' one sense which more than any other properly touches on the problematic of the sense of art? We have seen how the proper of touch is put into question, and we cannot ignore the concomitant problem of the propriety of touch over the domain of sense. In my view, it is in what he would call the *style* of his writing, and thus how he performs the question, that we find Nancy grappling with this. It is a style which we should call 'the risk of styles', an 'interminable alteration of style', the plural way in which Nancy puts the sense of touch to work in his writings about art, exposing them to the address of artworks in the name of opening up possibilities of world. Nancy, *The Sense of the World*, p. 198, n.156, and p. 56; italics in original. We will not analyse what 'style' means for Nancy, merely emphasise how his writing style walks the surface between sense and signification. To affirm from within philosophy, as Nancy does, the break between sense and signification is to call for the end of philosophy, and the end of philosophy is this affirmation. Ibid., pp. 22–3. It is not simply that Nancy philosophises about art, it is that he does so in such a way that philosophy's distinction from art is put into ques-

tion through the style of his writing. It is not just that Nancy argues through philosophical argumentation for the necessity of style. It is that he puts the argument into practice such that its argumentative force is suspended in favour of questioning the disciplinary distinctions upon which it might otherwise rest. Nancy exposes philosophy to the excess of signification of art, and thereby does philosophy confront the excess of its, philosophy's, meaning. This extends to giving some of his works specific visual forms; thus do Nancy's writings become 'too close' to literature, 'too close' to art. As a consequence, questions are invited as to the discipline of his work, discipline in both senses – or rather discipline in that singular sense in which the normative force of rigour is put to work in the name of reinforcing and policing disciplinary borders, in this case, and from both sides, between the disciplines of art and philosophy – and such questions are always political, for discipline in this latter sense is irreducibly a function of institutional signification. In the face of such institutional signification it is the 'responsibility' of thinking to carry itself out in a writing which is in excess of its 'discipline', a writing which the discipline cannot assume propriety over, but which that discipline nonetheless has a responsibility for.

71. Nancy, *The Ground of the Image*, p. 25.
72. Alain Badiou, 'Can Change be Thought? A Dialogue', with Bruno Bosteels, in Gabriel Riera (ed.), *Alain Badiou: Philosophy and its Conditions* (Albany: SUNY Press, 2005), p. 239.
73. An achievement which we might say is performed more on the side of the visual by Simon Hantaï in his foldings of Nancy's texts into works of visual art, bringing them to the point of irreadability in order to visibilise an essential sense of them, something that Nancy, in his correspondence with the artist, affirms. Simon Hantaï, with Jean-Luc Nancy and Jacques Derrida, *La connaissance des textes: lecture d'un manuscrit illisible (correspondances)* (Paris: Edition Galilée, 2001). For how, over time, Nancy puts into question the identity and difference between writing, or discourse, and painting, see his encounter with the paintings of François Martin. From 'On Painting (and) Presence', a 1988 catalogue essay on Martin's exhibition *Le Semainier*, in *The Birth to Presence*, to a 2006 paper entitled 'Catalogue', on the catalogue for Martin's 1979 *The Air Show*, in *Multiple Arts*.

8

The Separated Gesture: Partaking in the Inoperative Praxis of the Already-Unmade[1]

John Paul Ricco

The work of Jean-Luc Nancy is driven by a three-part exigency that is at once political, ethical, and aesthetic. Over the past forty years, his work has been equally exacting in thinking the relation between these three spheres and registers of praxis. While no single essay can ever do proper justice to this work in terms of its scope, diversity, and precision, and while my own contribution to this collection of essays will primarily focus on questions of aesthetic praxis, nonetheless I am guided by the conviction that when reading almost any text written by Nancy, one must remain attuned to the political, ethical, and aesthetic dimensions that shape it. Together they point to the innumerable decisions and actions in which nothing less than a sense of the world is created. As the three 'principles' for a shared sustaining in (and of) the separated spacing – between, amongst, and around bodies, places, and things – the political, the ethical and the aesthetic are the prepared conditions and distinct affirmations of the sense of existence as incommensurable and immeasurable.

Even when seemingly solely devoted to questions of sovereignty and community, or art and assemblage, or decision and justice – or when written without any one or more of these signifying markers of politics, aesthetics, and ethics, few texts by Nancy are devoid of thinking the political, aesthetic, and ethical together. This is because these three spheres, which Nancy himself understands to be separate and non-determinative of each other, are, nonetheless, also understood as coextensive in their mutual heterogeneity. It is this relational tension without resolution between the political, aesthetic and the ethical – of being at once inextricably tied to each other and yet irreducible and incommensurable to each other – that is, for Nancy, the very spacing of sense as shared-separation, or to appropriate terms central to his thinking: *le frayage du partage* (the frayed path, passage, edge and opening of sharing-out).

The task set for us by the work of Jean-Luc Nancy, then, is to think this infinite rapport and never-to-be-finalised relation between the spheres of the political, the aesthetic and the ethical, in terms of what he has referred to as 'the condition of nonequivalent affirmation'.[2] Yet the first step in doing so is not to confuse or conflate the political with the *affirmation* of this nonequivalence. For as Nancy makes clear in the opening lines of the chapter 'A Space Formed for the Infinite', in his recent book, *The Truth of Democracy*:

> The condition of nonequivalent affirmation is political inasmuch as politics must prepare the space for it. But the affirmation itself is not political. It can be almost anything you like – existential, artistic, literary, dreamy, amorous, scientific, thoughtful, leisurely, playful, friendly, gastronomic, urban, and so on: politics subsumes none of these registers; it only gives them their space and possibility.[3]

But just as much as the political does not subsume these various affirmations underneath it, I want to suggest that we also need to understand Nancy as saying that while the political prepares the space for the *condition* of this nonequivalence, this condition is, nonetheless, also not identical with the political. Instead, we might understand this 'condition' according to Derrida's reading of Nancy as: 'the spacing of a presubjective or precratic freedom, that is all the more unconditional, immense, immeasurable [*démesurée*], incommensurable, incalculable, [and] unappropriable ... in exceeding all measure'.[4] Which is to say that the condition of nonequivalent affirmation – as the spacing of (the) sense and (of) existence – is the incommensurable itself, and that it is this incommensurability that the political prepares the space for, and that in doing so, gives art, love, thinking (etc.) the possibility to affirm this condition of nonequivalence.[5] As Nancy underlines: 'To be sure, politics is the place of an "in common" as such – but only along the lines of an incommensurability that is kept open ... It does not subsume the "in common" under the kind of union, community, subject, or epiphany.'[6]

It is in this way that Nancy affirms the ontological priority of the political, by defining it as the spacing or *spaciosity* of sense and existence, rather than as a pre-given space in which politics takes place *as* the place, substance or essence of the political.[7] As transitive verb, 'spacing' is the word for the praxis of configuring space. Yet a 'configuration of space' that, as Nancy has formulated it, would not be the equivalent of a political figuration (fiction, myth), but instead and perhaps more literally, a figuring of the 'con' (with). This 'with' is taken to be neither the place, substance, identity or essence but the very spacing of existence, as sharing in the separation and retreat from (and in excess of) any common unifying figure (e.g. sovereign subject, master, genius) or common measure. For Nancy, it is this incommensurability and incalculability that is the political measure of being-common. What this means is that the political prepares the space and condition of non-equivalent affirmation as the place in common, through the retreat and withdrawal of all common essence, substance, presence and destination in the forms of community, identity, figuration, homeland, and so on.

In the *retreat* from these various ways of establishing political origin, foundation, authority, and principle, political praxis traces the infinitely finite contours and passages of existence. In turn, the ethical corresponds to the decision and stance that each time affirms this scene as separated in its spacing, while the aesthetic corresponds to the techniques of configuration and assemblage through which the separated-spacing is re-traced, presented, sustained and shared in any number of forms, including a work of art. Yet in defining politics as 'the antecedent of a condition of access, not a foundation or determination of meaning', what immediately arises and still needs to be thought is the question of 'the specific space-time of initiality' or antecedence itself.[8] In other words, it is a matter of describing, if not the pre- or fore-space of the political, then of the political as the force of opening or of 'spacing space' that is neither 'a matter' as Nancy states, 'of an originary multiplicity and its correlation . . .' or 'of an originary unity and its division'. Instead, as he goes on to write 'one must think an anteriority of the origin according to some event that happens to it unexpectedly (even if that event originates within it)'.[9]

Based upon our reading of various texts by Nancy, it would seem that this is something like the force of birth, intrusion, surprise, partition, and withdrawal, each of which names what Nancy might mean by 'the first thrust of freedom',[10] and hence is the antecedent spaciosity of the political, just here now, each time. For instance, 'intrusion' might be one such force, understood as a simultaneous breaking open and stepping or leaping out that is originary, rather than secondary or ancillary; not the intrusion into an already established place, but intrusion as the very rhythmic spacing-out that, as Nancy argues, is the very 'birth' or inauguration of freedom as initiality-in-act of which the political is the name for this praxis. As Nancy states,

> the opening of this scene . . . supposes a breaking open, a strike, a decision: it is also as the political that freedom *is* the leap. It supposes the strike, the cut, the decision and the leap onto the scene (but the leap itself is what opens the scene) of that which cannot be received from elsewhere or reproduced from any model, since it is always beginning 'each time'.[11]

Freedom for Nancy is the initiality of a step, leap, or gesture that is measured against nothing, and for this reason freedom is incommensurable. This nothing, or more properly, this *ex nihilo* is, as we shall see, at once the source of the experience of freedom's immeasurable measure, and of atheological creation. Creation is thus redefined as the praxis and technique of sustaining this incommensurable freedom and equality, by sharing in separation, in which separation is defined and understood as the irreducible spacing of sharing, equality, and freedom. As Derrida states, 'this equality in freedom no longer has anything to do with numerical equality or equality according to worth, proportion or *logos*. It is itself an incalculable and incommensurable equality; it is the unconditional condition of freedom, its sharing, if you will.'[12] In addition to being not equal to any numerical equivalence (it is an incalculable equality) or to any common measure (it is an incommensurable equality), this equality is strictly *equality* in the sense of being measured against nothing, not even itself. It is equality not equal to itself.

This is also the condition of nonequivalence that the political prepares the space for, and that various forms of affirmation such as the aesthetic and ethical seek to sustain. These are forms of praxis that are measured against nothing, nothing but the sharing-dividing of freedom. Which is to say that they are techniques for accessing the 'spacing' that is free of any common measure.[13] So while Nancy states that, 'the element in which the incalculable can be shared (out) goes by the names of art or love, friendship or thought, knowledge or emotion, but not politics'[14] he nonetheless simultaneously avows that, 'to think the manner in which these spheres are heterogeneous to the properly political sphere is a political necessity'.[15] Finally, in order to do so, it is equally incumbent to think these other forms as 'numberless and unfinalizable forms'.[16]

In what follows, I argue that the way to think art and ethics as numberless and unfinalisable forms is in terms of an inoperative aesthetic praxis that sustains the space prepared and opened up by the political, such as in works discussed below by the artist Felix Gonzalez-Torres – specifically his gallery installations and the invitation that is offered through them to partake in the decision to withdraw a piece from the assembled heaps of candy or stacks of paper, and thereby sustain the incommensurable separation of things, bodies and places. Gonzalez-Torres' work enables us to redefine art as an inoperative praxis of sharing in the incalculable. It enables the affirmation of the political as a spacing that is not a pre-given or ready-made ground, but instead is always the taking place – or better, a partaking place – that is already-unmade. In the decision to sustain the non-self-sufficiency of this scene as a decision that remains no place other than just between us, this inoperative praxis responds to an exigency that is at once aesthetic, political, and ethical.

As Nancy has noted: 'Art has hitherto been considered, in all possible ways, in terms of both "creation" (*poiesis*, genius, and so on) and "reception" (judgement, critique, and so on). But what has been left in the shadows is its befalling or devolving, that is to say, also its chance, event, birth, or encounter.'[17] My chapter is dedicated to thinking this befalling and devolving of art – of its presentation as already-unmade.

1. Rendering Two Duchampian Paradigms Doubly Inoperative

Here is a scene. A heap of candy is piled up in a corner. Each piece is wrapped in its own clear, shiny and glistening monochromatic cellophane wrapper. It is through the literal accumulation (from the Latin verb *accumulare*: heaped up) of these pieces that a polychromatic pyramid is presented in contrast to the smooth and stark white surfaces of the walls and floor. Walls and floor so immaculate in their surface that by way of what we might describe as an architectonic of aesthetic intuition, we immediately recognise this heap of candy as a work of art, exhibited in a modern art gallery.[18]

One might even further recognise this to be an image of a work by the American, Cuban-born artist Felix Gonzalez-Torres. It is one of his candy pile installations, titled, *'Untitled' (Portrait of Ross in L.A.)*, 1991. The parenthetical subtitle refers to Ross Laycock, Felix's boyfriend of eight years, who, while they were living together in Los Angeles (1990–1) died of complications related to AIDS (from which Felix would die five years later). Obviously this work does not convey the physical appearance of Ross through a representational and figural form of commemoration; but as Jean-Luc Nancy has pointed out, the portrait is always the presentation of the subject in retreat, perhaps best captured by *ritratto*, the Italian word for portrait. With this work by Gonzalez-Torres then, we are presented if not with an image, than a scene of this retreating portrait (*ritirato ritratto*).

As a scene of retreat, the work sustains – rather than puts to rest via a memorialising form of final return and remembrance – a sense of loss through an inoperative praxis and technique, in which an endless supply of ready-made pieces of candy is offered for the taking. Those that encounter the work are invited or, at least, offered the decision to partake in its infinite withdrawal, and thereby come to share not in the completion of the work, but rather in its incompletion. 'Incompletion' in the precise sense of the infinite opening and sharing of the work's multiplying finitude and division, or what might be described as *in-finishing*, a term we have inherited from Nancy. In its hyphenated form, *in-finishing* is to be read, at once, as the sense that the infinite is finite (i.e. actually rather than virtually infinite), and as the infinite opening of finitude, right at its limit (and never-ending end).

Depending upon the particular gallery installation, the invitation to take a piece of candy is either more or less pronounced; for instance, by a particularly hospitable museum guard or via instructions printed on an accompanying wall label, or in many instances without any sign or indication whatsoever. This varying and oscillating degree of explicitness and ambiguity is indicative of any invitation, and the invitation to partake in this work is as inoperative as is any invitation, given that, as Derrida notes:

> An invitation leaves one free, otherwise it becomes constraint. It should [*devrait*] never imply: you are obliged to come, you have to

come, it is necessary. But the invitation must be pressing, not indifferent. It should never imply: you are free not to come and if you don't come, never mind, it doesn't matter.[19]

An invitation opens up a space of decision and leaves one free: free to decide, as in the case of the work by Gonzalez-Torres, to touch, to take one piece or more than one piece of candy, to eat it or to save it, or perhaps even to give it to someone else, and to let them decide what to do with it – accept it, eat it, keep it, or give it to someone else, in turn. I have a small collection of pieces of candy from various installations of these works that have been given to me by friends as souvenirs of their encounter with the work. These small inadvertent gifts are *symbols* – in the full etymological sense of the word – of a separation that is shared between us. As noted earlier, such shared-separation is the very spacing of any relation, of which friendship is perhaps one of its most acutely felt forms.

The invitation that is offered by the Gonzalez-Torres to partake in the work – to take part in its presentation and spacing of decision – does not operate by way of imperative, obligation or necessity, yet at the same time its non-insistence is not indifferent, since it does not imply that if you don't partake in the work by taking a piece of candy, it doesn't matter. I wish to contend that it does matter that pieces of candy are taken, and in ways that extend beyond simply transgressing a whole series of written and unwritten taboos concerning coming into contact with, or touching a work of art on display in a gallery.

What might be called the decision of participation is here in rapport with the decision of invitation. Yet, as I have tried to suggest, it is a rapport (e.g. between audience and artist), that forever will remain incommensurable, because the offer to participate in the work and the partaking in the work are both dedicated to sustaining the work's disappearance. Through this inoperative praxis, not only is the traditional notion of the artist/author undermined – whether thought in terms of the author as creator or author as producer – but also, two principal aesthetic paradigms inherited from Duchamp are reversed, at once and in relation with each other: namely, the ready-made, and the notion that 'the audience completes the work'. Here we might remind ourselves of the principal means by which Marcel Duchamp, through his 'invention' of the ready-made, radically shifted and disrupted the discourses of art, artist, artistic production, and the work of art. No doubt this will be familiar to most readers, but a reiteration of this aesthetic logic is worthwhile, since I want to argue that Gonzalez-Torres went several steps beyond Duchamp, and rendered his (Duchamp's) workless work, doubly inoperative.

By defining the ready-made as an index of a rendezvous or encounter between himself and an industrially manufactured commodity about which he had no interest – aesthetic or otherwise – and as a trace of his act of choosing the anonymous object, Duchamp shifted artistic practice from making to selecting – which is to say, towards an act or praxis that is not the work or *poietic* production of the work of art (oeuvre), but rather the *désoeuvrement* (borrowing a term from Maurice Blanchot). Such a workless praxis is nothing more (or less) than an art of the gesture. Given that any form of praxis effects a transformation or reconfiguration of the doer, the doing and what is done, Duchamp's ready-made rendered workless, the notions of artist, art making, and the work of art, and if not by putting them completely out of work, certainly by putting them into question, including as the very question: Is this art? Duchamp's gesture dissolved the notion of work; yet, as Octavio Paz pointed out in an essay from around 1970 on Duchamp's ready-mades, this 'an-artistic' gesture, remained an artist's gesture – and not just any artist's gesture, but specifically that of Marcel Duchamp. Paz writes: 'If the object is anonymous, the man who chose it is not. And one could even add that the "ready-made" is not a work but a gesture and a gesture which only an artist could realize and not just any artist but inevitably Marcel Duchamp.'[20]

This persistence of the signatory is no doubt ironic, given that, as Paz goes on to explain: 'The act of Duchamp uproots the object from its significance and makes an empty skin of the name: a bottle-rack without bottles.'[21] While it can be said that Duchamp's workless gesture renders the ready-made object anonymous and useless, it must also be noted that the very same gesture runs the risk of being perceived as invested in the author, deposited in the object, or retained as though a medium or technique – all of which would draw the ready-made back into the discourse of artist, work of art, and *poietic* production. We might take Octavio Paz's words as cautionary when he writes: 'The transition from worshipping the object to worshipping the gesture is imperceptible and instantaneous: the circle is closed.'[22] Indeed, in our thinking of an art and aesthetics of gesture, we will want to keep the 'circle' open, and as I have already briefly suggested, the way to do that is to think the gesture that art is, as separated and open, rather than as the closed circle of either the work, reciprocal exchange, or even hermeneutic interpretation.[23] Yet in order to do so, one must also put into question, and perhaps resist the Duchampian aesthetic paradigm mentioned earlier, namely that 'the audience completes the work'.

There is no other artist I can think of whose work puts into question and undoes the notion of completion than Felix Gonzalez-Torres. In the installations of candy piles and paper stacks, Felix's work retains Duchamp's notion of the ready-made as index of encounter and trace of selection, but extends this encounter, decision and selection, so that it now includes the audience,[24] and therefore is no longer limited to the artist's gesture of choosing. In turn, the decision to accept the offer and to partake in the work by withdrawing a part of it, not only opens up the space and event of decision beyond that of artistic intention, the index of the moment of encounter lies not (or not only) in the presentation of the object as ready-made, but also and perhaps more subversively, in the ready-made's withdrawal and erasure. In this way two principle Duchampian principles are reversed and Duchamp's own workless work is rendered doubly inoperative. By partaking in the incessant withdrawal and disappearance of the work, that is, by taking a piece of candy or sheet of paper, the audience can be said to incomplete the work. A partaking that due to the work's always already, yet never complete withdrawal and disappearance, we can say is a partaking in the work as already-unmade.

Yet we also more simply can understand the work as already-unmade in the sense that – at least in terms of its exhibition – there is no moment prior to the work's withdrawal, given that withdrawal is operative in the very presentation of the work. So much so, that it does away with any notion of original plentitude prior to the work's withdrawal. The work exists at no moment prior to its withdrawal, and you can never be in any way confident that you are the first one to take a piece from the pile. We might say that withdrawal is *a priori* or originary, and that it is this that makes the work (perhaps any work in terms of the idea of origin) inoperative, which is to say, already-unmade. In other words, the work only exists in its never-ending loss, a finitude that is infinite to the precise extent that Felix Gonzalez-Torres indicated the quantity of candy shall be an 'endless supply', and, to the precise extent that any number of those who encounter the work partake in its withdrawal, by taking candy, each piece singular in its finitude and in relation to the incessant disappearance of the work. The praxis and technique of the work lies in the 'absence of beginning and "exhaustion of ends"'.[25]

Felix's pieces of candy (*singuli*) are not fragments of the work of art, but parts outside of parts (*partes extra partes*), in which no one piece of candy, nor the totality of pieces, constitutes the work. Gonzalez-Torres clearly specifies this in the certificates of authenticity that accompany the purchase and ownership of the work. For instance, if you were possessed by a hubristic impulse and were to take all of the candy piled up in the gallery, you would not have a work by Gonzalez-Torres, and, in turn, if you were to take just one piece, you also would not have a Gonzalez-Torres. This then raises the question: If the pieces of candy do not equal the work, then what does the work consist of?

In their offering of an endless supply of pieces of candy and the decision to take a piece or part, Felix's candy installations are scenes of an infinite offering and partaking of finitude. An overflowing offering and a partaking in withdrawal as two forms of fulfillment that, at the same time, are the impossibility of converting finitude into finish (i.e. of transforming the piece into a fragment and then the fragment into a whole/work). If to take a piece of candy is not to take the work or even a part of it, then to partake in the work can only mean to 'take a part' that is not a part, and thereby to share not secondarily and through a mode of participation, but primarily through a shared-separation, which is semantically borne by the French word *partager* meaning to share, to divide. It is this semantic double meaning that I wish to retain in my use of the English word 'partaking'.

The work – its praxis and technique – exists neither in author, audience or produced object, but rather in the gestures of offering and partaking, and more precisely, in the inoperative offering via an invitation (it too is 'inoperative' as we have seen) to act in a way that remains to be decided (to take, to keep, to eat, to transmit), and to partake in the withdrawal and disappearance of the work. In other words, it is to partake in sustaining the *worklessness* of the work, through a shared exposure to the exposition of art as vestige. I argue that these gestures of shared-separation are inoperative aesthetic praxis and techniques of those anonymous some-ones withdrawing those equally anonymous ready-made some-things and thereby partaking – not in the destruction, reduction or shattering of the work into fragmentary pieces – but in what Nancy at one point describes as 'the in-finite explosion of the finite',[26] or in-finishing. 'Anonymous' is obviously the name of no one, and yet at the same time that it is no one's name, it is also the name of any and every one, a multiplicity that in the coexistence of non-totalisable singularities, goes by no one (proper) name, but simply perhaps only as 'we', or 'us'. We might say that anonymity is structured by a tension between a sense of absence (no one . . . there) and of multiplicity (no one name, but always more than one).

2. Community, Number

In his recent essay 'The Confronted Community', Jean-Luc Nancy reminds us that his widely read essay 'La Communauté désoeuvre' (The Inoperative, Workless or Unoccupied Community), was originally published in the journal *Aléa* (Spring 1983), edited by Jean-Christophe Bailley. The theme of the issue was 'La communauté, le nombre' (Community, number). As Nancy describes it: 'The perfectly executed ellipse contained in this statement [Community, number] – where prudence rivals elegance, in the manner that was Bailly's great art – gripped me as soon as I received the call for papers, and I have never ceased to admire its aptness.'[27] Indeed, the aptness of the statement – especially for us in the context of our discussion – is the way in which it writes the tension between community and number, a tension that structures all of the various ways in which we think about the relations between the *common* and the *numerous*. These are the terms by which to understand how the innumerable (in the form of the endless supply of ready-made candy), and infinishing (in the form of each piece of candy being taken from the pile by anonymous some-ones), is a partaking in the infinite withdrawal and retreat of finitude.[28]

Just as Nancy enables us to imagine 'the perfectly executed ellipse' as drawing the single orbit traced by the two foci of community and number, in their mutual and constant distance from each other, Derrida enables us to further understand how the multiplicity of this 'more than one' is inextricably tied to the subtraction of 'minus one', through the very spacing and sense traced out by the ellipsis. As he writes at the very outset of his book *Rogues*,

> For a certain sending [*envoi*] that awaits us [or the offering and partaking that we are discussing here], I imagine an economic formalisation,

a very elliptical phrase, in both senses of the word *ellipsis*. For *ellipsis* names not only lack but a curved figure with more than one focus. We are thus already between the 'minus one' and the 'more than one'.[29]

It is precisely in the praxis of subtraction/division and addition/multiplication that is (inoperatively) operative in Gonzalez-Torres's candy and paper installations, that we are always 'already between the minus one and the more than one', which is to say, in the indissociable relation between withdrawal/separation and dissemination/circulation.

It is to such metaphors from arithmetic that John Cage resorts, in his '25 Statements re Duchamp', in order to describe three of the principal artists and achievements in twentieth-century art; and a fourth that at the time, according to Cage, was anticipated and yet to be fulfilled. Cage writes: 'Duchamp showed the usefulness of addition (moustache), Rauschenberg showed the function of subtraction (De Kooning). Well, we look forward to multiplication and division. It is safe to assume that someone will learn trigonometry.'[30]

I want to suggest that when it comes to that artist who will show us the 'usefulness and function' of multiplication and division, we need not wait any longer. Indeed, since the early-1990s and his first installations of paper stacks and candy piles, Felix Gonzalez-Torres has offered just that. In these works of art, 'multiplication' might be said to take the form of the endless supply of ready-made objects, and 'division' is three-fold: 1) the ongoing act of their taking, 2) the dividing up of parts, and 3) the shared-separation of those who decide to take part in the infinite withdrawal of the work's finitude. Which is also to implicitly note that Gonzalez-Torres' aesthetic praxis and technique of multiplication and division at the same time relies upon addition and subtraction.[31] Thus we are led to consider the ways in which the replenishing and withdrawing of candy is more than a simple matter of addition and subtraction, or perhaps even how endless acts of shared subtraction can generate 'the in-finite explosion of the finite' – which is to say, shared-separation as the spacing of sense in all directions at once.[32]

Like the ellipsis, the praxis of withdrawing is at the same time an opening up to the outside and an infinite sustaining of this spacing-out, right at the finite limit, edge or point. It is what renders any sense of an absolute end impossible, while at the same that it is what remains when nothing comes back to itself. It is what Nancy means by 'form' when he writes that 'form is a ground that withdraws', and as he further clarifies, 'a form is the force of a ground that sets apart and dislocates itself'.[33] This form and force is a division/separation and a dissemination/multiplication. In this chiasmic relation of force, form and ground, we can locate Nancy's definition of the image as that empty place of the absent that is not empty. This empty place is that which might be more properly thought less in terms of a thing, than as a scene, and even more specifically as the supplement (excess, more than one) that divides actuality (minus one), and thereby comes to constitute sense as that which is shared-divided (*partage*).

For Nancy, this praxis of sharing-dividing that is at the heart of his thinking of co-existence, has always raised the question of technique, technicity, and the event of technology; and while the issue is far too vast to tackle in the space that remains here, I would like to point to at least three places where Nancy broaches the topic in terms of the politics, aesthetics and ethics. Given our preceding discussion of the place of absence, we might begin with what I take to be a definition of ethics, as presented in his essay, 'Creation as Denaturation':

> This implies above all not a knowledge, but an *ethos*: *logos* itself as *ethos*, that is to say, the technology or the art of *standing in and abiding* in the escape of the *absence*. The art of standing, or what permits in general having or maintaining a standing in, including, and especially, where there is no longer any support or firm basis for whatever stance there is.[34]

In the second chapter of *The Sense of the World* (1993) dedicated to politics, and the question of 'one' as we have already briefly encountered it, Nancy writes:

> Politics of (k)nots, of singular interlacings, of every *one* as the interlacing, relaying, and recasting of a (k)not, and of every (k)not as a *one* (one people, country, person, and so on), but as a *one* that is *one* only by virtue of concatenation: neither the 'one' of a substance nor the 'one' of a pure distributive count.[35]

This means that, for Nancy, the 'one' is neither the 'one' as absolute singularity nor as the 'one' of additive serial succession, one thing after another (1 + 1), but is defined in terms of singular multiplicity (+1) as 'more than one'. Finally, in *The Muses*, Nancy provides a definition of aesthetic technique when he writes:

> The technicity of art dislodges art from its 'poetic' assurance, if one understands by that the production of a revelation, or art conceived as a *phusis* unveiled in its truth. Technicity *itself* is also the 'out-of-workness' [*désoeuvrement*] of the work, what puts it outside itself, touching the infinite. Their technical out-of-workness *forces* the fine arts, dislodges them endlessly from aestheticizing repose. This is why art is always coming to its end.[36]

The 'touching the infinite' that Nancy speaks of in terms of technicity's essential inoperativity, is the rapport with the infinite that happens right at the singular plural thing/image/body in its finitude; an infinite finitude or complete incompletion that affirms that singularity as already-unmade. It is curious that more recently, Nancy has distinguished politics and art in terms of their relation to ends that would seem to go against what he put forth in 1994. While we understand what Nancy means when he states that 'politics never attains ends' whereas 'art, love, and thought are entitled each time to proclaim themselves accomplished', I want to suggest that we might nonetheless want to reconsider to what extent such 'registers [as art, love, and thought] belong to the order of a "finishing off of the infinite", whereas politics pertains to indefinition'.[37] How might art, love, and thought be their own forms of in-finishing, if not of 'indefinition'?

It is in terms of this non-productive praxis, distinct from poiesis, that Nancy has reconceptualised the notion of creation, in a wholly a-theological sense. For instance, when he writes in his book *The Creation of the World or, Globalization*:

> If 'creation' means anything, it is the exact opposite of any form of production in the sense of a fabrication that supposes a given, a project, and a producer ... The idea of creation ... is above all the idea of the *ex nihilo* ... The world is created from nothing [*ex nihilo*]: this does not mean fabricated with nothing by a particularly ingenious producer. It means that it is not fabricated, produced by no producer, and not even coming out of nothing (like a miraculous apparition), but in a quite strict manner and more challenging for thought: the nothing itself.[38]

In other words, since the source, reason, principle and ground of the world is nothing, it is the nothing itself from which creation comes (ex) and towards which it goes (ex), and it is this outside and opening from nothing that is written as *ex nihilo*. As the withdrawal and retreat of any given or ready-made ground, creation is not the *poietic* production or work, and asymptotic relation to ends (as in certain weak versions of ontologies of 'becoming'), whether this is in terms of 'process' (absolutely infinite production/work) or 'progress' (ultimately finite production/work). Rather, creation is to be understood as the inoperative praxis of the already-unmade. By this we mean to say that the sense of existence and its place, is neither ready-made, nor yet-to-be-made, but already-unmade 'here and now every moment', each time, just this once, as Nancy has said of each and every decision.

It is in this way that Nancy has argued that existence is always created, yet not by some distanced and detached creator or author (God), but solely by existents in their very existence. Such that, as he states in a section of his essay 'Being Singular Plural' titled 'The Creation of the World or Curiosity': 'Existence is creation, our creation; it is the beginning and end that we are. This is the thought that is the most necessary for us to think.'[39] As he has argued, the relation between the numerous, community, and being-together never lies in a thing (for instance in the form of a common substance, figure or identity), and it is this *no-thing* that the *nihilo* of *creation ex nihilo* refers to. Here, the *nihil* is not reducible to either the One or to zero – that is: neither to absolute unity nor to nihilism (which is perhaps even less than zero) – but is to be thought in terms of multiplicity. Which is also to say: in terms of the *numerous* distinct from *number*, and thus *multiplicity* distinct even from *multiplication*. An innumerable, incalculable and incommensurable multiplicity – what in English is perhaps most aptly expressed as 'a lot of' (French: *beaucoup de*).

3. An Economy of the Separated Gesture

I want to suggest that what is shared between artist and audience – that is, what is offered by Felix and partaken in by those who encounter his work – is not a ready-made commodity, object of exchange or symbolic communion, a gift or even a souvenir, but rather a decision to sustain this scene (or spacing) of decision, through the incessant withdrawal and retreat of ready-made objects. It is a sustaining – by sharing together – in the separation between us. A spacing out of nothing (and to nothing), that thereby is the *nihilo* (nothing) from which ex-istence is sensed and takes place as opening and outside (ex-). Another word for this is 'creation'. What remains is not a thing, but the 'ex' of *creation ex nihilo*, and as Nancy has said: something like a gesture. Gesture as a partaking in the 'extra' of *partes extra partes*, by taking a part or piece that is not one part of a greater whole (i.e. a fragment), but a singular multiplicity or again, as Nancy has named it: a vestige.

As we shift our thinking and language from fragment to gesture, let us note that there is no such thing as a fragmentary gesture. Every gesture is the infinite index of finitude, or what we might take Nancy to mean when he refers to the 'infinite in act'. Prior to any signifying function, a gesture is first and foremost the index of spacing, and the incommensurable relation or shared-separation between here and there. A gesture signals (it gestures to) the 'there is' (*il y a*) of existence and its sense, as here, now, this. At the same time, a gesture is a grasping of what is not (or no longer) possessed or what can be given. We might say that the mode of having or giving particular to the gesture is a grasping of that which is slipping through one's fingers. In other words, distinct from substance and property, the propriety of the gesture is wholly inappropriable and this in-appropriability is precisely what the gesture gestures towards. At the same time, we might speak of an 'emptying' of gesture (e.g. kenosis of the divine), all the while affirming that there is no such thing as an empty gesture (even though we often speak of such terms, yet in doing so, we negate the very notion of the empty gesture). Like Nancy's definition of the image, a gesture is 'the empty place of the absent as a place that is not empty'.[40] In turn, there are no static gestures, all gestures are moving, they are the transiting and transmission, the rhythm and emotion, of existence.

In his 'Notes on Gesture', Giorgio Agamben tells us that according to the ancient writer Varro, gesture is neither acting (*praxis*) nor making (*poiesis*), but carrying on or sustaining. In the context of our discussion, we might specify gesture to be the shared-sustaining of the spacing of the 'with' (of being-together) as already-unmade. As I suggested a moment ago, gesture is this very spacing of shared-separation. Thus gesture – as *ars* and *teknē* – is mediality without means (i.e. process – finite or infinite) and without ends (i.e. completion, finish). In other words, gesture is the deconstruction of what Hannah Arendt refers to as the 'means and ends chain'. It is the spacing or what Agamben describes as 'the sphere of a pure and endless mediality [and, as he goes on to say] ... The gesture is, in this sense, 'communication of a communicability',[41] another name for which is 'art'. In light of this, we might understand that such phrases as 'the gesture of art' and 'the art of gesture' are pleonasms: expressions that even in their limited use of two key terms, use one word too many – as is even the case with the phrase 'the separated gesture' in the title of my chapter.

I now want to pose the following question: Is there an economy of gesture? That is: in the reversal of aesthetic value inaugurated by Duchamp exactly one century ago, and extended more recently (as we have discussed in the work of Felix Gonzalez-Torres), in which art as inoperative praxis opens up aesthesis as a spacing of infinitely finite withdrawal and retreat – which is in part to say, beyond use-vale, exchange-value, and perhaps even exhibition-value in the more limited sense of that term – we might not only ask what is it that gesture sustains, but also, *what is it that sustains gesture?*

Through my reading of Nancy alongside the gallery installations of Gonzalez-Torres, I would argue that what sustains gesture – and hence a shared aesthesis or sense of existence as already-unmade – is precisely this reversal of the relation and the value of production. This 'reversal of the relation of production' is what Nancy has identified as Marx's revolution. Yet, as Nancy explains: 'Marx's revolution presupposed that this reversal was equivalent to a conversion of the meaning of production (and the restitution of created value to its creator).'[42] In other words, it remained committed to an economy of production while, as Nancy argues: 'What we have begun to learn is that it is also a matter of creating the meaning or value of the reversal itself [i.e. inoperative praxis]. Only perhaps this creation will have the power of the reversal' [i.e. *creation ex nihilo*].[43]

We might then say that what sustains gesture is the very gap and separation of its spacing, the *nihil* or nothing from which creation happens. The gesture of creation is always an inoperative praxis, 'in excess or in deficiency with respect to its work'. As Nancy writes: 'the work of art is always also a meaning at work beyond the work [*à l'oeuvre au-delà de l'oeuvre*], as well as a work working and opening beyond any meaning that is either given or to be given'[44] [ready-made or gifted, but instead is the infinitely finite opening of the already-unmade]. As Nancy goes on to write: 'But the opening without finality is never a work nor any product: it is the enjoyment of which Marx spoke, as enjoyment by human beings of what opens their humanity beyond all humanism.'[45]

For Marx and others, this sense of enjoyment and pleasure is found in naïveté and play, and in particular those forms of naïve play without 'a goal of mastery (domination, usefulness, appropriation)' and that 'exceeds all submission to an end' belonging to childhood and the gestures, offering and sharing of separation that would seem to be the specific *ars* and *teknē* of a child's pleasure and enjoyment. For while Marx notes towards the end of the introduction to the *Grundrisse*, that 'a man cannot become a child again or he becomes childish', he immediately goes on to ask: 'But does he not find joy in the child's naïveté, and must he himself not strive to reproduce its truth at a higher stage?'[46]

It is this 'effect of perpetual childhood freshness' (as Nancy describes it) that led Freud to resort to examples and scenarios such as the mystic writing pad and the fort/da enunciation. Yet once we note that both of these forms of play are structured through techniques of erasure, withdrawal, disappearance and the retracing of these acts of retreating and departure, we realise that there is a sense of loss intimately located at the heart of children's play, and that this loss can be, nonetheless, a source of pleasure and enjoyment. Joining this insight with Marx's own, we can understand what Nancy means when he writes that: 'Perhaps art is the *infans* par excellence, the one who, instead of discoursing, fragments instead: fraying [*frayage*] and fracture of the access.'[47]

It is precisely this fraying of the path and fragmenting of the course of things, including any discourse *'which takes'* or appropriates, that Roland Barthes described as his method of teaching in his inaugural lecture at the Collège de France in 1977. As he stated: 'I am increasingly convinced, both in writing and in teaching, that the fundamental operation of this loosening method is, if one writes, fragmentation, and, if one teaches, digression, or, to put it in a preciously ambiguous word, *excursion*.'[48] *Excursion* (this word): which we take to literally mean 'the course or path out', *excursus* as a fracturing and fraying of discourse and its appropriating gestures of fragmentation, and a *gesturing* that might also be the art and technique of partaking in departing, of sharing in separation. For Barthes, this is the work of the child at play that is not invested in the object or perhaps even in the giver or receiver, but in the gesture of offering itself.

> I should therefore like the speaking and the listening that will be interwoven here to resemble the comings and goings of a child playing beside his mother, leaving her, returning to bring her a pebble, a piece of string, and thereby tracing around a calm centre a whole locus of play within which the pebble, the string come to matter less than the enthusiastic giving of them.[49]

Like the child in Barthes' image and scenario, those who partake in the infinite incompletion of the work of Gonzalez-Torres's candy pile art installations, partake in a gesture of offering the meaning or sense of which does not lie in any one or all of the pieces of candy, but in the offering itself, the offering of *no-thing* that is *res* (thing), at once *res omnium* (thing for everyone) and *res nullium* (thing for no one).

To conclude, we might say that this is an originary ambiguity that all gestures possess. Such that, as Maurice Blanchot explains, ambiguity is more essential than negation, since before the beginning [that impossible space-time] nothingness is not equal to being, but is only the appearance of being's concealment.[50] Therefore, existence in terms of separated-sense is more a matter of dissimulation than of negation. We have come to understand that the separated gesture is not a matter of the dialectic, and that in its ambiguity and dissimulation, gesture gestures towards existence as not a question of being or becoming, but towards existence as unbecoming, which is to say: already-unmade, and that the praxis, art, and technique of existence is inoperative. For if, as Blanchot argues, dissimulation is more original than negation and cannot be captured by negation, this is because existence has been already-unmade before it can be negated.[51]

When it comes to the work of Felix Gonzalez-Torres, each of us and the artist as well, is the young girl who succeeds the muses, the child who, as Nancy writes: 'exposes art that consents to its own disappearance: not in order to be resuscitated but because it does not enter that process'.[52] With respect to this Nancy, but perhaps Gonzalez-Torres and any other artist asks, 'What if art were never anything but the necessarily plural, singular art of consenting to death, of consenting to existence?'[53] It is in this sense that art is always coming to an end because it is never anything but unbecoming, and it is this infinitisation of ends, that is a political, aesthetic, and ethical exigency, at once. This non-dialectical doubled consenting (to existence, to death), in its syncopated rhythm (black-out, gap, contact) is what I have been trying to think in terms of 'the separated gesture'.

I want to close with the following question and possible response: What if the 'glue' that cements parts of an assemblage of bodies and things – the 'con' or *with* of construction – is not simply a part of the assemblage of bodies and things that constitute the ethical and aesthetic scenes of our coexistence, but more precisely is the part outside of all parts, the *extra* of *partes extra partes*, the outside that is precisely nothing, nothing but its spacing? A spacing that, as the only 'substance' of our being-together, is separated and incommensurably shared, as the decision between us. It would mean that these are not only scenes of deconstruction, in which, as Nancy and Alexander Garcia Düttmann have recently defined the latter, a construction is disassembled such that 'the assemblage remains but disassembled, in pieces, on its way to chaos',[54] but that what remains in and as the disassembled assemblage, is 'a mound, a pile, a heap without order', which as the authors reminds us, was once designated in French by the word 'struction'. Yet in this chapter and in other places, what I have tried to argue is that the piles of candy and stacks of paper, like any number of other withdrawn and disseminated assemblages in which the everyday disappears into the everyday – including ready-made things – are scenes of shared-separation and shared-exposure. Not parts of a whole or a single totalised amassing, but heaps or *structions* of separated gestures as the very *con*, (glue) or 'with', itself. It is this *nihil* spaciosity and inoperative praxis that affirms the relation between aesthetics and politics to be inextricable and incommensurable, at once.

Notes

1. I want to thank Sanja Dejanovic for her invitation to contribute to this collection, and for her patience and editorial care. I would also like to thank the participants and those in attendance at two conferences at which I presented earlier versions of this chapter. The first is CEP2013 – II Congress of Aesthetics and Politics: On Jean-Luc Nancy's Thought, convened at the Polytechnics University of Valencia, Valencia, Spain in May 2013; the second is the annual

conference of the Nordic Society of Aesthetics, convened at the University of Oslo, Norway, also in May 2013. I owe a special debt of gratitude to Professor Bente Larsen, for her invitation to present one of the keynote lectures, and for all of her warm and generous hospitality during my stay in Oslo.
2. Jean-Luc Nancy, *The Truth of Democracy*, trans. P.-A. Brault and M. Naas (New York: Fordham University Press, 2010), p. 26.
3. Ibid., p. 26.
4. Jacques Derrida, *Rogues: Two Essays on Reason*, trans. P.-A. Brault and M. Naas, Meridian: Crossing Aesthetics (Stanford: Stanford University Press, 2005), p. 47.
5. In a recent essay, Nancy writes that, 'politics [as though responding to its own exigency] . . . must permit spheres that are, strictly speaking, foreign to it, to expand on their own'; Jean-Luc Nancy, 'Finite and Infinite Democracy', in *Democracy in What State?* (New York: Columbia University Press, [2009] 2011), p. 64. As he goes on to state in this same essay: 'politics is in charge of space and of spacing (of space-time), but [it] is not in charge of figuring', and therefore is less a form than a force, or specifically, a force and 'form of access to openness of the other forms', ibid., p. 73.
6. Which in terms of the latter means thinking aesthetics not in terms of *poietic* production and revelation, but as inoperative technique and praxis, as I argue below. Nancy, *The Truth of Democracy*, p. 50.
7. 'There is no space previously provided for displacement (which is why the images of the agora or forum could be misleading), but there is a sharing and partitioning of origin in which singularities space apart and space their being-in-common.' Jean-Luc Nancy, *The Experience of Freedom*, trans. B. McDonald (Stanford: Stanford University Press, 1993), p. 74.
8. Nancy, *The Experience of Freedom*, p. 78.
9. Jean-Luc Nancy, 'Being Singular Plural', in *Being Singular Plural*, trans. R. D. Richardson and A. E. O'Byrne, Meridian: Crossing Aesthetics (Stanford: Stanford University Press, 2000), p. 39.
10. Nancy, *The Experience of Freedom*, p. 75.
11. Ibid., p. 78; emphasis in original.
12. Derrida, *Rogues*, p. 49.
13. This sense of absolute equality should be familiar to readers of the work of Jacques Rancière as well as that of Nancy. In my book *The Decision Between Us*, in a chapter titled 'Name No One Name', I discuss Jean Genet's experience of sensing the absolute equality with all other singular beings, as presented in his essay, 'What Remains

of a Rembrandt Torn into Little Squares All the Same Size and Shot Down the Toilet'. John Paul Ricco, *The Decision Between Us: Art and Ethics in the Time of Scenes* (Chicago: University of Chicago Press, 2014). For Nancy, as for Arendt and Ranciere (and others), politics has no a priori or proper place, but is instead the sharing-out (partitioning) of the spacing of sense as nothing but interrupted, separated, and divided. And it is in this non-ontological technique (and *ars*) of shared-separation (*partager*), that a politics of being-together can be said to take place as interval and passage. Yet not in an Arendt-like space of appearance of the in-between of being in common, but of a Nancy-inspired space of exposure (as Philip Armstrong's work on Nancy and the political has made clear) to an irreducible incommensurability that is 'us' – *partes extra partes*. Which is to say, a being-together that is not defined in terms of identity, but of separated spacing. Hence political practice is not a matter of *poiesis* in terms of either the revelation or production of a space deemed political, but of *praxis* (Arendt fully understood this), yet a praxis that is as much inoperative as it is operative, given that it consists in sustaining (retracing) the space between-us, in and as its withdrawal, retreat and disappearance – in other words: *compearance*. Not spontaneity, but simultaneity and a certain intrusiveness of coincidence or what Nancy describes as 'the instant itself as exteriority: the simultaneous'. See Nancy, 'Being Singular Plural', pp. 67–8.
14. Nancy, *The Truth of Democracy*, p. 17.
15. Nancy, 'Finite and Infinite Democracy', p. 64.
16. Ibid., p. 72. Hence Nancy's practice, as we have already encountered, of listing 'these other places . . . where incommensurability is in some way *formed* and *presented*: they can go by the names "art", "religion", "thought", "science", "ethics", "conduct", "exchange", "production", "love", "war", "kinship", "intoxication" – and the list could go on ad infinitum'. See: Nancy, *The Truth of Democracy*, p. 50.
17. Jean-Luc Nancy, *The Sense of the World*, trans. J. S. Librett (Minneapolis and London: University of Minnesota Press, 1997), p. 133.
18. Images of Felix Gonzalez-Torres' work can be found online at: <http://www.andrearosengallery.com/artists/felix-gonzalez-torres> and <http://felixgonzalez-torresfoundation.org/>.
19. Jacques Derrida, *On the Name*, ed. Werner Hamacher and David E. Wellbery, trans. D. Wood, J. P. Leavey Jr, and I. McLeod, Meridian:

Crossing Aesthetics (Stanford: Stanford University Press, 1995), p. 14.
20. Octavio Paz, 'The Ready-Made', in *Marcel Duchamp in Perspective*, ed. Joseph Masheck (Englewood Cliffs, NJ: Prentice-Hall, 1975), p. 86.
21. Ibid., p. 87.
22. Ibid., p. 86.
23. When it comes to an inoperative praxis of the already-unmade, such as in the gallery installations by Gonzalez-Torres discussed below, it is perhaps not even a matter of a circle (open or closed) but more precisely of that which is without closure, including in terms of being without end ('bad' infinity). Instead, Gonzalez-Torres's candy pile and paper stack installations are always in rapport with 'end' (i.e. finitude) yet infinitely so, and hence are the opening up or dis-enclosure of the circle – opening or dis-enclosure, right at the limit of their presentation/disappearance, and not simply in terms of the repetition of difference that infinitely repeats itself.
24. Although, as we will see, the notion 'audience', as receivers (whether passive or active) of the work of art, is one of the things, the status of which, Gonzalez-Torres's work puts into question, and in ways beyond 'relational aesthetics' with which he is so often associated in the contemporary discourse that goes by that name.
25. From the Translators' Introduction to Jean-Luc Nancy, *The Creation of the World, or Globalization*, trans. F. Raffoul and D. Pettigrew (Albany: SUNY Press, 2007), p. 15.
26. Nancy, *The Sense of the World*, p. 132. I would contend that most contemporary engagements with Jean-Luc Nancy's anti-productivist aesthetics and politics have not gone far enough in their rethinking of the author and the audience, and the 'collaborative work' that can occur between them. For any theorisation of aesthetic praxis that retains the language of participation, process, making, and construction (and destruction for that matter), thereby remains committed (implicitly or other wise) to a modernist ideology of work, including the hope and goal of the end of work in the form of the ultimate completion of the work.
27. Jean-Luc Nancy, 'The Confronted Community', in Andrew J. Mitchell and Jason Kemp Winfree (eds), *The Obsessions of Georges Bataille: Community and Communication*, SUNY Series in Contemporary French Thought (Albany: SUNY Press, 2009), p. 27.
28. Or as Nancy might put it, 'infinitely singularizing the ends'. Nancy, *The Creation of the World, or Globalization*, p. 61.

29. Derrida, *Rogues*, p. 1.
30. John Cage, *A Year From Monday* (Middletown, CT: Wesleyan University Press, 1967), p. 71.
31. The endless supply of mass-produced candy and their being taken, again and again, might also recall for us the language of multiplication and repetition in Hannah Arendt's philosophy of work and labour. However, whereas for Arendt 'Multiplication should not be confused with repetition', given that, as she goes on to state: 'Multiplication actually multiplies things [and hence belongs to work], whereas repetition follows the recurrent cycle of life in which its products disappear almost as fast as they have appeared' (and hence belongs to labour), we must recognise the extent to which these distinctions are blurred, and the chain of means and ends are deconstructed by the inoperative praxis that I am seeking to theorise here. See: Hannah Arendt, *The Portable Hannah Arendt* (London: Penguin, 2000), pp. 174–5.
32. 'Elle est multiplication de fins sans fin, plûtot que moyens ajustés à des fins: errance, distinerrance (Derrida). Elle est aussi moins "oeuvre" que mise hors de soi, ex-position.' Jean-Luc Nancy, 'Hors Colloque', *Figures du Dehors: Autour de Jean-Luc Nancy* (Nantes: Éditions Nouvelles Cécile Defaut, 2012), p. 535.
33. Jean-Luc Nancy, *The Muses*, trans. P. Kamuf (Stanford: Stanford University Press, 1996), p. 32.
34. Nancy, *The Creation of the World, or Globalization*, p. 90; emphasis in original.
35. Nancy, *The Sense of the World*, p. 113; emphasis in original.
36. Nancy, *The Muses* p. 3; emphasis in original.
37. Nancy, 'Finite and Infinite Democracy', pp. 73–4.
38. Nancy, *The Creation of the World, or Globalization*, p. 51; brackets added. 'The withdrawal of any given thus forms the heart of a thinking of creation', ibid.
39. Jean-Luc Nancy, *Being Singular Plural*, ed. Werner Hamacher and David E. Wellbery, trans. R. D. Richardson and A. E. O'Byrne, Meridian: Crossing Aesthetics (Stanford: Stanford University Press, 2000), p. 17.
40. Jean-Luc Nancy, *The Ground of the Image*, trans. J. Fort, Perspectives in continental philosophy (New York: Fordham University Press, 2005), p. 68.
41. Giorgio Agamben, *Means without End: Notes on Politics*, trans. V. Binetti and C. Casarino, Theory out of bounds (Minneapolis: University of Minnesota Press, 2000), p. 59. It is in this way that, at

one point, Nancy also defines art as distinct from both a poiesis and a praxis, as when he writes: 'What art does is to *please:* (is it supposed to say that "art pleases"?: and so it is neither a *poiesis* nor a *praxis*, but another kind of "doing" altogether that mixes together with both of the other kinds an *aisthesis* and its double entelechy.' See Nancy, *The Sense of the World*, p. 134. (This is the actual form of the quote. I have corrected the missing italics.)
42. Nancy, *The Creation of the World, or Globalization*, p. 54.
43. Ibid., p. 54.
44. Ibid., p. 54.
45. Ibid., p. 54.
46. Karl Marx, *Outline of the Critique of Political Economy* (Grundrisse der Kritik der Politischen Ökonomie), trans. M. Nicolaus (1857; repr. New York: Penguin, 1973), p. 111.
47. Nancy, *The Sense of the World*, p. 132.
48. Roland Barthes, 'Lecture', *October*, 8, Spring 1979, p. 15.
49. Ibid.
50. Maurice Blanchot, *The Space of Literature*, trans. A. Smock (Lincoln, NE: University of Nebraska Press, 1982), p. 264.
51. As Blanchot writes in a note to his chapter 'Sleep, Night:', 'So ambiguity does not consist only in the incessant movement by which being returns to nothingness and nothingness refers back to being. Ambiguity is no longer the primordial Yes and No in which being and nothingness would be pure identity. The essential ambiguity would lie, rather, in this: that before the beginning, nothingness is not on equal standing with being, but is only the appearance of being's concealment, or again, that dissimulation is more "original" than negation. So, one could say: *ambiguity is all the more essential because dissimulation cannot quite be captured in negation.*' Blanchot, *The Space of Literature*, p. 264; emphasis in original.
52. Nancy, *The Muses*, pp. 54–5.
53. Ibid., p. 55.
54. Jean-Luc Nancy and Alexander Garcia Düttmann, 'Picking Up', in Olivier Richon (ed.), *Picking Up, Bouncing Back* (London: Royal College of Art, 2010), p. 12. I am grateful to my colleague Brian Price, who gave me a copy – through his friend Alexander Garcia Düttmann – of this beautiful catalogue of graduate thesis work in photography at the Royal College of Art.

The Political Between Two Infinities: Evaluations

9

Im-mundus or Nancy's Globalising-World-Formation

Jean-Paul Martinon

In an attempt to make sense[1] of the world, Jean-Luc Nancy writes in *The Sense of the World*, one of the most abyssal paragraphs possible:

> I would like here to open up an exploration of the space that is common to all of us, that makes up our community: the space of the most extended generality of sense, at once as a distended, *desolate extension* – the desert that grows – and as a broadly open, *available extension*, one that we *sense* to be an urgency, necessity, or imperative. This common space is infinitely slight. It is nothing but the limit that separates and mixes at once the *in-significance* that arises out of the pulverization of significations and the *archi-significance* encountered by the *need* of being-towards-the-world. This limit separates and mixes the most common, most banal of senses – the evident inconsistency of the justification of our lives – and the most singular, the evident *necessity* of the least fragment of existence as of the world *toward* which it exists.[2]

Let me begin by trying to make sense of this dense paragraph: on the one hand, there is a distended and desolate *extension* of sense *and* non-sense ('*in*-significance'), created by the pulverisation of significations. On the other hand, as it were, there is an open and available *extension* (of) archi-sense ('*archi*-significance') stemming from the *need* to be towards the world.[3] With this juxtaposition, Nancy is *not* interested in pitching one facet of the world (the *in-significance* of the world) against the other (the *archi-significance* of the need of being-towards-the-world).[4] He is interested in thinking the *common* limit that paradoxically brings together and yet also separates the two apart. This *common* limit is not something that can be singled out, objectified, analysed, dissected, and discarded. It is a multi-faceted liminal operation that, as Nancy says, knows no stable referent *and yet* still manages to generate the world.[5]

But what is the point of focusing on such an abyssal and liminal operation that, evidently, takes place every second of time? As is well known, Nancy's aim is not to provide yet another picture of the world, but to actually embody its making, its creation; that is, in one Heideggerian expression: to work out how the world 'worlds'.[6] How is one to make sense of the way the world 'worlds'? Could the 'worlding' of the world be this common limit or double extension (in-significance/archi-significance)? If yes, how is one then to make sense of this liminal operation that is curiously at once ontological and ontical? Finally, but most importantly, once we make sense of this limit, how can we affect it politically so that it escapes its very own annihilation? These are the questions that will be addressed in this chapter. The aim is not to present once again an exhaustive overview of Nancy's interpretation of the world or its relationship to the three Abrahamic religions. There is enough scholarship already on that topic.[7] The aim is instead to evaluate the political *potential* of this liminal operation 'made up' of in-significance and archi-significance. This does not mean that what follows will demonstrate how Nancy's work can be seen to have a political *agenda*.[8] This simply means that Nancy's interpretation of the world perhaps gives us a radically new political *potential* for the world: to politically embody, what he overall calls the stance of the world.

In order to address this aim, the following chapter will *first* explore the sense of the world, the way it makes sense to us, especially as it is understood when the word 'globalisation' is mentioned. This will reveal a slightly different reading of globalisation.[9] Globalisation is usually understood as a 'uni-totality'[10] ruled by a de-regulated set of markets (commodities, capital, and labour) that has over the years partially phased out all unitary systems, including the nation-state.[11] However, if one focuses on the political dimension of Nancy's thought, a different understanding of globalisation comes about, one which curiously, and contrary to what many believe does not come across as specifically *alter-mondialiste*,[12] as if he were an advocate fighting to go 'beyond' globalisation. As the prefatory note to his book, *The Creation of the World*[13] clearly intimates, Nancy's understanding of the world is much more nuanced, taking, both, the world and

Im-mundus or Nancy's Globalising-World-Formation   221

globalisation, its archi-signification and its deepening in-signification, into account.

The *second* section will elaborate on this stance or liminal operation (in-significance/archi-significance), by exploring how Nancy pushes the argument further with the crucially split word *im-mundus*. With this split word, Nancy brings together this double extension or liminal operation. *Im-mundus* will be the way we create and produce the world, a gesture that stems paradoxically from out of no-*thing* and yet is some-*thing* that is with *and* without reason. With this approach, this chapter will hope to show that Nancy's attempt to expose the liminal stance of the world is an eminently political gesture that helps us to reopen, as he says, 'each possible struggle for a world',[14] and in the process to fight against this pernicious growth of the wasteland, to recall Nietzsche's famous cry.[15]

1. Globalisation: A World At and As the End

Globe, global, globalising, globalisation, globality: all these words have the same Latin root: *globus*: round mass, sphere, ball. The main characteristic of such etymological root is that, however divergent their meanings, all of the derivatives assume a circumscribed *whole*. They all associate the word 'globalisation' with the spherical shape of the earth, as if the two were necessarily mutually dependent. The shape of anything related to *globus*, and by extension, the shape of globalisation is therefore always – in most people's minds, at least – a physically limited round thing. However, if one discards the cliché juxtaposition earth/globe and imagines another shape, the limit of this shape suddenly becomes problematic: What shape does globalisation have? How is one to understand a limit to globalisation? Even if one can identify a limit, what would make it remain stable and/or comprehensible not just 'once and for all', but at least for the time it is articulated? Furthermore, if the solar system, the galaxy, and the universe are not what constitute an outside, then what exterior is really conjured up when thinking the limits of what is global? Is there such a thing as a non-globalised world? The questions about the limits of globalisation abound, but the answers are always short in coming.[16] This lack of answers shows that when it comes to the idea of globalisation, it is always the very idea of limit that is effectively put in question.

Considering the fact that it is always un-ascribable, this question of limit is perhaps that of an end creating itself. Globalisation knows no limit because it spends its time shaping its own end. Although one cannot escape this sense entirely, this ending is not apocalyptic. This ending effectively refers to an always-postponed achievement. It is the process of the creation of the end itself.[17] Nancy talks about this at length when he references our globalised and technologised world. He writes, for example, 'the world is always a "creation": a *tekné* with neither principle nor end nor material *other than itself*.'[18] In this way, far from simply revealing the integration of markets, nation-states, cultures, identities, and, technologies, globalisation exposes ourselves to the creation of the end of the world, whereby we are exposed to the endpoint at which the globe as a 'comprehensible' achievement (social, cultural, political, economic, and so on) creates itself.

The curious consequence of this ever-renewed ending is that in the process, globalisation allows itself to be perceived as *an* object of analysis.[19] This does not revert back to the idea of globalisation as a round object floating in space. Globalisation becomes an object because, in the process of creating itself as the end, globalisation figures itself as 'an object that ends'. In this process, globalisation therefore continuously offers itself as an object that curiously isn't 'one'. It achieves itself as what is effectively incapable of achievement. As Christina Smerick rightly says, 'globalization is not merely an economic situation regarding trade and popular culture. Globalization is making One of the world, which is not one'.[20] There would be no worldwide discussion about this controversial term if this were not the case.

This has a further consequence: in order for it to be perceived as 'an object', globalisation also, inevitably, projects an *imaginary* outside perspective. The *imaginary* aspect of this projection is here important because what ends cannot extricate itself from this end; it can only *imagine* it can do so. In other words, the process of globalisation can only offer itself if it *imagines* an end to the process itself, even though there is no evidence for it. In this way, and this is the crucial aspect of this consequence, globalisation is entirely structured in the dependency of metaphysics or, more precisely, in the dependency of onto-theology to make sense. In other words, and however much it is tied to the process of ending, globalisation *imagines* that one can stand outside of it and look at it as a comprehensive whole as if a god or an alien. But if one discards gods and aliens, how is one to understand this onto-theological status? What gives globalisation its slippery representational power?

a) The Rule of Tautologies

In his book *Dis-enclosure: The Deconstruction of Christianity*, Jean-Luc Nancy provides us with one of the most comprehensive analyses of the link between globalisation and its onto-theological context. He says the following:

> We know – how could we ignore this – that the threefold monotheism of a threefold religion of the Book (with which one could associate ancient Manichaeism, as well) defines a Mediterraneo-European particularity and, from there, diverse forms of global expansion ... Globalization is, as I understand it, in more than one respect a globalization of monotheism in one or another of its forms.[21]

In other words, globalisation is the result not only of the global expansion of Abraham's three religions, but also, and perhaps above all, of the monotheic aspect of these religions. If one accepts Nancy's link, and therefore the intricate relationship between these one-god religions and globalisation, then the question that immediately springs to mind is this: What exactly brings together the secular process of globalisation that we know today, and the monotheic aspect of these three millennial religions? Nancy answers this question by telling us that what links globalisation and monotheism is the tautological nature of its principal value. In the case of religion, the principle value is God and its unique tautological sense: God = God. In other words, nothing can replace God and nothing can compare to Him. He is 'One', and as such He reigns alone and has no rival. With regards to globalisation, the principle value is money in its tautological sense: money = money. In other words, no other value can replace the value of money. Money reigns supreme and nothing, not even bartering, can be used in its place.[22] In this way, the relationship between globalisation and the monotheism of Abraham's three religions is the value attributed overall to the mono-valence of its absolute values:[23] God and/or money. But how is one to understand this concretely?

b) Tautological Mono-valences

Karl Marx tells us that a general equivalency is achieved when a relative social mono-valence (in his case, money, but with Nancy, both money and God) is given an abstract value that supersedes all others. There is therefore a general equivalence when one symbol or one commodity is excluded from all others and is subsequently used in order to regulate what is left behind as unelected. Marx argues that: 'a particular kind of commodity acquires the character of general equivalent, because all other commodities make it the material in which they uniformly express their value'.[24] The singled out mono-valence or commodity is the one that functions as the general equivalent regulating all exchanges. This means that nothing can effectively equate, replace, or disturb the worldwide reign of tautologies known as God or money. They stand for the only language referents able to mediate and regulate all other exchanges within language. They are the general equivalents of all other terms in the system.[25]

Nancy draws three main consequences from the prevalence accorded to these tautological mono-valences: *First consequence*: it inevitably implies *a leveling of all distinctions*. As he says in the context of an analysis of democracy: 'The democratic world developed in the context – to which it is linked from the origin – of general equivalence. This expression – from Marx – designates . . . the general leveling of all distinctions and the reduction of all forms of excellence through mediocratization.'[26] This should not be understood as a lament for hierarchies or quasi-religious orders. This should be understood simply as the impossibility of seeing beyond the reference to a general equivalence. Everything, from procreation to death and from inorganic events to natural disasters,[27] is regulated by a reference to these incalculable mono-valences. Once regulated by them, there are no more distinctions; everything becomes secondary, mediocre. The *second consequence* is that *globalisation can only be a homogeneous traffic* that results in a fundamentalism of values. In other words, in a situation where there are only two mono-valences and nothing distinguishes itself outside of the value attributed by these mono-valences, everything becomes torn apart by secular and/or religious fundamentalisms. As Nancy says:

> Value returns eternally, precisely because it has no price . . . This is why our homogeneous world presents evaluation now as an equiva-

lence of mercantile value, now as one entailing the sacrifice of existence to a supreme omnipotence. It is always a traffic. It is always one fundamentalism of value against another: one value being valued as a fundamental, a principle measure, God or money, spiritual or stock-market value.[28]

There is therefore no way to exclude or excuse ourselves from these ever-prevalent mono-valences. This lack of alternative leaves us stranded 'in a traffic' with the bank or with heaven; a situation that drives, for example, many of us to become wage-slaves and/or fundamentalists (religious and/or secular).

Stuck in a perpetual homogeneous traffic, we become (*third and final consequence*) a multitude in a pluriverse that prevents us from uniting and acting together. Going against authors such as Hardt and Negri,[29] Nancy retorts that a 'multitude' disperses everyone into individual singularities, thus failing to assemble around a common effort. In an article for the communist newspaper *L'Hummanité*, Nancy, for example, wonders

> whether [this] dispersion (and therefore the use of the word 'multitude') is not precisely due to the rampant globalization imposed by capitalism, which the anti-globalization movement is trying to denounce ... 'Multitude' ... multiplies individuals and small groups, but not in the sense of an increase, propelled by a force, for example. It multiplies individuals as if all of them were caught in a type of errancy.[30]

The argument is clear: globalisation leaves us stranded in a 'pluri-' or 'multi-verse' that has lost all political agency and potential.[31] Stuck in endless traffic, a devout or a slave to one, or both, of these two ever-prevalent mono-valences, we become, as Hannah Arendt remarked a long time ago,[32] isolated and unable to come together, form groups or coalitions. We all err alone with our tablets and androids, solitary social networkers of multi-verses.

c) The Unworld (Non-Sense)[33] and the World (Sense)

The overall outcome of this view of the process of globalisation (as a pluri-verse scattered throughout with errant singularities caught in an endless traffic regulated by two monovalences) is, as Nancy says, in one formidable word: the unworld [*immundus* or *l'immonde*]. The unworld is *not just* what is unclean, it is *also and above all*, what does *not* belong to the world. Globalisation leads us to the unworld, that is, to what is *not* a world. Here again, it is crucial to understand that, although contrasted, the unworld and the world are not engaged in a dialectical battle as if opposite forces. As Nancy clearly says, 'one must not oppose the world and the unworld'.[34] For him, the two take place not against each other, but simultaneously in the creation and destruction of the world. If they were understood against each other, then, the unworld would oppose itself to the world, and everyone would wish the world to absorb the unworld (i.e. recycle it). As Nancy says in *Corpus*:[35]

> The world of bodies is shared with and divided by *immundus*. Identically. This isn't a simple dialectical respiration form the 'same' to the 'other', finally gathering up the trash and sublimating or recycling it. In this world and its creation, something exceeds and twists the cycles. . . . (Neither our bodies nor the world are circular, and ecotechnical creation's most serious law is *not to come full circle.*)[36]

However malignant it may be, the process of globalisation takes place as the world exceeds itself; an excess that can never reabsorb itself. We encounter here something crucial, but rarely highlighted in the many commentaries on Nancy's work. There is indeed a strange parallel between globalisation and what Nancy calls 'world-forming' (*mondialisation*). This parallel shows that neither comes full circle, both exceed each other, thus never allowing for sense (world-forming) to make *absolute* sense or for non-sense (globalisation) to end in either a *parousia* of (scientific) meaning, or total annihilation. In this way, there is no escaping this impossibility to recycle properly because creation is what goes radically beyond the logic of production (and therefore recycling), and, yet, the possibility of this production never leaves the horizon of creation. The two always go together while always exceeding themselves. This is not a circular thought; it is the facticity of thought itself, that is to say, it is the facticity of the world itself. In this way, there is no pure creation or world-formation as such. There is an exposure or opening that both creates *and* for good or bad also produces. It creates by emptying itself (the *nihil* creating or, as we have seen, the available extension archi-signification), and it produces not as a positive positioning, but as spacing (the desolate extension of in-significance) and this with no possibility of hypostasis as the moment-point where this spacing or extension can be identified. This is what allows Nancy to write about the 'nothing growing *as something*',[37] that is, as an object that, in the end, can be analysed as such. In other words, there is a void emptying itself and, in the process, produces *the world* as we know it.

Through such a liminal operation (i.e. this creation / production-without-positioning or globalising-world-forming), the world becomes, as Nancy says, in another formidable juxtaposition of words: a subject-reject[38] [*un sujet-de-rejet*] or *im-mundus*, the latter crucially hyphenated in order to distinguish it from the unworld, i.e. *immundus*. As he says: 'A body expels itself: as corpus, as spasmic space, distended, subject-reject [*sujet-de-rejet*], "im-mundus" if we have to keep the word. But that's how this world takes place.'[39] In other words, the unworld (*immundus* in one word) comes as the world forms itself (*mundus*): *im-mundus* (hyphenated). The word *im-mundus* is now crucially open: the world is at once a globalising phenomenon *and* a world-forming itself; an odd juxtaposition that can only be allergic to both sublation and deconstruction, precisely because it is the facticity of the self-de-*construction* of the world.

The consequence of this crucial juxtaposition of words, and therefore of this view of globalisation/world-formation, is that Nancy is not asking us, as is so often mistakenly commented upon, to choose between globalisation and world-formation (i.e. between *immundus* or *mundus*).[40] He is simply asking us to take both into consideration (*im-mundus*). Again, as he says: 'The intrication of world and filth [*du monde et de l'immonde*] cannot be, for us, either disintricated or dissimulated.'[41] Beyond the impossibility of recycling, the reason is simple: neither world-forming nor globalisation are 'destinies' as such; they are stances. One fabricates; the other creates.[42] One can be (just about) represented, the other cannot. The two sustain each other in their own stance. This is the only way the stance of the world can *make* sense, *is* sense. There would be no *authors* such as Jean-Luc Nancy, and there would be no commentators on his work happily engaging in the eco-technology of books, if this were not the case. The sense they impart is our sense.

This impossibility of disintricating one from the other is precisely what makes the world to 'world'. Caught in an endless traffic ruled by a couple of general equivalences, *our* 'growth takes care of itself';[43] *we* take care of ourselves, and the only way we can do this is to *both* create *and* produce – that is, to participate in the creation of the world *and* of its globalised eco-technological productions. There cannot be an alternative because the un-reflective and un-recyclable stances of the world do not allow it. And this is precisely what leads us *to erase* the world, *that is*, paradoxically *to create* a world that is always already *not* the world, i.e. not yet: *immundus*. With Nancy, the world as we conceive it today does not *just* slowly wither into nonsense (as in Heidegger),[44] and it does not *just* space us apart (as in Arendt); it remains, together, in-significance and archi-significance, subject-reject: *im-mundus, open*. As Christina Smerick rightly points out, inflecting the argument perhaps too optimistically: the structure that produces the nightmare – globalisation – is also the structure that produces hope.[45]

Inevitably, the question that arises as a result is this: Now that we have discarded the possibility of an alternative (globalisation as an inevitable socio-economic process that either benefits or harms the world, depending on the perspective *or mondialisation* as a creation *ex-nihilo* that exceeds the transcendental conditions of possibility of representation), how is one to understand the stance of this subject-reject, this *im-mundus* or globalising-world-forming?

2. *Im-mundus:* A New Non-Equivalence

Nancy's attempt to think a liminal subject-reject or *im-mundus* consists in fact in trying to find a new non-equivalence:[46] the always renewed affirmation of a unique, incomparable, and unsubstitutable 'sense' that would be *proper* to *im-mundus*, that is, *proper* to a world that perhaps for the first time asks itself whether it is worth saving, or more precisely, saluting in a Derridean sense. How is one to understand this 'properness' based on a radical non-equivalence? Nancy writes:

> The challenge is thus to introduce a new non-equivalence that would have nothing to do, of course, with the non-equivalence of feudalisms or aristocracies, or of regimes of divine election or salvation, or of spiritualities, heroisms, or aestheticisms, etc. It would not be a matter of introducing another system of differential values; it would be a matter of finding, of achieving a sense of evaluation, of evaluative affirmation, that gives to each evaluating gesture – a decision of existence, of work, of bearing – the possibility of not being measured in advance by

a given system but of being on the contrary, each time the affirmation of a unique, incomparable un-substitutable 'value' or 'sense'. Only this can displace what is called economic domination, which is but the effect of the fundamental decision for equivalence.[47]

The proposal is clear: the world needs a sense of evaluation that does not foster further traffic and fundamentalism, but gives experience a kind of value that is free of onto-theological constraints. The challenge is to give each human gesture the possibility of not being made into a commodity, or being tied to an absolute. Furthermore, the challenge is to give experience the chance of affirming itself as its own evaluation.[48] This new value is not intended either to create a new realm (in this world or another), or to (re)discover the unity immanent to the world, as if there could be some underlining sense to a fragmented multiplicity.[49] The value to be found should be that of the sense of our own *im-mundus*, subject-reject.

The reason Nancy insists so much on sense (and specifically the sense of *im-mundus*) is because, as he says, 'there is no longer a back-world [*un arrière-monde*] as Nietzsche would say'[50] that would metaphorically give sense to (or guarantee the meaning of) our existence. In other words, the reason we need to focus on sense is because we need to make sense for ourselves, as subject-rejects of this subject-reject that is *im-mundus*. We can no longer afford to create meaning only to latch it on one or two peerless mono-valences. God and money need to be thought *not otherwise, but for the first time without guarantees, that is, unhinged from their assumed tautological truths*. As such, this new value must be not only allergic to any kind of trafficking, it must also be without measure (absolute or otherwise). As Nancy says, referring to Georges Bataille's non-productive expenditures:

> Value must have value without measure. Bataille expressed this by calling value 'heterogeneous': The homogenous is the exchange of values, a general equivalence. In order to have value properly, it is necessary that value be heterogeneous to that equivalence ... The heterogeneous is not a matter of usage or of exchange, it is a matter of experience.[51]

Unique and unrepeatable, untradeable and unpreservable, the sense of *im-mundus* is therefore a general economy – in a Bataillean sense – that must risk itself in all its radical heterogeneity. This risk is incalculable because it is 'external to all numeration, to any counting',[52] and this is precisely the measure of this in-significance / archi-significance that is *im-mundus*.

The extraordinary consequence of this vision is that the sense of this heterogeneity is effectively worth nothing. The new non-equivalence can have neither an absolute value (God), nor an incomparable value (money). This does not mean that this new non-equivalence is worthless, something that can only be discarded because it cannot be compared to God or exchanged with or for money. The subject is *not just* a reject; it still retains itself as subject. *Im-mundus* is not just *immundus*; it is also *mundus*. As such, the sense of *im-mundus* is its own worth. As Nancy says, '[a] heterogeneous value is worth nothing, or it is worth what the "valent" [*valoir*] in itself is worth: an exposure to some measure when that measure is but the other of all measure, or its infinity in act'.[53] In this way, the sense of *im-mundus* or subject-reject is effectively a heterogeneity that knows no equivalent and, indisputably, no price-tag. This does not refer to the banal fact that life has no price (while knowing all along that this life can be traded, bartered, or insured, for example). This refers instead to the happenstance of a heterogeneity that is indeed worth nothing or is its own worth.

3. To Desire to Remain in Desire

But how can anyone make sense of this *im-mundus*, at once the process of globalisation and that of world-forming, without automatically re-absorbing it as some 'thing' with an onto-theological value? What concrete example can one choose to make sense of this non-sense (of the world, of existence) whose heterogeneity never allows it to have any worth in the conventional sense of the term? In order to make sense of this, it is necessary to go back to the way Nancy re-articulates Heidegger's understanding of Being. He writes:

> To the letter of Heidegger's texts, one could not substitute being with world. However, in spirit, things are different ... [For Heidegger,] being is, in one word, a verb. Being is no longer Being or a being, but 'to be', that is, a transitive verb: to be Being. Heidegger formulates this transitive request with the use of a non-grammatical expression.

He also formulates it (in *What is Philosophy?*) by giving a kind of equivalence: being takes (*legein, logos*) Being. I would prefer to formulate this transcription or translation differently. I would say that to be desires Being ... To be is thus simply this: let it be [*que l'étant est*]. Being is being: tautology in which Being resolves itself in being.[54]

The difference is clearly exposed here: instead of the tautological 'being takes Being' with which the early Heidegger ends his existential analyses, Nancy proposes to focus instead on the way 'to be' *desires* Being. The focus on desire is an attempt to ex-pose *concretely* the sense of existence or *im-mundus*. Desire is a crucial expression, because it is that which is sought after, coveted, called for. It is a movement; the movement of the *conatus*: desire for Being/World.

But the question remains: How could one desire without automatically appropriating it as need? In other words, how can one create the world without also effectively letting globalisation produce it as yet more meaningful/less surplus atomising us even more? In the end, we all want something, so how can one desire something other than general equivalence, that is, more money, more God? Nancy answers these questions in this way: 'How does one name the object of a desire that is not a general equivalence? I call it "sense", but I will also name it "desire": we desire to remain in desire, in the tension towards ... in the leap. This is the only way there can be something beyond equivalence.'[55] The world thus desires the world. The subject-reject thus desires itself as subject through its own rejection. Again, this is *not* a theme for thought. *Im-mundus* is a thrust or a throw, but not in the sense whereby we would go from one place to another. It is an unpredictable surge that can only be understood or heard, as Nancy says in Manchev's interview above, with the saying, 'let there be' [*que l'étant est*].[56] This expression does not refer to the biblical *fiat* (as in *fiat lux*: 'let there be light') because no dispelling of ignorance is implied. *Que l'étant est* implies being's surge in being-ness (as Nancy says in French: '*que l'étant en étant cherche et accroît en même temps son étantité*').[57] However, this does not simply take place at a pure ontological level. It also occurs in being's embodiment, the way the body surges in its bodily or material form. As such, it describes the embodiment of our very own stance or that of the world, as we *know* it. The expression 'let there be' therefore refers to a *fact*, the stance of the world or globe, an excess of significance and insignificance sustained [*sous-tendue*], by an archi-significance that desires to remain in desire. This is what *concretely* takes place here, now, 'in' this globalised world-forming or being/Being, and this without necessarily staining or straining it with metaphysical meaning.

A Demand for Reason

But let's push this further and ask: How does this thrust maintain itself? In other words, how can anything whatsoever sustain itself in this manner? An answer to these questions is precisely what should give us the *general* stance of *im-mundus*; the way *im-mundus* desires to remain in desire, the way globalisation and the world ex-pose themselves without referring to any given principle, nor to any assigned end by an outside or inside value.[58] Nancy writes:

> The world is . . . a fact: it may well be that it is the only fact of this kind (if it is the case that the other facts take place within the world). It is a fact without reason or end, and it is our fact. To think it, is to think this factuality, which implies not referring it to a meaning capable of appropriating it, but to placing in it, in its truth as a fact, all possible meaning.[59]

This is not a banal forensic thought: 'let's focus on the facts not on interpretations or reactions'. Nancy is a concrete thinker; the factuality of *im-mundus* is its sense, its non-equivalence, what desires sense, including interpretations and reactions. But how do we place *im-mundus* in its truth as a fact?

Once again, when it comes to the factuality of *im-mundus*, Heidegger's influence on Nancy's thought is unmistakable.[60] This is particularly acute when reference is made to Heidegger's *Principle of Reason*. In order to demonstrate that there is something without reason or entirely its own reason, Nancy, like Heidegger, quotes from the spiritual poem of Angelus Silesius, *The Cherubic Wanderer: Sensual Description of the Four Final Things*; the famous line taken from that text being, 'the rose grows without reason'.[61] The crux of Nancy's argument is that as soon as there is world, there is a demand for reason; there is *a demand* to frame or limit the world as vision, as globe, as a globalising phenomenon. But before this demand, the appearance of the world itself, like that of the rose, is without reason. Heidegger argues the same thing when he says that, 'the character of the demand to render, the *reddendum*, belongs to reason',[62] while the rose and the world pay no attention to itself, asks not whether it needs a reason. Accordingly, humans are the *animal rationale*, the creatures that require accounts (and in the process globalise their world-formation); they 'are the reckoning creature',[63] reckoning understood in the broad sense of the word *ratio*. In this way, world-forming comes to be experienced not as something rendered (by God or a Leibnizian principle of reason, for example), but as a demand that always gives accounts of the world as globe.

Im-mundus is thus at once without reason (like the rose) *and* (unlike the rose) a demand for reason that can never be properly rendered (again). This does not easily justify or equate globalisation with nature (the unworld, like a weed, spreads and nothing can be done to prevent it), and it does not reabsorb everything under human agency (humans are the only reckoning creatures on earth). Neither reason nor ground sustains *mundus*, and, yet, *mundus* demands, even commands its global account, its *immundus*,[64] for example with this demanding question: What is one to do with this globalised world? This explains why the world, as world, as the whole of what appears (always multiple, open, untotalisable) is concrete, which means that it never explains itself as it deploys itself, never presents itself as a factual intelligible necessity. As Nancy says in a recent collaborative book with Arelien Barrau, 'the world never matches its "being-thought"'.[65]

Without Grasp

There is no doubt that Nancy's understanding of the world and of globalisation is unique inasmuch as it never allows itself to veer into a fixed interpretation of the topic. The world and the globe never cease to defy themselves, both as representation and as creation. Once again, this does not make of *im-mundus* a quasi-representational vitalist movement that knows no rest. Part of Nancy's efforts is precisely to counteract this idea, and to propose instead the participation in the making of this subject-reject. This necessarily includes our participation in the making of this world and a non-messianic openness to what is radically unexpected or incommensurable.[66] The former does not sublate the latter, and the latter is not a mystical prayer. The stance of the world is our stance, how we choose to conduct the world, for good or bad, not as multiplicity or individual singularities, but as people, not in an empty populist sense, but as a grouping[67] 'able' to express anarchically an 'us' (*im-mundus*) with or against nature or earth, space or the universe, these empty totalities that momentarily and artificially demarcate our horizon.

Obviously, the main problem with this vision is that, however much it flirts with communism in its attempt to derail the stubborn logic of equivalence itself (and therefore of the logic of both religion and capital), it does not put forward a conventional political plan of action. It is true that if one challenges Nancy's thought on this topic, the result is obviously problematic. Indeed, the question that really needs to be addressed and that Nancy always eschews from answering, is this:[68] How can this *im-mundus* be affected politically so as to prioritise *mundus* over *immundus*? In other words, how is one to respond to this demand for reason that 'we' (that is, *im-mundus*) impose on ourselves in a way that encourages the growth of the subject-world *over and above* its reject, and therefore, potentially, its very real annihilation? These questions are crucial because they do not simply ask for a political statement with a delusory potential achievement;[69] they ask for the manner in which, according to Nancy, the liminal operation of *im-mundus should* really take place. After all, as Nancy himself recognises, 'one needs at least a modicum of representation: what or who do we want to be?'[70]

Perhaps the problem with *im-mundus* is that it does not address the problematic of its embodiment, and therefore of its enunciation, seriously enough. This is not a criticism, but a way of finishing this reflection on Nancy's *im-mundus* by taking it elsewhere. I am thinking here of Heidegger's words about the fact that humankind is always already transposed into its own possibility and, as such, can never hold itself long enough in order to be able to understand how its own possibility *actually* 'transposes' itself. In other words, and to use Nancy's own vocabulary, the world can never properly hold its own stance; it is always prey to the incommensurable and therefore to a certain indeterminacy of form and content. Never matching our own 'being thought', 'we' – this heterogeneity – can only therefore fail to capture, captivate, or control our own stance. Here is Heidegger's memorable passage:

> Man is that inability to remain and is yet unable to leave his place. In projecting, the Da-sein in him constantly *throws* him into possibilities

and thereby keeps him *subjected* to what is actual. Thus thrown in this throw, man is a *transition,* transition as the fundamental essence of occurrence . . . Transposed into the possible, he must *constantly be mistaken* concerning what is actual. And only because he is thus mistaken and transposed can he become *seized by terror.* And only where there is the perilousness of being seized by terror do we find the bliss of astonishment.[71]

If one transposes this passage and rethinks all of the above, then one can only conclude that any attempt to make sense of *im-mundus* is an attempt to absent ourselves from one's own transposition into the possible. In other words, *im-mundus* cannot *actually* be understood because, if we did, we would absent ourselves *not* from 'it' as such, but *from having been and from any futural projection.* This does not imply the absence of yet another onto-theological perspective, but the impossibility of extracting ourselves from what led us to the decision of understanding and the consequence of such a decision. Furthermore, the impossibility of eschewing the path that *leads us* to understand *im-mundus*, and the task that *stems from* it, effectively *also* prevents us from *affecting it.* Again, this does not relegate Nancy's *im-mundus* to the dustbin of philosophical ideas; this only highlights the difficulty of what he is asking us to achieve.

Mistaking

The other thing that Heidegger's crucial passage highlights is, of course, the fact that, even if one could, any attempt to think *im-mundus* can *only be* mistaken. Why mistaken? It is mistaken because our inability to absent ourselves from *im-mundus* prevents us from being right about it. We are always already immersed in its creation/production. It is true that Nancy himself acknowledges the importance of the mistake when he writes, for example:

> Praxis is not measured by a given, predetermined Idea. Yet, it is not measured against nothing. Let's try saying that it measures itself based on the Idea of what will be unable to saturate the Idea itself . . . At each possible point of [measurement], a mistake is not out of the question . . . To accept the risk is also part of the chance. Those, curiously, that take the risk of being mistaken leave open the greatest chance for the real chance.[72]

But how does one become one of those who take such a risk? Nancy remains silent. What is therefore lacking in Nancy's work on *im-mundus* is perhaps the fact that its very writing is never enough an openly mistaken subject-reject. Again, this does not mean that Nancy is wrong. This simply means that *im-mundus* is effectively always already a mistake, because its absencing never allows it to be rightly understood in its factuality. This is the only way one can think of our *im-mundus*, that is, seized by terror and astonishment, just as *im-mundus* (we) seize ourselves in our terrifying and astonishing absencing.

The question we are left is then this: *Once the error of our ways is held up each time as what partially makes us,* could the political as a task to be accomplished finally begin? If the answer is yes, then a much more difficult task opens up ahead of us because it implies that 'mistaking' is also part of this *im-mundus* that we create/fabricate; part of this subject-reject that we are, and thus part of this very writing *and reading*. At the level of exegesis, we can probably say that it is precisely the error of Nancy's statements about *im-mundus* or about this subject-reject that allows us to embody them and therefore risk yet more future mistakes. Indeed, with his mistaking comes a resistance against his thought; a resistance that gives thought another chance or opens up a new heterogeneity of contents that, properly speaking, knows no limit. Similarly, as a commentator, I'm no doubt mistaken here, but my mistakes allows for a resistance and a new indeterminate linking of phrase (by me or others), and thus to a new Nancy 'on' the world.

If we therefore hold the error of our ways as what makes *im-mundus*, then we also *begin*, more broadly, to resist against the world's worst threats (pollution, unbridled greed, fundamentalisms, terrorism, overpopulation, genocide – the list goes on). Our mistakes shape our resistance; it is what precisely breaks sense and renders it possible *both* as inevitable fabrication (or repetition) and as creation: the stances of our world. Nancy's political thought lies precisely in this world-forming, that is, *this (for now) major global mistake* that defies belief and yet forces us to resist, thus giving us a new *im-mundus*, one yet again allergic to any definition, delimitation, or end. And this is what we have/are: a world enhanced and polluted, heavy with a burdensome history of extreme violence, and dizzy by its inability to come up with a global strategy that would secure a better future for all. We carry these stances without any form of support or firm basis. These stances are our transient 'systasis',[73] this political-standing-together that makes us quiver between sur-vival (world-forming) and de-struction (globalisation). It is high time we assume our subject-reject, the errors of our way that make and shape our future.

This world, whose world is it? It's no longer God's, it's no longer Man's, it's no longer Science's. So? It's ours. What does that mean? Ours ... if you'll allow me to make a joke using free-association: Le Nôtre was the name of Louis XIV's gardener, who designed the park at Versailles ... Could our [notre] world be a royal park? Must it be a wasteland? Or will we be able to create a waste-park?[74]

Notes

1. 'Sense is not just the way in which meaning goes, it is also – and this is what shows the richness of this word – a sensation, sensuality, sentiment, common sense, critical sense. In this way, sense is not something to be owned or to be felt; it is the relation to the other and, as such, always already remains to be invented.' Jean-Luc Nancy, 'Nous avons accès à la parole, il n'y a qu'à parler!', *Libération*, 2 June 2009; my translation. See also Ian James, *The Fragmentary Demand: An Introduction to the Philosophy of Jean-Luc Nancy* (Stanford: Stanford University Press, 2006), p. 149.
2. Jean-Luc Nancy, *The Sense of the World*, trans. J. S. Librett (Minneapolis: Minnesota University Press, 1997), p. 9; my emphases, translation modified.
3. Ignaas Devisch describes this second extension clearly when he says that 'it' is 'the spacing between us, from being placed together in and through (a) space'. Ignaas Devisch, *Jean-Luc Nancy and the Question of Community* (London: Bloomsbury, 2013), p. 91.
4. Jean-Luc Nancy's work often refers to this two-fold issue. There is no space to survey it properly. I only give here another example: 'How are we to re-pose the question of the proper? ... I'm especially interested in two ways of tackling this question ... on the one hand the ordinary common, the anonymous, the everyday, the indeterminate, the substitutable, and on the other hand, the common-with, being next to and sometimes face-to-face with, being among, in the middle of, or mixed up with ... Both aspects are linked: everyday and go together.' Jean-Luc Nancy, 'Our World', interview with Peter Hallward, *Angelaki*, 8:2, August 2003, p. 52.

5. There is no space here to unpack the context in which Nancy comes up with this idea. Suffice to say that it obviously has its origin in his reading of Marx's *Capital*, especially in 'The Compearence from the Existence of Communism to the Community of Existence', *Political Theory*, 20:3, 1992, pp. 371–98. See also Jean-Luc Nancy, 'Rien que le monde', interview with Stany Grelet and Mathieu Potte-Bonneville, *Vacarme*, 11, 2000, pp. 4–12.
6. Martin Heidegger, 'The Origin of the Work of Art', in *Off the Beaten Tracks* [*Holzwege*], trans. J. Young (Cambridge: Cambridge University Press, 2002), p. 23.
7. For such an overview, see, for example: Ignaas Devisch, 'A Trembling Voice in the Desert. Jean-Luc Nancy's Rethinking of the Political Space', *Cultural Values*, 4:2, 2000, pp. 239–55; Ignaas Devisch, 'Being Mondaine: Jean-Luc Nancy's Enumerations of the World', *Cultural Values*, 6:4, 2002, pp. 385–94; Ignaas Devisch, 'The Sense of Being(-)With Jean-Luc Nancy', *Culture Machine*, 8, 2006; François Raffoul and David Pettigrew, 'Introduction', in Jean-Luc Nancy, *The Creation of the World, or Globalization*, trans. F. Raffoul and D. Pettigrew (New York: SUNY Press, 2007); François Raffoul, 'Le rien du monde: Une lecture de La création du monde ou la mondialisation', *Mondes Francophones: Revue Mondiale des Francophonies*, March 2007; Véronique Bergen, 'Struction', in *Jean Clet Martin's Blog*, 20 March 2011; Pierre-Philippe Jandin, *Jean-Luc Nancy: Retracer le politique* (Paris: Michalon, 2012).
8. The distinction made here between a political potential and a political agenda faithfully follows Nancy's own distinction between the French masculine word for the political [*le politique*] and the feminine word for politics [*la politique*]. For Nancy's distinction between *le politique* and *la politique*, see: Jean-Luc Nancy and Philippe Lacoue-Labarthe, *Retreating the Political*, ed. Simon Sparks (New York: Routledge, 1997), especially pp. 109–10 and, very recently, Jean-Luc Nancy, *Interroger la politique, interroger le commun* (Toulouse: Université de Toulouse le Mirail – France Culture, 2013). For a definition of the political in contrast to politics, see Jean-Luc Nancy, *The Experience of Freedom*, trans. B. McDonald (Stanford: Stanford University Press, 1993), especially p. 75. For a commentary, see Oliver Marchart, *Post-foundational Political Thought: Political Difference in Nancy, Lefort, Badiou and Laclau* (Edinburgh: Edinburgh University Press, 2007), especially, pp. 61–84.
9. In this chapter, the word globalisation will not be conflated with capitalism or, more precisely, capitalist globalism. As this chapter

Im-mundus or Nancy's Globalising-World-Formation   239

will strive to demonstrate, the singular plural extension of the world constitutes a global phenomenon that cannot simply be reduced to the circulation of commodities with profit as the only goal, however much this phenomenon is currently dependent on it. The hope with this focus is not to ignore or diminish the real geopolitical and ecological cataclysm that capitalist globalism leads to, but to better understand the potential of Nancy's political thought in its worldly *or* global dimension. See also endnote 10.

10. In doing so, this chapter will *also* not focus on the usual reading of globalisation as a Western monotheistic glorification of its supposed rational universality. Aware of the worldwide injustice that ensues from such glorification, this chapter will focus more precisely on this liminal operation that Nancy encapsulates with the conjunction 'or' in the title of his book *The Creation of the World, or Globalization*. See also endnote 13.

11. There is no space here to explore and analyse the scholarship on globalisation as a uni-totality. I give here, as an example, Gayatri Chakravorty Spivak's formulation: 'Globalization is an attempt to impose a unification on the world by and through the market.' Gayatri Chakravorty Spivak, *A Critique of Postcolonial Reason: Towards a History of the Vanishing Present* (Cambridge, MA: Harvard University Press, 1999), p. 357.

12. Following B. C. Hutchens, Jane Hiddleston, for example, writes that Nancy's world-forming is 'an alternative ethics' to the contemporary reign of capitalism. Jane Hiddleston, 'Nancy, Globalization, and Postcolonial Humanity', in B. C. Hutchens (ed.), *Jean-Luc Nancy: Justice, Legality, and World* (London: Continuum, 2012), p. 150.

13. '"The creation of the world *or* globalization": the conjunction must be understood simultaneously and alternatively in its disjunctive, substitutive, or conjunctive sense.' Jean-Luc Nancy, *The Creation of the World, or Globalization*, trans. F. Raffoul and D. Pettigrew (Albany: SUNY Press, 2007), p. 29. For a commentary on this note, see Séan Hand, 'Being-in-Common, or the Meaning of Globalization', in Hutchens, *Jean-Luc Nancy: Justice, Legality, and World*, pp. 131–45.

14. Nancy, *The Creation of the World, or Globalization*, p. 54.

15. Friedrich Nietzsche, *Thus Spake Zarathustra: A Book for All and None*, trans. T. Common (Minneapolis: Penn State Electronic Classic, 1999), pp. 268–71.

16. On the impossibility of ascribing a limit to globalisation, see also,

for example, Jan Aart Scholte, *Globalization* (London: Palgrave Macmillan, 2005), especially p. 53.
17. On the fact that globalisation is a limit continually forming itself, see also, for example, Philip Cerny, *Rethinking World Politics: A Theory of Transnational Neopluralism* (New York: Oxford University Press, 2010), especially p. 98.
18. Nancy, *The Sense of the World*, p. 41; my emphasis.
19. As François Raffoul and David Pettigrew rightly say: '[Globalization] supposes . . . the representation of . . . an end of the world, the world ending in such a view; it devotes itself, in the end, to the reduction of the world to the status of an object, a world regarded as "objective".' Raffoul and Pettigrew, 'Introduction', in Nancy, *The Creation of the World, or Globalization*, p. 4.
20. Christina M. Smerick, 'No Other Place', in Peter Gratton and Marie-Eve Morin (eds), *Jean-Luc Nancy and Plural Thinking: Expositions of World, Ontology, Politics, and Sense* (Albany: SUNY Press, 2012), p. 28.
21. Jean-Luc Nancy, *Dis-Enclosure: The Deconstruction of Christianity*, trans. B. Bergo, G. Malenfant and M. B. Smith (New York: Fordham University Press, 2008), p. 31.
22. See Nancy, *Dis-Enclosure*, p. 31.
23. And as such they become the value of all values. On this theme, see Jean-Luc Nancy, *L'équivalence des catastrophes (Après Fukushima)* (Paris: Galilée, 2012), especially pp. 16–17.
24. Karl Marx, *Capital: Vol 1*, ed. Friedrich Engels, trans. S. Moore and E. Aveling (New York: Lawrence & Wishart, 2003), p. 79.
25. For the way this relates to language, see Paul J. Thibault, *Re-Reading Saussure: The Dynamics of Signs in Social Life* (London: Routledge, 1996), especially p. 205.
26. Jean-Luc Nancy, *The Truth of Democracy*, trans. P.-A. Brault and M. Naas (New York: Fordham University Press, 2010), p. 23.
27. On the way natural disasters are recuperated by the principle of general equivalence, see Nancy, *L'équivalence des catastrophes*.
28. Nancy, *Dis-Enclosure*, p. 80; translation modified.
29. See Michael Hardt and Antonio Negri, *Multitude: War and Democracy in the Age of Empire* (New York: Penguin, 2004).
30. Jean-Luc Nancy, 'Nouveau Millénaire, Défis Libertaire: Interview with Jérôme-Alexandre Nielsberg', *L'Hummanité*, 26 December 2006, p. 16; my translation.
31. On this topic, see Nancy's remarks in Jean-Luc Nancy and Aurélien

Barrau, *Dans quels mondes vivons-nous?* (Paris: Galilée, 2011), especially p. 13.

32. 'The modern growth of worldlessness, the withering away of everything *between* us, can also be described as the spread of the desert.' Hannah Arendt, *The Promise of Politics* (London: Schoken Books, 2005), p. 201.

33. As can be expected in the context of Nancy's work, the word 'nonsense' should *not* be understood as what has no meaning or is simply gibberish. The hyphen clearly indicates that it is both sense and what has no-sense that is intended here. This does not imply an undecidability, but the impossibility of ascribing an absolute meaning or rationale to sense as such.

34. Jean-Luc Nancy, 'The Commerce of Plural Thinking: An Interview with Jean-Luc Nancy', in Gratton and Morin, *Jean-Luc Nancy and Plural Thinking*, p. 235.

35. There is no space to explore here the way Nancy understands the body and its role in and as the world. For a good analysis, see Boyan Manchev, 'Ontology of Creation: The Onto-aesthetics of Jean-Luc Nancy', in Alena Alexandrova, Ignaas Devisch, Laurens Ten Kate and Aukje Van Rooden (eds), *Re-treating Religion: Deconstructing Christianity with Jean-Luc Nancy* (New York: Fordham University Press, 2012), especially pp. 268–72.

36. Jean-Luc Nancy, *Corpus*, trans. R. A. Rand (New York: Fordham University Press, 2008), p. 103.

37. Nancy, *The Creation of the World, or Globalization*, p. 51.

38. If there was enough space, one should really evaluate this subject-reject with Nancy's earlier analysis of the German Romantics' subject-work. The latter implies an aspiration to foster an immanent communal identity that always runs the risk, as Arendt noted in *The Origins of Totalitarianism*, of ending up cleansing what fails to meet this aspiration. By contrast, the former can only challenge the validity of any aspiration precisely because such aspiration is itself always-already a subject-reject. For Nancy's analysis of the subject-work, see Jean-Luc Nancy and Philippe Lacoue-Labarthe, *The Literary Absolute*, trans. P. Barnard and C. Lester (New York: SUNY Press, 1988), pp. xi–xiii.

39. Nancy, *Corpus*, p. 107.

40. François Raffoul is perhaps the most prominent author advocating this interpretation. Although, as we have seen, Nancy clearly says that 'one must not oppose the world and the unworld', Raffoul, for example, writes: 'Nancy will oppose to the un-world a "creation"

of the world ...' François Raffoul, 'The Self-Deconstruction of Christianity', in Alexandrova et al., *Re-treating Religion*, p. 48. For other examples of this interpretation, see also François Raffoul, 'The Creation of the World', in Gratton and Morin, *Jean-Luc Nancy and Plural Thinking*, pp. 13–26 and Raffoul, 'Le rien du monde', p. 1.
41. Jean-Luc Nancy, *The Muses*, trans. P. Kamuff (Stanford: Stanford University Press, 1996), p. 85.
42. In a really problematic essay – mainly because it falls so lazily for clichéd male posturing: 'I'm right, he's wrong' – Martin McQuillan quips that 'what is required here is not the creation of an *ex-nihilo* without producer, but the recognition that production as such is always only ever a reproduction'. While it is true that production necessarily implies reproduction, Nancy never imagines the 'disappearance of the producer'. Any careful reading of his work clearly reveals that creation cannot take place without (re)production, and this is precisely what, overall, reveals the heterogeneous experience of lived globalisation today. Martin McQuillan, 'Deconstruction and Globalization: The World According to Jean-Luc Nancy', in Gratton and Morin, *Jean-Luc Nancy and Plural Thinking*, pp. 71–2.
43. Nancy, *The Creation of the World, or Globalization*, p. 51.
44. I'm thinking here specifically of the way Heidegger interprets Nietzsche's famous saying, 'the desert grows'. See Martin Heidegger, *What is Called Thinking?*, trans. J. G. Gray (New York: Harper Perennial, 2004), p. 49.
45. Christina Smerick, 'No Other Place', in Gratton and Morin, *Jean-Luc Nancy and Plural Thinking*, p. 34.
46. Nancy also uses the expression un-equivalence [*inequivalence*] in Nancy, *L'équivalence des catastrophes*, pp. 64–9.
47. Nancy, *The Truth of Democracy*, p. 24.
48. As Christopher Watkin rightly says: 'The challenge, Nancy notes, is one of not introducing another system of differential values, but of achieving a sense of evaluation, of evaluative affirmation, that gives to each evaluating gesture – a decision of existence, of work, of bearing – the possibility of not being measured in advance by a given system but of being, on the contrary, each time the affirmation of a unique, incomparable, unsubstitutable "value" or "sense".' Christopher Watkins, 'Being Just? Ontology and Incommensurability in Nancy's Notion of Justice', in Hutchens, *Jean-Luc Nancy: Justice, Legality, and World*, pp. 26–7.
49. See, for example, the way Nancy evades any non-theological discourse for this imperative in Nancy, *Dis-Enclosure*, p. 39.

50. Jean-Luc Nancy, 'La pensée est le réveil du sens, Interview with Nicolas Truong', *Philosophie Magazine*, 13, 1 October 2007, pp. 13–14.
51. Nancy, *Dis-Enclosure*, p. 76.
52. Jean-Luc Nancy, 'Preamble', in Alexandrova et al., *Re-treating Religion*, p. 19.
53. Nancy, *Dis-Enclosure*, p. 80.
54. Jean-Luc Nancy, 'La Métamorphose, le monde: Entretien avec Boyan Manchev', *Rue Descartes*, 2:64, 2009, p. 79.
55. Jean-Luc Nancy, *Politique et au-delà: Entretien avec Philip Armstrong and Jason E. Smith* (Paris: Galilée, 2011), p. 20.
56. On this theme, see Raffoul, 'Le rien du monde', p. 7.
57. Nancy, 'La Métamorphose, le monde', p. 79.
58. See Nancy, *The Creation of the World, or Globalization*, pp. 43–7.
59. Ibid., p. 45.
60. For a good analysis of the relationship between Nancy and Heidegger, see Daniele Rugo, *Jean-Luc Nancy and the Thinking of Otherness: Philosophy and Powers of Existence* (London: Bloomsbury, 2013).
61. See note 20 in Nancy, *The Creation of the World, or Globalization*, p. 120.
62. Martin Heidegger, *The Principle of Reason*, trans. R. Lilly (Bloomington: Indiana University Press, 1991), p. 39.
63. Ibid., p. 129.
64. Nancy, *The Creation of the World, or Globalization*, p. 47.
65. Florian Forestier, 'Aurelien Barrau, Jean-Luc Nancy: Dans quels mondes vivons-nous?', *Actu Philosophia*, 2012, p. 2; my translation.
66. On the non-messianic dimension of Nancy's thinking, see Boyan Manchev, 'Ontology of Creation: The Onto-aisthetics of Jean-Luc Nancy', in Alexandrova et al., *Re-treating Religion*, especially pp. 264–6.
67. As Nancy says: 'Although I realise that the word "people" has been high-jacked by populism, I don't see why one should be impressed by such high-jacking. Why should one renounce using the word "people" if one uses it in such a way that it indicates not an identity, but a pleb? A pleb that claims its right to exist ... [People] puts forward the idea that a common statement can be made, that an "us" can be expressed.' Nancy, 'Nouveau Millénaire, Défis Libertaire'; my translation.
68. The most remarkable and subtle attempt to get Nancy to put forward a political strategy is perhaps Boyan Manchev's excellent interview: Nancy, 'La Métamorphose, le monde', pp. 78–93.

69. As such, I distance myself from the way certain commentators have dismissed Nancy's political strategy because 'at the end of the day' it is only a desperate call to rescue absolute immanentism. For an example of such dismissal, see Seán Hand, 'Being-in-Common, or the Meaning of Globalization', in Hutchens, *Jean-Luc Nancy: Justice, Legality, and World*, especially p. 143.
70. Nancy, *Politique et au-delà*, p. 18.
71. Martin Heidegger, *The Fundamental Concepts of Metaphysics: World, Finitude, Solitude*, trans. W. McNeill and N. Walker (Bloomington: Indiana University Press, 1995), p. 365; my emphasis.
72. Nancy, 'The Commerce of Plural Thinking', in Gratton and Morin, *Jean-Luc Nancy and Plural Thinking*, p. 234.
73. 'What makes an individual's holding together, is the "systasis" [its political standing together] that produces it. What makes its individuality is its capacity to produce, and to produce itself, first of all, by means of its internal "formative force . . .".' Nancy and Lacoue-Labarthe, *The Literary Absolute*, p. 49.
74. Nancy, 'Our World', p. 52.

10

Precarity/Abandonment

Philip Armstrong

> How does this singularization that is *suffered* torment a *posited* sovereign?
>
> Reiner Schürmann

Precarity *and* abandonment? Precarity *or* abandonment? Or precarity as abandonment's worldly condition and abandonment as precarity's ontological condition? Or conversely, precarity as ontological and abandonment as worldly? This chapter addresses two terms that appear to sustain different critical trajectories, two discourses that open towards quite separate, critical domains. It also addresses two distinct fields of operation – two forms of experience – that one might characterise provisionally as social and economic on the one hand, ontological and philosophical on the other; but two terms in which their political presuppositions, at once shared and incommensurable, also remain to be thought. The chapter's concern, then, is with problematising this opening distinction between precarity and abandonment, beyond or prior to the established heuristic between precarity – understood as a condition of labour, work, or social reproduction – and those forms of precarious life marked by vulnerability, dependency, and exposure to the Other. (As I will suggest, the sense of alterity implied by abandonment is not a relation to the Other but thinking, with Nancy, 'the other of the *with*'.)[1] The chapter thus works towards other ways of thinking what binds and unbinds precarity and abandonment to and with one another, and so towards other dispositions in which to discern the relation – the rapport as such – *between* precarity and abandonment. In short, the chapter seeks to address other arguments that turn on precarity and abandonment's shared or irreducibly singular worldliness, their shared potential or impotential for what Nancy terms the creation of a world.

Central to this chapter is Nancy's 'Abandoned Being', a brief and tightly wrought text first published in 1981.² Given that the chapter resonates strongly with the section of Heidegger's *Contributions to Philosophy* on *Seinsverlassenheit* or 'abandonment', it would be important to note, as others have done, that Heidegger's volume was first published in 1989, *after* Nancy's text.³ No doubt references to abandonment appear with some frequency throughout both Heidegger and Nancy's writings. But Nancy's essay can be read as marking its critical distance from a series of Heideggerian propositions it simultaneously inherits, as if disinheriting Heidegger's thinking at the very moment in which Nancy's proximity and fidelity to his thought appears most evident. If *Seinsvergessenheit* or the 'forgottenness of being' emerges for Heidegger, at least since *Being and Time*, from out of a more originary abandonment, then Nancy's own appeal to abandonment takes its point of departure from Aristotle's *pollakōs legetai*, 'of being spoken in multiple ways', in order to transform two related problematics: the established philosophical quandaries animating Aristotle's phrase (does the dictum refer to different senses of being, in the sense of different meanings, or different types or kinds of being?) as well as Heidegger's subsequent terms for thinking being in light of its forgottenness and originary abandonment. As Nancy states, the oblivion of being that characterises Heidegger's thinking is in turn 'oblivious of being's abandonment'.⁴ In this sense, Heidegger is read back through Aristotle as much as Aristotle is read back through Heidegger. Rather than motivated by any form of 'return' – whether framed as Heidegger's return to Aristotle or Nancy's return to Heidegger – and rather than demanding that that we 'remember' the abandonment of being 'in its long, hidden, self-hiding history', as Heidegger intimates, Nancy's essay seeks to touch the limits of Aristotle and Heidegger's 'shared' thinking of being, the point where this thinking at once exhausts and exceeds its own claims, opened up once again from out of its own closure.

The reference to abandonment also opens towards other thinkers close to Nancy, including Emmanuel Lévinas and Giorgio Agamben, both of who refer with precision to the same term (in Agamben's case, with specific acknowledgement in *Homo Sacer* of Nancy's early essay).⁵ At the same time, however, the reference to abandonment also opens towards other thinkers at some remove from Nancy's writings or closest interlocutors. I'm thinking here of Elizabeth Povinelli's *Economies of Abandonment*, where rethinking abandonment in light of 'late liberalism' considerably distorts the distinctions addressed in our opening outline.[6]

If we take up again Nancy's essay, it is less in order to offer another commentary on the text – tracing out its infra-philosophical conversations or its extraordinary engagement in rethinking a number of foundational philosophical and metaphysical presuppositions – than an attempt to *graft* the text onto critical engagements at some remove from its more philosophical echoes.[7] No doubt this distinction between commentary and graft, philosophy and non-philosophy, also remains deeply suspect, too easily wedded to conceptions of text and context, discipline and (mis)translation, that remain untenable. Or the rapport between precarious existence and Nancy's rethinking of 'abandoned being' already opens towards a continual intertwining of these terms (one might say that the stakes here imply more a chiasmus than a dialectic). In other words, the appeal to abandonment also displaces these very distinctions, drawing us towards what has been usefully described as Nancy's 'materialist ontology'.[8] It is precisely such an ontology that also translates for Nancy as the fact – and not simply some idea or hypothesis – of worldly existence as co-existence.

Situating Nancy's text in light of recent engagements with precarity, notably in relation to contested emphases on thinking precarity in local or global struggles, and taking into account the increasingly widespread appeal to abandonment in both philosophical and political thought, I want to ask what begins to open up or close off when we trace out the displacements between precarity and abandonment. This tracing out aims not simply to resurrect or condemn these terms, nor to find some dialectical resolution, but to rethink some of their presuppositions, or to gesture towards the force that still inheres in each of the terms, and a force that appears in light of their contamination of one another's engagements, their opening towards other inflections of 'shared' existence. No less decisively, there remains the permanent possibility that the rapport between precarity and abandonment is also marked by a fundamental incompatibility, or a sense of radical incommensurability, even failure, and this would also be in need of acknowledgement, instructive in other ways too. We thus offer a series of ten brief remarks on rethinking precarity and abandonment, remarks that remain necessarily preliminary, less the positing of established theses than working proposals on Nancy's thinking of abandoned being.

I.

It has been a decade since appeals to precarity were first capable of mobilising tens of thousands of people in the streets of Europe, a decade since precarity was the key term around which protestors took to the streets in Euro May Day parades or strikes against Villepin's 'youth contracts', the mock effigy of St Precario leading demonstrations against forms of life characterised by the very precarity of social existence. And it has been a decade since precarity was prominent enough as a guiding political concept to generate not only several open-access journal issues devoted to the subject, but the felt need to create precarity websites, like the 'WebRing for Communication and Militant Research on Precarity' that sought to connect militant research on precarity and the activism of the Euro May Day mobilisations.[9] Situated today in light of the austerity state, Occupy, the Arab Spring, or Taksim Square – the terms that appear to sustain our contemporary political imagination – it might seem that precarity is now a little dated, a once useful slogan that has had its day. Or that it has been appropriated – perhaps congealed – into an established sociological category for which 'the precariat' would constitute a new, identificatory emblem. The events around precarity a decade ago also resonate within conjunctures that have only distant critical pertinence in relation to contemporary situations, conjunctures already overshadowed at the time by the anti-war demonstrations that pointed towards forms of violence for which precarity remained woefully insular as a term. These events are also now separated from us today by a global economic crisis given over to more local austerity measures – indeed, Austerity States – barely imaginable just ten years ago.

Addressing precarity today is certainly not to address a political cadaver, but it might not be out of place to suggest that the term also encourages a sense of closure, nostalgia, if not, mourning. Or perhaps, more simply and soberly, an acknowledgment that precarity *failed* to do the work it was once intended to do, and we are left with a few vestiges, left with the recognition that it was precisely the increasingly academic study of precarity that was once read (if no doubt a little too conveniently) as coinciding with the demise of its contestatory force. The desire to conceive of precarious workers as the creation of a new political subject looks more like a body in pieces – more nearly, a body barely struggling to survive – than a new form of political subjection or collective organisation. As Gabriel Giorgi evocatively suggests, rather than ushering in a new collective force, 'subjectivity now has to create, to invent, to design ways to affirm its own indeterminacy, which neoliberalism has turned into an explicitly, manifest condition' of the precarious subject's very existence.[10]

While this opening narrative makes sense from the point of view of possible mass mobilisations against the state or forms of governance, precarity nevertheless continues to offer a useful description for thinking contemporary existence and forms of life. Opening itself up to conceptual reinvention, of late there has been a resurgence of interest in the term, and precarity has survived its initial occasion or incoherence, sustained in light of the austerity measures whose increasingly precarious effects appear only too resonant in our contemporary moment.

The early debates concerning the differences between precarity and precariousness thus continue to offer a useful heuristic for thinking through the increasing contingency, not just of labour but also of social relations and the reproduction of life in what Zygmunt Bauman terms modernity's increasingly 'liquid' state. Whatever the distance from these conjunctures and events a decade ago, we still confront – and perhaps exponentially so – the conditions that made precarity once viable as a critical term: emphasis on short-term non-contractual work and 'flexiblisation'; the dissolution of welfare provisions; the increasingly sparse conditions of accessible and affordable healthcare, childcare, and education; the increasing dependence of social reproduction on private and public debt within the contexts of debt crisis management; cuts in public services and the growing everydayness of bankruptcy, foreclosure, homelessness; as well as debates concerning poverty, the privatisation of risk, and the financialisation of life – in short, conditions for which precarity offers not just a description but a *measure* of defining contemporary existence. Precarity still makes visible what largely remains hidden from contemporary life (ten years on, these are still the lessons of *Dirty Pretty Things*).[11]

However – and this is our first claim, simple as it is – addressing precarity today demands a distinct broadening of the term from anything suggested ten years ago, extending beyond the increasing insecurity of work to people who had always imagined their lives protected, beyond arguments that precarity demands that we adjust the limits or potentials of civil society, even beyond the need to think of precarity as a critical response to those various 'governmental and academic rationalities for which employment is the solution to all social ills'.[12] For what precarity addresses is not just the conditions of work, labour, and class composition under neoliberalism, but the conditions informing mass incarceration; immigration and refugee status; new forms of exclusion and the new governance of inclusion; conditions related to health, disease, and malnutrition; new forms of vulnerability, dependency, and disability; and all the shifting meanings of social difference and its governance, all the distinctions and categories pertaining to the effects of precarious existence on race, ethnicity, age, gender, sexuality, and their multiple and irreducible intersections. What demands acknowledging here are thus the conflicts, inequalities, and discrepancies – a differential distribution – within and across a broad range of subjects whose lives and identities are defined as precarious. Indeed, as Judith Butler argues, what is in need of acknowledgment are also the *creative* and not merely negative conditions of precarious existence, 'to call "precarious" the bonds that support life, those that should be structured by the condition of mutual need and exposure that should bring us to forms of political organisation that sustain living beings on terms of equality'.[13] At the same time, what remains at stake in rethinking precarity is capitalism's capacity to capture not just the conditions of labour and work, but knowledges and bodies, affects and languages, communication and the common. If sustainability rather than security was once usefully opposed to precarity, precarity now names the possibilities and impossibilities of offering fully sustainable solutions to any number of crises. In short, what is required is a more rigorous mapping of precarity's actual conditions, a mapping in which we are still learning to write (still wondering whether to believe in) precarity's grammar.[14]

In this sense, the broadening of precarity as a term would also need to acknowledge all the non-human as well as human conditions of precarious existence, including the environment, different ecologies, climate conditions, animal life, and so on. For precarity also blurs any neat distinctions between the human and non-human. As Jasbir Puar suggestively asks: 'Can we think of precarity "beyond" the human? What would an interspecies politics or vision of precarity entail?'[15] No doubt, this broadening of precarity comes with some political cost or focus, at least when situated in light of the mass mobilisations around precarity ten years ago. At the fullest extension of the term, however, we might well follow Kathleen Stewart, who refers to precarity suggestively as 'one register of the singularity of emergent phenomena', which she further describes in terms of their 'plurality, movement, imperfection, immanence, incommensurateness, the way that they accrete, accrue and wear out'.[16] Addressing precarity as an 'emergent form' is to address what 'starts to take form as a composition, a recognition, a sensibility, some collection of materialities or laws or movements'. 'Reattuning' ourselves to the ordinariness of the existence of people and things understood in terms of their shared contingency and vulnerability, it is precarity's forms that, in their simultaneous composition and decomposition, 'magnetize attachments, tempos, materialities, and states of being'.[17]

2.

If the broadening of precarity to 'states of being' appears to come at some political cost or focus, it also coincides with the realisation that our opening narrative also only makes sense from a predominantly European perspective. For this initial story about precarity was, in fact, closely bound to historically and geopolitically specific dismantling of the welfare state within Europe, notably within post-war Keynesian state economic planning, and so further suggests a necessary broadening of precarity's global as well as conceptual reach. Less a problem of political cost or focus, what is demanded here is a fundamentally different reckoning of precarity's global pertinence.

Situated in light of such claims, the broadening of precarity would now need to coincide not just with precarity's more global reach, but its profoundly uneven global distribution. More pointedly, the broadening of precarity reveals peoples or zones of the world that are left in shadow and abandoned. These are not simply understood as a structural and constitutive condition of global relations, but as sites of precarious existence in which 'precarity' does not even figure as applicable or pertinent in the first place.[18] Or if precarity is considered at all, it becomes significant only when read through humanitarian aid, relief, neocolonialist appropriations of poverty, or peoples or zones deemed so impoverished that the only solution appears to come from outside investments and intervention (if 'structural adjustment' becomes the key emblem here, one notes the absence of the discourse of precarity in its numerous critiques). When we take into account the new divisions and hegemonic conflicts that emerged *within* labour in European contexts, the ways work itself is redefined in the transition to immaterial labour, and the ways in which the global migration of labour has transformed established geopolitical distinctions beyond accustomed recognitions – in short, when we take into account the myriad displacements that have occurred in relation to the norms and affective investments in work – it becomes obvious that the recomposition of work and social existence, or the recomposition of who lives and who becomes disposable, is not an exclusively European phenomenon. And it becomes blindingly clear even as we recognise that precarity as a term has little critical resonance outside that limited geopolitical terrain (even its reception in North America is remarkably belated), and even as we recognise that it *still* does not function as a critical description or measure of historical or contemporary existence outside an extremely limited geopolitical axis.[19]

Lauren Berlant's compelling recent work becomes symptomatic in this larger context, notably the deep insight that precarity becomes 'a way to recognize and organize the ongoing class/group antagonisms/nostalgias/demands that symbolize the causes, effects, and future of the post-war good life fantasy'.[20] The references in which this post-war good life fantasy is then played out become telling. As Berlant goes on to acknowledge, 'xenophobias, autonomias, Tea Parties, Occupy Wall Street, the rise of Third Way "liberalism", and precarity movements all can be said to participate in a structure of feeling, a desperation about losing traction that is now becoming explicit and distorted politically'. If precarity becomes 'an idiom for describing a loss of faith in a fantasy world to which generations have become accustomed', then the examples to which Berlant refers intimate that a transatlantic axis appears to become the guiding measure of precarity's geopolitical reach.[21] No doubt, the terms of the argument briefly gesture towards the effects of precarity on 'smaller immiserated nations to India and China', even if the conditions there seem only a belated consequence of transformations within Europe and North America. But what do 'desperation about losing traction' and 'a loss of faith in a fantasy world' signify when wrenched out of this transatlantic context? In what ways does governance through insecurity play out when situated in light of struggles for post-colonial independence or the necropolitics of the post-colony, rather than Zuccotti Park? Indeed, in what ways does this emphasis on the post-war period close off longer historical trajectories that are not removed from the loss of post-war fantasies in European or North American countries (now connected to the rhythms and conflicts surrounding immigration), but which cannot be separated from longer colonial and post-colonial histories, including the various fates of indigenous peoples?

In a phrase that we owe to Brent Nielsson and Ned Rossiter, rather than understand precarity as a new 'state of exception', it becomes necessary to see labour and social relations under Fordism as the exception and precarity as the norm, thus rearticulating social reproduction in the global north in light of a more widespread condition of social existence, now situated on a fully trans-national and global scale.[22] What comes into relief is thus a recognition that response to changes in welfare in Europe was in fact part of a broader reconfiguring of a number of related factors, including the specificities of colonial and post-colonial histories and their continued effects, transformations in the state and neoliberal governance, and the becoming global of capital – in short, nothing less than a reconfiguring of the world as world. Broadening precarity in this way gestures towards an exacerbation of the conditions informing precarious existence that touches the limits of the existing discourses of precarity. As Nielsson and Rossiter argued some time ago, what is demanded is a renewed task of *translation*, which is also to say, a renewed recognition of the permanent possibilities of *mistranslating* precarity once removed from its more familiar historical and geopolitical trajectories.

3.

Taking into account both the broadening and simultaneous (mis) translation of precarity as both description and measure of contemporary existence, the question thus remains how these initial gestures relate to the distinctions addressed in our opening outline between precarity and abandonment?

First, the displacement between precarity and abandonment suggests a series of identifiable shifts in emphasis: from a more economic or sociological category to a term that appears more existential in its significance, or more existential than the shift from precarity to precariousness already wanted to suggest; from transitions in the nature of work or employment to a condition that appears more ontological or philosophically overdetermined;

from a militant discourse capable of mobilising masses of people to a term strongly resonant in theological contexts (to be sure, it is not just Christianity that shares a sense of abandonment as dereliction but it does seem to over-determine the phrasing); from precarity's emphasis on a social condition to an abandonment that suggests a stronger psychological effect, even a term to which an almost unbearable pathos or tragic affect adheres (as Berlant and others have forcefully demonstrated, affect already plays a decisive role in the workings of precarious existence, but abandonment seems to suggest a degree of pathos that the analysis of the affective conditions of precarious existence either avoids or delimits in more identifiable or culturally and politically recognisable ways).

Rather than distinct shifts in emphasis, the displacement from precarity to abandonment might be read instead as implying an intensification of precarity and its conditions, as if echoing the distinction between the governance of life and letting die, or as Zygmunt Bauman proposes, between being 'unemployed' and being 'made redundant'.[23] Whether a shift in emphasis or an intensification, abandonment nevertheless appears to betray the critical purchase of precarity, the ways precarity could intervene in established political discourses, in forms of governance or the social norms, expectations, and investments regarding work and labour, and so ways in which a sense of conflict and constitutive antagonism pertinent to precarity becomes muted, at worst, rendered 'merely' ontological.[24] Above all, what we lose sight of in the displacement from precarity to abandonment is already implied in the suggestion that we need a considerable broadening or translation of the term, a more carefully articulated, expansive, differential, or nuanced sense of the conditions informing precarious existence, or a more ordinary, embodied, or phenomenal understanding of precarious affects – in other words, *not* precarity's displacement or overcoming in abandonment, not its subsumption under the assumed nihilism or tragic mode that appeals to abandonment invariably suggest. At the very least, the distinction and implied hierarchy between precarity and abandonment needs to be parsed out differently, leaving the question open whether precarity and abandonment in fact touch one another rather than the one displacing the other.

What remains decisive here is not simply pointing to a broadening of precarity and its frames of reference, however useful and critically necessary such gestures might be. Nor is it a question of seeing in the displacement from precarity to abandonment an historical narrative, or of being for and against precarity, as if weighing out its pros and cons into livable and unlivable proportions. For the critical gesture that remains decisive is how to push precarity to the extreme. In other words, there is a sense in which precarity has not been thought through far enough, not worked through to its conceptual limits or exhaustion, not thought through to its extremity, to an utter dereliction that Nancy has phrased as 'the extreme poverty of abandonment'.[25] By this, we do not mean to say – this should be evident – that there has not been enough precarity in the world. Rather, the argument here is not to resist precarity as such, but to think precarity in and at this limit or extremity. Or the argument seeks at this limit or extremity not just the condition in which precarity conceptually exhausts itself but inaugurates the limits of its constituent or transformative force, the limit in which to think what it opens and closes off, and so a limit-thought that brings into relief precarity's potentiality or impotentiality. What is disclosed at this extremity is not an intensification defined by negation – at least in the sense that abandonment might be understood as the increasingly negative condition of precarity – but an intensification in and at this limit, and an intensification experienced as an affirmation, not negation. Which is to say, an intensification and affirmation experienced as excess or abundance, the way one abandons oneself at a limit, in excess of one's self – as Nancy writes, 'one abandons oneself in excess, for there is no other modality of abandon'.[26] This is not the same intensification that Berlant describes, and no doubt quite justly, when she refers to the alienation of bodies under capitalist forms of labour 'lived as exhaustion plus saturating intensity'.[27] For the intensification of this excess or abundance – what Nancy phrases as this 'profusion of possibles' – is what abandonment also names. Indeed, this excess or abundance is what abandonment *is*. As Heidegger will insist in the *Contributions*, excess (*Übermaß*) should be understood not as quantitative surplus, but as a measure without measure, as a measure that 'refuses to be evaluated and measured'. It is excess that 'opens the *strife* and keeps open the space for every strife'. Taking us beyond – or prior to – questions of description, measure, and calculation, this excess is abandonment's gift, its sense of exposure, or its worldliness.

4.

In 'The Ambivalence of Disenchantment', Paolo Virno argues: 'Today's modes of being and feeling lie in an *abandonment without reserve to our own finitude*. Uprooting – the more intense and uninterrupted, the more lacking in authentic "roots" – constitutes the substance of our contingency and precariousness.'[28] These modes of being are not reducible to a representation or a desire for a more authentic life, for they emerge from modalities of experience that Virno describes in terms of 'the degree zero of the sentiments connected with the end of the society of work'. Indeed, 'the radical abandonment to finitude that characterizes the contemporary emotional situation demands that we submit ourselves to finitude as a limit that cannot be contemplated 'from outside', an 'unusable limit that can be employed neither as a motivator of "decisions" nor as a skeleton of a well-structured identity'.[29]

What interests us in Virno's characterisation of this abandonment as an 'unusable limit' or 'perceptual excess' is the way it opens to an extreme paradox. For the abandonment to finitude 'is inhabited by a vigorous *feeling of belonging*':

> What kind of belonging could I mean, after having unrelentingly insisted upon the unexpected absence of particular and credible 'roots'? True, one no longer 'belongs' to a particular role, tradition, or political party. Calls for 'participation' and for a 'project' have faded. And yet alienation, far from eliminating the feeling of belonging, empowers it. The impossibility of securing ourselves within any durable context disproportionately increases our adherence to the most fragile instances of the 'here and now'. What is dazzlingly clear is finally *belonging as such*, no longer qualified by a determinate belonging 'to something'.[30]

Abandonment thus opens towards a fundamental ambivalence. On the one hand, it gestures towards a sense of belonging that turns into an 'adhesion to every present order, to all rules, to all "games"' – a cynical tendency which is demonstrated in 'strategies of self-affirmation' and, more often, 'simple social survival'. On the other, it opens for Virno towards a 'formidable critical and transformative potential'. This potential is expressed in forms of defection, lines of flight, and 'exodus' (from wage labour), all of which are not negative conditions but conditions of possibility

Precarity/Abandonment   257

for action, responsibility, or 'an affirmative "doing"'. In short, drawing from a motif that informs much recent political thought – a motif often phrased around the relation without relation – Virno appeals to 'a feeling of pure belonging that is typical, in Bataille's terms, of the community of all those who have no community'.[31]

5.

How are we to think this sense of abandonment as both limit and excess? Situated within neoliberal tendencies, what abandonment continues to expose is its irreducibility to capitalism's capacities to appropriate precarity, its way of turning precarity into a determinable condition. Or rather, what abandonment illuminates is capitalism's capacity for producing precarious existence and then seeking to appropriate precarity by transforming it into risk and calculation, oriented towards outcomes in which an individual invests (state lotteries would be a useful emblem). This transformation is capitalism's way of making individuals responsible for their own precarious existence, responsible not simply for being precarious but for demonstrating and performing it, so that precarious jobs are now understood as the means through which creative self-employment can lead to industrious self-entrepreneurialism (and as work on derivatives suggests, this transformation is not about rampant 'speculation' but risk adjusted rates of return). By subjecting precarity and volatility to various forms of risk and calculation, and so recognising capitalism's investments in crises and volatility as the condition of value and exchangeability ('capitalism *is* crisis'), what emerges in this transformative appropriation of precarity is capitalism's demand for permanent management and assessment, for strategic planning and accountability, for guaranteeing and legitimising its stratagems of efficiency, streamlining, action plans, contingency planning, crisis management, evaluation, policy, insurance, security, control – in short, all the metrics and measures that seek to turn precarity into something productive, oriented, destined, something like a project.

To be sure, when these practices of appropriation fail, when the glorification of work becomes an unobtainable, widely shared and not individualised fantasy, then we begin to see the force of neoliberal management and control, the rampant exploitation of fear, insecurity, trauma, and shock, all bolstered by authoritarian pressures and state sanctioned violence. The Austerity State now occurs as the measure of precarity's limits. But if precarity is always what exists prior to, and in excess of, the capitalist affirmation, capture, and investment in risk, then abandonment names that refusal to lend precarity to any project, categorisation, cause, substantiality, ground, or principle (metaphysical or transcendental). As the term already implies, it opens towards a different sense of passivity, belonging, or withholding, and the gift that abandonment *is* withdraws or subtracts itself from giving and from all reciprocal exchange.[32]

6.

This emphasis on extremity, limits, and excess reopens further ways of thinking about the larger discourses of work and employment, discourses framed by the assumed dignity of work, a work imperative that is said to open a destiny – that work will make one free.[33] For if work can be defined as a policy-driven norm (a norm shared traditionally by both 'left' and 'right'), if capital repeatedly presents itself as the answer to 'job creation' (the answer to restoring full employment), then, abandonment removes work from its destinal calling. Or rather, it installs a fundamental *destinerrancy* at the heart of precarity, an insecurity more radical than anything claimed by the precariousness of social existence.

The emphasis on extremity, limits, and excess equally exposes conflicts and discriminations *within* labour, notably around questions of immigration, race, and gender (voiced by segments of the working class whose jobs have become precarious, it is not just the 'right' that demands authoritarian policies). As Franco Barchiesi notes, 'rhetorics of citizenship predicated upon "virtuous" employment feed, for example, anti-immigration sentiments that realign – in South Africa as in Europe or the US – workers, politicians and entrepreneurial strata around the legalities of national belonging'.[34] A similar conflict emerges across gender lines, where 'insecurity is expressed as male discomfort (when not overt fear) of depending on female income, even when it practically alleviates that insecurity'.[35] These various conflicts and discriminations are then set against a larger backdrop, evocatively suggested by André Gorz:

> Never has the 'irreplaceable', 'indispensable' function of labor as the source of 'social ties', 'social cohesion', 'integration', 'socialization',

'personalization', 'personal identity' and meaning been invoked so obsessively as it has since the day it became unable any longer to fulfill *any* of those functions.[36]

If Gorz's argument strips social existence back to a limit or extremity, abandonment in turn removes work and labour from any assumption of its 'functional' capacities in the first place. Or rather, abandonment opens towards an excess over any function, whether understood as an assigned role or duty that one is expected to perform – the action for which a person or thing is particularly fitted or employed – or as a determinant value or significance.

In light of this larger backdrop concerning the transformation in the values of work, Papadopolous, Stephenson, and Tsianos refer to 'an excess of sociability and subjectivity in precarious lives which does not directly correspond to the immediate conditions of work', an excess created in the 'unbreachable gap between work and its remuneration, a gap in which people have to live their actual lives' – 'the embodied experience of precarity *exceeds* the conditions of production entailed in precarious labor'.[37] No doubt capital seeks to appropriate, invest in, and normalise this excess. Or forms of governance seek to control this excess and the more 'dangerous' elements of embodied experience are put back to work.[38] But an excess exists within the regime of control, an excess that emerges in the tension between 'neoliberal imperatives to transform the self' and 'the *embodied experience of precarity*'; it is this excess of experience that opens towards 'a surplus of freedom'.[39] Indeed, if this excess is characterised by its circulation in 'an unspecified space of purposelessness' rather than a production, abandonment exposes through this purposelessness both 'the most sophisticated form of exploitation of the worker's body' as well as 'the speculative possibility of a new coming common'.[40] In other words, abandonment empties this speculation of any dialectic, purpose, function, and destination, opening towards an exposure whose purposelessness is then the enabling condition of thinking this 'coming common' in the first place.

7.

Rather than pursue the question of *community* organised around a transformed sense of feeling or affect, what precarity and abandonment force us to reconsider are the ways in which we might consider both a *condition*, as in Hannah Arendt's sense of 'the human condition', or in Judith Butler's understanding of precarity as a 'shared condition',[41] or in Nancy's sense that 'abandoned being has already begun to constitute an inevitable condition for our thought, perhaps its only condition',[42] which François Raffoul suggestively paraphrases as abandonment's 'incondition'.[43] But in what sense are both precarity and abandonment said to be a *condition*? And if 'being is thus abandoned to the being-there of man, as to an order', then how are we to read Nancy's comment that this categorical imperative 'submits to no condition'?[44]

If both precarity and abandonment expose us to a sense of the condition in which a subject is said to exist, then the term turns around a fundamental ambivalence. References to a condition suggest a potentially unlimited signification that oscillates between a condition that is internal to the subject, and a condition that is imposed from above or outside the subject. Thus, the repeated references to precarity as a 'condition' point towards the conditions that inform an identity, and so towards specific attributes, behaviours, comportments, or conducts. Condition in this sense refers to a particular mode of being of a person or a thing. But condition also connotes a situation, position, circumstance, social status, or estate, as if responding to the conditions that stipulate, govern, or rule a subject, and so capturing a compact, stipulation, agreement, or contract. Like subject or conduct, and echoing some of the received distinctions between precarity and precariousness, condition points us towards the decisive problem of modern, liberal government, in which liberalism asserts the sovereignty of the free individual, yet simultaneously demands that individual behaviour be regulated and controlled. Such would be the 'condition' in which the precarious subject is said to exist.

There exists, however, another sense of condition, of *con-dicere* understood as a 'speaking-with'. For the situation of a specific 'mode of being' that we call a condition finds its originary force not in defining the attributes of a being, and then measuring their social and political effects, but in a speech articulated through the speaking subject's own exteriority to itself, and specifically in this way of con-versing that is irreducibly a speaking *with*. This is not an individual voice that appeals or addresses others, and it is not the mutual communication or connection between two people. For the condition that is a speaking-with is a *dia-logue*, understood specifically as the rhythmic spacing or sharing of the logos, of the speaking-with of beings-one-with-the-other or being-in-common. If, as Nancy writes, 'in languages, as between languages, the very being of abandonment is abandoned'[45] – a phrasing that rewrites Heidegger's claim for language as 'the house of being' – then, abandonment is the laying bare of precarity understood as this 'condition' of speaking-with, this irreducible sharing of voices (which is indissociably the very *inscription* of this sharing, and which finds its origin in and as the abandonment that sustains it).[46] Here we begin to mark an irreducible difference between the 'irremediable scattering, a dissemination of ontological specks' that follows the *pollakōs legetai* understood in terms of the abandonment of being – what Nancy phrases as a 'simple plurivocality' – and the speaking-with inaugurated by this very abandonment.[47] As Nancy remarks elsewhere, this is not a question of 'mutual understanding' but of learning to 'speak anew', and of speaking anew when 'the voice is already in abandonment'.[48]

When we consider that precarity also refers to prayer – *precarius* is what is 'obtained by asking or praying' – then abandonment suggests a close rapport between the 'conditions' informing precarious existence and the 'prayers' in which such existence is articulated. Nancy writes:

> The fact is, 'poor humanity' may have nothing else to say but its own wretchedness, nothing else to pray. Prayer thus conceived does not enrich, does not remunerate the 'poor humanity' that we today have just as many reasons to bemoan ... It carries poverty over to saying – and it isn't poverty but saying that is obliterated in prayer. Does not the same apply (isn't it the same thing) to ... the saying of speech itself?[49]

Prayer in this sense has nothing to do with an elevation or rising up, like 'the freeing of the word in its very obliteration', and it has nothing to do with a worshipper 'hoisted above his or her condition', for the task is:

> to empty and let be emptied out all prayers that negotiate a sense, an issue, or a repatriation of the real within the narrow confines of our faded humanisms and clenched religiosities, in order that we may merely open speech once again to its most proper possibility of address.[50]

8.

Abandonment – or rather, an abandoning – thus suggests laying bare or stripping away. This laying bare is not reducible to bare life, at least in the sense that laying bare implies a sense of transitivity (and a transitivity of sense), not an emptied or evacuated substantiality. What the displacement from precarity to abandonment thus reinforces are the ways in which precarity is not to be understood either in terms of the conditions of representation, or as the failure of representation, or again as a condition that could be subsumed under an alienation. Neither is abandonment a model or the product of a will. In excess of itself, the laying bare implied by an abandoning is instead the 'condition' in which something or someone comes into existence or appearance – exposed – rather than identified, figured, or represented.

Here, the well-known etymology of abandonment as an exposure to the law comes to the fore. For abandonment is to turn over to the law and its ban, not to such and such a law in its application, but the law as such and in its totality. As Nancy will argue:

> abandoned being finds itself deserted to the degree that it finds itself remitted, entrusted, or thrown to this law that constitutes the law, this other and the same, to this other side of the law that borders and upholds a legal universe: an absolute, solemn order, which prescribes nothing but abandonment.[51]

This lack of prescription, which is the 'other side of the law' that makes the law possible, gestures towards thinking existence as 'no longer produced or deduced, but simply posited'. And as Nancy will argue, 'this simplicity arrests all thought' – 'once existence is abandoned to this positing at the same time that it is abandoned by it, we must think the freedom of this abandonment'.[52]

In the exposure to this 'other side of the law', two aspects of Nancy's argument come into focus. First, the abandonment towards which Nancy gestures is not simply abandonment *of* and *from* the world, but abandonment *to* the world. As François Raffoul has demonstrated, it is in this abandonment *to* the world that Nancy comes to articulate his discussion of freedom, world-making, and the creation of the world.[53] Second, prior to any distinction between the possession and dispossession of the world that sustains or constrains precarious existence, if 'the law of abandonment is the other of the law which constitutes the law', then Nancy claims that in being's abandonment, 'being is not entrusted to a cause, to a motor, to a principle; it is not left to its own substance, or even to its own subsistence. It is – in abandonment.'[54] Our question is how, or indeed whether, the discourse of precarity is capable of sustaining this relation to the law of abandonment, and so thinking the freedom of abandonment as an exposure to the world and its creation. Or the question remains how and whether precarity sustains a positing that refuses all cause or principle, refuses the production and deduction of existence, notably within forms of neoliberal governance that demand that precarity show and reveal itself, demonstrate and identify itself, produce and perform itself.

9.

Franco Barchiesi argues:

> Exactly because work under capitalism is always precarious to varying degrees, demands for the eight-hour day or a living wage were about taking life back from the workplace. Later social compacts and welfarist deals recuperated those passions under the aegis of liberal, nationalist or social productivism. But now that those compacts are finally gone, liberation from work can regain centre stage. What are, for the precarious multitude, the modern parallels to the 'eight-hour day' or a 'living wage'?[55]

He then asks, more pointedly, how liberation from work might resonate in a context, such as in South Africa, 'where so many struggle on a daily basis to survive', for it is in 'the failure of work to ensure decent lives – as for only a shrinking minority "job" and "survival" can comfortably sit in the same sentence – that thinking life beyond work becomes necessary'.[56] The question here concerns this appeal to 'thinking life beyond', to thinking life not just beyond work, but thinking a more originary 'beyond' that characterises survival as such.

In her interview with Judith Butler, Athena Athanasiou argues that survival is:

> configured and differentially allocated by normative and normalizing operations of power, such as racism, poverty, heteronormativity,

ethnocentrism, and cultural recognition. It denotes the subject's avowal of the losses and foreclosures that inaugurate her emergence in the social world and, at the same time, her reworking of the injurious interpellations through which she has been constituted and upon which she depends for her existence.[57]

In light of this allocation, how then does the subject 'survive recognition' and the 'regulatory power' upon which recognition is premised? How are we to think 'the performative politics' of survival? Or again, how would the forms of resistance informing, say, the life of Palestinians under occupation relate to these same questions of survival? As Athanasiou forcefully argues, these myriad forms of resistance pertain to:

> the ordinary and extraordinary forces of endurance and survival, emerging from, and potentially dissolving, the political condition of enforced precarious living. And yet, in their ordinary and extraordinary forms of surviving, Palestinians do not merely survive occupation and apartheid (although there is nothing *mere* about surviving), but they also defy and trouble the colonial foreclosure of the possibility to live. 'Survival', therefore, refers not to an existential drive of mere self-preservation, but rather to the collective contingencies of exercising freedom, even in structurally unfree conditions, that produce contexts of survival as merely, or barely, living.[58]

The argument turns on a distinction articulated earlier in the interview between 'the political struggle for the possibility of living (and not merely or barely surviving)'.[59] In other words, a distinction is made between a survival that opens the possibility of living, resisting, and collectively exercising freedom, and 'merely or barely' surviving, even if the former finds its force from the assumption that there is 'nothing *mere*' about surviving in the first place, nothing that ever constitutes 'barely surviving'. We might say that 'bare life' does not exist, or it does not exist temporally or ontologically prior to its contamination by a life of engaged resistance and the possibility of enduring, living, and surviving. But in what sense is this distinction itself problematic? Or in what sense is the positing of bare life, of merely surviving, perhaps more of a theoretical fiction, a way of opening up an analytic space in which the thought of survival become possible in the first place, a way of pushing survival to a limit or extremity? Opening itself up to other

Precarity/Abandonment   265

tenses in which survival is endured, in what sense does bare life also open towards an abandonment for which there is no ontology of being that is not in excess of itself, open to relationality or belonging as such?[60]

If abandonment can be rephrased as a question of surviving or of living on, then, surviving is not just the act of one person outliving another, as in a legal inheritance, but 'living beyond' (*supervivere*), that is, not just living life but existing above, over, beyond, besides, in addition to life (which is why it differs from subsistence). Surviving is the excess of life over and beyond life itself, at once beyond *and prior* to the 'mere fact' of life. Survival is the mere condition of co-existence.[61] Removed again from the pathos that surrounds the term, survival opens life to a different sense of tense or temporality, or a different sense of the life and death, finite and infinite, in which the distinction between life and disposable life becomes pertinent in the first place. Survival is not the dialectical overcoming in which one person succeeds another, nor structured by an opposition between life and death, but the opening of another temporality within the present tense of life itself. In short, survival opens a different sense of finitude understood in its disjunctive duration, another sense of what is sustained or endured.[62]

10.

References to time, temporality, and tense punctuate the literature on precarity with repeated insistence, from Pierre Bourdieu's early argument that precarity concerns the 'destructuring' of existence deprived of a 'temporal structure', to the critical meditation on the phrase 'I don't have the time' in *Escape Routes*, to Virno's focus on enduring the 'fragile instances of the "here and now"', to the compelling responses to questions of temporality in the 'Precarity Talk' virtual roundtable organised by Jasbir Puar.[63] Also pertinent here is Elizabeth Povinelli's extraordinary discussion of tense and the 'durative present' in her *Economies of Abandonment*, or Lauren Berlant's exploration of 'slow death' in *Cruel Optimism*, of precarious life situated within the 'elongated *durée*' or the 'ongoing now' of the present moment.[64] If the promise of the good life no longer masks 'the living precarity of this historical present', then, the temporal rhythms of existence are now defined by different senses of impasse, imminence, stasis, endurance, belatedness, refrain, interruption, emergence, seriality, sequence (the cinematic becomes our condition).

The emergence of these different temporalities and tenses continually confront the specificities of capitalism's temporal rhythms, from Fordism, Taylorism, and time and motion studies, to the different temporalities implied by insurance, investment, futures, and derivatives. We might also usefully refer here to colonialism, understood not simply as the governance of space and the spatial redistribution or dispossession of people and their lands, but the establishment of rituals and routines based on strict adjustments of time.[65] Those temporal practices in colonial contexts could then be introduced back into the workspaces of the metropoles (and not simply vice versa), so that the opening of different temporal rhythms of existence is as much the experience of colonial and post-colonial order and resistance, as it is a measure of the rhythms of precarious life in the global north.

But what exactly is the time of abandonment? And how does the opening of precarity to abandonment suggest other ways to parse out the tempos, tenses, and temporal rhythms of existence? Nancy writes:

> The time of abandonment is not a time full of questions, this time that is uplifted, distended with expectation, marshaling the future under the direction of the question, promising and finally projecting into that future the rectitude of a response. It is not the artificial time of anticipation, but it is time, the only time – the time that never suspends its flight.
>
> The time of abandonment is the time, the wavering, of the instantly abandoned instant; time abandons itself, and that is its definition. And in time we are abandoned to time, just as time abandons us. Thus our time – our epoch – is more than ever the time of time, the time of the temporal ontology of abandonment, and of the end of History in the sense of History's desperately holding on to time, resisting it, sublating it. This History is abandoned by history. What is abandoned, what abandons itself, *is* only in the transition, the tilt, the teetering – 'between the ungraspable and the grasp' – and in the skip of the beat [*syncope*], of a heartbeat; and even the transition, the defection, the swoon, *is* not. One cannot even say *the* transition, *the* flow, *the* duration, much less *the* heartbeat or *the* skipping of the beat. Time's duration, which constitutes time, has no other fixity than its incessant vanishing. Time does not fly, but a flight constitutes time. Time's

system is not the skipped beat [*syncope*]; rather, time skips, and skips itself: suspension, pulsation, continuity broken off and started up again on its very disjunction, thus the same (the same time) and never the same (*never* the same time). Which does not mean: abandonment *always*, for there is no permanence in abandoned being.[66]

The most 'untimely' question thus remains: within 'conditions' articulated in terms of precarious existence, within 'conditions' sustained by this 'temporal ontology of abandonment', how do we invent a temporality *between* us – once again, here and now?

Notes

1. In preparing the chapter, my deepest thanks go to Jason Smith and Daniele Rugo, and for conversations with Shannon Winnubst, Mat Coleman, and Franco Barchiesi, my colleagues in the 'Precarity and Social Contract Working Group' at The Ohio State University. See Jean-Luc Nancy, *Being Singular Plural*, trans. R. D. Richardson and A. O'Byrne (Stanford: Stanford University Press, 2000), p. 81.
2. See Jean-Luc Nancy, 'Abandoned Being', trans. B. Holmes, in *The Birth to Presence* (Stanford: Stanford University Press, 2000), pp. 36–47. Nancy has described the text as written when he no longer co-authored texts with Philippe Lacoue-Labarthe, and so assumes his 'independence'. See Jean-Luc Nancy, 'D'une "mimesis sans modèle": Entretien avec Philippe Choulet au sujet de Philippe Lacoue-Labarthe', in *L'animal*, 19–20, Winter 2008, p. 109.
3. See Martin Heidegger, *Contributions to Philosophy: (From Enowning)*, trans. P. Emad and K. Maly (Bloomington: Indiana University Press, 1999).
4. Nancy, 'Abandoned Being', p. 39. David Farrell Krell suggests that Heidegger's *Seinsverlassenheit* be thought in proximity to Derrida's portmanteau term, *destinerrancy*, which he paraphrases as 'the radical insecurity to which all destining, sending, and writing are exposed'. See David Farrell Krell, *The Purest of Bastards: Works of Mourning, Art, and Affirmation in the Thought of Jacques Derrida* (University Park: Pennsylvania State University Press, 2000), p. 206.
5. See Giorgio Agamben, *Homo Sacer: Sovereign Power and Bare Life*, trans. D. Heller-Roazen (Stanford: Stanford University Press, 1998), pp. 28–9.
6. See Elizabeth Povinelli, *Economies of Abandonment: Social*

Belonging and Endurance in Late Liberalism (Durham, NC: Duke University Press, 2011).

7. Even though he does not refer to Agamben's reworking of Nancy's argument – an argument informing the pages that follow – François Raffoul offers an incisive commentary on Nancy's text in 'Abandonment and the Categorical Imperative of Being' in Benjamin Hutchens (ed.), *Jean-Luc Nancy: Justice, Legality, and World* (London: Continuum, 2012), pp. 65–81.
8. See Anne O'Brian, 'Nancy's Materialist Ontology', in Peter Gratton and Marie-Eve Morin (eds), *Jean-Luc Nancy and Plural Thinking: Expositions of World, Ontology, Politics, and Sense* (Albany: SUNY Press, 2012), pp. 79–94.
9. Available at <http://precarity-map.net/index.html> (accessed 3 October 2013).
10. See Gabriel Giorgi, 'Improper Selves', *Social Text*, 115, Summer 2013, p. 69.
11. We recall the scene in Stephen Frears's *Dirty Pretty Things* – to the question: 'Who are you people? Why haven't I seen you before?' Okwe responds: 'We are the people you don't see. We are the ones who drive your cabs, we clean your rooms, we suck your cocks.'
12. See Franco Barchiesi, 'Precarious Liberation: A Rejoinder', *South African Review of Sociology*, 43:1, 2012, p. 98.
13. Judith Butler, 'Post Two' in 'Precarity Talk: A Virtual Roundtable with Lauren Berlant, Judith Butler, Bojana Cvejic´, Isabell Lorey, Jasbir Puar, and Ana Vujanovic´', *TDR: The Drama Review*, 56:4, Winter 2012, p. 169.
14. It is the same problem of grammar that Butler has posited as precarity's 'shared condition'. See Butler, 'Post Two', p. 170.
15. See Jaspir Puar, 'Post Three', in 'Precarity Talk', p. 171.
16. See Kathleen Stewart, 'Precarity's Forms', *Cultural Anthropology*, 27:3, 2012, p. 518.
17. Ibid., p. 524.
18. See James Ferguson, *Global Shadows: Africa in the Neoliberal World Order* (Durham, NC: Duke University Press, 2006).
19. There are a few exceptions, including Franco Barchiesi, *Precarious Liberation: Workers, the State, and Contested Social Citizenship in Postapartheid South Africa* (Albany: SUNY Press, 2011); Elizabeth Povinelli, *Economies of Abandonment*; and Gabriel Giorgi, 'Improper Selves'.
20. See Lauren Berlant, 'Post One' in 'Precarity Talk', p. 166.
21. The exchanges around precarity in 'Precarity Talk' frame the dis-

cussion in terms of 'the transatlantic contours of the geopolitics of precarity' (163), but the question of 'the uneven and disenfranchising distribution of precarity across different strata of beings' (169), or the gestures towards thinking 'the utility of the term in Asian, African, and American contexts' (170) remain largely unaddressed. As a critical response to this general lacuna, see Franco Barchiesi, 'Precarity as Capture: A Conceptual Reconstruction and Critique of the Worker–Slave Analogy', *UniNomade 2.0*, <http://www.uninomade.org/precarity-as-capture/> (accessed 3 October 2013).
22. See Brett Neilson and Ned Rossiter, 'Precarity as a Political Concept, or, Fordism as Exception', *Theory, Culture & Society*, 25:7–8, 2008, pp. 51–72.
23. See Zygmunt Bauman, *Wasted Lives: Modernity and its Outcasts* (London: Polity, 2004), pp. 10–13.
24. The argument, of course, can be reversed, as in Povinelli's emphasis on economies of abandonment, even as she refuses 'ontotheoretical' solutions to the social projects addressed in her account of late liberalism.
25. Nancy, 'Abandoned Being', p. 39. The terms of the argument can also be extended through a reading of Heidegger's commentary on Hölderlin's phrase: 'we have become poor in order to become rich'. See Martin Heidegger, 'Poverty', trans. T. Kalary and F. Schalow in F. Schalow (ed.), *Heidegger, Translation, and the Task of Thinking: Essays in Honor of Parvis Emad* (New York: Springer, 2011), pp. 3–9. See also Philippe Lacoue-Labarthe, 'Présentation' in Martin Heidegger, *La pauvreté (die Armut)* (Strasbourg: Presses Universitaires de Strasbourg, 2004).
26. Nancy, 'Abandoned Being', p. 37.
27. See Berlant, 'Post One', p. 166.
28. See Paolo Virno, 'The Ambivalence of Disenchantment', trans. M. Turits in Michael Hardt and Paolo Virno (eds), *Radical Thought in Italy: A Potential Politics* (Minneapolis: University of Minnesota Press, 2006), p. 31.
29. Paolo Virno, 'The Ambivalence of Disenchantment', p. 32.
30. Ibid., p. 32.
31. Ibid., p. 33. We should recognise the importance of Agamben's affirmation of 'whatever singularities' in Virno's argument. See Giorgio Agamben, *The Coming Community*, trans. M. Hardt (Minneapolis: University of Minnesota Press, 1993).
32. The argument resonates with Derrida's reading of gift-giving in *Given Time: I. Counterfeit Money*, trans. P. Kamuf (Chicago:

University of Chicago Press, 1994), notably its rethinking of the distinction between gift and economy.
33. See Kathi Weeks, *The Problem with Work: Feminism, Marxism, Antiwork Politics, and Postwork Imaginaries* (Durham, NC: Duke University Press, 2011) and Barchiesi, *Precarious Liberation*.
34. Barchiesi, 'Precarious Liberation: A Rejoinder', p. 100.
35. Ibid., p. 102. For an extended analysis in terms of gender, see Weeks, *The Problem with Work*. Cited in Weeks, *The Problem with Work*, p. 77.
36. Cited in Weeks, *The Problem with Work*, p. 77.
37. See Dimitris Papadopoulos, Niamh Stephenson and Vassilis Tsianos, *Escape Routes: Control and Subversion in the Twenty-first Century* (London: Pluto, 2008), p. 231.
38. This brings us back to Guy Standing's *The Precariat: The New Dangerous Class* (London: Bloomsbury, 2011). For a damning critique, see Franco Barchiesi, 'Precarious Liberation: A Rejoinder.'
39. Papadopoulos et al., *Escape Routes*, pp. 235 and 237.
40. Ibid., p. 258.
41. Butler, 'Post Two', pp. 169–70.
42. Nancy, 'Abandoned Being', p. 36.
43. Raffoul, 'Abandonment and the Categorical Imperative of Being', p. 67.
44. Nancy, 'Abandoned Being', p. 46.
45. Ibid., p. 40.
46. We note the proximity of Nancy's argument to the writings of Adriana Caverero. Near the conclusion of 'Abandoned Being', Nancy insists on the 'here' that is the writing of the text itself – 'Here: most strictly, there, where it is written, before you. Here is written here, here is never more than an inscription. Here lies its abandoned letter.' (p. 47).
47. Nancy, 'Abandoned Being', p. 39.
48. See Jean-Luc Nancy, *Dis-Enclosure: The Deconstruction of Christianity*, trans. B. Bergo, G. Malenfant, and M. B. Smith (Fordham: Fordham University Press, 2008), p. 128.
49. Nancy, *Dis-Enclosure*, pp. 137–8.
50. Ibid., p. 138.
51. Nancy, 'Abandoned Being', p. 44.
52. See Jean-Luc Nancy, *The Experience of Freedom*, trans. B. McDonald (Stanford: Stanford University Press, 1993), p. 9, quoted in Raffoul, 'Abandonment and the Categorical Imperative of Being', p. 71.
53. See Raffoul, 'Abandonment and the Categorical Imperative of Being'.

As Stanley Cavell will argue in another context, Emerson also thinks this 'abandonment of and to ... the world'. See Stanley Cavell, *In Quest of the Ordinary: Lines of Skepticism and Romanticism* (Chicago: University of Chicago Press, 1994), p. 175.
54. Nancy, 'Abandoned Being', p. 44.
55. Barchiesi, 'Precarious Liberation: A Rejoinder', p. 105.
56. Ibid.
57. See Judith Butler and Athena Athanasiou, *Dispossession: The Performative in the Political* (London: Polity, 2013), p. 79.
58. Ibid., p. 181.
59. Ibid., p. 99.
60. On the ban as a form of relation, or the 'simple positing of the relational with the nonrelational', see Agamben, *Homo Sacer*, p. 29.
61. Agamben writes: 'only if we are able to decipher the political meaning of pure Being will we be able to master the bare life that expresses our subjection to political power, just as it may be, inversely, that only if we understand the theoretical implications of bare life will we be able to solve the enigma of ontology' (see Agamben, *Homo Sacer*, p. 182). It remains to be seen how Nancy's insistence on thinking 'pure Being' in light of an originary 'being-with' transforms the very terms of Agamben's argument.
62. This rereading of survival resonates with Martin Hägglund's appeal to 'the radical finitude of survival' in Derrida' writings, in *Radical Atheism: Derrida and the Time of Life* (Stanford: Stanford University Press, 2008).
63. See Pierre Bourdieu, 'Job Insecurity is Everywhere Now', in *Acts of Resistance: Against the Tyranny of the Market*, trans. R. Nice (New York: W.W. Norton, 1998), pp. 81–93; Papadopoulos et al., *Escape Routes*, pp. 242–4; Virno, 'The Ambivalence of Disenchantment', p. 32; and 'Precarity Talk: A Virtual Roundtable'.
64. See Povinelli, *Economies of Abandonment*, and Lauren Berlant, *Cruel Optimism* (Durham, NC: Duke University Press, 2011).
65. See Giordano Nanni, *The Colonization of Time* (Manchester: Manchester University Press, 2012).
66. Nancy, 'Abandoned Being', pp. 41–2.

11

'A Struggle between Two Infinities': Jean-Luc Nancy on Marx's Revolution and Ours

Jason E. Smith

Jean-Luc Nancy's *La création du monde* was published in 2002. It is comprised of three long essays written between 1999 and 2001, devoted either in whole or in part to the theme of 'creation'. The collection also includes three shorter interventions addressing classical or contemporary 'political' themes or conceptual fields: biopolitics, sovereignty, and justice. All of these essays can be said, however, to take on the theme of the 'world' from a variety of angles and, more specifically, what happens to the figure of the world in a period characterised beginning in the 1990s as a period of *mondialisation*. And yet it is the lead essay in this collection, 'Urbi et Orbi', that takes up this question most directly.[1] Originally presented in a first version at a conference in March 2001, Nancy's essay should be seen as a contribution to, and an intervention in, the debates on 'globalisation'.

This word and concept was forged in Anglophone debates during the 1990s, after the collapse of the old Soviet bloc. It was a moment marked both by the expansion of market relations to formerly 'socialist' enclaves, and by an array of military incursions on the periphery of the new imperial arrangement, whether in the name of a 'new world order' (Iraq), or through the mobilisation of an instrumentalised and cynical conception of human rights (the former Yugoslavia). The opening movement of Nancy's essay draws some attention to the distinction between the English 'globalisation' and its misleading French equivalent, *mondialisation*. Emphasising the distinct roots of the two terms, and the difference between the idea of a *globe* and the formation or the 'making' of a *world*, Nancy implicitly registers (without mentioning the phenomenon by name) not only the definitional distinction, but the growing antagonism between the two movements: between the neoliberal triumphalism exhibited by the political classes guiding and steering this globalisation of capitalist social relations – an expansion escorted, as noted, by military force on occasion and if necessary – and another conception of the world or the formation of worlds. If globalisation might be defined, in Nancy's terms, as 'the domination of an empire bringing together technological power and pure economic reason', then, the struggle against this figure of domination will take the form of opposing a privative notion of the world – the *worldless world* of the globe – to the movement of 'making a world [*faire monde*]'."[2] If the process of globalisation is one in which the world, in becoming unified under the sign of capitalist social relations, and in particular the domination of a certain abstract regime of 'value', is – to cite Nancy's rather dramatic formulation – a world that is in the process of 'destroying itself', then, Nancy's essay can be seen as an attempt to contribute to the emergent struggle against this process of self-destruction.[3]

Nancy's essay, then, outlines what in 2001 was a still mobile front between the forces at work in the destruction of the world – the above-mentioned 'empire'[4] – and those that might surface in a struggle against this empire. But what would be at stake in such a struggle? Not simply a defeat of these forces, but the reconstitution of a capacity to *faire monde* ('the world has lost its capacity to make [up] a world')[5] or, more specifically, and with reference to the book's title, the capacity to 'create' worlds or the world (and whether one can speak of 'world' in the singular is an implicit tension in Nancy's essay and work more generally); a struggle between the destruction and the creation of the world, *tout court*. This struggle will take on different contours throughout the essay. Towards the close of his essay, Nancy clarifies the distinction between globalisation and *mondialisation* through recourse to the classical Hegelian distinction. This distinction is between the 'bad infinity' of a process in which a limit is posited and overcome only in order to be reposited in that same movement of *dépassement*, and the properly *actual* infinity that consists, as Nancy formulates it (still enigmatically), as the 'finite inscription' of the infinite.[6] On this basis, Nancy then clarifies the nature of the struggle he regards as structuring – or tearing apart – the worldless world of globalised capitalism: 'It is a struggle between two infinites, or between extortion and exposition.'[7]

I will return to this distinction and conflict between two infinities in a moment. What I want to emphasise in the meantime is Nancy's use of the term 'struggle' here. It must be noted that it was in the period during which these texts were written – 1999 to 2001 – that the first signs of a mobilised, if still incoherent, resistance to the process of globalisation appeared in the West – that is, within the walls of the imperial 'centre'. The duration of the anti-globalisation movement that became visible for many with the large demonstrations in Seattle in 1999, and in the violent confrontation between demonstrators and the Italian state at the July 2001 G8 summit, coincided with the period during which the texts for *La création du monde* were written.[8] (This movement, though it ran up against its own immanent limits in the confrontations in Genoa, can nevertheless be said to have met its end with the attacks of September 11, and the subsequent response on the part of the 'empire'.) Nevertheless, Nancy's intervention works on a different historical scale. And the manner in which he defines what he calls 'our task'[9] takes on multiple dimensions. If our 'task is a struggle', he notes, this struggle is an obscure one, defined less by one force confronting another, but by the internal struggle of 'capital against itself': a formula that explicitly avoids formulating the struggle against capital as one undertaken by a given social fraction or class. 'Urbi et Orbi', however, which both cites and to some extent *assumes the form of an address* to 'the city and the world', explicitly makes reference to an enigmatic 'us' ('our task'). Our task and our struggle, as he initially sketches it, is first of all a struggle at the level of thought (*'un lutte de pensée'*).[10] What we must think – think anew, *after* Marx – is the form that the 'annihilation or overcoming of capital will take'. To do this, we must think through the difference between 'Marx's revolution' and the revolution that we are 'perhaps already' caught up in, signalled as it is by 'a thousand revolts, a thousand rages, a thousand creations of signs'.[11] In addition to this necessity to rethink the turn 'our' revolution would take, Nancy underlines that this struggle has a concrete form as well. Our task, in addition to rethinking the nature of the 'communist revolution' – these are Nancy's words – is to 'reopen each possible struggle for a world, that is, for what should form the contrary of a globality of injustice founded on a general equivalence'.[12] Such a struggle, finally, would involve – and this is the thought Nancy concludes with – 'seeking power' and 'finding forces' capable, if not of 'creating the world', then of creating the space or forcing free the opening in which making or creating a world becomes possible.[13]

I.

From a certain perspective, 'Urbi et Orbi' can be understood as a long exegesis of, and meditation on, a carefully chosen passage from Marx's *The German Ideology*. The passage is concerned – as many of Marx's texts from the same period were – with the linked development of what Marx calls 'the productive forces', and the concomitant expansion of capitalist markets to every point on the surface of the earth (the 'world market'). But the term 'exegesis' is not quite right. Rather, Nancy has recourse to this text or fragment in order both to think the contemporary completion of the process Marx could only have obliquely anticipated, and to reactivate and work over certain terms in Marx's text that were not given much conceptual pressure by Marx himself. In some cases, Marx either takes the term for granted – for example, the notion of a or the 'world' – or the term has no real technical or scientific value in the fully developed analytical model the mature Marx will later arrive at (for example, 'enjoy' and 'creation'). In turn, Nancy will introduce concepts into his reactivation of this rather early Marxist text that will only be developed later by Marx, such as 'value': a category that will, in its distinction from 'material wealth', constitute the conceptual keystone of *Capital*.

I will return to these strategies and operations later in this chapter. For the moment it is sufficient to underline a few aspects of the passage in question. Appearing in the 1845 manuscript of *The German Ideology*, the passage represents a snapshot or freeze-frame of a thought in motion, undergoing significant mutations under the influence of both Marx's contacts in Paris during his exile, as well as the material pressure of history itself: the rapid development of the capitalist mode of production, the nascent formation of an organised workers movement that would later see itself as the negation of that social form, and the inklings of the first open and concerted rebellion, on a continental scale, of this same movement just a couple of years later, in 1848. And while this text – importantly, it was never published in Marx's and Engels' lifetime, and remained in a disordered state – can be said to delineate what Althusser famously described as an 'epistemological break' with the Hegelian and Feuerbachian matrix of his earlier, 'young' work of just a year or two before, it retains traces of the teleological orientation necessitated by that matrix, while lacking almost the entire battery of Marx's properly 'scientific' categories (not least, value and surplus-value, absolute or relative).

The passage chosen by Nancy has at its core two fundamental concepts: 'world market' and 'communist revolution'. Marx thinks these two concepts in their necessary relation: no communist revolution without, as its material and historical condition, the development of a world market. Without further ado, here is the rather long passage in question, around which Nancy develops his recasting of Marx's concept of the world, or the becoming-world of the world:

> In previous history, to be sure, it is every bit as much an empirical fact that by the extension of men's activity to world-historical dimensions separate individuals have been increasingly subjugated under a power alien to them (whose pressure they then also imagined to be the chicanery of the so-called World Spirit, etc.), a power that has become every greater and in the end shows itself to be the *world market*. But it is just as empirically grounded that the overthrow of the existing social conditions by the communist revolution (of which more later) and the suppression of private property, which is identical to that revolution, will dissolve this power, so mysterious to the German theoreticians, and then the liberation of each single individual will be achieved in the same measure that history is completely transformed into world history. It is clear from the above that the actual spiritual wealth of the individual depends entirely on the wealth of his actual relationships. Only by these means are single individuals liberated from various national and local limitations, placed in a practical relation with the production [including that of spirit] of the entire world, and thus capable of acquiring the ability to enjoy this multiform production of the entire globe [the creations of men].[14]

On the face of things, the schema proposed by Marx is familiar enough. We should recall that just a few pages before this particular passage, Marx utters one of the more famous lines from *The German Ideology*, a line as enigmatic as it is decisive: 'Communism is for us not a *state of affairs* to be established, an ideal to which reality must conform. We call communism the *real movement* that supersedes the present state of affairs.'[15]

The lines cited by Nancy seem to clarify, in an unequivocal fashion, the nature of this 'real' movement that abolishes or overcomes the present state of affairs. This movement is in fact double:

on the one hand, it is the expansion of capitalist market relations to the entire globe; on the other, it is the overthrow of these same relations, once they reach a certain level of development. What is meant by 'markets' here? Marx is quite clear that this term does not simply mean the exchange of commodities on a global scale, but rather the twofold process whereby technological innovation is paired with a global division of labour, a 'division of labour between various nations'. It is only with the fragmentation of production process and its being distributed across global supply chains – a process properly initiated after the global capitalist crisis of the 1970s – that one can speak of a global division of labour in the sense Marx here predicts. The real movement spoken of by Marx is, therefore, first and foremost the expansion of this global division of labour on a planetary scale: this is what is meant by the 'multiform production of the entire globe'. And yet Marx insists that, *up to a certain point*, the social relations that form the necessary condition for this development – namely 'private property', the private ownership of the means of production – will fuel this expansion. The powers of 'multiform production' will remain, for the vast majority of humanity, a 'power alien to them', as Marx puts in classical Hegelian terms. It is only with – and this line comes just after Nancy cuts Marx off – a communist revolution that will abolish these relations that the mass of humanity up to then 'fettered' by them can assume 'conscious mastery' of these powers: it is then that this humanity will be able to 'enjoy' the 'creations of men'. Such is Marx's vision: a communist revolution will necessarily be the overthrow, at the level not of the individual nation but of the 'world' itself, of the capitalist relations of production.

There is nothing novel or particularly striking in this particular passage, as I have presented it thus far. On the one hand, a global expansion of capitalist social relations (all labour transformed into waged labour, all production oriented towards exchange) will occur 'behind the backs' of the mass of humanity whose activity, nevertheless, makes this expansion possible; on the other hand, a communist revolution, at some point in the development of these productive forces (technological innovation, global division of labour), will make possible the seizure of these powers that have developed behind the backs of the producers. The 'conscious' deployment of these forces, predicated on the destruction of private property, will open the world in its all multiformity to all. In this way, an 'actual spiritual wealth'[16] of individuals can be developed, a wealth measured not by the quantity of exchange value appropriated by a given individual, but the multiplication of 'relations' developed between individuals: their capacity for exposition, each to all the others. This process is, to use Nancy's own terms that I cited early, the movement from 'extortion' to 'exposition'. From one infinity to another.

Now, my contention is that Nancy's own use of this particular passage in Marx complicates or rewrites this schema. The strategic choice of this text should, I hope, now be clear. If in this passage Marx identifies the link between the development of a world market and the possibility of a communist revolution, then Nancy is suggesting that the emergence of the phenomenon of 'globalisation', however poorly conceptualised it might have been – both by its proponents among the global capitalist class *and* its enemies among the nascent anti- or counter-globalisation movement of the late 1990s – should not only be seen from the perspective of the ravages unleashed on the globe by this process. It must also be thought as putting the final touches on the material conditions that must be in place for the irruption of a 'communist revolution'. And it is this communist horizon that structures the movement of Nancy's own text, a text that ends – it must be underlined, given how rare this term is in his work – by invoking a certain figure of 'struggle'. Nancy invokes, more precisely, the intimate relation between the activity of 'creation' (the creation of a world, of the world) and the conflictual process of a struggle that would involve 'seeking power, in finding forces'.[17]

It is here, to anticipate, that Nancy's real conceptual labour begins. What is a communist revolution? It is nothing less than the abolition of the categories that organise the capitalist world. It is the emergence of a form of 'creation' – this is the term Marx uses, *Schoepfung* – that will replace the metaphysico-economic figure of production while in turn being inseparable from, to the point of converging with, its seeming other: 'enjoyment', as Marx puts it, or in Nancy's French, *jouissance*.[18] Communist activity emerges at the point where one can no longer distinguish the struggle for communism, the creation of the world, and the enjoyment – rather than appropriation – of this same creation.

2.

In Marx's conception of the revolutionary transformation of society, what is at stake is first of all a mutation in what Marx called the 'relations of production', that is, the form in which the socialised production of the capitalist mode of production is distributed. As is well-known, Marx makes a distinction between the forces and the relations of production, between the production process itself – the bringing together of masses of wage-labour and machinery, raw materials and so on, in view of producing commodities for exchange – and the property relations that entail the private ownership of the means of production. Marx always characterised this tension between the socialisation of production and the private confiscation of surplus-value (what Nancy refers to as 'extortion') as a contradiction that, if a structural characteristic of capitalism, would eventually intensify to the point that these relations would become a *fetter* on the development of the forces of production. It is, for this reason, that Marx could characterise the revolutionary overturning of the capitalist order as a 'reversal of the relations of production'. Nancy writes that in:

> thinking of itself as a reversal of the relations of production, Marx's revolution presupposed that this reversal was equivalent to a conversion of the sense of production (and the restitution of created value to its creator).[19]

The reversal of the relations of production amounts, in fact, to a redistribution of the social product in a more equitable form. With the dissolution or sloughing off the increasingly constraining relations of exploitation characteristic of a class society, the value produced or 'created' by the labour that is poured into the production process will be restored to those who produce it, rather than being diverted towards the social fraction holding the keys to the means necessary for the survival of these same creators. This is a version of a motif found in the earliest Marxist texts: the producers reappropriate what they produce, and in so doing, transform production itself into the *self*-production of a humanity that is no longer separated from the means of existence, no longer deprived of control over the conditions of its becoming. It is also a motif that is found historically throughout the history of the worker's movement: the productive class will, in a revolutionary transforming of society, seize the means of production and assume control over the production process, eliminate the property relations that secure the extraction of surplus-value, and restore all the value produced socially equitably to the producers themselves. This redistribution of socially produced wealth can take two forms: either to each according to the quantity of labour-time he or she has contributed (the so-called 'lower' stage of communism) or 'from each according to ability, to each according to his need' (the 'higher' phase).

However, we should remember that Nancy's text is not simply a meditation on Marx and his conception of revolution. On the contrary, it sets itself the task of differentiating between the conception of revolution proposed by Marx and a new 'sense' of revolution that will, if one likes, *revolutionise revolution* itself. At stake is the difference between Marx's revolution, and our own: 'The difference between Marx's revolution and the one we are perhaps already in.'[20] I will argue that the place where this distinction becomes clearest is in the way Nancy conceives of and transforms Marx's theory of value.

In the opening pages of 'Urbi et Orbi', Nancy makes reference to Marx's analysis of the commodity-form – what Nancy calls the 'fetishized' form of value – from the opening chapters of the first volume of *Capital*. It should be recalled that these opening chapters of *Capital*, which examine the 'dual-character' of the commodity (its being the bearer of both use-value and exchange-value), the form of value, and the relation between value and money, are often neglected by Marxists who consider them either as relics of Marx's early Hegelianism (cf. Althusser), or as merely a restatement or refinement of the labour theory of value as Marx inherited it from Ricardo, and more generally, the very science of (classical, or bourgeois) political economy whose critical undoing *Capital* intends itself to be. From this perspective, it is only with the chapters examining the transformation of *money into capital* and the production of surplus-value that the *properly* Marxist 'critique' begins. This apparently theoretical debate will have deeply political consequences, however. By separating Marx's analysis of the nature of value from the process of extracting surplus-value, many figurations of social transformation that emerged in the history of the worker's movement neglected the real stakes of Marx's critique, namely his critique of the value-form or the nature of value itself. What this meant in strategic terms was a conception of a reputedly non-capitalist society in which the 'relations of production' are indeed transformed: the ownership of the means of production now collectively controlled (meaning, *de facto*, in the hands of the state and a bureaucratic or technocratic managerial class) and the conditions for the extraction of surplus-value by a specific social force removed. But such a vision leaves entirely intact the labour theory of value developed by classical political economy: the idea that the value of a given commodity or good is determined by the quantity of abstract, or 'socially average', labour time incorporated into the product. It is this conception of a society that has eliminated the mechanisms of exploitation, but *maintains the law of value* as the norm regulating social production that Marx so vigorously critiques in his famous 'Critique of the Gotha Programme'. And yet it remains the case that Marx's conception of a *lower* stage of communism – his conception of 'revolution' as a gradual transition from capitalism, through a socialist planned economy, to full communism – is still organised around the calculated value of the goods socially produced and distributed. It is a society in which money has been replaced by labour vouchers that give access to social production through a mechanism of *equivalence*: the quantity of goods a given producer can consume is determined by the quantity of labour-time represented by the vouchers he or she received in exchange for his labour time. The elimination of money (replaced by labour vouchers) and markets (through centralised, produced co-ordination of production and consumption at the level of society as a whole), would leave intact the principle of equivalence that governs capitalist society; it leaves intact the mechanism of abstraction that allows what Marx calls 'concrete' labour in all its diversity (the paving of a road, the composing of a symphony, caring for small children, and so on) to be compared and exchanged with one another, by reducing each to a purely formal envelope: the quantity of abstract labour employed in each activity.

This brief detour through Marx's treatment of the theory of value he inherits from classical political economy is necessary if we want to understand the precise sense of Nancy's zeroing in on the theme of 'value' in 'Urbi et Orbi'. Indeed, if the question that orients Nancy's essay is the distinction between Marx's revolution and our own, we must develop a critique of Marx's own treatments of the theory of value, sketching out a new theory of value that would in some way exceed Marx's own stated, and in many ways ambiguous, account. Commenting on the long passage from

The German Ideology around which Nancy is gravitating in this text, he writes:

> The global development of the market ... creates by itself the possibility of making the real connection of existences appear as their real sense. The commodity-form, which is the fetishized form of value, should be dissolved, sublimated or destroyed – in any case, revolutionized, whatever the exact concept might be – into its veritable form that is not only the creation of value, but the value of creation ... Consequently, the 'communist revolution' is nothing other than ... the liberation of value as real value of our production in common.[21]

As I have stated, Nancy's recasting of the passage from Marx's *German Ideology* introduces elements that are absent from Marx's own theoretical framework in the mid-1840s: not least, his theory of commodity fetishism or his analysis of value. Nevertheless, these terms form the centre of Nancy's revision of the notion of communist revolution. The fundamental revolutionary activity is identified with the process whereby the 'form' of the commodity-itself is dissipated or destroyed in view of 'liberating' value: a formulation that Marx himself would find unintelligible insofar as his theory of value requires that value be inseparable from equality, equivalence and exchange. That is, Nancy proposes releasing the notion of value from the idea of exchange-value and, more generally, with the idea of equivalence (a 'circulation of value not caught up in equivalence').[22] This is not all, however. The inversion proper to the communist revolution is, Nancy suggests, an inversion of the relation between value and creation. If the labour theory of value determines the value of a commodity on the basis of the labour-time incorporated in it – labour is the 'creation of value', in short – then the revolutionary inversion he proposes (and that he intimates is lurking here and there in Marx himself, for example, in his later notes on Adolph Wagner, referred to by Nancy briefly)[23] would impose the 'value of creation'.

This remains enigmatic, as do most inversions of this sort. Nancy underlines that what is at stake in the 'real movement' he is trying to describe is not simply the abolition of value – of exchange-value – in view of a form of society in which production would be *solely* concerned with the production of what Marx, in *Capital* and elsewhere, calls 'material wealth': that is, the production of use-values. The distinction and even contradiction, what Marx calls the 'antagonistic' discrepancy between material wealth and the logic of value, can be considered the matricial contradiction organising capitalist societies.[24] Luc Boltanski and Eve Chiapello clarify this distinction in the following terms, placing particular emphasis on what they call the 'detachment of capital from material forms of wealth', that is to say, the at times antagonistic relationship between material wealth understood as 'concrete forms of wealth' or use-values, and capital understood as value that is not a static property of a given thing, but a process of valorisation which 'uses' use-values in a process of self-expansion:

> Capital accumulation does not consist in amassing riches – that is to say, objects desired for their use-value, their ostentatious function, or as signs of power. The concrete forms of wealth (property, plant, commodities, money, etc.) have no interest in and of themselves and can even, by dint of their lack of liquidity, represent an obstacle to the only objective that really matters: the constant transformation of capital, plant and various purchases ... into output, output into money, and of money into new investments. This detachment of capital from material forms of wealth gives it a genuinely abstract character, which helps make accumulation an interminable process.[25]

It is this transformation of value into capital – that is, self-valorising value, value that is not a property or thing but a movement of self-expansion – that is in fact at the heart of Nancy's reflection on communism. Communism for him becomes the overcoming of value understood as a general equivalent and its replacement in the form of 'real value' (in a sense still to be determined).

The decisive discovery made by Marx, namely this antagonism between the production of material wealth (here: 'concrete forms of wealth') and the logic of value (as self-valorising) has its own limits, however. Capital is a social force that, for the first time in the history of humanity, renounces every figure of the limit (even the contours of the globe itself) in view of an indefinite expansion at the expense of any and every use-value or concrete form of wealth it can posit as a mere 'moment' of its own return into self, its immanent self-mediation. Nancy implies that Marx's understanding of the 'communist revolution' is, nevertheless, caught in the tension between the indefinite self-expansion of capital as self-valorising value – what Nancy calls an 'autistic process with no end or goal [*sans fin*]'[26] – and the production of *finite* use-values whose measure is always what we might call the finitude of (human) need. For capital, 'there exists no limit, no possible satiation'.[27] Its limit is always ever a mere horizon; a threshold constantly re-posited each time it is transgressed. Such is the nature of capitalist growth: always ever itself even as it grows quantitatively with each completion of its cycle, each circular return back into itself.

Nancy casts this 'autistic' process, with neither end nor goal, in terms Marx does not use in his account of the self-valorising aspect of value (in the fourth chapter of the first volume of *Capital*). Namely, in Hegelian terms: the so-called 'bad' or spurious infinity whose infinity is never *actual*, real, concrete, since it is only ever the mere negation of the finite or a specific limit. Nancy writes that 'value' valorises itself 'by means of this autistic process without end or goal, and this infinity has no *actuality* [acte] other than the reproduction of its power or potentiality'.[28] This endless form of the non-finite can never come to rest in itself since it is always defined by an external determination it must constantly overcome, only in order to re-posit this limit in the very movement of its negation. This process never ends, but it can be suspended, namely in those moments Marx characterised as *crises* of accumulation, when a given limit or concrete form of wealth cannot be overcome as a mere moment in the circuit of valorisation, the process getting hung up on a particular moment (for example, commodities that can not have their exchange-value realised in the market, or money that stands idle rather than being invested in the production process).

Following Hegel, this spurious infinity is, in turn, opposed by Nancy to a 'good' or actual infinite, which would be proper to what Nancy identifies not simply with communism, but with the *jouissance* – *Genüss* – Marx speaks of in the passage on the world market Nancy is here elaborating. The 'real' or 'veritable' value that is at stake in the communist revolution such as Nancy conceives it must therefore be distinguished from, both the 'finitude' of use-values or material wealth, and the in-finite self-reproduction of value: 'it is neither value measured by its useful use nor value giving itself as general equivalence'.[29] In short, the real value of our production will not oppose the finite to the infinite self-reproduction of value; it will not oppose the 'satiety' encountered in the consumption of use-values to the insatiable expansion of capital. *Communism must be measured against the ambitions of capitalism itself: it must oppose its own infinite to that of capitalism*, its 'good', concrete, actual infinity to a movement that merely negates, over and over again, the limit posed by any concrete determination. It opposes the enigmatic *jouissance* of communist enjoyment to both the implacable hunger of capitalist expansion – to the limits of the earth, and beyond – and to the stubborn, meager satisfaction of mere use.

The question Nancy poses is therefore: what is the exact relation between these two infinities? Nothing less than the nature of the 'communist revolution' is at stake. Nancy offers two different formulations. First, he characterises the actual infinite as the 'exact reverse' of the spurious infinite set into motion by the capitalist mode of production and, a few lines later, identifies what Marx 'names "revolution" – and here we are no longer sure whether this is indeed Marx's revolution, or "ours" – as the process of 'turning over one infinite into the other, and potentiality into act'.[30] How are we to understand these images – if they are indeed just that, images rather than conceptual determinations – of one infinite being the 'other side' of the other, and the process of revolution (a word that, etymologically suggests turning over or around) as a '*retourner*', a turning over, as one does a card? More importantly, just how does one carry out such a turning or flipping over or around? Who or what could perform such an operation?[31]

Nancy suggests a different kind of relationship between these two infinites later in his text. I have alluded to this passage in an earlier part of this chapter. In so doing, he implicitly responds to these questions. In the final pages of Nancy's essay, he characterises these two infinites not simply as two sides of a single coin ('exact reverse'), with a point-by-point continuity that might be overturned in a single, simple gesture, but as a messier or at least implicitly protracted and uncertain 'struggle'. Speaking of 'our task' when confronted with the spectre of globalisation, Nancy describes this task as one of struggle; but immediately after having spoken of our task ('our task is a struggle'),[32] he qualifies this formulation: 'In a sense, it is a struggle of West against itself, of capital against itself. It is a struggle between two infinites, or between extortion and exposition'.[33] Why a struggle? And what form of struggle is this?

Once again we see that, for Nancy, the 'antagonism' – to use the term Marx's translators use – is not between use-value and exchange-value, but between two determinations of the infinite: between the self-valorising value of capitalist expansion (founded on the extraction or 'extortion' of surplus-value in the production process) and, in an expression that makes little sense within Marx's analysis of capital, the 'circulation of value freed from equivalence'.[34] This use of the term struggle displaces it from the classical imagery that we associate with Marxism. 'Class struggle' is generally conceived of as a war, at times open and at times implicit, between two social forces over control of both the state and the apparatus of production: that is, between two classes over two forms of power. But already Marx, as I have already underlined, used the term 'antagonism', or rather 'antagonistic movement', in the opening pages of *Capital*, in his account of the twofold character of the commodity:

> An increase in the quantity of use values is an increase of material wealth. With two coats two men can be clothed, with one coat only one man. Nevertheless, an increased quantity of material wealth may correspond to a simultaneous fall in the magnitude of its value. This antagonistic movement has its origin in the twofold character of labour.[35]

The term antagonism, as it is used by Marx, is meant to displace the site of struggle away from two social forces or classes over the state or the economy in order to locate a rift or confrontation at the heart of the very form of the commodity. It is therefore perfectly in keeping with the movement of Marx's thought to conceive of a struggle that would not be mapped onto two classes, but would be located at the heart of capital (or, the 'West') itself. The actual infinite of communist *jouissance* – *jouissance* because the 'infinite' produced by our 'production in common', not being a 'quantity of equivalence', could not be 'appropriated', only enjoyed;[36] it is not, therefore, some force, place or activity outside of the nexus of capitalist society, but lurks within it or is woven throughout, in a conflictual relation that both spurs capitalist development itself, and threatens it with a sudden overturning into its opposite, that is, its hidden face or truth.

What then is *our task*? What role do *we* play in this conflict that is both our struggle and a struggle between capital and itself, between the two infinites at war within this world that Nancy dramatically describes as in the process of 'destroy[ing] itself'[37] at the very moment it becomes worldwide, global? This is an answer that the course of this struggle alone can provide.

Notes

1. Jean-Luc Nancy, 'Urbi et Orbi', in *La création du monde or la mondialisation* (Paris: Galilée, 2002), pp. 11–64; translations are my own.
2. Nancy, *La création du monde or la mondialisation*, pp. 15, 16. There is a perhaps misleading proximity between this 'privative' experience of the world – a world that appears *as* worldless, a world that is only insofar as it destroys itself – and Heidegger's characterisation of the animal's mode of relation to its world or to worldness. It has a world by not having it. It is 'poor' in world. It should be noted, moreover, that one of the central nexuses explored by Nancy in this essay is the relation between world and wealth, between wealth and poverty.
3. Nancy, *La création du monde or la mondialisation*, p. 17. Nancy even invokes Freud's theory or speculative fiction of the 'death drive' – the *pulsion de mort* – when describing this phenomenon (p. 16).
4. While Nancy hardly fashions a systematic conception of 'Empire' (complete with majuscule) in the manner of Michael Hardt and Antonio Negri, he cites their contemporary *Empire* in a later essay in *La création du monde* (p. 171, n.1). In 'Urbi et Orbi', Negri's *Kairos, Alma Venus, multitude* is equally cited, and Nancy notes some of the resonances between Negri's reflections and his own. Another powerful conceptualisation of the concept of Empire that borrows equally from Nancy and Negri (as well as Giorgio Agamben and Foucault) can be found in Tiqqun's *Introduction to Civil War*, trans. A. Galloway and J. E. Smith (Los Angeles: Semiotext[e], 2010).
5. Nancy, *La création du monde or la mondialisation*, p. 17.
6. Ibid., p. 27.
7. Ibid., p. 60.
8. To my knowledge, the only commentary to articulate the relation between Nancy's thought and the anti-globalisation movement is Philip Armstrong. See his *Reticulations: Jean-Luc Nancy and the Networks of the Political* (Minneapolis: University of Minnesota Press, 2009), as well as his chapter in this volume. See equally Nancy's own discussion of the relationship, in terms that anticipate some of themes of 'Urbi et Orbi', in 'Nothing but the World: An Interview with *Vacarme*', *Rethinking Marxism*, 19:4, October 2007, pp. 521–35.
9. Nancy, *La création du monde or la mondialisation*, p. 59.
10. Ibid., p. 60.
11. Ibid., p. 61.
12. Ibid., p. 62.

13. On Nancy's sparing references to the idea of politics as the deployment of a force that would not 'create a world' so much as create spaces in which the emergence of a world – the production of a 'common' – might take place, see my 'Nancy, Justice and the Idea of Communism', in B. C. Hutchens (ed.), *Jean-Luc Nancy: Justice, Legality and World* (London: Continuum, 2012).
14. Karl Marx, *Early Political Writings* (Cambridge: Cambridge University Press, 1994), p. 136.
15. Ibid., p. 133.
16. As will be seen, Nancy places particular pressure on this phrase, which has no real conceptual place in Marx's later theoretical framework. Indeed, Nancy will invoke this idea of a wealth that is refractory to the basic categories organising Marx's 'mature' theory of capitalism, namely the bifurcation and 'antagonism' between the logic of value and what Marx calls 'material wealth'.
17. Nancy, *La création du monde or la mondialisation*, pp. 63–4.
18. Marx's term here is *Genüss*, a term that in this text is at times simply used as a synonym of 'consumption', or *Konsumtion*. Nancy's use of *jouissance* here deliberately recalls Lacan's account of *jouissance*. I cannot unpack, here, the fate the term undergoes in Nancy's essay. I simply want to underline that for Nancy the term 'enjoyment' cannot, despite Marx's own usage, be identified simply with consumption, that is, a term opposed to production. The recasting of the antinomy production/consumption as creation/enjoyment is meant to displace Marx's categories.
19. Nancy, *La création du monde or la mondialisation*, p. 61.
20. Ibid., p. 61.
21. Ibid., p. 21.
22. Ibid., p. 22. Value is, in short, a 'relational' concept; there is no 'absolute' value, no 'priceless' value in Marx's theory, save a few indications referred to by Nancy.
23. Nancy, *La création du monde or la mondialisation*, pp. 25–6.
24. Marx uses the term *gegensätzlich* to describe the rift or opposition, indeed 'antagonism', between the production of use-values and the logic of value: 'An increase in the quantity of use values is an increase of material wealth. With two coats two men can be clothed, with one coat only one man. Nevertheless, an increased quantity of material wealth may correspond to a simultaneous fall in the magnitude of its value. This antagonistic movement has its origin in the twofold character of labour.' (Marx, *Capital*, I, chapter 1, section 2.)

25. Luc Boltanski and Eve Chiapello, *The New Spirit of Capitalism* (London: Verso, 2005), p. 5.
26. Nancy, *La création du monde or la mondialisation*, p. 29.
27. Boltanski and Chiapello, *The New Spirit of Capitalism*, p. 5.
28. Nancy, *La création du monde or la mondialisation*, p. 29.
29. Ibid., p. 28.
30. Ibid., p. 30.
31. Elsewhere in 'Urbi et Orbi', Nancy uses a similar image or terminology: 'in a certain way, profit and *jouissance* are placed back to back, acting as two faces of the infinite: on the one side, that of the interminable growth of accumulation . . . on the other side the actual infinite, the one by which a finite existence accedes, as finite, to the infinite of a sense or of a value which is its own sense or value'. Nancy, *La création du monde or la mondialisation*, pp. 44–5.
32. Ibid., p. 60.
33. Ibid.
34. Ibid., pp. 21–2.
35. Karl Marx, *Capital: Volume One*, trans. B. Fowkes (London: Penguin, 1976), pp. 136–7; translation modified.
36. Nancy, *La création du monde or la mondialisation*, p. 59.
37. Ibid., p. 17.

Index

abandonment, 6, 9, 12, 23–4, 27–8, 36, 68, 94, 103, 245–7, 253–67
Adorno, Theodor, 81–2
affect, 72, 107, 140, 143–4, 160, 173–4, 250, 252, 254, 256–7, 259
affirmation, 6, 8–9, 13–15, 38, 82, 157, 182, 190, 192–6, 228–9, 255–7
Agamben, Giorgio, 207–8, 246
alienation, 13, 142, 169–70, 255–6, 262
Althusser, Louis, 90, 275, 280
anarchy, 24, 49, 95, 98
animal, 9, 43–51, 57, 59–60, 72, 233, 287n2
   animal / human, 36, 48, 50–8
   animal monstrans, 53–4
   humanism, 7, 26, 36–7, 45, 54–6, 72–3, 84, 94–6, 209, 233, 250, 261
anthropocentrism, 43, 47–8, 52, 61, 91–2, 108
Antigone, 77, 82–3
appropriation, 8, 10, 13, 21, 34, 41n29, 83, 95, 165, 170–1, 185, 207, 231–2, 251, 257, 278
Arendt, Hannah, 208, 212n13, 215n31, 225, 228, 260
Aristotle, 43–6, 48–50, 52, 83, 246
   political animal, 44, 49

Badiou, Alain, 43–51, 56–7, 61, 159, 185
Barthes, Roland, 209–10
Bataille, Georges, 14, 97, 229–30, 257
becoming, 5, 21, 34, 37, 70–1, 73, 78–9, 80, 155, 206, 210–11, 276, 279
being-in-common, 80, 94, 101, 109, 119, 150, 153–4, 158, 169, 171, 193–4, 202
being-in-the-world, 180, 219
being-together, 1, 50–1, 76, 102, 105, 155, 206–7, 211, 213n13
Benjamin, Walter, 1, 81
biopolitics, 130–1, 272
Blanchot, Maurice, 199, 210, 216n51
Blocher, Sylvie, 174
body, 43, 45–6, 57, 77, 92, 97, 124, 140, 143–4, 154, 167, 177–9, 205, 220, 226–7, 231, 234, 248–9, 254, 259
Bourdieu, Pierre, 265
Butler, Judith, 250, 260, 263

capital / capitalism / capitalist globalism, 11–14, 100, 103, 142, 144, 150, 156, 158, 160n16, 167, 169, 172, 223, 234–5, 238n9, 250, 253, 255–9, 263, 266, 273, 275–86
Centre for Philosophical Research on the Political, 2, 117, 125
Christianity, 54, 58–61, 139, 142–4, 146, 151, 159n9, 160n16, 231, 254
chronos, 98; *see also* time
citizen, 92, 130, 258; *see also* people (*demos*)
commodity / commodification, 166, 172, 199, 206, 220, 224, 229, 277–86
communism, 21, 46, 52, 56, 80, 101, 105, 234, 276–8, 280–4

290

community, 3–4, 15, 21, 34–5, 49–50, 68, 75–6, 80, 101–5, 152–5, 192–4, 202, 206, 219, 257–9
compearance / co-appearing, 5, 7, 37, 150–1, 154–6, 186, 212n13
corpus *see* body
creation, 6–7, 18, 103, 121, 181, 195–6, 205–8, 222, 226–8, 233, 235–6, 262–3, 273–82
Critchley, Simon, 132

Debord, Guy, 141, 144, 169
decision, 8, 14, 22, 32–3, 37, 72–3, 77, 80, 94, 109, 192–8, 200–1, 206, 211, 212n13, 228–9, 235, 256
deconstruction, 117, 146, 159n9, 207–8, 211, 227, 237
Deleuze, Gilles, 48, 179
  and Guattari, Felix, 189n41
democracy, 13–15, 31, 57, 66–8, 70–1, 80, 88–110, 122–8, 131–3, 152, 157, 166–8, 224
denaturation, 204, 112n41
Derrida, 29–30, 90, 97–9, 110n13, 117, 175, 177–8, 180, 183, 189n41, 193, 195, 197–8, 202, 228
  différance, 29–30, 90–1
desire, 21, 29, 46, 53, 81, 101–2, 108, 157, 173–5, 177, 231–2
dialectic, 68, 176, 210–11, 226, 247
doxa, 43–5, 93, 145
Duchamp, Marcel, 198–200, 203, 208

economy, 166–7, 170, 222–3, 229, 249–51, 253, 278
ecotechnics, 51–2, 56, 58–61, 226–8
ellipsis, 202–3
enjoyment, 12–13, 144, 209, 278, 285–6, 288n18, 289n31
equality, 43, 55–6, 59–60, 87, 91, 102, 195, 212n13, 250
equivalence, 21, 37–8, 102–3, 158, 195, 224, 227–32, 234, 274, 281–6
eroticism, 143–4
Esposito, Roberto, 1, 58
ethics, 4, 8–10, 22–3, 30–1, 34–6, 84, 193–4, 204, 210
evaluation, 224–5, 228–9, 255; *see also* affirmation

event, 2, 9, 14–15, 26–7, 48–9, 53, 67, 84, 89–94, 98–103, 108–10, 142, 181, 194, 196, 200, 248–9
ex nihilo, 23–4, 36, 97, 195, 205–8, 228
excess, 12–13, 55, 90, 94–5, 170, 172, 173, 204, 226, 231, 255, 257–8, 265
  surplus, 231, 255, 259
existence, the fact of, 8, 23–4, 28–9, 33, 35, 37, 75–6, 94–5, 230–1

face, 177; *see also* surface
figure, 59, 78–9, 82, 90, 92, 94, 98, 100–1, 105, 129, 143, 152, 155, 157, 168, 177, 184–6, 194, 206, 278, 283
finite, 8, 67, 73, 100, 176, 182, 194, 197, 200–3, 256, 265, 273, 283–4
Foucault, Michel, 45, 48, 116, 124, 128–32
foundation, 10, 31, 52, 78, 94–9, 109, 117, 123–4, 142, 194, 247; *see also* ground
freedom, 7–9, 24, 26–30, 36, 66, 72–4, 77–8, 84, 193–5, 198, 258–9, 262–3
  letting beings be, 8, 24–5, 53, 231
Freud, Sigmund, 209
friendship, 166, 195, 198

gaze, 59–60, 70, 75
gesture, 174–5, 199–200, 207–10
gift, 206, 209, 229, 255, 258
globalisation, 11, 99, 103, 220–1, 222–3, 226, 230–1
God, 7, 24, 45–8, 50, 56, 143, 147–8, 159n9, 206, 222–5, 229–30, 233, 237
Gonzalez-Torres, Felix, 196–210
ground / groundlessness, 23, 26, 33, 77, 80, 95, 97–8, 161n18, 182–4, 196, 204–6

Hardt, Michael, and Negri, Antonio, 225, 287n4
Hegel, G. W. F., 12, 68–71, 73, 76–9, 81–3, 107, 273, 275, 277, 280, 284
  restlessness of the negative, 68–71
  speculative remark, 69–71, 76

Heidegger, Martin 5, 22–7, 30–6, 52–3, 71, 74, 75, 83, 106–8, 143, 145, 161n17, 171, 174, 177, 220, 228, 230–4, 235, 246, 255, 261, 287n2
history, 81, 142, 148, 171, 266, 275–6
Holderlin, Friedrich, 25, 82–3
human / non-human *see* animal

identity, 73, 75, 84, 100, 151, 155, 164, 259
image, 74–5, 79, 93, 139–49, 150–8, 207
image-politics, 151, 156–8
imaginary, 222
immundus, 225–8, 230, 234
inequality *see* equality
infinite, 12–13, 76, 80, 100, 194, 197, 200–3, 205, 207, 211, 273
  bad infinite, 12, 38, 214n23, 273, 284
  two infinities, 11–15, 273, 278, 289n31
interval, 10, 179, 182, 184, 213
intrusion, 67, 194–5

jouissance see enjoyment
justice, 9–10, 15, 103, 120–2, 274

kairos, 98
Kant, Immanuel, 23, 29, 49, 68–9, 71–5, 99, 145, 149, 154, 160n15
Kierkegaard, Soren, 59
knots, 14, 204
knowledge, 2, 4, 76–7, 79, 82, 126–8, 204, 231, 250, 275

labour, 201, 215n31, 249–50, 252–3, 257–9, 263, 280; *see also* precarity
Lacoue-Labarthe, Phillippe, 1–2, 49, 117
language, 54–6, 165, 175, 173–4, 180, 261
  silent protest, 173–4
  speech, 49–50, 54–5, 60, 175, 260–1
  voice, 55, 175, 260–1
law, 29, 96, 97, 109, 120–1, 126–7, 134n12, 262–3
Lefort, Claude, 112n51, 116, 124–8
  empty place of power, 124–7
Leibniz, Gottfried, 95, 233

Levinas, Emmanuel, 246
liberalism, 247, 252, 259–60, 272
limit, 84, 175–6, 184, 219–20, 227, 232, 234, 255–8
logos, 21–2, 96, 195, 204, 231, 261
love, 47–8, 59–61, 78, 195, 205

Machiavelli, Niccolo, 129, 131
Marx, 12, 81, 102–3, 170, 208–9, 224, 274–86
Marxism, 12, 49, 118, 141, 286
post-Marxism, 141, 144
May '68, 3, 90, 92, 100–1, 151
Merleau-Ponty, Maurice, 54
metaphysics, 14, 21–2, 26–7, 30–1, 49, 75, 89, 142, 222, 232, 258, 278
monotheism, 223
mono-valence, 223–5, 229
multiplicity, 75, 100, 102, 105, 122, 194, 202, 205–7, 229, 234
multitude, 105, 225, 263
mythos, 96

Nietzsche, Friedrich, 2, 4–5, 9, 13, 46, 67, 93, 104, 159n9, 229
nihilism 1, 9, 93, 102, 124, 158, 206, 254
nihilo / nihil, 1, 3, 6, 24, 97–8, 206–8, 211, 226; *see also ex nihilo*; nihilism
non-equivalence, 9, 13, 102–4, 193, 228, 230, 232; *see also* equivalence
nothing, 27–8, 97–8, 205, 207–8, 221
number, 105, 195–6, 202, 205–6, 230

Occupy, 248, 252, 262
Oedipus, 83–4
ontological difference, 27–8
ontology of sociality *see* social ontology
onto-theology, 1, 147, 222–3, 230, 235
opening, 26, 31–5, 76, 143, 165, 168, 174, 206–8, 219, 228, 233, 246
originary / original ethics *see* ethics
other, 29, 50, 75, 245
  stranger, 67, 107–8

Pascal, Blaise, 14, 94
people (*demos*), 91, 97–8, 104–8, 124–7, 243n67

Plato, 95, 139, 141, 146, 149
poiesis, 170, 185, 196, 199, 205, 207, 212–13n, 215–16n41
polis, 21–2, 38, 44, 48–9, 90, 101
political philosophy 2, 21–2, 117, 119, 122–3, 155
Povinelli, Elizabeth, 246, 265
power, 8, 15, 90, 96, 98, 112n51, 122–33, 278
 biopower, 130–1
 power of reversal, 15, 208, 285
praxis, 2–3, 7–8, 12, 14–15, 21–3, 28, 30, 32, 34–6, 38, 73, 76–7, 82–4, 109, 118, 140–3, 149, 152, 167, 170, 185, 194–211, 212n13, 215n41, 235
 praxipoietic, 170, 185
 see also decision
precarity, 245–66
predicate, 23, 180
pre-political, 66, 67, 77, 81, 119, 124
production, 12–13, 36, 103, 146, 199, 205–6, 208–9, 226–8, 235, 259, 263, 275–86
Puar, Jasbir, 250, 265

Ranciere, Jacques, 48, 109, 212n13
relation, 3–4, 10–11, 27–8, 30–1, 34–6, 46, 50–1, 56, 72, 74, 76, 79, 80, 96–8, 121–5, 127–8, 140–1, 145, 149, 156, 198, 245–51, 257, 265, 273, 276–80
resistance, 4, 9, 105, 172–3, 216, 236, 247, 252, 263–4, 266, 273–8, 285–6
responsibility *see* ethics
retreat of the political, 3, 117–18, 123, 155–6, 185–6, 194
revolution, 38, 49, 78, 92, 97–9, 123, 125, 132, 167, 208, 274
Rousseau, Jean-Jacques, 14, 92, 96, 101, 141, 153–4

Sarkozy, Nicolas, 92
Sartre, Jean-Paul, 29, 45, 87n52
self, 29–30, 34–7, 72–4, 79–80, 82–3, 90, 97, 106–7, 124, 150, 155–6, 170, 227, 255–6, 264, 279
sense, the flight of, 1, 123, 142, 148, 173
sensible, 70, 140, 143, 146, 148–9, 154, 169
sensuousness, 175

sign, 165, 173–4, 184
signification, 8, 28, 79, 144, 150, 165–7, 168, 170, 173–5, 183, 231
 loss of power, 66, 88, 123, 219–21, 226, 228, 230–1
Silesius, Angelus, 232
Situationism, 141, 153–4, 169–71, 185
social ontology, 3, 49, 116, 120, 123, 132, 141–2, 153
socialism, 101, 105, 119
sovereignty, 14, 80, 82, 90–1, 96–8, 109, 117–18, 126, 129–32, 152, 192, 260
space / spacing, 4, 6, 14–15, 30, 35, 38, 74, 81–2, 100, 102, 105, 110, 131, 155, 157, 167–8, 176–8, 183, 189n41, 192–6, 198, 200, 203, 207, 210–11, 212n5,13, 219, 227–8, 255, 266, 274
Spinoza, Baruch, 49, 161n25
state, 68, 78, 81, 93–4, 99, 101, 127, 129–31, 152, 157, 220, 222, 248–9, 251, 253, 257–8, 274–5, 281, 286
state of exception, 97, 253
style, 180–1, 190n70
subject / subjectivity, 35, 43, 73–4, 79, 81, 87n52, 94, 96–7, 144, 153, 227, 229–31, 233–6, 249, 260
surface, 53, 143–4, 181–4
surplus *see* value

technology, 25, 36, 58, 100, 103, 204–5, 222, 228, 277
theology, 47, 56, 60, 96, 98, 156, 151, 195, 205
thinking, 7–9, 46, 81, 84, 95, 118, 150, 155, 206, 232, 234, 249, 274
time, 6, 9, 72, 74, 80, 98–103, 151, 176, 194, 206, 265–7, 280
 future, 9, 11, 72–3, 90, 93, 103, 110, 236–7, 266
 iteration, 67, 79, 171, 199
 past, 67–8, 71, 80–1, 266
 presence, 5–6, 28–31, 35, 139–41, 145, 148, 154, 158, 178, 185
 see also history
totalitarianism 88–9, 105, 117, 122, 124–5, 127–8, 168

touch, 10, 33, 35, 76, 83–4, 144, 170, 175–86, 189n41, 190n70, 198, 205, 254
transcendence, 80, 176, 179, 180–2
transimmanence, 74, 76, 176, 179–81
   immanence, 4, 91–2, 180–3, 265
transvaluation *see* value

unworld *see immundus*

value, 2, 7, 9, 11–15, 23, 38, 56–7, 75, 93, 102–3, 145, 150, 160n16, 166–7, 170, 172, 195–6, 208, 211, 223–5, 228–32, 242n48, 257–9, 273, 275–86, 288n16,22,24, 289n31
violence, 79, 95, 183–4, 235–6, 257, 274

wink, 174

EU representative:
Easy Access System Europe
Mustamäe tee 50, 10621 Tallinn, Estonia
Gpsr.requests@easproject.com

www.ingramcontent.com/pod-product-compliance
Lightning Source LLC
Chambersburg PA
CBHW052152300426
44115CB00011B/1641